TO MAKE NEGRO LITERATURE

TO MAKE NEGRO LITERATURE

WRITING, LITERARY PRACTICE &
AFRICAN AMERICAN AUTHORSHIP

ELIZABETH McHENRY

DUKE UNIVERSITY PRESS   DURHAM & LONDON   2021

Printed in the United States of America on acid-free paper ∞
Project editor: Lisa Lawley
Designed by Aimee C. Harrison
Typeset in Adobe Jenson Pro and ITC Franklin Gothic
by Westchester Publishing Services

Library of Congress Cataloging-in-Publication Data
Names: McHenry, Elizabeth, [date] author.
Title: To make Negro literature : writing, literary practice, and African
American authorship / Elizabeth McHenry.
Description: Durham : Duke University Press, 2021. |
Includes bibliographical references and index.
Identifiers: LCCN 2020054043 (print)
LCCN 2020054044 (ebook)
ISBN 9781478013594 (hardcover)
ISBN 9781478014515 (paperback)
ISBN 9781478021810 (ebook)
ISBN 9781478091745 (ebook other)
Subjects: LCSH: American literature—African American authors—
History and criticism. | American literature—19th century—
History and criticism. | African Americans—Intellectual life—
19th century. | African Americans—Books and reading. |
African Americans in literature. | BISAC: SOCIAL SCIENCE / Ethnic
Studies / American / African American & Black Studies | LITERARY
CRITICISM / American / African American & Black
Classification: LCC PS153.N5 M37 2021 (print) | LCC PS153.N5 (ebook) |
DDC 810.9/896073009041—dc23
LC record available at https://lccn.loc.gov/2020054043
LC ebook record available at https://lccn.loc.gov/2020054044

Cover art: *Exhibit of the American negroes at the Paris exposition*,
1900. Prints and Photographs Division, Library of Congress,
Washington, D.C.

This book is freely available in an open access edition thanks to TOME
(Toward an Open Monograph Ecosystem)—a collaboration of the
Association of American Universities, the Association of University
Presses, and the Association of Research Libraries—and the generous
support of New York University. Learn more at the TOME website,
which can be found at the following web address: openmonographs.org.

For Electa and Quinn,
and for Gene, who makes every moment count

CONTENTS

ACKNOWLEDGMENTS

MY THINKING ON THIS BOOK BEGAN OVER TWO DECADES AGO, WHEN I first came upon Mary Church Terrell's cache of short stories in her archive at the Library of Congress. I did not know at the time why these stories felt important to me. I only knew that there was something poignant about them, something they wished to communicate that remained unaccounted for in traditional narratives of Terrell's life and her activism. It was not until I returned to them years later that they began to appear to me as vital elements of an alternative or unwritten aspect of African American literary history. Of this book's many tentative beginnings, none was more important than the paper on Mary Church Terrell that I delivered at the Print Cultures Symposium at the University of Illinois in 2005. For his invitation to speak about my "new project" and, later, to expand on that paper in print, I thank Gordon Hutner. This book's fourth chapter reflects an earlier form of my thinking on Terrell and her fictional writing that appeared in *American Literary History* 19, no. 2 (Spring 2007), 381–401; any overlap between the old and new versions appears by permission.

Along the way, as each of the book's chapters took shape, I benefited immensely from the intellectual companionship and impassioned writing of fellow travelers working at the intersection of Black studies, African American literary studies, print culture and book history scholarship, and archival and material studies. Over the years, I have learned from and been inspired by the scholarship of Brent Hayes Edwards, P. Gabrielle Foreman, Eric Gardner, Jacqueline Goldsby, Saidiya Hartman, Laura Helton, Shirley Moody-Turner, Kinohi Nishikawa, and Britt Rusert, as well as by many others in the field of Black print culture. I remain indebted to Frances Smith

Foster, the allure of whose scholarship first drew me to Black print culture and to the archives. Carla Peterson has been a fierce supporter from the beginning, and early conversations with her helped to lay the foundations for this book. Randall Burkett continues to feed my curiosity for what the archives hold, and I am grateful to him for his willingness to think with me about materials that have been dismissed by others. I am especially grateful to those who stepped in when I most needed them. This includes Priscilla Wald, who listened with such great care and, in doing so, helped me to reset the course of this project; Joycelyn Moody, who advocated for me on a moment's notice; and Kimberly Blockett, who, when the book refused to follow its plan, helped me to muster the patience its writing required.

A fellowship from New York University's Humanities Initiative (now the Center for the Humanities) in 2012 allowed me write what became the first chapter of this book and more generally provided the time and space to begin to understand the logic of what I wished to do. I am certain that this project would have remained unfinished without the generous support of the American Council of Learned Societies, and I have NYU to thank for a much needed sabbatical leave that, coupled with the ACLS fellowship, allowed me the true luxury of two full years of writing and revision. I received invaluable assistance from a number of archivists and librarians, including Charlotte Priddle, director of NYU special collections; Amanda Watson, the librarian for English and comparative literature at NYU; and Lynn Farrington, senior curator of special collections at the Kislak Center for Special Collections, Rare Books and Manuscripts, at the University of Pennsylvania. Along the way I tested my ideas before many audiences, whose comments, criticisms, and suggestions were critical to moving the project forward. For their invitations to visit, I'd like to thank in particular the Center for Literature and the Public Sphere at Seton Hall University, the Grolier Club and the Rare Book School, Yale University's Program in the History of the Book, the National Humanities Center, and the Black Bibliography Project. I'd also like to thank NYU's Print Culture Working Group, where a vigorous conversation about genre helped me to come closer to understanding the books sold by subscription that I address in my first chapter. There I connected with Ellen Gruber Garvey, whose generosity in talking with me about this project certainly helped to make it better.

The true constant across the years in which most of this book was written was my students at NYU. Every step of the way, the classroom has been an invigorating place to pursue interests, to try out arguments, and to take in ideas. It has been my privilege to work with an extraordinary group of students whose love of the archives overlapped with my own. Conversations in particular with Matt Bruen, Jane Greenway Carr, Laura Fisher, Laura Helton, Kristen Highland, Rob Koehler, and Autumn Womack sustained me over the years and certainly enriched this book. Their rigorous engagement with obscure documents, their questions about collecting and archival practice, and their dedication to collaboration and scholarly community inspired me to think more deeply and more productively. Many NYU students have also provided much-needed help as research assistants, and their work—in tracking down sources, organizing references, and making PowerPoint presentations—eased my load immeasurably. In particular I would like to thank Laurie Lambert, whose folder of notes on Daniel Murray I returned to again and again during the writing of this book, and Olivia Howard, who did all that I asked of her and more. Ryan Healey also deserves special mention for working with me to bring order to the endnotes and the bibliography.

The English Department at NYU remains for me an ideal intellectual home, and I am grateful to my colleagues for what feels like a lifetime of camaraderie and support. Phil Harper remains my truest ally and most loyal advocate, and over the years he has generously given me—in terms of time, openness, and wisdom—more than I can ever thank him for. His careful reading of the earliest drafts of the book helped me to unlock its purpose and its arguments, and I have him to thank for pushing me to take on (rather than shy away from) Booker T. Washington's authorship. Pat Crain volunteered to read the manuscript in its most inchoate and unruly form, and her insightful comments and vital encouragement gave me the courage to keep going. Sonya Posmentier worked with me to design a road map for my fellowship year and, in doing so, helped me to launch what was the most inspired and enjoyable period of my writing life. She has been a constant source of productive conversation about this book and so much more. Over a series of lunches, Gene Jarrett asked all the right questions about the project and in the process helped me to clarify my vision of it. I am grateful to Lisa Gitelman for listening as I sketched out the final shape of the book, and for telling me, one fall afternoon over cocktails, that the book was done. John Archer was a reassuring presence and an outstanding mentor just when I needed it most. Along the way Tom Augst, Jennifer Baker, Nick Boggs, Chris Cannon, Patrick Deer, Carolyn Dinshaw, Juliet Fleming, Lissette Florez, John Guillory, Lenora Hanson, Isabel Hofmeyr, David Hoover, Alyssa Leál, Wendy Lee, Paula McDowell, Peter Nicholls, Patricia Okoh-Esene, Crystal Parikh, Cyrus Patell, Dara Regaignon, Catherine Robson, Martha Rust, Simón Trujillo, and Greg Vargo provided encouragement in ways small and large.

Una Chaudhuri, Maureen McLane, and Jini Kim Watson deserve special mention for their warmth and for their willingness to be leaned on, as colleagues, mentors, and friends: their support has made all the difference.

It is my good fortune to have found my way back to Duke University Press and, more specifically, to editor Courtney Berger, who from the start has been dedicated to moving this project forward. My thanks to her for believing in it, and for expertly navigating me through each step of the review process. Britt Rusert and an anonymous reader for the press offered extraordinary feedback on the manuscript: what a privilege to be read so generously, so carefully, and so well. In particular, Britt Rusert dared me to be bolder and more precise in my claims about *failure*, and her insistence that the manuscript needed to be trimmed helped me to produce a stronger and more focused book. Sandra Korn was a constant source of good advice, and her patience for my endless questions is much appreciated. I am grateful to Lisa Lawley for overseeing the production process, and to Emily Shelton, whose attention to detail and thoughtful suggestions on style made this a better book. Special thanks also go to the marketing team at the press and to Lalitree Darnielle, who generously made it a priority to scan images for me in her home under the most difficult of circumstances. The book's production costs were supported by the English Department at NYU, through its Abraham and Rebecca Stein Faculty Publication Fund. I am also grateful to the NYU Center for the Humanities for a generous TOME (Toward an Open Monograph Ecosystem) grant, which made it possible for this book to be freely accessible online.

I finished *To Make Negro Literature* in the midst of a global pandemic and at a time when racial violence and anti-Black sentiment has made the precarity of Black lives ever more apparent. The reverberating turmoil and loss that defined the year 2020 has only underscored the importance of friends and family in my everyday life and, certainly, in the completion of this work. I did not always want to be asked, "So, how's the book coming?" But I fully appreciate the love and the moral support that lay behind the question. To all the communities I call home: thank you for caring for me over the years, in ways large and small. I am especially grateful to Betsy Michel, whose thoughtfulness, kindness, and love epitomize what it means to be neighborly. I am also grateful for the friendship of two extraordinary women who have become like family to me. It is now unimaginable to think about cooking the Thanksgiving bird without Elena Lüthi, who approaches this project and all other things with fierce determination and an abundance of good humor. It is equally unimaginable to eat Sunday night dinner without Alison Magruder, whose cheerful presence has brought so much laughter and joy to our lives. My special thanks also go to

Annie Simmons (all-around champion of everything) and Sonya Browne (for the endless supply of printouts that let me see my words on paper).

In the final two years of writing, the remarkable Vera Keller saw me through countless bumps and bruises: she knows every joy and every frustration that was related to finishing this book. She is a top-notch writing partner whose wise counsel and incisive suggestions (despite the distance that separates us) moved this book forward in incalculable ways. Ashraf Rushdy was sure that this book would be written long before I was, because, he said, the obvious sequel to a book called "Forgotten Readers" is one called "Forgotten Writers." While I did not adopt his title for this book, he was of course right that those aspects of literary history that had fallen by the wayside would continue to capture my attention and inspire my scholarship. Each word of this book has benefited from Ashraf's high standards as a reader and his sharp eye for that which must be expanded, deepened, and connected. There was never a time when I lost my way that he was not there to help me to find it. As a scholar, I have gained immensely from his profound commitment to reading, to writing, and to intellectual companionship, but I am also an infinitely happier person for his kindness, his generosity, his sense of humor, and his friendship.

During all the years this book was being written, Alleah Shareef held down our fort, taking care of all of us and making it possible for me to be a scholar and a mother. She has enriched our lives in ways that are impossible for me to enumerate. Nancy Stone and Adelia Moore quite literally opened their doors to me and to our small children, becoming the New York City family we needed. Penelope McDonnell has always embraced me, lifting my spirits and buoying my confidence when I needed it most. It is impossible for me to imagine life in New York City or parenthood without Indra Chitkara, Kim Holden, and Caroline Hubbell, three extraordinary women who have been by my side every step of the way. Electa Sevier, Anja Hanson, Phoebe Brown, Rachel Simons, and Cori Field are my original squad, and our spirited girls' weekends never fail to leave me refreshed and relaxed. Quick visits and long conversations with Jenny Kelso Smith and small, quiet talks with Monica Thomas at her kitchen counter have restored my equilibrium. Cara McCaffrey never failed to remind me what warmth and generosity feels like. Cocktails "on the orange" with Lee Michel was a ritual that brightened my days. And Susan Chamber's infectious smile and her warm hugs lifted me up and kept me going during my most difficult moments.

This book was quite literally written in the presence of two extraordinary dogs, Blossom and Mabel, whose endless patience and enormous capacity for sleep provided me with good company on even the longest and hardest days. It is a true gift that I was never alone when writing, and I have come to believe that I am incapable of doing my best thinking if Blossom and Mabel are not by my side. My thanks to Laura Cooper Davidson for loving them as much as I do, and for all the joy and beauty she brings to our world.

My family has surrounded me and cared for me from the very start, and their love and support is key to all that I do. I think of my grandparents, Elizabeth and Alphonso Williamson, every day, and each day I gain greater appreciation for what they accomplished as African Americans born in the opening years of the twentieth century. I cannot begin to fathom what they endured, and yet my most vivid memories are of their laughter, their optimism, and their love. I am a literary historian because of my mother, Mary Williamson McHenry: the example of her daily work, as a teacher and a scholar of African American literature, showed me the value of Black history and literature and of thinking through written words. She also modeled for me how to live a life of adventure, of courage, and of faith. My dad, Donald F. McHenry, is an extraordinary father and grandfather who makes it clear every day that, of all life's accomplishments, family is the most important one. I know that he learned this from his own mother, Dora Brooks McHenry, who died too soon but whose impact was so great; his ardent love for and dedication to us, and his insistence that all our goals are reachable is a tribute to her. His faith that this book would get written helped me to reach the end.

Chrissie McHenry has made everything in my life—from my childhood to my adulthood—better for her presence. In many ways she absorbs all the worst of me: my fears, my frustrations, my disappointments, my sadness. And yet she remains a model of kindness, love, good humor, and true generosity. I am grateful to be her sister, and so fortunate to have her. Sharing in the lives of her extraordinary children, Claire, Caroline, and Daniel Lempres, continues to be one of my greatest joys. Strong, smart, independent, kind, conscientious, and hardworking: each one is destined to do great things and make huge and necessary contributions to this world. To them I owe thanks for sharing so much with me, in terms of adventure, laughter, distraction, fellowship, love, and, of course, computer assistance. I am indebted to them for being always "on call," to fix weird formatting, to remove strange lines that wouldn't go away, and to catch all the typos that I didn't see.

The most important environment for the creation of this book was the one that I found every day with my husband, Gene, and our two children, Electa and Quinn McHenry-Assaf. Quinn and Electa have truly grown up with this book and their constant presence—first as babies, then as children, and now as teenagers—serves as a daily reminder of what is most important. I cannot imagine my life without Electa's astute fashion advice or Quinn's basketball wisdom or without their unique ways of seeing the world around them. Electa and Quinn are my greatest gifts and deepest inspirations, and their energy and enthusiasm has sustained me over the long haul. I know that they will be happy to hold this book and see that, yes, it is finally finished. My final and most profound thanks go to Gene Assaf, whose love makes everything possible and infinitely more worthwhile. Gene holds me steady in the most fundamental ways, and what he has done for me, for us, and for this book is inestimable. There are no words that can possibly express all that he means to me. He is an outstanding friend, partner, and father who reminds me each day that the point is not to cross the finish line but to taste, and to remember the taste, of all that is good along the way.

TO MAKE NEGRO LITERATURE

WRITING, LITERARY PRACTICE & AFRICAN AMERICAN AUTHORSHIP

SOMETIME IN THE SUMMER OR EARLY FALL OF 1903, AS HE WORKED
to find a balance between his life as a scholar and his aspirations as a civil
rights activist, W. E. B. Du Bois quietly purchased a printing office at 163
Beale Street in Memphis, Tennessee. He did not live or work in Memphis,
nor did he have experience in or knowledge of the business of printing. In
theory, there were plenty of printing offices in Atlanta that would have been
accessible to Du Bois, and as a professor of sociology at Atlanta University,
he also would have had some access to the university's printing office. Described
in the *Catalogue of Atlanta University* for 1901–2 as "large and well appointed,"
the printing office was used as a place of instruction, where students learned the
printing trade by working on publications for both the school and the larger
Atlanta community.[1] But it was also where two monthly newspapers were
published: the *Bulletin of Atlanta University* and a student newspaper called
the SCROLL. It also housed Atlanta University Press, which, beginning in
1896, had produced the proceedings of the annual Conference for the Study of
Negro Problems as well as related publications. And yet Du Bois invested his

entire life savings—some $1,600—in the Memphis print business, entering into an unlikely partnership with two former students who had recently graduated from Atlanta University. He hoped to make the printing office the home of a national Negro journal and the "basis of a publishing house" that would produce "supplementary reading for Negro schools, text-books, works of Negro authors, etc." By taking control of a printing press, Du Bois was determined to give voice to Negro writers and artists, who would "be encouraged to write of themselves and depict the things nearest to them and thus speak more naturally and effectively than they usually do."[2]

These were lofty goals, and, to Du Bois, the printing business represented a significant literary intervention. He used its presses to manufacture a broadside of his own poem "Credo," which, distributed by Black clubwomen in places like Tuskegee, Alabama, would reach a wider and more diverse audience than it had through its original printing in the *Independent* in the fall of 1904. He also produced a journal, the *Moon Illustrated Weekly*, which had a limited distribution in Memphis and Atlanta beginning in December 1905. But the journal never had anywhere near a national readership, or the ten thousand subscribers that Du Bois had estimated he could potentially attract when planning the venture. The *Moon's* demise sometime in the summer of 1906 went largely unnoticed, except by fellow journalists who took it as an occasion to ridicule Du Bois for what they considered an arrogant effort to venture outside the realm of academia. "With the pompous air and assumed dignity of a peacock . . . the Moon reached its zenith a few weeks ago and has fallen behind the veil," wrote a correspondent for *Alexander's Magazine*, playing on the image Du Bois mobilized in *The Souls of Black Folk* to theorize the dynamics of race and racism in the United States and across the globe.[3] Du Bois himself attributed the demise of the *Moon* to the mismanagement of his younger colleagues, who, in turn, perhaps recognizing that Du Bois would never see or acknowledge his own "blunder in the matter," blamed each other.[4] Du Bois effectively walked out on the whole Memphis printing enterprise, deserting his partners and threatening them with legal action to recoup his investment in the business.[5]

I begin with the story of Du Bois's short-lived experience as the owner of a printing business because it illustrates the sorts of narratives, rarely told about African American literary history, that are the subject of this book. Relatively few critics have focused their attention on this episode in Du Bois's career, and those who have generally agree that the most we can say about the *Moon* is that it was a precursor to the *Crisis*, the highly successful journal for which Du Bois served as the founding editor. This perspective insists that we quickly shift our attention forward, not only to the *Crisis*, a publication that is more readily accessible and more easily contextualized than the *Moon*, but also to the familiar ground of the Harlem Renaissance, the historical moment about which we literary critics are perhaps the most well versed. The *Crisis* was the official organ of the NAACP, and its primary purpose was to be a political and news publication that broadcast, according to its inaugural editorial, "those facts and arguments which show the danger of race prejudice."[6] It was launched in 1910, but the *Crisis* is more commonly associated with the key role it played in the development of Black literary voices during the Harlem Renaissance, the literary and artistic movement of the 1920s. Under the editorial direction of Jessie Fauset, the *Crisis* celebrated the talents of a generation of young African Americans by publishing their art and their writing. It was a crucial means through which Black literature found cohesion and visibility during a decade that awakened both white Americans and African Americans themselves to the place and purpose of racial art.

But by assessing the *Moon* as a precursor to the *Crisis*, we have subsumed its story as well as crucial lessons about how African American literature was made in the first years of the twentieth century into a larger and already written narrative, one that obscures the particularities of the *Moon* as a product of a specific literary historical moment that remains underappreciated. The years with which I am concerned in this book lie between two cultural heydays that are the subject of a great deal of scholarship. In recognition of the literary ambitions and accomplishments of Black women during the 1890s, we have dubbed this decade the "Woman's Era," identifying it as a moment that resulted in an impressive body of literary work appearing in various print formats. The inclusion, in 1988, of a number of texts from the 1890s as part of the set of thirty reprinted and then–newly discovered texts as *The Schomburg Library of Nineteenth-Century Black Women Writers* drew considerable attention to individual authors like Anna Julia Cooper, Frances E. W. Harper, Gertrude Bustill Mossell, and Emma Dunham Kelley-Hawkins, while also encouraging scholars to look at and think of these writers as a part of a larger tradition of nineteenth-century African American literature.[7] This series was widely celebrated and enticed a generation of researchers to appreciate in new ways the contributions of Black women to intellectual history and to the history of African American literature. Curiously, a *Supplement* to the series, published in 1991, included several texts by Black women from the early twentieth century; bundled together in a series on nineteenth-century writers, those volumes appear out of context and, as Frances Smith

Foster notes in a review of the series, include no explanation of the "reasons for or the implications of [their] inclusion . . . in a series about nineteenth-century literature."[8] Scholars are even more likely to subsume the literature of the first two decades of the twentieth century in an extended understanding of the Harlem Renaissance, as do Henry Louis Gates Jr. and Gene Jarrett in their collection of writings from the years 1892–1938, *The New Negro*. By organizing the collection around the "trope" of the New Negro, they point to a coherent narrative of racial uplift and creativity, refiguring the Harlem Renaissance as the "long New Negro Movement," a continuum that runs from the nineteenth century well into the twentieth.[9] The volume is an important and effective anthology that exposes students to a sampling of how the concept of the New Negro was mobilized over the course of almost four decades. But, like the *Supplement* to *The Schomburg Library of Nineteenth Century Black Women Writers*, it only reinforces my observation that the literary projects of the early twentieth century are rarely allowed to claim their own independent space.

In fact, most scholars that address this body of literature do so across a wider "postbellum, pre-Harlem" time frame. This is the case with Dickson D. Bruce Jr.'s foundational *Black American Writing from the Nadir: The Evolution of a Tradition, 1877–1915*, which provides an invaluable survey of the fiction and poetry produced by African Americans in the years between the end of Reconstruction and the beginnings of World War I. More recently, Barbara McCaskill and Caroline Gebhard's edited collection *Post-Bellum, Pre-Harlem: African American Literature and Culture, 1877–1919* revisited these years, not to survey them but to illuminate the "unresolved contradictions" of the post-Reconstruction era. This volume brought much attention to a number of understudied authors and texts. The novelist Sutton Griggs was barely mentioned in that collection, but since its publication interest in his novels has spiked. His literary career is the focus of a collection of essays, *Jim Crow, Literature, and the Legacy of Sutton E. Griggs*, edited by Kenneth Warren and Tess Chakkalakal, which is dedicated to "mov[ing] Griggs from the margins to the center of African American literary history." Another notable contribution to the field is James Smethurst's *The African American Roots of Modernism: From Reconstruction to the Harlem Renaissance*, which focuses on the influence of African American artists and intellectuals on the development of literary modernity in the United States.[10]

All of this notable scholarship is "on" African American literature at the turn from the nineteenth to the twentieth century. But none of these studies focus as tightly on the years that surround the turn from one century to another—years that carried great significance for African Americans, as the trope of the New Negro shows—or illuminate the kinds of texts, literary practices, or modes of authorship that constitute the subject of *To Make Negro Literature*.[11] I am not suggesting that the turn from the nineteenth century to the twentieth should be considered a discrete period, isolated or disconnected from the years that surrounded it. But I do believe that our tendency to group the years from 1877 to 1919, from the end of Reconstruction to the Harlem Renaissance, has prevented us from identifying the specificity of the intervening years. Without lingering on those years that surround the turn of the century, it is difficult to recognize and come to critical terms with an aspect of literary culture that is all too rarely the subject of study: *failure*.

Literary history seldom privileges that which is unsuccessful, whether in terms of writers and texts never recognized by publication, or projects that remained incomplete or unfulfilled. But these writers, texts, and projects are no less a part of literary history. The *Moon* is not just a precursor of the *Crisis*, where the failure of the former is eclipsed by the success of the latter; it is an event that demands we examine the scope and shape of literary culture at the moment in which Du Bois launched his printing business and conceptualized the *Moon*, and in which it failed. A more nuanced understanding of the *Moon's* content, the specific conditions of its publication and its failure, and the overall history of Du Bois's ownership of a job printing business is one component of this.

We do well to remember that Du Bois's printing business, as well as every other aspect of his life and his intellectual work, was supposed to fail: he worked to build what was intended to be simultaneously a Black business and a Black intellectual institution in the midst of what was a veritable assault on Black lives and livelihood. The fact that African Americans were deemed by whites to be incompatible with such institutions serves as a reminder of the *queerness* of Black life during the Jim Crow era: Black people were, to say the least, "cast out of straight time's rhythm," to borrow José Esteban Muñoz's phrasing.[12] Excluded from American social, cultural, intellectual, and political institutions, African Americans' literary and intellectual efforts during this time must be seen as a remarkable historical record of the road maps of their rejection of this positioning. In recent years, the idea of success and, more specifically, the attendant category of failure have proven to be a rich site of theorization for scholars of queer studies. My attention to the ways that failure resonates queerly is particularly indebted to Muñoz, who usefully understands queerness as a forward-looking mode of critique. In this context, queer failure is a rejection of what is, or, in Munoz's words, a manifestation of a "brilliant offness" that is "not so much a failure to succeed as it is a failure to participate in a system of valuation that is predicated on exploitation and conformity." To see Du Bois's failure in these terms allows us insight into the ways that African Americans around the turn of the century "productively occupied" failure because it was a way to audaciously reject and refuse the place assigned to them and the disrespect shown to their intellectual lives as segregation and disenfranchisement were formalized and codified.[13] This perception of failure suggests the importance of our reevaluating those texts, genres, institutions, and forms of authorship that we have dismissed as unsuccessful, unproductive, unconventional, anomalous, or irrelevant; they are an important archive of the queer literary practices through which African Americans rejected a system of racial categorization that deemed them socially intolerable, intellectually inferior, and politically unqualified.

The objective of *To Make Negro Literature* is to reorient our understanding of African American literary culture at the turn from the nineteenth to the twentieth century by taking account of a variety of projects and conditions of authorship that have been dismissed or gone largely unnoticed in traditional accounts of African American literary history. A key to doing this work is to focus on a specific historical juncture. While the framework of the "long nineteenth century" has done much to center that century within a trajectory of capitalist modernity, my book suggests the ways that the *longue durée* poses problems for recovering the unfamiliar and now mostly obscure cultural artifacts that existed in the seams of these historical folds. My aim is to turn our critical attention away from the usual markers of literary achievement (known authors and traditionally published works of poetry and fiction), not to dismiss their importance but as a means of expanding and supplementing our knowledge of the complex literary landscape in which our African American ancestors lived. At no point in history was that landscape more complicated than in the last years of the nineteenth century and the opening decade of the twentieth. This interval lies at the very heart of the period historian Rayford Logan famously termed the "nadir" of race relations in the United States.[14] The generation of literary practitioners that animates this study experienced the promise of Reconstruction firsthand, but they matured intellectually during the years that saw the loss of the civil rights gained during Reconstruction and theoretically guaranteed by the Thirteenth, Fourteenth, and Fifteenth Amendments. In addition to the erosion of Black political leadership, they witnessed the

rise of lynching and other forms of anti-Black violence, the systematic disenfranchisement of Black voters, the legalization of segregation, and the nor-
malization of patterns of racial discrimination. By 1896, the Supreme Court
decision in the *Plessy v. Ferguson* case only gave legal confirmation to what
was social fact: that the full rights of citizenship would remain elusive for
African Americans, and that racism was becoming ever more deeply embedded in American culture. It would become only more so in the first decades
of the twentieth century, when Jim Crow laws expanded, white supremacist
groups like the Ku Klux Klan flourished, and racial violence in the South
drove African Americans to seek refuge in Northern cities.[15]

To use the word "Negro," as I deliberately do in this study, is to evoke
a particular moment in which African Americans embraced the word, insisting that its first letter be capitalized as a means of both controlling its
meaning and signifying the recognition and respect due to people of African
descent. By capitalizing the "N," they meant to overturn popular and social
tradition and defy the insult and negative connotations of the word "negro."
"Negro" with a capital "N" was a term of dignity, one that was forward-
looking in that it spoke to African Americans' determination to construct
positive images of themselves in the hardening racial atmosphere of the late
nineteenth and early twentieth centuries. That the word appears throughout
the early decades of the twentieth century with a lowercase "n" offers an indi-
cation of just how entrenched racism was in the nation. Even the *New York
Times* did not adopt a policy of using an uppercase "N" in the word "Negro"
until 1930, when they noted of this long-overdue policy: "It is not merely a
typographical change; it is an act of recognition of racial self-respect for those
who have been for generations in 'the lower case.'"[16] The refusal to capitalize
the "N" in "Negro" has always been indicative of social custom and popular
opinion that African Americans were unworthy of the dignity afforded by
the typographical gesture of respect and recognition. And yet, in the post-
Reconstruction landscape of racial violence and disintegrating rights, African Americans' insistence that it be capitalized was a means of asserting
themselves in a world that remained determined to break them down.

While for some African Americans the shift from "negro" to "Negro" did
not appear overly significant, and the term "Afro-American" was already in
wide use, for many Black intellectuals of that generation the capitalized title
constituted nothing less than what Henry Louis Gates Jr. and Gene Jarrett
call "a sign of plenitude, regeneration, or a truly constructed *presence*" that
countered how the lowercase usage had symbolized "lack, degeneration, or a
truly negated *absence*."[17] For the most part, then, the writers that I attend to

in this study considered themselves to be Negro writers, and the literature that they were concerned with making they considered, in a wholly new and radical way, Negro literature.[18]

At the moment in which they wrote, the successful literary appearance of any African American was a significant achievement. Scholars have noted that the years surrounding the turn of the century were "remarkably productive for African American imaginary literature."[19] In doing so, much of their attention has been directed to a handful of writers. By far the most well-known of these and the two writers who were the most visible during these years were Paul Laurence Dunbar and Charles W. Chesnutt. Both writers are usually hailed as the first to publish their work with mainstream, white publishers—Dunbar with Dodd, Mead and Chesnutt with Houghton, Mifflin. They are also among the first to be recognized by the American literary establishment, in this case both of them by the "dean" of American letters, William Dean Howells. What is equally important to their successes, though, is what that entrée to American letters required of them, and in what ways it reveals even more starkly the precarious instability of African American literary culture. In his reviews of their work, Howells had emphasized color—Dunbar was "of the pure African type," while Chesnutt's Negro blood was "diluted"—and clearly indicated how that feature of their life, their race, should limit what they represented in their literary productions. Dunbar was "most himself" when he wrote "entirely black verse," by which Howells meant verse written in dialect rather than the formal literary English that made up over half of the poems in *Majors and Minors*.[20] And, while Chesnutt's two collections of short stories, *The Conjure Woman* and *The Wife of His Youth*, were entirely palatable because the first had Uncle Julius speak in dialect, and the second because it allowed white readers to "acquaint" themselves with "those regions where the paler shades dwell as hopelessly with relation to ourselves, as the blackest negro," Howells was dismayed by the subjects Chesnutt chose for his next works: in *The House Behind the Cedars*, passing, and in *The Marrow of Tradition*, the 1898 Wilmington race riot. He did not review the former and called the latter "bitter, bitter."[21]

Both writers keenly felt the restraints those expectations cast on them. Chesnutt recognized that "the public as a rule do not care for books in which the principal characters are colored people, or with a striking sympathy for that race as contrasted with the white race."[22] Likewise, Dunbar spoke of the "irrevocable harm" embedded in the "dictum" Howells had "laid down regarding my dialect verse," which Howells had praised as vibrant and authentic expressions of Black culture, while the rest of his poetry, written in standard form, Howells deemed "not very interesting."[23] Dunbar desperately "searched for strategies to counter the influence" of his dialect writing, which threatened to play into public demand for the demeaning images of African American minstrelsy.[24] Dunbar was deemed at his best when he wore a mask of Blackness, which was most readily characterized by the racially explicit dialect that, for Howells, worked in tandem with Dunbar's complexion to define the authenticity of his Blackness. Other critics followed suit, one sensing that "Mr. Dunbar should write about Negroes" and "sound" Black while doing it.[25] When he didn't do either—when he wrote about white people and did not use dialect—reviewers thought that he was writing about people and experiences "alien" to him.[26] What the fuller story of Chesnutt's and Dunbar's publishing careers reveals, then, are the paradoxes of authorship and literary production around the turn of the century: even those authors we associate with *success* during these years struggled to place their literature amid a literary landscape that was, for Black writers, still very much under construction.

This same instability also marked the careers of those writers who published their work in less prestigious and Black-owned venues. Pauline Hopkins, for instance, published all four of her novels with the Colored Co-operative Publishing Company, a Black-owned press that also published, from 1900 to 1904, the *Colored American Magazine*. In this case, what created instability for Hopkins and the publisher were the racial politics of late nineteenth-century America. Finding Hopkins and the magazine she edited too critical of his political positions, Booker T. Washington took control of the *Colored American Magazine* and derailed Hopkins's career.[27] Sutton Griggs, as Du Bois would do later, established his own press, the Orion Publishing Company, which issued five of his novels between 1899 and 1908, but found that it was wholly unprofitable.[28]

The importance of these authors and their literary accomplishments are undeniable. And yet what surfaces in this brief review are the inconsistencies of African American literary culture around the turn of the century. Despite the obvious degrees of success of these writers, a deeper look at their stories only begins to reveal the complicated, qualifying questions about Black authorship and the reach and possibilities of African American literature that lay beneath the surface of their achievement. It is this history of a fundamental instability in African American literary culture that I wish to excavate in *To Make Negro Literature*. To do so, I turn to a series of texts, projects, and practitioners that make visible the *unsettledness* of the category of Black literature at the turn of the century, even to those working in the field. Many of these are now largely unfamiliar or discounted in importance, but, I argue, taken together, they begin to reveal African American literature's workspaces and its working conditions. My study is guided by the kinds of questions that these practitioners were asking at the very moment that a modern understanding of African American literature was taking form. How should that literature be defined and structured, and what were its proper parameters, practices, and subjects of attention? What were the viable venues for its publication, and what was its intended readership? How was authorship imagined and pursued, and in what ways was it compensated? What, in a word, was Negro literature?

It bears remembering that, at the turn of the century, variations on these questions were being asked not only by African American literary practitioners in their own circles, but also in intellectual communities and institutions of higher learning throughout the United States; they exemplify a moment when the place of literature and the meaning of literary study were being reconsidered and reconceptualized. Institutional histories of the professionalization of literary studies tell us that, at the end of the nineteenth century and into the first decade of the twentieth century, the study of literature was consolidating as a formal practice, and "English" as a discipline was taking shape. In the United States, preacademic literary culture (which took place in drawing rooms and literary societies, most often in the form of public oratorical performances) gave way to academic literary culture, and intellectuals began to imagine, develop, and debate particular scholarly and critical practices. The literary education provided by traditional colleges, where literary study was conceived as an extension of grammar, rhetoric, and elocution, was giving way to the democratic modern university's sense that literature could and should be organized and "taught." As Gerald Graff and others have argued, the turn of the century was when "English" was being conceptualized as an academic discipline and the organization, methods, and directions of the study of literature were being debated and reconstituted.[29] The questions that shaped this inquiry were both small and expansive. What were the parameters of literature and literary practice? How should literature be organized? What might a "literary curriculum" look like, and what vocabulary of terms should it use? How should a tradition of humanism and cultural values be considered and taught? What were the new branches of knowledge, and how should they be harmonized with the old? The fundamental questions that I argue were being asked about Negro literature at the turn of the century, and the intellectual work of mapping its parameters that I illuminate in this book, in fact reflect a larger unsettledness of literature as a category in the United States.

By evoking the question "What was Negro literature?," I echo (with a signal difference) the title of Kenneth Warren's much-discussed, provocatively titled monograph, published in 2011. I share with him an interest in developing a greater appreciation for the distinctiveness of literary practice and production at different historical moments. But my concern in *To Make Negro Literature* lies not in arguing for a new periodization of African American literature, as Warren does in that work, or in linking the racial coherence of African American literature during what he identifies as the Jim Crow era to a political response to segregationist thought and practice. Instead, I wish to attend to the *literariness* of literature in the years immediately following the institutionalization of Jim Crow, in order to provide a more granular account of African American literary and print culture. It is a time, I argue, when African American literature *doesn't* cohere. That is one reason why this particular moment in African American literary history resists being written: it cannot be accounted for in a smooth, consistent, or cohesive narrative. What we must attend to, I contend, is not only what appears on the surface of this literary moment in its most visible published authors and major texts, but also those elements that are anomalous and that speak in another register to the infrastructure being built to support African American print culture.

To use the word "infrastructure" here is to evoke a world of building and of architecture. In doing so I wish to suggest the ways in which we might expose the blueprints of Black literary culture—that is, those literary projects and people that laid practical and conceptual frameworks for African American literature and the transmission of literary culture and that lie just beneath the surface of the known world of African American literary history. What kinds of writing and conditions of authorship have underwritten what has been valued as African American literature? What sorts of investments stand behind the most visible literary productions, and what kinds of interactions have played supporting roles in the era's literary landscape? In what structures can we see the intellectual bases of literature and literary culture taking shape? The goal of this book is to bring to the fore what lies hidden—often in plain sight—in the background of literary history, as a way to rejigger both our understanding of turn-of-the-century African American literary culture and our conception of the appropriate objects of African Americanist literary inquiry.

At the time of this writing, the known world of African American literary history is more expansive than ever before. This is due in no small part to scholars working at the intersection of African Americanist inquiry and print culture studies, who have made strong arguments for centralizing what in the past might have been considered peripheral sites of literary history. Fueled by the "archival turn" in American studies generally, literary scholars have effectively shifted our attention from a focus on Black literature to one on Black print. Perhaps the most dramatic result of this shift has been our attention to the early Black press and to periodicals, which abound with examples of the breadth of African American writing and literary activities. These new directions have opened windows onto the habits of Black readers and transformed our understanding of Black authorship, editorship, circulation, and reception of print. They have even revitalized studies of what was long privileged as the principal form in which African Americans found literary expression: the slave narrative. Scholarship on slave testimonies that appeared "piecemeal in anti-slavery newspapers, almanacs, and pamphlets" now complement our understanding of the "exemplary" narratives of Frederick Douglass and Harriet Jacobs that were published as bound books under the supervision of well-known abolitionists.[30]

Today it hardly seems worth mentioning that the archives of Black literature have never been more readily accessible or more fully discussed than they are now. Recent critical attention to the scholarship of Dorothy Porter illustrates the extent to which such research would be unthinkable without the foresight of generations of librarians and archivists who fought to preserve and make accessible the records of Black history.[31] We are reaping the benefits of their work to organize these records in ways that would make Black studies an expansive field and facilitate robust investigations of the history of Black print. Nothing matches or can replace the benefit of working in the presence of rare documents and manuscripts, but the exponential increase in digital materials is providing scholars with unprecedented access to texts that were once largely unreachable or hard to find. This has only made more visible the broad range of materials, formats, texts, and genres that have been considered literary in different historical moments and further challenged us to locate the full variety of sites where literature appeared and literary culture unfolded. As Eric Gardner's inquiry into the nineteenth-century African American periodical the *Christian Recorder* illustrates, lingering over those locations in which literary culture was not only embedded, but also supported, discussed, and debated, reaps extraordinary insights into the ways African Americans used and appreciated Black literature and print culture.[32] Digital projects such as the "Just Teach One: Early African American Print" initiative are making readily available such texts as the novella "Theresa," written by "S" and published in the pages of *Freedom's Journal* in 1828, or William J. Wilson's "Afric-American Picture Gallery," published in 1859 in the *Anglo-African Magazine* under the name "Ethiop."[33] The fact that we can engage our students in ongoing recovery projects and the "hands-on" process of archival research ensures that the task of recuperating the full breadth and depth of African American literary history will be valued and taken up by the next generation.[34]

All of these things mitigate the extent to which silence haunts the archives of African American literary history, but they can't resurrect the missing records of African American lives. Central to working in the archives of Black history are the challenges presented by their omissions and gaps. In the past decade, scholars have aptly assessed these archives as spaces of power, facing head-on the paralyzing dilemmas of how to effectively embody the Black past while at the same time respecting what cannot be known. Much of the theoretical work on archives and archival recovery and on the ways that Black archives are entangled in the politics and practices of institutionalization has focused on the archives of Atlantic slavery. But examples of these concerns in the areas of literary and print culture study abound. None have been more influential for scholars of Black print culture and African American literary history than the foundational scholarship of Frances Smith Foster and Carla Peterson. Both Foster and Peterson have been instrumental in guiding researchers to methodologically sound ways of approaching and contextualizing "recovered" histories and texts, not only in terms of their provenance, but also their place in the archives of Black print. Central to what their scholarship communicates is the importance of working productively across the gaps in our knowledge of the African American past and the silences of the archive by capitalizing on partial knowledge and modes of speculation. They have challenged us to work in slow, patient, and meticulous ways with bits or "scraps" of information, rather than rapidly move on to projects that seem easier or are more firmly aligned with familiar narratives of Black literary practice.[35]

But part of what we are missing in African American literary history is a result of our own scholarly neglect. We have dismissed as unworthy of attention certain kinds of productions—texts and events that are not lost, then, but disregarded. It is four such events on which I focus in *To Make Negro Literature*: books sold by subscription; forms of print long considered reference tools rather than a genre of any literary value in themselves; forms of authorship that are today disrespected; and writing that simply failed to appear in the venues we think of as "publication." These kinds of events constitute undertheorized elements of Black print culture, their histories difficult but not impossible to excavate and explore. The work of this book is to restore these stories and re-place them where they belong: as interventions that merit attention for the ways that they contributed to the making of African American writing and Black literary culture in their own time.

To Make Negro Literature, then, intends to expand the scope of literary studies. In doing so, it builds on a growing body of scholarship from across the humanities and social sciences that challenges popular concepts about what constitutes relevant archives and objects of study. In addition to looking beyond the printed book for our understanding of African American literary history, many scholars are now broadening our understanding of the "actors who are central to the production of black texts, but rarely make their way into scholarly studies, from black printers and compositors to papermakers, engravers, editors, subscription agents, and readers."[36] These actors, as Britt Rusert insightfully notes in her survey of the state of African American print culture studies, are deservedly becoming—and will continue to be—objects of study. Never before have scholars come together more fully or assessed more thoughtfully the vast history of African Americans' interaction with print, from the eighteenth century to the twenty-first, in a series of monographs, conferences, symposia, recovery and editorial projects, and special issues of periodicals dedicated to the study of African American and Black print culture. Perhaps most important, they are finding ways to pass on to graduate and undergraduate students both the skills necessary to responsibly do archival work and a dedication to the expansive scholarship of Black print culture. In short, Black print culture studies have never been more vibrant or plentiful. Still, as Joycelyn Moody and Howard Rambsy II note in MELUS's 2015 special issue on Black print culture, we "simply need more such work."[37]

This book responds to that call and participates in the project of creating a more nuanced, more detailed history of African American literary culture in the historical folds between the nineteenth and the twentieth centuries by focusing on the circumstances of literary production and publication; on authorship's sustainability and literature's form and function; on the relationship between Black writing and emerging audiences and agendas; and on the frameworks that structure ways of organizing how to talk and think about literature and the literary.

I begin with an assessment of a difficult-to-define genre that I call "racial schoolbooks," which were sold by subscription throughout the South and the Midwest around the turn of the century. This provides me with a lens through which to see a readership that literary history does not yet adequately recognize. It is unsurprising that much of what we know about

Black readers and print culture is centered on the urban North, where before and after emancipation African Americans had greater access to education and to the materials that advanced both literacy and literary culture than did African Americans in the South. It has proved far more difficult to illuminate print and literary cultures across the South, where African Americans were generally less privileged, less well-educated, and less likely to have access to the sort of organized literary activities and periodicals from which we have drawn much of our understanding of the literary cultures of the North. The racial schoolbooks I explore in the first chapter illustrate the kind of reading material that was available to late nineteenth- and early twentieth-century African Americans living in Southern states. I focus in particular on one book, *Progress of a Race*, a volume that was composed in large part of previously published bits, loosely connected by an authorial voice that walks readers through the history of the race and its progress. The volume reveals a mode of authorship akin to curatorial work, suggesting how books of this sort emerged from and also replicated other institutions of learning and representation. By locating *Progress of a Race* in a tradition of African American self-education, I illuminate the ways that it reproduced and even replaced the schoolhouse as the site of the advancement of literacy and literary education.

Christopher Hager has insightfully made the point that the acquisition of literacy is a process that "unfolds over time."[38] *Progress of a Race*, I argue, stands as important evidence of the ways that literacy was extended, developed, practiced, and supported in African American communities across the South. It is an example of the kind of literature that was dismissed by highly literate people but embraced by the less literate, for it provided them with the means of both practicing literacy and seeing literary culture at work. Here I emphasize an important distinction, between the acquisition of basic literacy and the considerably more elusive idea of developing the analytical and critical skills associated with the literary. The schoolbooks I examine offered a framework through which African Americans—who might in fact be illiterate or semiliterate when they bought the book—could advance sequentially through a trajectory that began with "reading" the book's illustrations, moved forward into reading curated bits of text, and finally ended with mastering the depth of thinking and critical analysis associated with the literary. This was the sort of pedagogical intervention that African Americans needed to unsettle the racial status quo and to activate the skills necessary for negotiating the precarious position in which they found themselves at century's end, but it was certainly not an aspect of the

South's structures of segregated industrial education or vocational training that most Black Americans received. In considering this text, I bring to our attention a genre that has been considered an undistinguished literary form, hardly worthy of serious scholarly attention. I also illuminate a mode of selling books, by subscription, long associated with cheap and gaudy productions deemed without literary value or intellectual worth. In suggesting the importance of critically reassessing these texts, I argue that they make visible not only the important authorial project that is realized through acts of selection and compilation, but also the intellectual community established and authorized by the volume itself.

The second chapter of *To Make Negro Literature* is again interested in another kind of curatorial work and the development of intellectual community—namely, the ways turn-of-the-century literary practitioners thought bibliographically, which is to say how they returned again and again to the genre of the list as a means through which to catalog and frame Black print culture. One objective of the cluster of lists and bibliographies created in this period was clearly enumerative: they document an ongoing effort to announce Negro literature and to resolve questions about its existence and its historicity. But they were also powerful instruments of investigation, used by practitioners to test and stabilize how African American literature would be seen, defined, and used. Bibliography forms an important branch of literary study, but as scholars we are more apt to think of bibliographies themselves as tools that we make use of, rather than as documents worthy of our critical attention. And yet the bibliographies that I explore in *To Make Negro Literature* clearly reveal the precise ways literature was being conceptualized in the late nineteenth and early twentieth centuries. The chapter brings to the fore the extent to which lists and bibliographies were a crucial mode of African American intellectual practice: as structures through which their creators worked to assemble and sort elements of Black print culture and make it both visible and useable. In this, Black bibliographers participated in what was a national movement to establish the parameters of American literature, which advanced alongside the professionalization of bibliographic studies and library work that took place toward the end of the nineteenth century. African Americans were largely excluded from the organizations that spearheaded these efforts, but they were nevertheless committed to the project of shifting literary culture from an idle pastime of the privileged few to an intellectual pursuit associated with increased access and organized study. The array of lists I look at here—which includes those published in the context of the period's racial schoolbooks like *Progress of a Race*, Daniel Murray's bibliography projects for the 1900 Paris Exposition and the Library of Congress, and the series of bibliographies through which W. E. B. Du Bois worked to create a population of "general readers" equipped to study the problem of the color line in academic ways—help us to see lists and bibliographies as important elements of Black print culture. Their authors themselves authored Negro Literature, not only by guiding readers to it, but also by showing how Black print culture should be valued, historicized, and read.

If the first two chapters of *To Make Negro Literature* focus on authorship that is curatorial in nature, the following two chapters shift their focus to two different kinds of authorship, both of which might best be described as *hidden*. In chapter 3, I consider a form of authorship that hasn't received scholarly attention in African American contexts: those who "author" not themselves, but others. It is no secret that T. Thomas Fortune wrote much of what was published under Booker T. Washington's name around the turn of the century, but little attention has been paid to Fortune's experience writing for Washington, or to the ways that he quite literally orchestrated Washington's career as an author of books. The sheer number of books that Washington published between 1899 and 1901 reveals that book authorship—as opposed to publication in newspapers or periodicals—was high on Washington's agenda around the turn of the century. This chapter looks at Fortune's role in setting that agenda and in the labor of writing that went into the fiction of Washington's authorship. Fortune's career as an important journalist is well known, but both his vision for Black literature and his dogged crafting of Washington's image as a leader whose ideas, he believed, needed "permanent preservation in book form," have been overlooked. In addition to offering an expanded history of the façade of Washington's authorship, the chapter explores the ways that Fortune worked to give shape and definition to Black literature and literary culture by manipulating Washington's career as an author. What the chapter makes visible is Fortune's wish to *organize* Black literary culture around the turn of the century by giving it a textual and geographic center as well as a public face. This was one way, he believed, to define Black authorship and negotiate its parameters. In the end, Fortune knew, it was irrelevant that Washington did not write what he authored. Through establishing for Washington a posture of authorial presence, Fortune was able to activate a concept of Black authorship, one that projected the centrality of literature to Negro leadership and generated a public with an interest in the kinds of racial authority, information, and insight literature could convey.

This concept remained provisional and, in the case of Fortune's own never-completed book projects, came at a price, but even the story of Fortune's frustrations as an author of fiction serves as an important reminder that the sum total of African American literary history includes not only what was written and published, but also those literary attempts that were imagined and never realized. The final chapter of *To Make Negro Literature* is centered directly on literary failure, one of the threads that unifies the chapters of the book and drives my analysis of African American literary culture between 1896 and 1910. As my discussion of the publishing success of Paul Laurence Dunbar and Charles Chesnutt indicates, there are certainly literary success stories from these years, but in turning to the story of Mary Church Terrell, I illuminate one writer's painful recognition of her own failure as an author, and what she did with that failure. Terrell was a successful lecturer, activist, and journalist at the beginning of the twentieth century, and yet she believed that, more than any other form, imaginative literature generally and the short story specifically had the potential to speak to the race problem and to the lives and struggles of African Americans in ways that nonfiction and journalism could not. Whereas her journalism appeared in African American print sources throughout the first decade of the twentieth century, her archives at the Library of Congress are full of the unpublished short stories she wrote and sought to place in the nation's elite literary magazines. The collection also includes a dispiriting series of rejection letters from the publishers of these magazines that made clear to her that she lived in a political climate unsupportive of literary ambitions like her own. The chapter explores the ways Terrell used this knowledge and indeed, the form of the cover letter, to mount a protest against a publishing industry that refused to accept the creative works of African Americans. By continuing to submit stories that she knew would be rejected, she challenged editors to establish rather than acquiesce to public opinion and open up their pages to stories that might counter the influence of the racist narratives they widely circulated. It was not a campaign waged for her own benefit; she realized that her own writing would not be published. But from her own failure she was trying to make future failures by African American authors less likely. That she purposefully saved these letters illustrates her decision to value, preserve, and curate materials that would give voice to her own understanding of the way the literary market worked for Black writers.

The focus of my interest in Terrell—her unpublished short stories and the letters she wrote to communicate to editors her disappointment in the network and cultural values of mainstream American magazines—brings to the fore the central arguments of this book. *To Make Negro Literature* contends that the unsettledness and the complexity of turn-of-the-century literary culture needs to be revisited, so that we may read the stories of lesser-known and uncelebrated authors, messier and unpublished texts, and unsuccessful or underrealized projects alongside and against those that have received substantial critical attention. Materials of the sort I examine in this book demand close reading and critical analysis, for the simple reason that they broaden and complicate what is often perceived (and too often taught) as a seamless march from the past to the present.[39] In the faltering efforts, the failed strategies, the instability and the discontinuity that *To Make Negro Literature* brings to the fore is an important genealogy of African American literary culture, one that pushes us to expand our analytical rubrics and critical frames of reference in important ways.

One of the things I advocate for in this book is that we remain conscious of the still-limited kinds of works that receive our critical attention. While the focus of print culture studies has expanded tremendously in the last decade, it needs to expand further to include those components of African American literary history that did not appear in print and never made it to the stages of publication that we have traditionally associated with literature. Christopher Hager's patient, meticulously researched account of the manuscript writing of African Americans who were only marginally literate has much to tell us about the kinds of literary culture that existed outside of the realm of "highly literate people."[40] So too do the books sold by subscription that I examine in *To Make Negro Literature*, which have rarely warranted critical reading. One reason for this is surely because the profession of literary scholarship prizes what is original and creative, not what is manifestly unoriginal or utilitarian. Historians of Black print culture continuously lament not knowing more about those Black readers who were less highly educated, less cultured, and less privileged, but in dismissing books sold by subscription we have surely closed off one avenue through which to expand our understanding of the literary habits of those African Americans whose access to reading material was limited to the unexceptional and pedagogically oriented. Our own critical biases, then, have played a part in circumscribing our perspectives on African American literary history.

In writing *To Make Negro Literature* and thinking through its implications, I have been mindful of a key question: How can scholars make the fleetingly popular, the hidden, the forgotten, or the obscure aspects of African American literary history *legible*? My purpose in examining the particular authors and materials I look at in this book is not to resurrect them as accomplished, in the terms usually used by literary critics. I doubt that T. Thomas Fortune and Mary Church Terrell's writing will ever garner critical acclaim, or that the racial schoolbooks of the late nineteenth century or the lists and bibliographies generated at the same moment will claim the same place in literary history as, say, Du Bois's *The Souls of Black Folk*. My turn to the archives is not for the purpose of changing this. Rather, it is for the purpose of allowing these elements of literary culture to be seen as repositories of knowledge about the literary past that stand for themselves. Writing about the need to develop an appreciation for "*lostness, or condition of being lost*" as a mode of "archival discovery that attends to the conditions that would produce textual absence," Kinohi Nishikawa reminds us how much there is to learn about the literary culture of a specific moment by looking at a text's ephemeral appeal and the conditions that surrounded its appearance in and then disappearance from the literary landscape.[41] It need not always be that the materials we draw from the archives be added to a literary canon, or fit into a prewritten narrative of literary history. In the case of Terrell, her stories had no appeal for specific reasons, and never appeared in print. Nevertheless, outlining the story of her writing, of her aspirations to have her short fiction published, and of her failure to achieve this goal is crucial to seeing both the obstacles Black writers faced in the early twentieth century and the ways they sought to maneuver around them. Framing the failure of African American writers, texts, institutions, publications, and projects and, in Nishikawa's terms, charting the "path toward [their] becoming obscure," promises to significantly expand what we know about African American literary history.[42]

In the end, then, this is an account of the "making" of Negro literature in the sense of accounting for some of the ways African American intellectuals at the turn of the century made that literature possible by focusing more clearly on its infrastructure. As Du Bois claimed in a handwritten 1905 assessment of the value of developing his job printing business into a full-fledged publishing house, a Black-owned publisher could both manufacture "supplementary reading for Negro schools" and allow Negro writers the space to "speak more naturally and effectively" about the "things nearest to them."[43] My attention in *To Make Negro Literature* is drawn to both the readers and the writers about whom Du Bois was concerned at the beginning of the twentieth century. In the first two chapters, I explore the infrastructure for *readers* first by looking at a specific kind of text, the "schoolbook," that in many ways attempted to supplement the Negro school itself for its potential readers, leading them from literacy to the threshold of the literary. I then turn my attention to how those readers were directed to particular bodies of texts in the lists and bibliographies that cataloged, categorized, and made comprehensible the concept of "Negro literature." In the next two chapters, I explore the conception of emergent *authorship* in these same years, of those who were striving to speak more naturally and effectively in print, but were constrained by different forces that kept them from being able to do just that. Both Fortune and Terrell are "hidden" authors whose writing exists in the texts of another or in the archives of their own making. These two processes together—the emergence of the Negro reader and the halting and hidden work of the Negro writer—were the conditions that rendered possible the making of Negro literature.

Writing in 1913, Du Bois noted that, "despite the fact that the literary output by the Negro has been both large and credible," the "time has not yet come for the great development of Negro literature."[44] This foray into the history of African American authorship, writing, and literary practices at the very end of the nineteenth century and very beginning of the twentieth seeks a greater understanding of the disjuncture between the "large and credible" literary "output" of African Americans that Du Bois points to here and his determination that a time had "not yet come" that would allow for the "great development" of Negro literature. To focus on a time when something has not yet occurred may seem counterintuitive to historians of African American literature, whose research remains, for the most part, oriented toward moments that celebrate achievements rather than those that highlight shortcomings. But I am hopeful that, in shifting our focus, we will be able to set new terms for the critical appreciation of those shortcomings at the turn from the nineteenth to the twentieth century, while illustrating the sort of work that remains to be done to expand the map through which we see African American literary history.

"THE INFORMATION CONTAINED IN THIS BOOK WILL NEVER APPEAR IN SCHOOL HISTORIES"

PROGRESS OF A RACE & SUBSCRIPTION BOOKSELLING AT THE END OF THE NINETEENTH CENTURY

SOME OF THE MOST FAMILIAR WORKS OF AFRICAN AMERICAN LITERature from the turn from the nineteenth to the twentieth century illuminate the important place of literature and the literary in racial uplift ideology by fictionally replicating the process of literary learning as inherent in practices of political activism. These scenes of literary association, where characters come together to exchange ideas in the form of readings, lectures, and addresses, form the moral and intellectual centers of texts that are today most widely studied. In *Contending Forces* (1900), for instance, Pauline E. Hopkins casts Ma Smith's "parlor entertainments" as an example of a site of literary learning, where the community's Black women, led by those who are "well read and thoroughly conversant with all current topics," assemble for sewing and conversation.[1] Another example of this comes later in the book, in the chapter titled "The American Colored League," when its male characters assemble to share their views in a public forum. Frances E. W. Harper's 1892 novel *Iola Leroy* includes similar scenes, the most memorable of which is the conversazione that takes place in the chapter "Friends in Council." In the parlor of a private home, poetry, political addresses, and musical performance are placed in conversation in a way that move the novel's title character to both a clearer understanding of her own identity and a mandate to take action on behalf of her race: she is inspired, as was Harper herself, to write a book. Harper's parting note to the reader directly articulates her belief in the importance of literature to Black progress. While she acknowledges that African Americans have only just begun to "grasp the pen and wield it as a power for good," she identifies literary practices as key to the "brighter coming day" she sees on the horizon.[2]

These fictionalized scenes of literary and intellectual exchange are a part of what Hopkins readily identifies in the subtitle of her book as a "Romance," but there is ample evidence in the pages of African American newspapers and periodicals, as well as in the surviving records of literary associations, to illustrate that, by the end of the nineteenth century, similar forms of literary activity took place in enclaves of the Black middle and upper classes across the country.[3] In these contexts, literary study, broadly defined and taking place in a variety of forms, was one way African Americans distinguished themselves, not only from other, less highly educated, less ambitious, and less cultured African Americans living in Northern cities, but also from their Southern counterparts. If literary study became for African Americans in the North a marker of progress, it was also a marker of distance, distinguishing the prosperous, morally upright and intellectually vibrant lives of the middle and upper class from the vast majority of African Americans who remained in the largely rural South, where basic literacy itself was uneven. This less privileged, less highly educated population nevertheless also has a literary history defined by specific literary practices, albeit one that is difficult to recover.

We have grown familiar with narratives outlining the great progress made by former slaves in obtaining basic literacy skills after Emancipation, their learning facilitated not only by the network of primary schools formed through the Freedman's Bureau, but also schools organized through their own determination to teach themselves. But, as Christopher Hager has argued, literacy and education, like Emancipation itself, was a long, difficult, and uneven process.[4] Less easily accessible is a more extensive sense of how literacy unfolded around the turn of the century, when illiteracy rates among African Americans in the South hovered at around 50 percent. Researchers have noted the difficulty of definitively interpreting data related to literacy and illiteracy gathered at the end of the nineteenth century, citing, among other things, different perceptions of how literacy was defined and what it entailed between households and respondents.[5] But this was the figure that W. E. B. Du Bois settled on for the state of Georgia in 1900, as he prepared a series of maps, charts, and graphs that outlined statistical data on the Black population of Georgia that would form a large part of the Exhibit of American Negroes at the Paris Exposition Universelle. With its mix of rural and urban locations, Georgia presented itself to Du Bois as a "typical Southern State," and the steady decline in illiteracy across the forty years represented by the graph was certainly notable and indicative of the rise of literacy among African Americans across the South. But equally telling was the data presented in other charts that detailed how few African American students were pursuing courses of study outside of the industrial arts, toward degrees in business, the classics, the sciences, and "professional" subjects.[6] In the Atlanta University Studies' publication for 1900, Du Bois paid tribute to the network of Black colleges and universities that sprang up across the South after the Civil War by documenting the "number, distribution, occupations, and success of College-Bred Negroes." These institutions were certainly important to fostering certain kinds of literary production and producing readers for literature by writers like Frances Harper and Pauline Hopkins. But only a very small fraction of the Black population enrolled in these institutions, and, as Du Bois acknowledged, the number of Black students enrolled in the college curriculum at these schools was even smaller.[7]

These facts make it all the more important to think about the turn-of-the-century literary habits and practices that developed outside of schools, particularly across the South, through which African Americans moved beyond the acquisition of basic literacy skills to embrace an emergent concept of the literary. It is interesting to note that the term "literacy," as Raymond Williams reminds us, was "not in the language until the late nineteenth century," and that in fact its introduction was in part "made necessary by the movement of *literature* to a different sense."[8] In *Marxism and Literature*, Williams demonstrates how, before the eighteenth century, literature was simply "a condition of reading: of being able to read and of having read."[9] Only during the eighteenth and nineteenth centuries did the concept of literature evolve from its earlier, broader meaning, first to the neutral sense of a body of printed writings and, finally, toward the more specialized notion of a "'creative' or 'imaginative' work" of a certain quality that was distinct from utilitarian or nonimaginative writing.[10] Given the emphasis on the acquisition of literacy skills that emerged in part out of the massive effort to educate newly freed slaves, it is unsurprising that the word "literacy" is recognized as originating in the United States around 1880.[11] The hunger among former slaves for basic literacy in the aftermath of Emancipation was dizzying and, by the year 1900, illiteracy rates had dropped dramatically among the Black population. Distinguished from literacy, then, was the rise of a broader understanding of reading accomplishment and of the purposes and possibilities of literature that was located in an emergent idea of the literary. To be mindful of this distinction is to extend and expand our understanding of African American literary history in ways we have yet to fully acknowledge.

This chapter lingers over the transition between literacy and literary understanding as it took place among African Americans outside of Northern cities at the very end of the nineteenth and into the early twentieth century by attending to a specific kind of book. One of the most difficult aspects of my work with these texts has been simply giving them a name: they are at once compilations, anthologies, histories, biographies, and schoolbooks. I have settled on this last term—"schoolbooks"—for it captures the fundamentally educational quality of these massive volumes and their movement through various subject matters that, I argue, simultaneously gave shape and meaning to both Black identity and to literary study. Intended for instructional use, the books organized both racial knowledge and literary understanding. Indeed, they presented a coherent curriculum for a new logic of Black education, one that, at the end of the nineteenth century, did not have an established place in the formal educational settings available to African Americans. Sold door-to-door by agents who entered people's homes to show the book and talk to potential buyers about it before they purchased it, these schoolbooks made available to multiple generations both educational material and the cultural capital associated with books and the literary. In recognizing these books and their buyers, some of whom were likely to have been newly or semiliterate, or even illiterate, we extend our understanding of African American readers and Black print culture to include, among other things, the literary experiences of the less highly educated and less highly privileged, a culture of reusing and repurposing text, and a vibrant industry of subscription publishing. We also make visible a curriculum of literary study for African Americans that, through books, circulated within African American homes and local communities rather than in primary schools or institutions of industrial or college education.

Representative of this kind of book is William Crogman and Henry Kletzing's *Progress of a Race; or, The Remarkable Advancement of the Afro-American Negro, from the Bondage of Slavery, Ignorance and Poverty to the Freedom of Citizenship, Intelligence, Affluence, Honor and Trust*, which forms the focus of this chapter. *Progress of a Race* was copyrighted in 1897 and appeared in numerous editions between 1898 and 1929. At 664 pages, it reads now as an excessively bulky and largely uninteresting book focused on Black history and achievement that is entirely out of line with our own sense of the literary. On the surface, it contains little to help us understand its relevance to literary history. Indeed, few scholars have taken note of it or books of its kind, beyond general observations on their grandly narrativizing function, and even fewer have delved into the history of their publication, distribution, or reception. Henry Louis Gates Jr. cites the role of *Progress of a Race* and texts like it in crafting a new public image of African Americans that was intended to move "away from the stereotypes scattered throughout plantation fictions, blackface minstrelsy, vaudeville, racist pseudo-science, and vulgar Social Darwinism."[12] But his attention to the text itself is glancing, meant only to support his argument that African Americans created a metaphor of Blackness as a way of combating racist images that circulated in various popular cultural forms around the turn of the century. In *A Faithful Account of the Race*, historian Stephen G. Hall usefully places *Progress of a Race* in the context of the development of African American historical writing in the nineteenth century, but his brief analysis of the text as an Emancipation narrative places it in a long but limiting trajectory of disciplinary writing.[13] In contrast, I am interested in the literary value of *Progress of a Race*, not only in terms of the history of its emergence and distribution, but also its contents and use.

It's important to acknowledge the several interrelated reasons *Progress of a Race* and texts like it that were sold by subscription to African Americans around the turn of the century have been easily dismissed by literary scholars or deemed unworthy of sustained critical attention. Broad-ranging in scope and content, with a distinct and heavy-handed pedagogical quality, these books are easily excluded from what we now think of as literature, and this is the primary reason they have not been the subject of scholarly inquiry. One glance at *Progress of a Race*'s table of contents confirms that it resists identification by genre. It is, in fact, not one specific genre but a mixed bag of genres arrayed in an unstable hierarchy, an irregular and mysterious category of text that is difficult to contextualize. There are, however, antebellum antecedents of *Progress of a Race* and books like it that make visible a long history of racial schoolbooks produced by African Americans. The

PROGRESS OF A RACE

.. OR ..

THE REMARKABLE ADVANCEMENT OF THE AFRO-AMERICAN NEGRO

From the Bondage of Slavery, Ignorance and Poverty
to the Freedom of Citizenship, Intelligence,
Affluence, Honor and Trust

BY

H. F. KLETZING, A. M..

AND

W. H. CROGMAN, A. M.,

Professor in Clark University, Atlanta, Ga., Author of "Talks for the Times.'

❧ ❧

WITH AN INTRODUCTION

BY

BOOKER T. WASHINGTON,

Principal of Tuskegee Normal and Industrial Institute, Tuskegee, Alabama.

❧ ❧

PUBLISHED BY

J. L. NICHOLS & CO.

Atlanta, Ga.   Naperville, Ill.   Toronto, Ont.

(To whom all communications must be addressed.)

1898

☞ AGENTS WANTED.

1.1 Title page of William Crogman and Henry F. Kletzing's *Progress of a Race; or, The Remarkable Advancement of the Afro-American Negro* (1898).

mixed-genre and pedagogical valences, for instance, of Benjamin Banneker's almanac, which contains astrological, political, and religious material, included mathematical tables and calendars that gave Black readers resources to practice science, while also providing a treatise through which they could educate themselves on the tenets of both slavery and abolition. I have argued elsewhere that the earliest Black periodicals, such as *Freedom's Journal*, the *Colored American*, and Frederick Douglass's newspapers, served as "makeshift textbooks" by providing free African Americans in the urban North a variety of kinds of texts through which to practice literacy and display a commitment to literature. James. W. C. Pennington's *A Text Book of the Origin and History, &c. &c. of the Colored People*, published in 1841, serves as a reminder that African Americans understood the need to produce their own freestanding histories through which to counter racist thought and reconstruct the Black past long before the Civil War. Pennington's "text book" was directed to "families, and to students and lecturers in history," and his pedagogical mode—"to state facts, points and argument simply, rather than go extensively into them"—speaks to the urgent need he perceived for material that would, in a straightforward and effective way, "unembarrass the origin" and "show the relative position of the colored people in the different periods among the different nations."[14] Recent scholarship has begun to unpack and demystify the hybridity and the didactic quality of these texts, but we have been less able to see the value of doing the same for their late nineteenth- and early twentieth-century counterparts.

A second reason these books have been dismissed is that, whereas scholars are drawn to originality and creativity in literature, these books are highly unoriginal and uncreative, their content often taken from other texts without explanation or citation. As we will see, the authors of *Progress of a Race* copied, condensed, and abbreviated other literary texts rather than producing one from scratch. Rarely did they identify their sources, resulting in a text whose ambiguities necessitate the reevaluation of what counts as new and how authorship was understood and practiced at the end of the nineteenth century. Although *Progress of a Race* and books similar to it generally include prefaces by popular African American personalities, these individuals were usually figureheads, their words and images used because they were widely recognizable. But they were seldom responsible for the text's conception or construction. This is particularly true of Booker T. Washington, whose popularity as a spokesperson for the Black community made foregrounding his words and image a common means of selling books he did not author. "Authorship" is a particularly vexed idea in *Progress of a Race* and books like it published around the turn of the century. We might switch our emphasis to think about the role of the editor in these collections, as we often do when facing anthologies and compilations. But even the editorial hand modeled in books like *Progress of a Race* remains difficult to contain and understand. The individuals who did compile and edit the texts did not leave records of their purposes or processes.

A third reason for limited attention to these books is the fact that their mode of publication and their readership remains murky. While *Progress of a Race* helps make visible a moment in African American literary history when books became mobile and the audience for Black literature and literary learning expanded, it doesn't allow us access to these readers' impressions of what they read—or even offer evidence that they read these texts at all. The means of publication and distribution of these texts, printed by subscription book manufacturers whose records were not saved and marketed by anonymous agents who sold them door-to-door, often to uneducated, barely literate buyers, places them outside the conventional boundaries of quality literature (that is, the literature that we generally study). Although archives like the Zinman Collection of Canvassing Books at the University of Pennsylvania and Kent State University Libraries' collection of Publishers' Canvassing Books points to the prominence and the importance of subscription publishing in the United States, particularly in the nineteenth century, scholars have long deemed texts sold by subscription distinct from "real" literature. In the hierarchy of literary importance and literary power, these texts—cheaply produced, difficult to attribute to a specific author or even to a set of authors, not distinguished for their aesthetic accomplishment, and generally viewed as without status compared to those connected to "real" literature and its means of "official" distribution and consumption—bear all the markings of the subliterary. They have come to epitomize those apparently worthless texts, poorly printed and bought and valued by those who at times did not even have the ability to read them, against which we define the true "literariness" of other works, their scholarly value limited to the extent to which they help us determine a hierarchy of literary power that by definition excludes them.

How, then, are we to assess and appreciate these texts? In this chapter, I draw attention to *Progress of a Race* not to establish its literary value in our contemporary terms, but in order to better understand its historical, cultural, and intellectual significance to those who bought it in the last years of the nineteenth and first years of the twentieth century. In attending to *Progress of a Race* as a book that highlights the transition between the acquisition of elementary literacy skills that was the focus of African American education in the South in the aftermath of Emancipation and what I term an emergent concept of the literary, I am interested in the difference between basic reading ability and the more complex and layered learning experience and critical engagement with reading material implied by the literary. *Progress of a Race*, I argue, was structured to engage literacy in the pursuit of the literary—that is, to provide both a wider, deeper experience with reading and to communicate a set of methods for examining the richness and diversity of writing. It supplied primary documents through which to investigate African American history, culture, and achievements, and to study, evaluate, and interpret the wide body of writing on race and African American identity.

The biggest obstacle to understanding the importance of *Progress of a Race* lies in appreciating the context in which it was written. I therefore begin this chapter by mapping out my understanding of *Progress of a Race* as a schoolbook. In doing so, I place it in a long tradition of African American self-education, where books replicated and often took the place of schools as sites of learning. In the second part of the chapter, I look at the 1893 Chicago World's Fair and the Southern States and Cotton Exposition, held in Atlanta in 1895, to establish the ways that African Americans sought representation in the last decade of the nineteenth century. Here I lay the groundwork for my argument that the book *Progress of a Race* replicated the physical space of the Atlanta Exposition's Negro Building, offering, in a permanent and movable textual form, the educational logic of that temporary public display. The third part of the chapter looks at the mobility of *Progress of a Race* by focusing on both its publication history and the means by which the book was circulated. Published by subscription and sold door-to-door, *Progress of a Race* was simultaneously a display piece and a means of creating community and forging a collective sense of identity that located racial understanding and race pride in the space of books. Finally, in the last part of the chapter, I look at the contents and the structure of *Progress of a Race*, which, I argue, was intended to both highlight racial history and to chart the path forward from literacy to the literary.

The Schoolbook as Schoolhouse

While most histories of African American life at the end of the nineteenth century emphasize the debate between Booker T. Washington and W. E. B. Du Bois on the type of education best suited to advance the race, and the kind of institution best placed to meet that educational need, there is another story that remains relatively untold. The story of African American self-education helps us to understand the longer history of African American aspirations for learning and the different sites where that learning took place. Historically, for many Black learners, moving through a book either independently or in the company of other learners provided the only curriculum or structured education they received. Lorenzo Ezel's description of how he used his blue back speller confirms the influence of schoolbooks outside of the classroom. It also serves as a reminder that early African American education often took place both individually and on the margins of everyday life. "I ain't never been to school but I jes' picked up readin'," Ezel said. "With some of my first money I ever earn I buy me a old blue-back Webster. I carry dat book wherever I goes. When I plows down a row I stop at de end to rest and den I overlook de lesson."[15] This kind of movable, independent learning was especially important for Black adults, for whom attending school during the day may not have been possible.

This was the learner recognized by the African Civilization Society when, in 1866, it began publishing a schoolbook in newspaper form specifically aimed at teaching Black adults both literacy and literary skills. Founded in 1858 with the goal of encouraging the settlement of Black missionaries in Africa, the African Civilization Society was a Northern-based organization "officered and managed entirely by colored men."[16] During the Civil War, its aid efforts expanded to include providing assistance to the South's former slaves. The first issue of the *Freedman's Torchlight* appeared in 1866. Published in Brooklyn, New York, its creators meant for it to be distributed monthly among former slaves in the South as both a substitute for and supplement to formal schooling. Adult readers of the *Freedman's Torchlight* were to see themselves as the paper's primary audience. "We could not attend school in our youthful days," they were told, "and now we cannot spare a day for school. Yet we must learn how to read and write and understand figures." The *Freedman's Torchlight* presented itself as a solution to this dilemma, in both content and form. "Order your children to prepare for school, and proceed to work," the paper's first issue told its readers. During the day, the *Freedman's Torchlight* could be used in schools, as a supplement to more traditional schoolbooks. But for adults "without a knowledge of letters" who "must work during the day and go to school at night," the *Freedman's Torchlight* would be a "blessing," serving as instructional material that would take the place of a formal teacher-led classroom.[17]

In a form that combined an elementary curriculum with news that was better suited to the maturity of an adult reader, who aspired to read newspapers, than the imagination of a child, the *Freedman's Torchlight* stands as

THE FREEDMAN'S TORCHLIGHT.

"If God be for us, who can be against us?"--*Rom. 8: 31.*

| VOL. 1. | BROOKLYN, N. Y., DECEMBER, 1866. | NO. 1. |

THE FREEDMAN'S TORCHLIGHT
Is published Monthly on the following
TERMS:

One copy for one year - - 50 cts.
Eleven copies, for one year, to
one address - - - - $5,00
Twenty-five copies, for one year,
to one address - - - - 10, 00
Fifty copies, for one year - - 20, 00

☞ PAYMENT ALWAYS IN ADVANCE.

Money may be sent by Post-office order to "THE FREEDMAN'S TORCHLIGHT," African Civilization Building, Dean st. near Troy avenue, Brooklyn, N. Y.

ALPHABETS.

abcdefg
hijklmn
opqrstu
vwxyz
,;:..?!æœ

𝒜𝐵𝒞𝒟𝐸𝐹𝐺𝐻𝐼𝒥𝒦𝐿
𝑀𝒩𝒪𝒫𝒬𝑅𝒮𝒯𝒰𝒱𝒲𝒳𝒴𝒵
𝑎𝑏𝑐𝑑𝑒𝑓𝑔𝒽𝒾𝒿𝓀𝓁𝓂𝓃𝑜𝓅𝓆𝓇𝓈𝓉𝓊𝓋𝓌
𝓍𝓎𝓏,;..?!

A B C
D E F
G H I
J K L
M N O
P Q R
S T U
V W X
Y Z . &
1 2 3 4 5 6 7 8 9 0.

LESSON No 1.

ba be bi bo bu by
ca ce ci co cu cy
da de di do du dy
fa fe fi fo fu fy
ga ge gi go gu gy
ha he hi ho hu hy

LESSON No 2.

ja je ji jo ju
ka ke ki ko ku ky
la le li lo lu ly
ma me mi mo mu my
na ne ni no nu ny
pa pe pi po pu py

LESSON No 3.

ra re ri ro ru ry
sa se si so su sy
ta te ti to tu ty
va ve vi vo vu vy
wa we ya ye za ze
wi wo zi zo

LESSON No 4.

ab eb ib ob ub
ac ic oc uc
ad ed id od ud
af ef if of uf
ag eg ig og ak

SPELLING AND READING LESSONS.

1

bat, cat, rat, boy, top, run, sun, dog, hog, log, sing, wing, the, see, has, map, bark, and, can.

2

the bat can fly. the dog can bark, and the boy can run. the sun is up. I can see the sun. I see the map. the boy has a top.

3

free, life, live, fives, took, love, loves, man, now, will, thank, God, work, hard, good, house, right, learn, land, made, free, slaves, stand, God, should, ought, serve, read, stand, union, ever, now, and.

4

I am free and well. I will love God and thank him for it. and I must work hard and be good and get me a house and lot.

5

God made all men free. Then we should not be slaves to sin nor man. But we ought to love God and serve him. We should learn to read and write and be good. We will stand up for the union, now and for ever.

LESSON No 1.

Looking to God.

At night before I close my eyes
And in the morning when I rise,
I pray for safety, health and grace,
And still the Lord before me place.
Through all the business of the day,
He goes before, and points the way;
His goodness shews me what is right,
And makes me sleep in peace at night.

GOD SEES US.

God made our eyes, and can discern Which ever way we think to turn. He made our ears, and he can hear, When we may think nobody's near. In every place, by night and day He watches all we do and say. Then always be afraid, my dear, To tell a lie, for God does hear.

GOD

There is none like unto thee our God. He made us, and the heavens declare his glory. He is one God and the Father of us all. He sees all we do and hears all we say. If we are good he will love us and save us; but if we are bad he will punish us with eternal death.

MAN

God created man in his own image. He made man of the dust of the earth, and breathed life into his nostrils and man became a living soul.

ADAM

Adam was the first man. He had a reddish color. Adam lived nine hundred and thirty years.

EVE

Eve was the first woman. She was Adam's wife. Adam and Eve were our first parents.

THE BIBLE.

The Bible is the holy book of God; it tells us all about God and his works. It also tells us how the first people lived and where they lived; and about Jesus Christ the Son of God who died to save sinners. We must study hard and learn to read the Bible; for it tells us how to please God and get to heaven.

HISTORY

History will tell you all about the different nations, and great cities that ever have been. It will tell you who first came to this country, and all about the Colored people and every other people. It is delightful to read history. As soon as you can read all in this little paper, called the *Torchlight*, you will be able to read history.

ARITHMETIC.

Arithmetic is the science that treats of numbers. It is sometimes called a language of which there are ten different letters or characters, namely, 1, 2, 3, 4, 5, 6, 7, 8, 9, and 0, which is called a cipher. These may be combined so as to express every idea of numbers. *One* is the base of all numbers. Hence to *one*, every other number bears a certain relation. Numbers may be added together, subtracted or multiplied, therefore, there are four general divisions to Arithmetic, addition, subtraction, multiplication, and division.

Can you count?

GEOGRAPHY.

Geography is the science that treats of the outside part of the earth. If you can read well enough to understand it, you may turn to a lesson on Geography found at another place in this little paper.

GRAMMAR

English grammar teaches how to speak and write the English language correctly. If you wish to know more about it, you can find the lesson in it at another place in the *Torchlight*.

HITHERTO THE LORD HATH HELPED US."

BY REV. F. BOTTOME.

"Ebenezer! God is with us!"
Sang our fathers long ago;
"Ebenezer! God is with us,"
Sing their grateful children now,
Ebenezer!
Every knee to worship bow.

Blessing now and adoration
Young and old in concert sing;
Sing in lofty jubilation
To your great Redeemer, King;
Grace and mercy
His right arm alone did bring.

"Ebenezer!" God is with us!"
Echo down the stream of time,
"Ebenezer!" till the story
From the hills of glory chime,
And the angels
Swell the glorious song sublime.

an example of the way schoolbooks have been used to give sequence to instruction. The first page of the first issue included a listing of the alphabet in both upper- and lowercase and script letters, followed, first, by lessons one through four, all of which involved practice with "simple combinations of the vowels and consonants," then a "Spelling and Reading" lesson, moving readers from the simplest words like "cat," "dog," "the," and "see" to more complicated words and sentences. Embodied in these spelling and reading lessons are the African Civilization Society's political and religious instruction, for the *Freedman's Torchlight* also meant to order readers' social, religious, moral, and ethical priorities. Through careful study, by the end of the first page of the newspaper, readers would have mastered enough words to read the following passage: "I am free and well. I will love God and thank him for it. [A]nd I must work hard and be good and get me a house and lot."[18]

These sentences underscore the extent to which even those most basic lessons in literacy, created for African Americans in the South by their Northern counterparts, were ripe with social and political intent.[19] But, alongside this mission, the *Freedman's Torchlight* wanted to advance its readers beyond basic literacy skills by providing the materials of a literary education. Reading allowed learners to go places, not only in the world of material prosperity but also in the issue of the newspaper itself. Readers who were interested in English grammar, for instance, were directed to "another place in the *Torchlight*," and those pursuing knowledge in geography likewise to "another place in this little paper." In some cases, as in those interested in prosody, "the fourth and last part of Grammar," the paper promised that it was a subject "of which we will speak in due time." As a schoolbook, in other words, it directed students to different classrooms, and sometimes to future classes.

The *Freedman's Torchlight* supported the African Civilization Society's contention that "the black man is the better leader and teacher among his own people than the white man." Their effort to take control of Black education had, by 1866, already resulted in the organization of "twenty-two (22) day and night schools, employing thirty-three (33) teachers."[20] They intended that the *Freedman's Torchlight* be published monthly as a part of an effort to build an educational system that would educate African Americans outside of the physical and organizational structure of the schoolhouse; such an education, they believed, would facilitate social, political, and economic advancement even for those who could not attend school. Imagining this sort of advancement made the *Freedman's Torchlight* a very different sort of educational space than the freedmen's schools, where schoolbooks produced by the American Tract Society directed Black learners to accept white supremacy, economic subservience, and their own intellectual inferiority. Of course, the *Freedman's Torchlight* was also designed so as to instill in African Americans "proper" religious and moral values alongside lessons in spelling and geography. But, unlike the majority of early textbooks designed for African Americans by whites, it served as what Erica Armstrong Dunbar has described as a protected space, where those new to formal education could study and practice literacy beyond the boundaries of racist stereotype and public constructions of Blackness.[21] Likewise, it animates Kevin Quashie's useful concept of "quiet," which he describes as an invitation to consider Black cultural identity from somewhere other than the public discourse by which it has historically been defined. In the quiet of the pages of the *Freedman's Torchlight*, African Americans were able to begin the process of seeing possibilities and setting aspirations for themselves.[22]

The *Freedman's Torchlight* is just one component of a long history of efforts by African Americans to create intimate spaces in which to learn about themselves and to supplement what was missing from their education with texts of their own creation, making visible the processes of rethinking the tenets of Black education that came from within the race. Often this took the form of books that were intended to supplement through literature—that is, reading material—the education that they received in school. Increasingly, the area of Black history was identified as one of these needs, with books being produced that outlined the Black historical past and highlighted important members of the race while advancing the pedagogical imperative that Black identity be known through literary work. Exposure to literature became the base for programs of knowledge acquisition that would teach African Americans what they needed to know to be "awake to the new destinies which await them."[23] This was the intent of William T. Alexander's *History of the Colored Race in America*, which was copyrighted in 1887. In the preface, Alexander notes that the "subjects embraced in this work are of vast importance and need careful attention. It is only by a thorough knowledge of the past history of the race that the colored people will be better able to avail themselves of the blessings the future has in store for them." Self-consciously, these texts were considered teaching tools, necessary for an African American individual to engage with as a part of the process of "fit[ting] himself for the duties of life," including "ste[ping] forth into the political arena to do battle for himself."[24]

On the final page of the *History of the Colored Race in America*, in a chapter focused on the education of Black women, Alexander points to the importance of "self-education," which he realized was especially significant for them.[25] But his own book—and the proliferation of books like his—underscores the degree to which self-education was a central concern of all African Americans as the nineteenth century drew to a close. What Alexander proposes is that the book take the place of the school; it effectively organizes a curriculum of study and guides its reader at his or her own pace through the material without the need for a teacher. In doing this, texts that functioned as schoolbooks make visible a moment when African Americans were taking charge of key aspects of their own education, shifting the site of education, at least in part, from the public space of schools to the private space of homes, where it became a shared concern. Despite the proliferation of schools, the need for this supplemental and alternative mode of independently acquiring education was perhaps at no time more necessary than at the end of the nineteenth century. As Washington's influence as an educator and popularity as a spokesperson and a leader crystallized, more and more support was given to schools that championed industrial training, making fewer and fewer resources available to support college-level education, which was in any case available to only a slim minority of the African American population.[26] Schools oriented toward industrial education would continue to do little to support literary training beyond the acquisition of basic literacy, validating the charge that this form of education was a movement to "deprive the blacks of intellectual development."[27] As Hampton Institute's second president, H. B. Frissell, recalled in a 1907 article, "Negro conventions referred to Hampton as a 'slave pen and literary penitentiary.'"[28] This perspective illustrates the understanding among African Americans that Hampton and schools like it were not sites where extensive literary training would take place. This left African Americans to find these courses of study elsewhere. As we will see in this chapter, William Crogman's *Progress of a Race* was intended at least in part to move African Americans beyond the skills of basic literacy, advancing literature and its study as a means of claiming Black identity.

I have opened this chapter with an overview of the *Freedman's Torchlight* and an introduction to the idea that texts could provide a framework for crucial forms of African American self-education for several reasons. First, the *Freedman's Torchlight* is representative of a long history of African American self-education that predates Emancipation. As scholars have argued, African Americans have always had to take the matter of their education into their own hands. Before the Civil War, a combination of law and custom prohibited enslaved people from learning to read and write. Scholars have documented the ways that African Americans nevertheless went about learning "in secret places," to quote Heather Andrea Williams, as a way to access literacy and the written word.[29] As the *Freedman's Torchlight* illustrates, even as the number of schools for African Americans increased during Reconstruction, the means to a structured curriculum that advanced self-education coexisted alongside formal education. The newspaper was intended to serve the newly free Black population as both a supplement in the classroom during the day and a schoolhouse in its own right in the evenings. Organized around sequenced learning, where students could build from one level of success to the next, it provided a template for progress like the school. The trajectory of that progress was from the most basic building blocks of literacy to the literary—from learning the alphabet and how to put together simple words and sentences, to putting literacy to work as a means of studying academic disciplines, ethical issues, and politics.

Toward the end of the nineteenth century, as conditions for African Americans deteriorated throughout the country and opportunities to move beyond the most elementary forms of education in schools dwindled, the need for self-education became even more pronounced. The schools did not provide the sort of education that African Americans needed to learn to speak for themselves or, as Alexander puts it, to "step forth into the political arena to do battle for himself." This would only be achieved through what Alexander identifies as "self-education," a pursuit that takes place not in a school but, rather, in and through books. The word "schoolbook" usually points to a book that is used in schools. But here I am interested in the way schoolbooks took the place of schools. In this context, the book more than the school becomes the site of learning.

The Negro Building's Logic, in Textual Form

Alexander's explicit advice to make the book the primary site of self-education reveals not so much a suspicion of public education, which, after all, was still in its formative years when the *Freedman's Torchlight* was circulating and the *History of the Colored Race in America* was published, but a sense that there were supplemental "spaces" where education might be pursued. Those spaces could vary, from the "sewing circle" in Hopkins's novel to the parlor in Harper's, and to the end of the row where Lorenzo Ezel rested his plow and sharpened his mind. What distinguishes them all is that they were private spaces, or at least not public in the same way school buildings were public. These were spaces marked not by their specific location but by what happened in them—self-education—and the means by which that education was pursued: through the individual study of books. For Booker T. Washington, that type of education, which he had himself pursued with some devotion in his earlier years, sometimes and in some forms became the exemplar of folly. One of the "saddest things" he saw during his travels, he wrote, was "a young man, who had attended some high school, sitting down in a one-room cabin, with grease on his clothing, filth all around him, and weeds in the yard and garden, engaged in the study of French grammar."[30] What saddened Washington was the relatively abstruse subject the young man pursued, as well as the inattention that he gave to the manual labor of cleaning himself, his house, and his yard. For Du Bois, Washington was unable to appreciate the boy's aspirations for learning because Washington had succumbed to "triumphant commercialism, and the ideals of material prosperity."[31] What neither writer emphasizes is that this is a scene in which this young man was engaged in educating himself in a private, domestic space (a "one-room cabin"), attended only by the book of French grammar he had at hand. What replaced the buildings of the Hampton or Tuskegee Institutes, or Atlanta University, was a room and a book of his own.

What I have called the "schoolbook" is an object that divorces the text from the institution in which it is usually housed. The "book" does not need a "school." It becomes its own school. This dynamic in which the text replicates the task of the institution in which it is conventionally housed is important because of what it reveals about African American strategies of self-education. It is also important because of what it suggests about the ways that books could emerge from and also replicate other institutions of learning and representation. It is to those less permanent but equally significant structures that we can now turn. That story begins for us with the 1893 Chicago World's Fair.

The World's Columbian Exposition, as it was formally called, was the second World's Fair to be held in the United States. It was designed to dazzle the world with the progress and achievements of America, including its transformation from a mostly agricultural society to a strikingly modern, urban, and industrial one. African Americans saw this as an appropriate moment to represent themselves through a display of their own progress and citizenship. They lobbied for a physically separate space at the fair in which to represent themselves; they were, after all, key participants in the progress of the United States that was on display. This request, however, was denied. At the center of the protest against their exclusion was the widely circulated pamphlet *The Reason Why the Colored American Is Not in the World's Columbian Exposition*, which included contributions from abolitionist leader

Frederick Douglass, journalist I. Garland Penn, and lawyer and business leader Ferdinand L. Barnett. But it was fueled by Ida B. Wells's own fiery words and her vivid understanding of the importance of compiling a record of the violence and inequities to which Black people in the United States were subject. Her determination to "print [this record] in book or pamphlet form for *free* distribution at the world's fair . . . and lay the whole question in all its hideousness bare before the world" ensured that Black Americans had a vigorous and long-lasting textual presence, if not a centrally located physical one, at the fair.[32]

Despite the challenges of gaining representation in Chicago, a small set of African Americans did so successfully.[33] One of them was William H. Crogman, an African American professor of Latin and Greek at Clark University in Atlanta. The display of work he organized by students at Atlanta University was exhibited in the Liberal Arts Building, which showcased the "educational methods and systems" of leading colleges around the nation.[34] The Atlanta University exhibit highlighted Black students' academic accomplishments in grammar, rhetoric, logistics, and mathematics. It was deemed not worth mentioning by Trumbull White and William Igleheart, whose book *The World's Columbian Exposition* was advertised as a "Full Description of the Buildings and Exhibits in all Departments." Nevertheless, this display of African American intellectual work was there, tucked in among the exhibits of the best of the nation's colleges and universities, a list that included "Amherst, Bryn Mawr, Chautauqua, the University of Chicago, Johns Hopkins University, Columbia College, The Massachusetts Institute of Technology, Princeton, the University of Michigan, Vassar, Yale, and almost every one of the State Universities."[35]

William Crogman was an important if understudied participant in protests surrounding the lack of representation at the Chicago World's Fair. He was born free in 1841 on the island of St. Maarten and orphaned as a teenager. After his parents' death, a Massachusetts ship-owning family took him in; this began a decade-long period in which Crogman traveled the world while working as a hand on shipping vessels. Visiting ports in Europe, South America, Australia, and Asia, his education was informal but international. In 1868, with the support of his adoptive family, Crogman enrolled in Pierce Academy in Middleboro, Massachusetts. There he faced racial prejudice but still excelled at his studies: according to the school's principal, Crogman "accomplished in one quarter as much as the average student did in two, mastering almost intuitively, and with equal facility, both mathematical and linguistic principles."[36] Upon graduation, he was hired by the Freedman's Aid Society

1.3 *Portrait of William Crogman,* the frontispiece to *Progress of a Race* (1898). This is the same portrait used as the frontispiece in Crogman's collection of lectures, *Talks of the Times* (1896).

to teach "the English branches" at Claflin University, an all-Black school in Orangeburg, South Carolina, where he was the first Black teacher. According to his biography, it was during his tenure there that he became "impressed with the need of a knowledge of Greek and Latin, and began the study of Latin himself."[37] He enrolled in the "classical course" at Atlanta University in 1873, moving through the program in three years instead of the usual four. Crogman completed the degree in classics in 1876 as a member of Atlanta University's first graduating class. Even as he went on to become a founding member of the faculty at Atlanta's Clark University, he continued his studies, receiving in 1879 a master's degree from Atlanta University. An educator with a reputation for being able to "motivate even the dullest student," Crogman quickly advanced to the positions of senior professor and master teacher at Clark, where he was praised for his "scholarship in his department, literary ability, general culture and distinguished services."[38] He also made a name for himself as a popular public speaker whose lectures combined a sharp knowledge of the history of African Americans with a firm belief in their worthiness of the rights and responsibilities of citizenship.

Crogman's experience at the 1893 World's Fair was likely one reason why, in September 1894, he was appointed as one of fourteen African American men charged with forming a "Negro Exhibit" for the Southern States and Cotton Exposition, due to take place in Atlanta in 1895. His willingness to serve as the commissioner from Georgia is a testament to his belief in the importance of the forum of the world's fair, as well as his stature as a respected educator and leader. This World's Fair would yield what Chicago's had not: an African American representative space and site. The commissioners were keenly aware that, as I. Garland Penn, the head commissioner of the Negro Building, put it, this was "an opportunity to seek again what we wanted in Chicago."[39] A pavilion dedicated to the display of Black life, progress, and achievement would be a place to "show [the white people of the South] that we, the colored people of the south, have accomplished something, that we are indeed a great people, and that we have a future before us which very few of them dream of," as the African American doctor and businessman H. R. Butler argued in the pages of the *Atlanta Constitution*.[40] Crogman embraced the opportunity wholeheartedly. He spent the summer of 1894 traveling across the state of Georgia, as well as what he described as the "southern and southwestern states," not only to assemble the state's collection but also to talk up the exposition as an opportunity for African Americans to represent themselves.[41] In the end, the Georgia exhibit was representative of the pedagogical logic of the Negro Building as a whole: it positioned signs of African American expertise in manufacturing and industrial skills alongside proof of their intellectual activities. The handcrafts of its African American people were well represented, and next to evidence of African American talents in sewing techniques, woodworking, iron forging, and other products of school programs in industrial education was a display of materials from the college curriculum taught at Atlanta's African American colleges and universities, which included books on philosophical methods, Greek, Latin, physics, trigonometry, and political economy. Taken together, the contrasts inherent in these displays would lead to productive debates on the future of African Americans in the United States that would take on greater dimensions and visibility in the years ahead.[42]

Despite recent scholarly efforts to expand our understanding of the 1895 Negro Building and, more broadly, the racial dynamics at play in world's fairs, our knowledge of the 1895 Southern States and Cotton Exposition for the most part begins and ends with Booker T. Washington's infamous address. The Atlanta Compromise, as it is familiarly known, was delivered on September 18, 1895, as a part of the fair's opening day festivities. Washington's speech and the conciliatory philosophy it advocated has remained the most visible artifact from the Atlanta Exposition. It is there that Washington famously pronounced: "In all things that are purely social, we can be as separate as the fingers, yet one as the hand in all things essential to mutual progress."[43] But this was not the only influential address delivered by an African American at the exhibition. Here I want to draw attention to another speech, one that more fully identifies the tensions and contradictions between different educational philosophies that were articulated at the site of the exposition. The Reverend John Wesley Edward Bowen, a professor of historical theology at Atlanta's Gammon Theological Seminary in Atlanta, had been chosen as the keynote speaker for the opening ceremonies of the Negro Building itself, which, due to delays in construction, did not open to the public until October 21, 1895. Before a crowd of approximately five thousand African Americans and only five hundred whites, Bowen opened his address in a far different tone than that captured by Washington one month earlier. Whereas Washington had indicated that the Negro was content with relative stasis, Bowen declared in his address, called "An Appeal to the King," that "a new Negro has come upon the stage of action."[44] He invited African Americans to see themselves as actors in motion, their advancement the result of their intellectual performance. According to Bowen, nothing was more important than the intellectual work with which African Americans were engaged. Pointing to Washington, DC, artist W. C. Hill's "statue of a Negro with broken manacles on his wrists," Bowen rhetorically asked his audience what this man was doing: "He is thinking!" was his thunderous reply (7). In introducing his audience to the Negro Building and inviting them to enter and embrace it as their own "stage of action," he asked them to see it as a structure through which African Americans could make visible crucial skills of thinking critically. This critical thought, he advocated, should not be primarily about their relationship to white Americans but about their own racial history and emergent consciousness of what Bowen called a "racial personality" (8).

"The Negro wishes to put himself on record," Bowen told his audience. To do so, he said, "he will think off those chains," leaving him "free to build this country and make a grand destiny of himself" (2, 7).

It is notable that the king to which Bowen directs his appeal is not God, as historian Theda Perdue has suggested, but what he terms "American sentiment" (4), which he describes as that invisible force of prejudice that "occupies a front seat in the halls of legislation[,] dictates the political policy of the nation," and passes judgment on "acceptable" behaviors and appearances (1).[45] Bowen recognized the harmful and pervasive structures of power underlying this force, whose laws, he said, were "unwritten" but "executed with scrupulous exactness in the minutest detail" (1). Simply put, there was no room for silence or passivity in the presence of this king. In his speech, Bowen pointed to the Negro Building as a sign of what he called "unperceived but positive changes in society" (2) that would alter American sentiment toward the Negro. These would also lead to a deeper understanding of what lay beneath the South's so-called "Negro Problem." Understanding this problem, he implied, was one of the primary reasons that Blacks must become critical thinkers. Bowen recognized that racial strife was not a simple or isolated issue of Black-white relations in the United States, but one that needed to be attacked globally and systematically. He challenged African Americans to think deeply and expansively about what he termed the "so-called race problem," which, he noted, has been "popularly interpreted to mean the Negro race problem." Thinking critically about race—by which he meant studying it widely and deeply, to come up with a "truer and larger conception of the subject" (2)—would reveal an even more pernicious, pervasive global "human race problem": the problem of difference. Solving the race problem in the South would be one way for African Americans to contribute to the well-being of the country. But Bowen wanted African Americans to develop the critical skills needed to see beyond the illusion of what he called the "narrower Negro race problem" (2), to understand conceptually the structures of power and systems of marginalization, disempowerment, subordination, and exploitation that lay beneath the world's and the human race's inequities, discrimination, and distaste for difference.

One of the most important elements of Bowen's speech was his direction that African Americans needed to think critically about themselves. The Negro "has begun the study of himself," Bowen told his audience, defining this as an essential component of "seeking to locate himself as a crucial factor among men" (3). The term he uses here is an important one: "study." Whereas learning indicates the acquisition of a skill—we learn to read, for instance, or how to ride a bike—studying implies an ongoing intellectual process and practice. In Bowen's use of the term, that practice is a common, communal one that conjures up a sense of both racial community and collective endeavor. By simultaneously documenting the common scholarly practice that the Negro Building illustrates as already in motion and calling for the ongoing habit of critical inquiry that must be its legacy, Bowen presents the Negro Building as an intellectual workspace, identifying it as both an impetus for and an invitation to what Fred Moten and Stefano Harney have called "black study."[46] Only by engaging in deep and sustained study of themselves, Bowen argues, would African Americans be able to answer for themselves the series of questions that he challenged his audience to confront. Has the Negro any place in American life? If so, what is that place to be? How were African Americans to negotiate the relationship between racial and national belonging? How were they to simultaneously attend to equality and diversity? What shifts needed to occur—and was it even desirable—for the United States to become, in Bowen's words, a "sphere of nationality, and not of raceality" (3)?

In fact, the Negro Building was modeled as a generative place of Black study, where African Americans practiced and performed as critical thinkers; it was a context that sought to recognize the complex meanings of race and difference and to elevate conversations about them to advanced levels. The "question of equality of the races as familiarly understood and as commonly interpreted is a threadbare and musty saying and is groundless in reason and in the concrete facts of today," Bowen told his audience in the Negro Building's opening ceremony. In challenging African Americans to use the building as a "stage of action," he identified it as exactly what it was: an important site of Black intellectual practice (7). The exhibits confronted African Americans with a huge variety of material items as food for thought; placed alongside and in conversation with one another, they appear as an invitation to think critically about the politics of racial identity and the Negro past, present, and future. But the Negro Building was not only a place of display. It sponsored caucuses, debates, and conferences that took place throughout the fall of 1895, all of which initiated discussions, shared knowledge, and launched organizational efforts. The congresses ranged widely, focusing on African American professionals, businesses, and religion. Military Day highlighted the contributions of Black troops and, in doing so, made visible the centrality of Black patriots to the country's most important national narratives. The Negro Building hosted an event to honor the National Afro-American Press, as well as a meeting of the American Association of Educators of Colored Youth. A Congress on Africa exposed African Americans to knowledge of their ancestral homeland, providing a public forum for thinking about the relationship between Africa and African Americans. By far the largest event sponsored by the Negro Building was the Congress on Women. Barred from the Women's Building, Black women used this event to augment the visibility of their own education, creativity, leadership, and influence, supplementing the material signs of their productivity with evidence of their intellectual, social, and activist work. Coupled with the displays in the Negro Building, all of these events had the effect of illuminating questions about racial identity and American race relationships. The discussions that sprang from these forums were not limited to the immediate space of the Atlanta Exposition, but circulated throughout the nation, not only by visitors to Atlanta but also by both white-owned newspapers and the Black press.[47]

The Atlanta Exposition closed on December 31, 1895. But in the years that followed, I argue, when the bricks-and-mortar building that had housed the Negro Building had been emptied of its contents, collections like *Progress of a Race* re-created the pedagogical logic of the Negro Building, their literary, textual form offering displays and forums for discussion and debate that did not have to be dismantled but could enter people's homes on a permanent basis. There is a clear transition from 1893 in Chicago, where African American accomplishments were displayed in a limited way in the Liberal Arts Building of the Columbian Exposition, to 1895, where, for the first time, African Americans established their own Negro Building, and to 1897, when *Progress of a Race* provided in textual form the representation that had been absent in Chicago. Here, the book *Progress of a Race* supplanted the Negro Building just as books had supplemented, and sometimes supplanted, the schoolhouse. The physical building that housed displays of African American life and provoked Black intellectual thought was replicated in *Progress of a Race* and other massive text-based literary collections published at the end of the nineteenth century.

This development, from building to book, seems inevitable, since the designers of these exhibits sometimes used the format of the book as their pattern. Writing a few years later about the Paris Exposition, African American lawyer Thomas Calloway saw how such exhibits were already books in potentia. He would note that the organizers "decided to make the exhibit a social study, and to constitute each feature as a supplementary chapter, the whole forming a book or treatise on Negro progress and present conditions."[48] This way of framing the 1900 exhibit, as modeled as a book on "Negro progress," brings into perspective the ways that the book *Progress of a Race* was perhaps modeled after the programs and exhibits of the Atlanta Exposition's Negro

Building. Like the Negro Building, exposure to the text's curated "displays" and to the ideas and opinions that emerged from its contents served a pedagogical function: the book provided both a context for learning and an organized structure. As we will see, these books and the pedagogical practices they supported would largely defy the tenets of an industrial or a vocational model of education that was most widely available to African Americans at the end of the nineteenth century; they would also expand in a significant way the liberal arts education offered in Negro colleges by extending their reach and by including African American history and Black identity as a subject of study.

At the forefront of the effort to produce and distribute this sort of education to African Americans was William Crogman, the man who had successfully displayed evidence of Black intellectual achievement in Chicago and so carefully curated Georgia's exhibit in Atlanta's Negro Building. His book, *Progress of a Race*, which was copyrighted just two years after the close of the Atlanta Exposition, replicated the Negro Building as an instructional space in recasting intellectual training as a literary endeavor to be undertaken independently. With *Progress of a Race*, Crogman effectively relocated the site of African American education, from the temporary, public, and architectural space of the Negro Building to the permanent, domestic, and mobile site of the book. Proof of the urgency of his project would emerge just five months after the Negro Building and the Atlanta Exposition closed, when the equal rights guaranteed to Black citizens under the Fourteenth Amendment were rescinded by the U.S. Supreme Court's decision in *Plessy v. Ferguson*. By upholding states' rights to segregate public facilities, the court tacitly legalized it, authorizing white racist violence, and guaranteeing the injustice and the daily humiliations African Americans faced under Jim Crow's stringent regulation of urban and rural life. These deteriorating conditions made *Progress of a Race*'s alternative structures of knowledge and its mobility more necessary than ever.

A "Race Publisher"

In the first two parts of this chapter, I have offered a sense of the context out of which *Progress of a Race* appeared, arguing for the importance of seeing the text as a schoolbook and as a means of self-education that emerged from both Crogman's role as a commissioner of the Negro Building at the Atlanta Exposition and his status as an educator in a charged landscape where Black education was inadequate. I will return to the literary agenda communicated in the textual space of the book in the final part of the chapter. I now turn to what is arguably the most important feature of *Progress of a Race*: its mobility. *Progress of a Race* was not the only print form to emerge from the context of the Atlanta Exposition's Negro Building, but, significantly, this particular text was the result of a carefully calculated experiment, the story of which is embedded in a larger history of subscription bookselling. Crogman was passionate about the importance of public educational work, and *Progress of a Race* illustrates his desire to extend both the pedagogical value of the Atlanta Exposition's Negro Building and the reach of literature—which is to say scholarly material and the intellectual conversations that sprang from it, beyond the limits of what was typical for Black education. But it is important to remember that *Progress of a Race* was also a commercial venture. For its publisher, the collection's appeal was surely its potential for financial profit; its success would be measured in its ability to reach an as yet untapped Black book-buying public that the publisher calculated was eager to see themselves in print and to gain more and different perspectives on Black progress. In 1895, the illiteracy rate in Georgia and across the South was still high.[49] And yet it is during this time that the idea of marketing books specifically to African Americans and on African American subjects gained momentum. In the case of *Progress of a Race*, the success of this idea would depend on a midwestern publisher, who was essential to both the manufacturing and marketing process and who was willing to take the risk that such a line of books could succeed financially. That publisher was the J. L. Nichols Company, which was centered in Naperville, Illinois, a city just outside of Chicago. By the 1880s, Chicago had become the largest publishing center in the United States outside of the East Coast and an epicenter for subscription manufacturing and selling, a business that thrived in this particular location in part because of its ability to move books into the West, the South, and even up into Canada. The industry in Chicago expanded exponentially in 1893 as a direct result of the World's Columbian Exposition; an extraordinary number of publications were associated with this event, and many of them were manufactured in the Chicago area.[50]

But the idea of marketing "Negro History" did not initially come from this Northern hub of the industry. Significantly, the Nichols Company had an office in Atlanta, and a history of the company credits the venture that would result in *Progress of a Race* to an Atlanta employee, A. N. Jenkins. Jenkins began his working life as a subscription bookseller, clearing $780 in the first year that he marketed, primarily in western states, the company president J. L. Nichols's own publication—and the text with which he began his publishing company: *The Business Guide: or, Safe Methods of Business.*

Like many subscription booksellers, Jenkins rose up through the ranks; as a supervisor of booksellers in the South his agents sold over thirteen thousand books in a single year. He would eventually settle in Atlanta, beginning a company called Guide Publishers, which would be absorbed by the J. L. Nichols Company in 1898. In selling the Guide Publishers Company to Nichols, Jenkins took on a leadership position in the Nichols Company, becoming the local manager of an Atlanta branch of the company and, in doing so, extending the reach and influence of the Nichols business into the South. Jenkins appears to have worked most closely at the Nichols Company with John Hertel, who also got his start in the business as a canvasser of subscription books and who worked in the Naperville headquarters. Upon the death in 1895 of J. L. Nichols, who had first employed Hertel to sell his own publications as part of a "squad" of four canvassers in Colorado in the summer of 1891, Hertel took over the publishing company as its general manager, successfully expanding the "Nichols business" into a "large and permanent subscription house."[51] Hertel and Jenkins would eventually form a partnership, and the pamphlet that introduced their new company, Hertel, Jenkins & Co., offers the most complete account available on the origin of the idea of forming a line of books that would highlight the subject of African American history and their acquisition of *Progress of a Race*. "To Mr. Jenkins belongs the honor of suggesting and planning a Negro History," it reads. "At his earnest solicitation his publishers issued 'Progress of a Race,' which has been a great success and introduced him as a race publisher."[52]

Jenkins's Southern roots and his experience as a subscription bookseller, selling books to those who did not have access to bookstores or lending libraries, combined with the visibility of African Americans during and in the wake of the Atlanta Exposition, may have led him to believe in the marketing potential of a book like *Progress of a Race*. That both the concept and the fact of a "race publisher" could emerge from Atlanta, Georgia, at the end of the nineteenth century points to the intersection of a number of elements. It is clear that Jenkins believed a Black book-buying public existed, and that a book-manufacturing company such as the Nichols Company, selling exclusively on a subscription basis, could cultivate and profit from it. Indeed, the ability to find and tap into this sort of new or underrealized book-buying public was exactly the reason subscription bookselling was so popular and profitable in the United States by the end of the nineteenth century. According to John Tebbel, whose *A History of Book Publishing in the United States* outlines the U.S. publishing industry as it developed and differentiated, one important function of subscription selling has been the "selling of books to people who never bought them before, who have no library or bookstore service, or if they do, are not habituated to using them."[53] The push to expand to meet the needs of new markets, and interest in developing a specifically African American market, was a component of what Tebbel calls the "great surge of subscription selling that began in the late 1800s."[54]

In the case of the African American market for subscription books, few records of subscription publishing or the experience of book agents have survived beyond the books that they sold. Earlier in the nineteenth century, the African American author who had tapped most successfully into this burgeoning "surge" of subscription selling was William Still. As Stephen G. Hall illustrates in his history of Still's *The Underground Railroad* (1872), his "innovations in publishing and dissemination laid the groundwork for the subsequent explosion in the production of and market for black historical texts" at the end of the nineteenth century.[55] Scholars have agreed that there were many reasons for the success of Still's book: whereas most accounts of the underground railroad had been crafted to highlight the role of its white agents and the remote country homes that had served as the railroad's stations, Still's recasting of its history to emphasize the centrality of Philadelphia's free Black community to the railroad's success and his ability to give voice to fugitive slaves breathed new life into the story.

But most important to the success of the book was Still's ability to market it successfully through a network of agents. Porter and Coates, a white-owned publishing company, agreed in 1872 to produce ten thousand copies of the book, which were to be sold by subscription only. It was widely advertised in numerous newspapers during the 1870s, including and especially the Black press. With readers' interest in the book piqued, Still deployed a network of agents that virtually blanketed the nation in order to sell the book. Recruiting both male as well as female and white as well as Black agents (his connection with the latter group was through contacts in the AME Church and the Black schools), Still picked his canvassers carefully and compensated them generously. He also directed them extensively on how to sell *The Underground Railroad* by appealing directly to customers. Much of what we know about his instructions to agents and marketing strategies comes from letters he wrote to agents between 1873 and 1874, as well as his correspondence with other individuals. But he continued to market the book and sell it by subscription at least throughout the 1870s. After his one-year contract with Porter and Coates was up, Still purchased the plates for the book and thereafter had the book printed himself. He reissued the book as *Underground Railroad Record: With a Life of the Author* in 1883, establishing a new life for it a full decade after its initial publication.[56] Still's aggressive promotion and marketing of *The Underground Railroad* would prove valuable for other Black writers, even those who were veterans of book publication: William Wells Brown sought out and relied on Still's advice in reviving sales of *The Black Man*, which had been first published in 1863.[57]

Far fewer documents exist to recreate the story of *Progress of a Race*'s publication or distribution, or that of any of the other books sold by subscription throughout African American communities in the last decade of the nineteenth century. The story of these texts must be pieced together instead. A first step is to come to terms with the sort of book that was the specialty of manufacturing publishers and the subscription industry. Typically, books sold by subscription were thick, heavy, important-looking volumes, which some have considered "blown up by publishers to twice the size actually required."[58] One aspect of their appeal was their promise to look *significant* on a bookshelf, perhaps particularly next to a volume as weighty and substantial as an ornate family bible. That the volumes were, in Tebbel's words, "tricked out in flamboyant bindings," with covers that seemed etched in elaborate gold (or expensive-looking) decorations, contributed to their appeal.[59] Tebbel's description of these books as "tricked out" refers to the fact that, in appearance, they were heavily accessorized; his language, however, drawn at least in part from the world of prostitutes who get dressed up to perform their "tricks," unmasks Tebbel's own twentieth-century disdain for the products of subscription publishing. But at the end of the nineteenth century, new book buyers gravitated toward the substantial size and ornamental appearance of books sold by subscription, which was a part of their understanding of a book's value: the *look* of the book was a significant part of its appeal.

It was not that the content of the book was irrelevant. But, as J. L. Nichols's description of his own book, *The Business Guide; or, Safe Methods of Business* suggests, subscription book buyers were not always seeking originality or creativity in the books they bought. Nichols's introduction promotes the book as one valuable to "all that desire, in cheap form, full information as to methods of doing business. It contains all that is practical in Hill's Manual, Gaskell's Compendium, and other books of like character." Both *Hill's Manual of Social and Business Forms: A Guide to Correct Writing*, published in 1883, and *Gaskell's Compendium of Forms, Educational, Social, Legal and Commercial*, published in 1881, were massive guides to writing, social skills, and business habits for those "who wish to master at their own homes the most necessary forms and laws of business and society."[60] Nichols's book was significantly shorter and, by his own description, less expensive. But for buyers of the book, these features were selling points, in that Nichols's book promised to have gleaned the most relevant information from these longer, more expensive volumes and condensed it for readers seeking the knowledge they contained, but at a fraction of the cost. Nichols's promotion of his book relative to other, presumably more well-known titles did not necessarily imply that his readers would be familiar with these other books; instead, his advertising strategy relied on his buyers' perception that they were getting a wealth of pertinent information in a form that was both accessible and cheap. His book, then, provided its readers with information from an entire set of other books at a price point that was made to seem a bargain. This would appeal to a market of buyers for whom both time and money were limited, and for whom originality was unnecessary.

While bookstores and other retail outlets for book buying thrived in the Northeast and in densely populated cities, subscription publishers like the Nichols Company relied on an alternative business model for covering the vast expanse of the United States that was, for the most part, not urban and lacked access to retail venues. Under this system, subscriptions publishers hired regional agents, who in turn hired their own canvassers or teams of canvassers, who would be responsible for selling books door-to-door. Many booksellers got their start as young men or college students and, like Jenkins and Hertel, some worked their way up into management positions in the publishing industry. Canvassers, often equipped with only descriptions or prospectuses for books that had yet to see their way into print in their final form, were able to access homes and book buyers that trade publishers and traditional booksellers could not reach. Book agents were enterprising, and both they and publishers had a reputation for taking advantage of their buyers' situation at every stage of the process. Because their buyers did not have experience buying books, or access to bookstores or other outlets of the regular bookselling trade where they might compare volumes, they were receptive to the price point that was presented to them, and they could not tell in advance whether the book they were purchasing was of high quality—in terms of the paper and the bindings, for instance—or not. In fact, subscription books, including those manufactured and sold by the Nichols Company, were notorious for being rapidly produced and riddled with errors, small and large. But, like many subscription book publishers, leadership of the Nichols Company believed that their particular target audience would either not care about or even notice the sloppy writing or defective manufacturing of their books. "You know that nine-tenths of the people who buy subscriptions books are not very intelligent—that is to say, not very well-read," wrote Hertel in a letter to Booker T. Washington's close assistant, Emmett J. Scott, in correspondence about Washington's own foray into the subscription market with his autobiographical "The Story of My Life," which would be published by the Nichols Company in 1900.[61] In verbalizing the cynical belief that his clients were, by and large, a naïve group, Hertel revealed much about the marketing strategies of the company, whose ability to capitalize on both the inexperience of their clients as book buyers and their hunger for certain kinds of titles and the look of literary bulk and substance was a recipe for success in the late nineteenth- and early twentieth-century United States.

Although Still's correspondence suggests that *The Underground Railroad* found more success among white buyers than African American buyers, by the mid-1890s, Jenkins was right in thinking that there was a market for books sold by subscription in African American communities. And he was not alone in this realization. The publication of the *Afro-American Encyclopædia; or Thoughts, Doings and Sayings of the Race* in September 1895, which was produced by publishers Haley & Florida of Nashville, Tennessee, coincided with the opening of the Atlanta Exposition. The volume's editor, J. T. Haley, who is identified in the 1900 census as white and as a "book binder," told the story of its inception in the preface. During their twenty years in the subscription book business, the company's canvassers had "embrac[ed] both white and colored." But, Haley told the *Afro-American Encyclopædia's* buyers, the "scarcity of books by negro authors suggested the idea of the compilation of this book." Increasing literacy rates across the South and the rise of a Black middle class, particularly in cities like Nashville and Atlanta, surely made African Americans more visible as potential buyers of books. But the market also appears to have been driven by "the wants of the negro," which Haley described as "desirous of knowing more of the history of his race, and the achievements of its great men and women (but who are without the assistance of books that bear upon this subject)." Haley imagined that these readers might not always be entirely literate: he therefore designed the book in a way that it could "be dipped into here and there with the certainty of something being found capable of giving instructions to all classes of readers." Haley's comments in the preface suggest his belief that books produced for African American buyers did not need to achieve the same level of quality as those produced for white buyers, but in this case, he boasted that the "utmost care has been taken in the collation of the matter in this work, and no expense has been spared to make it not only acceptable to the colored people, but to all classes of readers as well."[62]

Like most book manufacturers—as subscription publishers considered themselves—no records of the company Haley & Florida are extant; nor do records exist to indicate how many copies of the *Afro-American Encyclopædia* sold, or whether white as well as "colored people" were among its buyers. But Haley's comments in the preface help us to appreciate the publisher's understanding of Black Americans' desire for materials that would supply them with an understanding of their own history and the people involved in making it. Regardless of the limited role of books and literature in Booker T. Washington's vision of industrial education for African Americans, regardless of the modest forms of education available to them, books held an increasingly important place in the African American imaginary. That place is perhaps best captured by the image, titled "Enlightening the Race," that appears opposite the title page of the *Afro-American Encyclopædia*: a drawing of the Statue of Liberty—or, as the statue was originally called, "Liberty Enlightening the World." In the *Afro-American Encyclopædia* rendering, the Roman liberty goddess holds in her left hand not the *tabula ansata*, or handled tablet evoking the law, that is inscribed with the Roman numerals for July 4, 1776, the date that the Declaration of Independence was signed, but a modern-day book. Held high in the air, a second book replaces the statue's torch. The book's titles are not apparent in the image. But by replacing both the tablet and, especially, the statue's torch with books, the image captures the understanding that books would show African Americans the path to freedom. What is perhaps most interesting about this image is the fact that it was included in the book's first edition, before the statue was dedicated in the fall of 1896. African Americans had been vocal in their criticism of the statue, which hardly represented their own experience in the United States.[63] Given this attitude, the image may have been poorly chosen by the publisher, carrying meanings he did not fully calculate; it nevertheless captured African Americans' association of books with enlightenment, freedom, and possibility at the end of the nineteenth century.

In view of the cosmetic and structural differences between the *Afro-American Encyclopædia* and *Progress of a Race*, and the fact that *Progress of a Race* drew heavily from the contents of the *Afro-American Encyclopædia*, it's likely that these texts were designed for sale in different markets defined most notably by different levels of education and income. The expensive leather binding of the *Afro-American Encyclopædia* leads me to believe that it was most likely limited to the African American middle and upper classes of Nashville, where it was published. But African Americans were commonly drawn to educational, inspirational books like the *Afro-American Encyclopædia* and *Progress of a Race*

ENLIGHTENING THE RACE.

1.4 *Enlightening the Race*, the frontispiece to James T. Haley's *Afro-American Encyclopædia; or the Thoughts, Doings and Sayings of the Race* (1895). This recasting of the statue known then as *Liberty Enlightening the World* accurately captures the turn-of-the-century understanding that books would illuminate for African Americans a path to literary understanding and to the rights and responsibilities of citizenship.

for a number of reasons. Some were interested in the content and wanted to read it. But others were drawn to a book's alleged popularity (as asserted by the selling agent), or to the very things that have led subscription books to be devalued: their size and decorative appearance.[64] Solid and orderly, the protection of a permanent binding and placement on a bookshelf dignified a collection of print (as opposed to a stack of yellowing newspapers), manifesting its importance for its owners and to visitors to the home as well. The sheer quantity of material inside was intended to entrance buyers as well: in the case of the *Afro-American Encyclopædia*, that quantity was relayed in the book's all-encompassing subtitle, which informed readers that the book contained "Addresses, Lectures, Biographical Sketches, Sermons, Poems, Names of Universities, Colleges, Seminaries, Newspapers, Books, and a History of the Denominations, Giving the Numerical Strength of Each." It is the additive value that this subtitle promotes: purchasing the *Encyclopaedia*, it communicates, would in essence bring multiple texts, and multiple kinds of texts, into the buyer's possession. In fact, the subtitle continues, promising that the volume will be instructive: "It teaches every subject of interest to the colored people, as discussed by more than one hundred of their wisest men and best women." The title of Crogman's book is much briefer, but was also well-selected so as to allure buyers, for whom it might have had a familiar ring. The "Progress of a Race" was a concept and, more specifically, a turn of phrase that was repeated so often at the end of the nineteenth century, particularly in association with the Negro Building at the Atlanta Exposition, as to become a catchphrase.[65]

So far in this section I have outlined the general business model of subscription books, and the strategies the industry used to sell them. I now turn more specifically to how *Progress of a Race* was sold by subscription. Like most subscription books, *Progress of a Race* was sold from a prospectus (sometimes called a canvassing book, or a sales dummy), which was an abbreviated replica of the book and a standard marketing tool for subscription booksellers. In fact, most books sold by subscription were not even printed until a significant number of orders had been placed. The prospectus would be given or sold as part of a selling package to a canvasser, or agent, to use in describing and soliciting sales of the book. Canvassers brought sales dummies of the book to African American communities, moving from door to door and receiving orders for the completed volume from customers. Lacking both mobility and access to retail venues, it was a happy coincidence that subscription booksellers brought thick, good-looking books into African American communities, providing them with easy access to the foundations of a family library that would signify their aspirations beyond the manual labor that was expected of them. Arriving at their doorsteps with samples of the books, subscription sellers conveniently came to them, sparing even middle-class buyers in urban areas the discrimination and humiliation that came with shopping and offering them a volume that was both aesthetically pleasing and intellectually promising.

The prospectus for the first edition of *Progress of a Race* is bound in red, with the volume's subtitle, "The Remarkable Advancement of the American Negro," written ornately across the cover, as it would be on the completed book. Produced in 1897, it includes the finished title page as well as a preface by "The Authors." But Booker T. Washington's introduction stops abruptly at the end of its second page, and the tremendously detailed table of contents runs only from chapter 1 until midway through chapter 14. The finished volume has a total of 17 chapters, but this abbreviated table of contents, the publishers felt, was enough to give buyers a sense of the content of the book they would be buying. The prospectus includes one poem, the complete text of George C. Rowe's "We Are Rising," which follows the table of contents in the prospectus but precedes it in the complete volume. In essence, what the prospectus provides is a sampling of the book; its disjointed but representative pages are a means of whetting the buyer's appetite for the whole. A very few pages from each of the book's first chapters is included.[66] These pages are all paginated, but the page numbers refer to the pages' placement in the longer, completed volume rather than the short prospectus, underscoring the sense that the excerpts are meant simply to offer a taste of the book's contents rather than a comprehensive reading experience. The sections are not cut in such a way as to give any sense of the narrative arc of the completed chapters; in fact, each chapter is fragmented and ends abruptly, according to the page break rather than, for instance, a paragraph break. Most often, the representative chapters end in the middle of a sentence.

The lack of continuity of its pages makes it clear that the prospectus for *Progress of a Race* was not designed for textual appreciation; rather, it is cast as a visual document, one for which agents were required to create the narrative arc of the book from pictures rather than words in order to sell it. Whereas the volume's text in the prospectus is abbreviated and minimized, its copious visual images are highlighted, with over forty-four pictures in a book of eighty-nine pages: in effect, an image appears on every other page. This serves to underscore the publisher's expectation of how the book would best be marketed—visually. Indeed, the convergence of visual and textual representation gave African American buyers two means of envisioning racial identity and, quite literally, new ways to see themselves as the nineteenth century turned into the twentieth. *Progress of a Race* made visible images of Blackness in a way that other, similar texts from the end of the nineteenth century did not. Unlike the *Afro-American Encyclopædia*, which features only a handful of formal portraits and drawings of important buildings, *Progress of a Race* foregrounds itself as an illustrated text: its images or illustrations were intended to be integrated into the published material in such a way as to interpret or explain the text. It includes formal portraits of famous Black personalities, present and historical. It is no surprise that Booker T. Washington's image was the first one in both the salesman's dummy and the complete version of *Progress of a Race*. Frederick Douglass's portrait is also prominently featured, as is that of author Frances E. W. Harper and the widely respected Black minister Alexander Crummell, whose autograph was deemed so coveted as to be reproduced under his portrait. These African American "heroes" were visual reminders of all that African American people were and could become; their visages alone, collected in one volume, spoke to the value and appeal of *Progress of a Race* for its potential buyers, who, the pictures promised, could learn more about the lives and accomplishments of Black leaders if they bought the printed text. But *Progress of a Race* also makes visible unknown individuals in an effort to make visual the narrative of Black history it tells.[67] There is no doubt that images expanded the potential "readership" of the book beyond those who were literate in the most conventional sense; this was a principal selling point of the volume. Agents were instructed to emphasize the "fine pictures" and repeatedly call attention to the book as "the best illustrated work ever published." They were told to read the "title page aloud slowly and deliberately" and to "always read the writing under the illustrations," bringing them to verbal life for those potential buyers who did not have extensive literacy skills.[68]

What these photographs do, arguably, is demonstrate the "progress" of the race, sometimes by creating productive contradictions between image and text, and sometimes by implicitly having the images reflect the larger message the book makes. In the section on slavery, for instance, the dominant images are of formerly enslaved people, casting visual priority on the more dignified renditions of African American life that compellingly juxtapose the dehumanizing textual descriptions of slavery. Likewise, the photographs of postbellum African American subjects show us people as people, defined by their individuality rather than by their domestic or industrial roles. Whereas Frances Benjamin Johnston's 1899 photographs of the Hampton Institute depicted its students anonymously consumed in labor, for instance, the reader of *Progress of a Race* is confronted with the presence of living bodies rather than the products of their labor, the immediacy of their racial features attesting to their Blackness and their humanity. In its visual work, *Progress of a Race* produced what Brett Hayes Edwards calls a "space of 'new creation,'" one that allowed its owners to see themselves as a part of the progress the book itself defined and illustrated.[69]

The material presentation of the prospectus was a powerful selling tool for *Progress of a Race*. But so too was the sales pitch the publishers advised their fleet of agents to employ. Toward the end of *Progress of a Race's* thin selling volume is a description of the work it represents, designed to help the agent present the book to potential clients. *Progress of a Race*, prospective buyers were to be told,

> not only gives the social, moral, political and intellectual advancement of the colored man in the last generation but also an account of his origin and descent, and a complete history from the time he was ruthlessly torn from his native Africa, and carried in a Dutch ship in 1619 up to the present time. His condition as a slave, his ingenious schemes for freedom and hair-breadths [*sic*] escapes enroute "The Underground Railroad," and later his bravery and heroism in the Civil War, are all graphically depicted, and the whole is both instructive and fascinating.[70]

By casting *Progress of a Race* as both instructive and necessary, buyers were invited to think of it as something they both needed and wanted: it would educate, and it would entertain. There was much that they didn't know about Black history, they were to see; *Progress of a Race* was a book that would give them the "real story" of the Black past and memorialize those events and people whose heroism should not be overlooked.

There is little extant information on the identities of the sales agents for *Progress of a Race*, and likewise not much textual evidence of what the actual experience between agent and potential buyer might have been like. Nonetheless, an elaborate set of selling tips, which includes a script to be used by agents in selling *Progress of a Race*, offers some tantalizing hints. First of all, the script assumes that both agents for the book and their buyers are African American. Phrases such as "the people of our Race" and references to "our people" become refrains in the sales spiel, connecting buyer and seller in a mutual embrace that agents hoped would result in a commitment to buy. Shared racial identity and shared history surely helped potential customers trust book agents and feel a connection to them; it also suggested common ground for investment in the book and its contents. But agents were pre-

1.5 & 1.6 These portraits of two "ex-slaves," from Crogman and Kletzing's *Progress of a Race* (1898), were included in a chapter on the history of slavery. While the surrounding text tells the story of slavery's brutalities, images like these gave visual priority to the dignity of freedom.

pared to make connections with their customers in other ways as well. First and foremost, they wanted to position themselves as known to the customers in their territory by immediately constructing and then capitalizing on an intersecting social network of potential buyers. Their goal should be to "call on prominent people in your territory" first: "Get their orders first and a written testimonial if possible," as "endorsements from ministers, teachers, etc., will be a great help to you in getting the business" of others throughout the area. They were told to "greet your customer pleasantly, and BY NAME IF POSSIBLE," suggesting not only an element of respect but also membership in the community and at least the beginnings of a personal relationship with their buyer. Conversations with one buyer would facilitate their relationship with the next. "It is easy to find out about folks who live in nearby houses," they were instructed.[71] All of these recommendations serve as a reminder that communities were created and reinforced through the purchase of *Progress of a Race*, not only of those who shared a deep respect for African American history and a commitment to learning, but also of those whose respect for, for instance, the community's clergy and teachers or even a neighbor was confirmed by buying the book that they had endorsed or themselves purchased. Aspects of character might be validated or membership in a social group guaranteed by who did or did not purchase the book.

The list of selling tips for *Progress of a Race* illustrates the extensive instructions the publishers provided for their agents, whose skills and performance in the field would determine if their books sold or not. An article on subscription book publishing that appeared in *Publishers' Weekly* in 1898, just after the marketing for *Progress of a Race* was likely to have begun, underscores this: "Success of a subscription book publishing firm does not so much depend on the merits of its books, or their 'get-up,' *i.e.*, the style of printing or binding, or quality of paper, as it does upon its manager's knack of selecting and retaining such agents as are particularly fit to sell books on the subscription plan. A good agent can sell almost any book."[72] Agents were often seen as "doing missionary work" rather than peddling merchandise, "by introducing literature, *i.e.*, good books and works of art, in circles that would never dream of buying these or similar works in a bookstore."[73] Speaking generally of the industry, the article continues:

> Many canvassers for popular or useful works often introduce the first books to the home of the mechanic or farmer, and create a taste for reading among people, who have perhaps paid no attention to books since their school days. . . . If these [people] are approached by a persuasive agent, they are apt to be seized with a desire for books, and consequently give the agent an order, vaguely hoping that in this way they may be doing something for their "neglected education." These people are seldom, or never seen inside of a bookstore, nor have they any idea of what books would be suitable for them, and know nothing about the prices, editions, bindings, printing, etc., of books.[74]

In the case of the African American buyers to whom *Progress of a Race* was marketed, "these people" were a diverse mix, for whom books and the acts of buying and owning them meant many things. Some of them would not automatically have seen themselves as book buyers, whether because they lacked the money to buy them, felt incapable of reading them, or saw their priorities as lying elsewhere. Agents broke down barriers of class, education and profession by advertising *Progress of a Race* as "a book alike for the laborer, mechanic and the professional man, all will find it interesting and instructive."[75] Indeed, what was common about their experience was more important than what divided them. More than anything else, agents were instructed to appeal to their buyers' sense of race pride. "Don't you agree that

Sales Talk for Progress of a Race

To the Agent:

If you are anxious to make a success of this work YOU MUST make a careful preparation before calling on your customers.

FIRST study these instructions until you know them by heart. Acquaint yourself with every page of the outfit. Be able to turn freely from one interesting section to another and YOU WILL FIND EVERYONE ANXIOUS TO GIVE YOU AN ORDER.

SECOND. Call on prominent people in your territory. Get their orders first and a written testimonial if possible. Endorsements from ministers, teachers, etc., will be a great help to you in getting the business.

THIRD. Always greet your customer pleasantly, and BY NAME IF POSSIBLE. It is easy to find out about folks who live in nearby houses. After a few introductory remarks say:

"I have been fortunate in securing the position as SALESMAN in this territory for "PROGRESS OF A RACE," the only true and complete history of the NEGRO RACE on the market." (Here produce your outfit and turning to the frontispiece say:)

"I want to call your attention first to this group of leading men. In the center is Booker T. Washington, who was entertained by presidents and royalty; Paul Laurence Dunbar (upper left), who is known the world over for his writings; Blanch K. Bruce (upper right) served in the Senate of the United States; Frederick Douglass (lower left), our great statesman and diplomat; and the Hon. John M. Langston (lower right), lawyer, diplomat and college president." (Next turn to title page—read it aloud slowly and deliberately. Call attention to the fact that the authorship is of the highest, and that each chapter has been prepared by an expert.)

(Turn to page 13 and read the dedication—say:) "I'll venture to say, Mr. ——, that you never knew there were Negroes in the United States who are paying more than $100,000 income taxes. I tell you the people of our Race have a right to be proud of their record, and you will agree with me when you have seen the whole book. Of course, Mr. ——, this is only a sample. The complete book contains almost 500 pages and there are over 200 illustrations. Let me show you." (Here show Principal Moton's picture and read parts of his Introduction on page 5.) "Dr. Moton, as you know, is carrying on the work of Booker T. Washington at Tuskegee Institute. To give you an idea of the wide scope of the book, I'll read the Table of Contents (page 7). This is the first page (page 9) of the List of Illustrations, and you can see that no money has been spared to make this the best illustrated work ever published."

"CHAPTER I gives a brief history of the Race and shows that 'God created of one blood all nations of men.' Notice these next fine pictures. They show that the book is right up to date." (Agent, always read the writing under the illustra-

1.7 This "Sales Talk for *Progress of a Race*" is included in the 1920 canvassing book for *Progress of a Race; or, The Remarkable Advancement of the American Negro*. Kislak Center for Special Collections, Rare Books, and Manuscripts, University of Pennsylvania, Philadelphia, PA.

we ought to be proud of our people, Mr. _____?," reads one suggested sales pitch. Another is this line: "You will laugh, Mr. _____, to learn how smart some of those slaves were. This one was shipped to safety in a box by freight." Scripted lines like, "You see, Mr. _____, we are represented in almost every industry" reinforced the façade of personal relationship and the veneer of the seller's respect for the buyer that was the hallmark of subscription book selling.[76] The stories highlighted by the selling agents promised to entertain and educate, all while underscoring the centrality of African Americans, not only to the text itself but also to American life. Agents represented the text as a defensive space, where positive portrayals of the Negro presented an alternative discourse, one that countered the dominant narratives of Negro stupidity and inferiority; it was a text through which African Americans could both revalue their Blackness and see themselves as a literary, which is to say, an intellectual, people. This made buying *Progress of a Race* an act of self-respect: to own it was to honor a set of values and gain new respect for the place of African Americans, regardless of the degradation that defined their everyday existence.

In 1898, this was not a literary or intellectual experience available to African Americans in the context of any formal school setting. Indeed, agents told prospective buyers "the information contained in this book will never appear in school histories." Collectively, then, African Americans were to take on this separate course of study as a responsibility to be met outside of the standard curriculums they found at school. "It is our duty to see that folks know what a wonderful record the Race has made in these few short years. You can do your share by reading this book, letting your children learn the truth, and giving the facts as wide a distribution as possible."[77] Note the collective mission that is inspired, not only by the words "our duty," but also by the notion of sharing in the work of racial progress by reading *Progress of a Race*. The phrase "A COPY OF 'PROGRESS OF A RACE' IN EVERY HOME" was not merely a sales slogan; it reflected the belief that the text was an essential way of transmitting knowledge that would be crucial to a reimagining of African American identity and life. Buying the book was cast as a way of participating in a "spirit of progress" that included developing more sophisticated literary skills. "You want your children to catch the spirit of progress and achievement. Give them a chance and yourself too," agents said, using the key word of *Progress of a Race*'s title to instill lofty goals in the minds and hearts of African American buyers.[78]

In this context, the fact that *Progress of a Race* was sold "exclusively by subscription" further substantiated its value by pointing to its exclusivity. Given the elaborate sales script provided to selling agents, many African American book buyers surely felt fortunate to have the opportunity to buy this volume. The "conditions" of sale addressed the book's quality (high), size (substantial), and price (reasonable). The description of the physical book would have sounded impressive: "This work is printed from clear new type, on fine calendar paper and contains over 600 pages and 100 beautiful half-tones and zinc engravings." Note the specificity: clearly, it was believed that the page and picture count mattered to potential buyers.[79] Buyers were allowed to survey two options for possible bindings for *Progress of a Race* and their corresponding pricing. The first was described as "bound in beautiful silk cloth (sprinkled edge)"; the "sprinkled edge" referred to the process of sprinkling or spattering colored ink on the three cut edges while a book is tightly clamped, resulting in ornamental book edges. The second, more expensive option was to have the book "bound in beautiful red Russia [cloth], gilt edge, litho end sheets, stamped on back in gold."[80] The price difference for the different bindings was 70 cents, with the first binding being offered for $1.55 and the second, more expensive binding being offered for $2.25; this more expensive version would yield a bigger profit for the sales agent. It would also increase the symbolic value of the book as an object. The prospectus included an example of the higher-priced binding in the form of a sample book spine that, mounted on the rear end paper, resembled a bookmark but was intended to illustrate how the book would look adorned in the more ornate binding.

At heart, the prospectus for *Progress of a Race* was a blank book, a category of book that, as Lisa Gitelman reminds us, was not intended to inspire reading but writing: it was where the financial transaction between buyer and seller was recorded.[81] At the back of each prospectus were columned, ruled blank leaves available for agents to fill up with the names of subscribers. Agents recorded sales by indicating the subscriber's name, address, and the style of binding they had chosen. The grid was a means of recording logistical information about the order and the site of the formal agreement between subscriber and agent; on the top of each blank page is written "We the undersigned do hereby agree to receive and pay for the copies set opposite our names."[82] But it was also the place where a sense of self and status were conferred, where buyers would see their names and locate themselves and others among the host of buyers of the book already listed. These pages recorded forever the people who signed on to buy *Progress of a Race*. It is an irony of history that they were also the pages deemed most disposable. In order to fill the orders, most of the books (or at least, their relevant pages) were likely turned in to the publisher as soon as the blank pages were filled

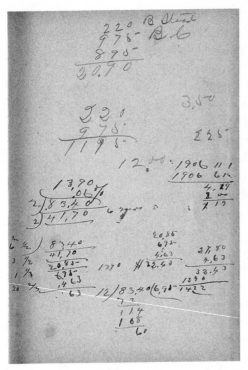
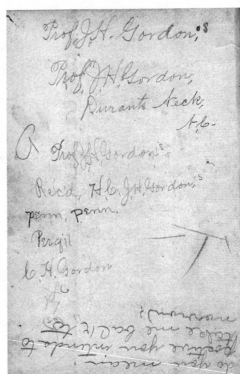

1.8 & 1.9 The blank pages of canvassing books for *Progress of a Race; or, The Remarkable Advancement of the American Negro* were often repurposed, as were these from a 1900 edition. A page at the front of the book was used to perform math functions, while a page at the back was used to practice handwriting.

up. These books were then likely to have been discarded: the Nichols Company would replace the used prospectus with new volumes so that the sales process could begin again. But canvassing books were also prime candidates for being repurposed in ways that seemingly had nothing to do with either *Progress of a Race* or the sales agents who sold it. Some were used for general note-taking or as scrap paper; others show evidence of use as a place to practice handwriting.[83] The absence of the pages of these "blank books" limits how much we can know about the readership of the book, the choices buyers made regarding type of binding, and the rate and pace of sales.[84] It also limits what we can know about the book's financial success.

We are left to gauge this venture's profitability from the fact that the Nichols Company, in relaying the company's history, called the venture into what they described as "race publishing" a "great success."[85] They continued to publish *Progress of a Race,* which appeared in at least five editions between 1897 and 1929. In 1902, the book was published under a different name, *The Colored American, from Slavery to Honorable Citizenship,* with J. W. Gibson replacing H. F. Kletzing as the coauthor. Changes to this edition included a simplified index and the addition of a list of illustrations. Later editions returned to the original title, but Gibson, who was, like Kletzing, white and a teacher, remained the coauthor.[86] The Nichols Company would continue to seek out texts by Negro authors to sell by subscription. By far the company's most prominent but also most problematic author was Booker T. Washington, whose *Story of My Life and Work* the Nichols Company published in 1900. I will return to the Nichols Company, the subject of Washington's authorship and, to some extent, the appeal of subscription publishing to African American readers in chapter 3. Despite Washington's prominence and the extensive records he kept of his correspondence and business affairs, even the story of his involvement with the Nichols Company remains incomplete. But it offers another lens through which to see the importance of subscription publishing to African American literary culture around the turn from the nineteenth to the twentieth century.

In 1898, *Publishers' Weekly* would describe the subscription publishing industry as composed of "unscrupulous publishers" whose "modern literary productions ... are utterly worthless."[87] Even to our twenty-first-century sensibilities, *Progress of a Race* and books like it seem to be poorly packaged and inferior literature. But the story I have reconstructed here suggests that, for scholars of African American print culture, this stereotype has outlasted its usefulness. As this chapter illustrates, despite their poor reputation, we would be wise to reconsider subscription books like *Progress of a Race,* to better appreciate the significance they held for their original buyers. We are always looking for ways to study the literary practices of those African Americans who were less privileged, less well educated, and less elite, and *Progress of a Race* and books like it provide a window through which to do so. African Americans without access to elite literary culture were drawn to the material appearance of the books, whose bindings and cover, however gaudy or cheaply produced, symbolized the subject matter's importance and contributed, by extension, to their own sense of themselves as an important people. They were inspired by the personal sales experience facilitated by the subscription process; indeed, the agent's ability to articulate the text's significance—its value—may not have been broadcast with the same vigor or been audible in the same way in a more anonymous selling situation. There was a collectivity that was inspired by the door-to-door selling process, where neighbors joined neighbors in championing the race by buying the text. Their shared support for the book and the race was made visible when they signed their names alongside those of their neighbors on the blank pages of the prospectus intended to record sales of *Progress of a Race*. Showing off a list of names to a potential buyer is a typical strategy used by sales agents to entice people to buy things that their neighbors have; assuredly, that was the case here, too. But we can also surmise that, in buying a book entitled *Progress of a Race*, consumers likely felt that they were engaging in something more than "keeping up with the Joneses": they were supporting and ensuring the very progress to which the book itself bore witness.

Progress of a Race

What, then, did *Progress of a Race* look like, and how, on a pedagogical level, did it "bear witness" to Black progress while simultaneously serving as a schoolbook that advanced the literary education of its buyers? In the final part of this chapter, I turn to the structure and content of *Progress of a Race*, a text that is itself enveloped in questions that are difficult to answer. Chief among these is how William Crogman became associated with H. F. (Henry Frick) Kletzing, his coauthor for the first edition of the anthology. Born in 1850 and a native of Fairview, Pennsylvania, Kletzing was not African American. He was a professor of mathematics at North Western College in Naperville, Illinois, the same suburb of Chicago where *Progress of a Race*'s publisher, the J. L. Nichols Company, was located. Interestingly, J. L. Nichols himself was also on the faculty at North Western College; he is listed as the principal of the "Commercial Department" in the *American College and Public School Directory* of 1893. The school was comprised of only seven departments and offered just four courses of study. With a total of only fourteen members of the faculty, it is reasonable to speculate that Kletzing and Nichols knew one another.[88] The Nichols Company would publish a book Kletzing coauthored with his brother, E. L. Kletzing, in 1899. The title page of that book, *Traits of Character Illustrated in Bible Light. Together with Short Sketches of Marked and Marred Manhood and Womanhood*, lists him as "author" of *Progress of a Race* and another inspirational book, *Stepping Stones to Success*, which was also coauthored by his brother. While my research suggests that the link between Kletzing and Crogman seems to have been through J. L. Nichols or the Nichols Company, there is no evidence that speaks to whether the partnership between Kletzing and Crogman in *Progress of a Race* was substantive or in any way a real collaboration.[89]

Can we, then, assume that Crogman, as a scholar of considerable stature and ability, as an African American dedicated to "public educational work" and as an experienced commissioner of the Atlanta Exposition for the state of Georgia's Negro Building, was primarily in charge of selecting contributors and texts, and was the main influence on the editorial choices made in the process of putting together the book?[90] Or was Kletzing a real collaborator, whose suggestions and opinion significantly determined the shape and scope of the anthology? This last possibility—that Crogman and Kletzing actually worked together as coauthors—might be one way to make sense of the patched-together quality of the book, the fabric of which, as I will discuss in this section, was composed of the remnants of many texts that were minimally woven together. But this prospect only further complicates the questions of authorship I attend to here. My own sense is that Crogman and Kletzing's partnership was in name only, recommended by or even insisted on by the publisher, and that Crogman was in effect the driving force behind and primary "author" of the volume. Crogman was not an insignificant member of the Black leadership class in Atlanta, and his collection of lectures, *Talks of the Times*, suggests the extent to which he traveled around the country, publicly addressing both Black and white audiences. The success of the Negro Building and his role as Georgia's commissioner most likely brought him even more visibility. But Crogman did not have anything near a national reputation, and Kletzman's whiteness, despite his own lack of renown, literary or otherwise, may have served as the insurance policy the Nichols Company felt it needed should book buyers turn out to have limited confidence in buying a book like *Progress of a Race* that was presented as authoritative but authored solely by an African American.[91] They also may have hoped that *Progress of a Race* would have an interracial audience, despite its subject matter, and that a white coauthor would suggest a symbolic partnership that would appeal to white buyers.

Crogman and Kletzing's silence on this subject is compounded by the fact that, although they refer to themselves as "authors" in the volume's preface, they reveal little about the extent or nature of their authorship in *Progress of a Race*, or what authorship meant to them. Nothing remains to provide insight into the "authors'" process of selecting subjects and texts to include in the book, or the logic behind their use or arrangement of material in the text, which is presented as both drawn from other people's words and ideas in solicited manuscripts but also "authored" by Crogman and Kletzing. "We have quoted largely from different authors, and wherever possible have given credit," they explain in the Preface. "But in some cases even this was not possible, as the author was not always known."[92] Most turn-of-the-century texts like *Progress of a Race* are made up of a series of complete essays attributed to individual authors, which were then assembled in a single volume. *Progress of a Race* differs dramatically from these texts in the way that the "authors" combine bits and pieces of previously published material, making sense of and ordering them with the addition of their own headings and commentary. They refer to others and even quote their words, but rarely do they offer formal citations of their sources. Extensive references are made to Crogman's own published work, *Talk of the Times*, but aside from direct references to that text, it is impossible to identify the extent of his contribution to *Progress of a Race*.[93] Although the authors refer to the solicitation of manuscripts (apologizing for omissions in the text's content, particularly in the chapter on "Noted Men and Women," because of "manuscript[s] that did not reach us in time"), they don't distinguish in the final text between their own prose and those texts, or scraps of texts, which originated elsewhere. While they offer *Progress of a Race* as an assembly of texts written at least in part by others, attributing authorship and identifying the sources of publication of the individual texts from which they worked is difficult. But it's clear from the texts that can be identified that *Progress of a Race* is, on its own terms, decidedly not an original book; rather, it is a book that calls into question some of the very ideas about authenticity, originality, and authorship that have long guided African American writing and literary criticism, particularly in the nineteenth century.

The previously published material the authors drew from for the initial chapter, "History of the Race," offers a sense of the variety of documents they turned to in composing *Progress of a Race*. A principal source was the array of race histories that had proliferated in the post-Reconstruction period, including William Wells Brown's *The Rising Son, or the Antecedents and Advancement of the Colored Race* (1874), Joseph Wilson's *Emancipation: Its Course and Progress* (1882), and George Washington William's *History of the Negro Race in America* (1885). The authors of these works have all been identified as amateur historians, who nonetheless initiated an important wave of historical writing that *Progress of a Race* was heir to.[94] Edward A. Johnson's *A School History of the Negro Race in America* was another source of the text of *Progress of a Race*; published in 1890, it had been written principally for primary school students and was used in the public schools in Raleigh, North Carolina, where Johnson was a teacher.[95] The authors also drew for that first chapter on more specialized sources, like A. A. Gunby's essay "A Statement of the Problem" and an essay by Henry W. Blair titled "A Problem in Civilization," both of which were printed in the National Education Association's *Journal of Proceedings, and Addresses* in 1890. Also included was material from Heli Chatelain's address "A Bird's-Eye View of African Tribes and Languages," which he had delivered as a part of the Atlanta Exposition's Congress on Africa in December 1895; it had been included in *Africa and the American Negro: Addresses and Proceedings of the Congress on Africa*, a textual product of the Negro Building's programming edited by J. W. E. (John Wesley Edward) Bowen and published in 1896. An entry on the Negro in *The New American Cyclopedia: A Popular Dictionary of General Knowledge*, published in 1870, was another source. Finally, the authors also took material from James T. Haley's *Afro-American Encyclopædia; or the Thoughts, Doings, and Sayings of the Race*, which had been published in 1895.

Frustratingly, the authors of *Progress of a Race* do not cite the sources of their material, though at times they casually gesture to different authors or speakers (referring, for instance, to "Professor Johnson, in his school history" [28], or to what "Dr. Livingstone says" [28]). For scholars interested in tracking down the sources of *Progress of a Race*, these tags do help, but this was obviously not their purpose. In *Progress of a Race*, identifiers of this sort are meant to add authority and weight to the text in a way that scholarly citation or comprehensive bibliographic detail would not. For these readers, it was likely unimportant who Dr. Livingstone or Professor Johnson were, or where, exactly, their words had originally come from. What was important was the authority inherent in their honorific titles. Prefixing a person's name was used as guidance in *Progress of a Race*: it told the book's users how to read and value ideas.

Another way the authors directed their readers and affirmed a particular world view was by editorializing, sometimes identifying a political position with which they disagreed, and, more often, defining and dismissing racist beliefs with authoritative comments. Some writers, like John P. Jefferis, they included even though they were "not friendly to the Negro," because the author in question "nevertheless makes a statement" (30). In other cases, though, there was no "statement" in question, and the only response to what they called a "preposterous idea"—in this case, that the "Negro is not a human being"—was utter dismissal (23). A "theory so absurd and contradictory to all history," they wrote, "need[s] no refutation," and in *Progress of a Race* it received none (23). By identifying what was and what was not "a question of debate," the editors clarified what was simply outdated racist bombast, and what was more important: the rise and progress of African Americans.

Of course, by introducing these ridiculous statements the authors did at least suggest that they were circulating in contemporary society, and the reason they did so, I argue, is that it provided a way of pushing African Americans to see and understand their own progress, not only in relation to Black accomplishment, but also in terms of literary advancement. Sifting through multiple perspectives and layers of information, learning to see the limitations, omissions, inconsistencies, oversights, and arguments in writing about African Americans was one way for them to see and practice the literary skills that would lead to what the authors called "The Proper Interpretation" (25). In the hands of these authors, the proper interpretation could only result from exposure to an array of literature on African Americans and racial history and to the critical and interpretive skills that were necessary to effectively evaluate and contextualize them.

It is important to note here that for the book to function pedagogically in this way, it did not have to be original, creative, or new. It bears remembering that schoolbooks are unique because of their specific instructional intent: to diffuse knowledge. In this, they are not valued for their originality or creativity, but because they contain useful knowledge that is well organized, effectively presented, and easily circulated. Noah Webster, whose name is synonymous with the schoolbook market in the early United States, made this argument in 1783 while in the process of compiling his first schoolbook and simultaneously advocating for copyright laws in the state of Connecticut. Speaking of the distinct purpose of schoolbooks in a letter to his friend, John Canfield, he said, "An attention to literature must be the principle bulwark against the encroachment of civil and ecclesiastical tyrants." It was the humble schoolbook that could do that important work, he continued, more effectively and more pervasively than a "folio on some abstruse philosophical subject." The folio might be original, but the unoriginal schoolbook cast a broader and more penetrating light.[96]

To make a valuable schoolbook, the authors of *Progress of a Race* only needed to bring together material that could be easily read, critically analyzed, and thoroughly discussed, increasing the spread of information and, with it, the likelihood that Black readers would develop their own ideas of Black identity and progress. In doing so, they created a text that made ideas about race and racial identity easily accessible and digestible. Ellen Gruber Garvey's work on scrapbooks and the practices of scrapbooking in the nineteenth and early twentieth centuries provides a useful way of thinking about authorship in this context. As she reminds us, "Pieces of information—whether in the form of articles, books, or snippets—are detachable, moveable, and classifiable under multiple headings." Extracted from their original source, items are free to take on different orders and interpretations, leading to different meanings. "Putting old sentences and passages into new relationships is a crucial part of writing," she observes.[97] This form of "writing with scissors," adopted by scrapbook makers throughout the nineteenth and into the twentieth century, is instructive, particularly as a means of gaining insight into the authorial practices of Black Americans. As so many of the texts that *Progress of a Race* draws from illustrate, African Americans were historically not able to serve as their own authors. Much that circulated about them, even that penned by African Americans themselves, reveals the long legacy of racist writing in which Black identities were tangled. In locating, excerpting, and fusing together an array of writings on race, the authors of *Progress of a Race* created something new and different out of a diverse range of texts that their readers were unlikely to have seen in their original context. By selecting, reproducing, and recirculating these texts, they preserved them in a form that allowed readers to study the range of discourse on race and the so-called race problem, giving them a context in which to use these texts to help them determine their own ideas and develop the skills necessary to become the author of their own texts.

This approach suggested that the authors of *Progress of a Race* were intent on designing a far different book than, for instance, the *Afro-American Encyclopædia; or the Thoughts, Doings and Sayings of the Race*. The *Encyclopædia* shared *Progress of a Race*'s goal of advancing the race by illustrating its achievements but differed in that it was composed of well-rounded essays that the book's editor specifically refers to as articles, all of which were included in their entirety. Only the author of the book's introductory essay is not identified. It is interesting to note that the editor for this volume, James T. Haley, speaks of himself as a collector and collator rather than an author, explaining in his preface to the volume that the "utmost care has been taken in the collation of the matter in this work." Indeed, specific citations confirm that Haley was not the *Encyclopaedia*'s author; he reinforces this understanding in his remarks, where he extends thanks to the "living authors, publishers and owners of copyrights" that allowed him to "make extracts."[98] *Progress of a Race* adheres to none of this decorum or legalese, dissembling and recycling bits of text from the *Encyclopaedia* and other texts in ways that paid little attention to copyright law or the original text's context or its specific location in the source document. In a practice akin to sampling—a musical term that describes the act of taking a portion, or sample, of one sound recording and using it as an instrument or sound recording in a different song or piece— they take freely from the words of others, organizing their source material in ways that served their own interests and agenda.

One of the most interesting aspects of *Progress of the Race* is the ways its authors drew on the notoriety of Booker T. Washington without endorsing his views. Indeed, Washington's presence in the book produces one of its most obvious tensions. Crogman and his partner clearly wished to capitalize on having an association with Washington, whose authority and political affiliations would certainly increase sales. For that reason, presumably, they used his introduction and placed a portrait of him at the front of the book, even though Crogman's own perspective differed significantly from that of Washington. The book and its introduction clash on several grounds. While Washington focused on African American life in the post-Emancipation era, *Progress of a Race* deals extensively with the history of slavery that Washington ignored. Likewise, Washington cites and celebrates the "wave of industrial feeling now extending over the country" (introduction), while *Progress of a Race* has a pedagogical imperative directed at producing a "wave" of intellectual curiosity and forms of literary study that ran counter to Washington's call for African Americans to see themselves as manufacturers and laborers. Washington's, in the end, was one possibility for an educational program that *Progress of a Race* considered, not one it endorsed.

Whereas Washington's prominence is supported by his status as the author of the book's introduction, there is little else about the way that the authors of *Progress of a Race* treat his writing that privileges it. Two of their strategies reveal how they created this dynamic. In some cases, by not identifying Washington as the author of a piece, they render his voice anonymous, his ideas represented as truncated bits and pieces that are controlled not by the text's original author, but by subsequent authors. He is, in other words, treated like almost all of the other writers anthologized in *Progress of the Race* and not given any special standing.[99] Second, where Washington is identified as the author, Crogman and Kletzing considerably alter the text to make it serve the educational purpose of their book rather than political purpose of the original essay. In one notable instance, they take out Washington's autobiographical anecdotes, omit his oratorical inflections, and introduce keyword subtitles for clarity, while reducing Washington's address to half its original length.[100] By identifying the "plot" of Washington's address and shortening it to a more manageable length and form, the authors make it more accessible to a wider set of learners. The effect of revising the text is to highlight what is distinctive about it.

Balancing Washington's perspective in the chapter on "Educational Improvements" was Alexander Crummell's "Prime Need of the Negro Race," a text that had originally appeared in the *Independent* on August 19, 1897.

Crummell is listed in *Progress of a Race* as the "Late Rector of St. Luke's Protestant Episcopal Church, Washington, D.C." But his remarkable career spanned much of the nineteenth century and included many other roles, including abolitionist, educator, and orator. His most recent accomplishment had been the founding, in March of 1897, of the American Negro Academy, an organization formed specifically to support "the genius and talent in our own race."[101] The American Negro Academy was intended to bring together Black intellectuals who, through lectures, conferences, and writing, would simultaneously repudiate the "facts" circulated by scientific racism that suggested Black mental inferiority and illustrate for Black and white onlookers the depth of Black intellectual thought. Crogman had been one of the masterminds behind the idea of bringing together a group of Black scholars, quietly communicating with Crummell about what he initially described as an "African Institute composed of say fifty colored scholars, the best we have; devoted to literary, statistical, ethnographical, folk-lore investigation, pertaining wholly and entirely to Africa and to the world wide Negro race."[102] Despite Crummell's age at the time talk of starting the "African Institute" began—he was seventy-four when Crogman first approached him with the idea—he was deemed essential to the success of the project precisely because he was respected for the depth and clarity of his thinking.

Featuring his words in *Progress of a Race* was a way for Crogman to show his admiration for this towering Black intellectual. "Prime Need of the Negro Race" can only be read as directly critical of Booker T. Washington, and the authors' decision to include it in *Progress of a Race* in its entirety, when many of Washington's texts were chopped up and unattributed to him, may have indicated their respect for Crummell and for his pedagogical position. Crummell believed that Washington's emphasis on industrial education for the Negro was misplaced and asserted, from the very first line of his article, that this error in emphasis would be responsible for "hinder[ing] the progress of the race" (361). Those wishing to solve the "Negro Problem," Crummell wrote, were divided into two groups or classes: "The one maintains that industrialism is the solution of the Negro problem; and another class, while recognizing the need for industrial skill, maintains that culture is the true solution" (361). For Crummell, the emphasis on industrial education represented an unwelcome continuation of the American "school of labor" to which Black people were confined under slavery. He described industrial education as simply "an alteration in the form of an old and settled order of life" (361): it maintained the basic structure and emphasis of the "old slave-labor system" (363). Crummell did not disagree with the importance of industrial skills; what he found objectionable was "an undue and overshadowing exaggeration of it in the case of the Negro" (363). He also believed that while industrial skills may provide a source of income for African Americans, they would not lead to real change. The Negro race, he said, "needs a new factor for its life and being, and this new factor must come from a more vitalizing source that any material condition. The end of industrialism is thrift, prosperity or gain. But civilization has a loftier object in view. It is to make men grander; it is to exalt them in the scale of being; and its main energy to this end is the 'higher culture'" (364). At the heart of higher culture, Crummell believed, was intellectual engagement, something that was not available through a standard "Negro curriculum."[103]

I have quoted at length Crummell's words from "The Prime Need of the Negro Race" because they illuminate the sort of intellectual engagement and critical thinking that Crogman hoped would emerge from the pedagogy embodied in *Progress of a Race*. W. E. B. Du Bois would eulogize Crummell in *The Souls of Black Folk* as one who was unafraid to "struggle with life that he might know the world and know himself."[104] This is precisely the combination of studied inquisitiveness and fearlessness that the literary education embedded in *Progress of a Race* was intended to promote. The importance of Crummell's words are perhaps signaled by the fact that his article was fully identified by its title and original place of publication, as well as its author's name and position. Another way the authors emphasized Crummell's significance is that they did not excerpt, truncate, or rearrange his article, as they did with Washington's address. What they did, then, in two of the rare pieces in which they identified the author, is make clear that the one who saw the "progress of the race" through pursuing a "higher culture," including literary culture, was to be read in full, while the other, who advocated the "school of labor," had to be read piecemeal and only in light of someone who was critical of that very position.

The one alteration the authors make to Crummell's essay is worth noting for what it reveals about the authors' sense of their readership, and their model for what a schoolbook was to do. As they did with other texts, including Washington's, they created bold-faced headings to announce the subject of each paragraph. These headings were sometimes single words identifying a subject (e.g., "Leaders"; "Enrollment"; "Civilization"), but most often they were short, catchy phrases that highlight its central subject or message. Evidence from other sources reveals that it was precisely this kind of organization that Black readers wanted. In a letter to the *Christian Recorder*, one reader praised a book for its "convenience," noting especially that a book that had clearly marked sections and short ones was most effective for "a people who have not the complete control of their time."[105] Clarity of outline mattered to Black readers. This was most obviously achieved in *Progress of a Race* through the authors' deliberate use of boldface subheadings, which authoritatively guided readers to and through discrete units of text that could be perused in short sittings or read more deeply in longer ones. A text punctuated in this way would have made the considerable length of *Progress of a Race* less intimidating and more manageable by offering ways for the reader to enter the text; the structural assistance communicated through the headings was instrumental to both breaking it up and navigating it. The headings also facilitated random access to the material collected in the chapter, and in the book, alleviating the need to read sequentially. This is also facilitated by the depth of detail in the book's table of contents, which guides readers through *Progress of a Race* not by indicating relevant page numbers, where chapters begin or end, but by indicating the topics covered in each chapter. In a text of over six hundred pages, this itemization was likely a welcome feature.

The way uniformity and order are imposed on *Progress of a Race* by its authors is notable, as is the authors' willingness to chop up and blend together literary texts in an effort to make them accessible to a wide range of readers. One of the main arguments inherent in the construction of *Progress of a Race* was that racial and literary knowledge could be made accessible to all African American men and women, regardless of their distance from pursuits traditionally associated with Black intellectualism at the end of the nineteenth century. *Progress of a Race* provided a template for the sustained study of both race and literature by stabilizing the presentation of both in one location. This was the sort of education that promised to prepare African Americans to enter the debate over Black identity and the future of African Americans in the United States. The fragmentary, disconnected composition of *Progress of a Race* distinctively served its purpose by breaking down what in their original forms were lengthy, complex literary texts in order to simplify and provide access to the scholarly discussions in which they participated. This intervention acknowledged the sizable body of race literature already produced by and about African Americans while also calling attention to the difficulty of making that literature usable by a wider community that did not have ready access to literature, or to the kinds of racial knowledge that would help them see themselves as part of a fragile but growing collectivity.

In book form, *Progress of a Race* exemplified what Crogman had tried to do first in the exhibit in the Liberal Arts Building in Chicago, and then in the Negro Building in Atlanta: to represent the work of the race as a sign of progress, and to make that material easily accessible by "curating" it. As Crogman insisted in the preface of *Progress of a Race*, it "put into permanent form" the story that had been housed in temporary buildings and displays in Chicago and Atlanta. One of the imperatives of his project in *Progress of a Race* is to show Black readers how to "progress" from literacy to the literary, which is exemplified in the movement from reading bits of condensed prose by anonymous authors to mastering the depth of thinking an Alexander Crummell could provide. In *Progress of a Race*, then, Crogman partially fulfills the trajectory he articulated as necessary for African Americans in one of his addresses from *Talks for the Times*: to offer the path from "the little world of the school" to the "larger world of action and responsibility."[106] This movement, from learning how to read to learning how to represent oneself, was crucial to the kind of progress that was sorely needed in Black communities—not primarily across the Northeast, where opportunities for intellectual community were more readily available, but across the South and the Midwest.

As I have argued here, buyers of *Progress of a Race* were participating in a crucial shift, from basic literacy to a more extensive understanding of the literary. For scholars, *Progress of a Race* offers invaluable insight into the sort of materials that facilitated this shift, helping us to see and understand the literary practices of African Americans who were not Northern, not urbane, and not elite as they came to be book buyers and to extend their grasp of the nuances of literature and the possibilities of literary study. We don't know the impact of this or similar books on individual Black learners or on the Black communities in which the book was sold. But critical attention to *Progress of a Race* and texts like it offers one way to enlarge the map through which we see African American literary history around the turn of the century. For its original consumers, *Progress of a Race* extended literary culture into Black communities and Black homes, locating racial identity and race pride in the space of books. In addition to expanding the reading material that was popularly available, it organized knowledge and served as a stepping-stone to a larger literary world bounded by race. One concrete example of this can be found in the six-page list of "Colored Authors and Names of Publications" that is tucked into the chapter of *Progress of a Race* on "Personages of the Negro Race." This list gave readers an additional 139 titles to supplement their understanding of the scope and parameters of Black literature. As I argue in the next chapter, lists such as this, which proliferated around the turn of the century, quite literally provided ways to physically locate and conceptually know Black literature. They facilitated the sort of literary consciousness promoted by *Progress of a Race* and helped make it more accessible to more people. In the context of the substantial length of *Progress of a Race*, this list appears relatively modest, but it was another important invitation to literary study and a means of putting forward a scaffolding of ideas about literature that would give it additional shape and purpose.

CHAPTER TWO

THINKING
BIBLIOGRAPHICALLY

IN THE PREVIOUS CHAPTER, I LOOKED AT THE WAY A CERTAIN KIND
of book—ornate and physically impressive in size, unoriginal in composition, pedagogic in nature, cheaply produced and sold by subscription, and
focused on racial history and achievements—established one kind of scaffolding for literacy among a segment of the African American population
with little access to fine works of literature or the reading material that would
advance their literacy. These books, I argued, represent avenues of education
that took place outside of schools and worked to promote racial identity as
they built bridges between Black literacy and literary understanding. In this
chapter, I explore another form of scaffolding that supported Black literacy
and the development of an appreciation for the literary at the turn from
the nineteenth to the twentieth century: lists. Lists are one of the most everyday and utilitarian forms of writing and as such are rarely the focus of
scholarly inquiry. But in this chapter I argue that lists of print—and, more
formally, bibliographies—emerge as one of the most historically important features of turn-of-the-century African American literary history; they

were, for the generation that created them, the framework that gave purpose and legitimacy to Black literature. At the same time, lists of "colored authors and names of publications" presented themselves as sites through which to grapple with the very idea of Black literature. Their very format asked important questions about African American literature and its parameters: What should it include? What should be excluded? How should it be categorized and conceptualized, and for what purposes? These questions lay at the heart of giving purpose to literacy and to the development of an expanding sense of the literary for African Americans. By their very nature, the lists make visible the process of assembly and contextualization that was ongoing in Black communities around writing and Negro authorship. But, as they recorded the literary milestones already achieved by African Americans, the very format of the list made lists simultaneously interactive, forward-thinking, and usable. They opened up the category of Black literature to inquiry and debate as they invited readers to add, subtract, redistribute, and otherwise revise them in ways that linguistically finished texts do not.

To fully appreciate the function of the lists of African American literature that proliferated around the turn of the century, one must give some thought to the list as a genre that is quotidian and practical as well as historical. The everyday appeal and practical efficiency of lists is everywhere apparent: we have all made shopping or packing lists, and the generic "to-do" list is a universal means of organizing and remembering tasks or errands that need to be completed. And yet, as Paul Tankard observes, we are wrong to think of lists as "an uninteresting and rather minimal function of written language: obvious, written usually in shorthand, using writing only for its capacity for storage."[1] This seemingly straightforward idea of lists does not begin to capture their extensive definitions and historical uses. We rarely think critically about lists in and of themselves, and yet their complex and contradictory nature demands attention. Lists are at once assertive and provisional; they are generated out of the needs of the immediate moment but also become, in some fundamental way, future-oriented. They are texts that seemingly drive toward closure (a completed or fully checked-off list) and yet also serve as invitations to revise, whether by adding to or subtracting from its entries or by regrouping and reordering the list as a whole. In fact, lists are not just a primitive means of collecting, remembering, or recording; they are also managerial devices and mechanisms through which to think. Lists help us to sort out and break down ideas and, in doing so, make them accessible to others. They appear to be authoritative and certain, but they are in fact forms that compel us into discussion, enticing readers to intervene by questioning a list's very existence or calling attention to the locations of its excesses and its gaps. The motion of a list's creation, then, is a discursive event, one that implicates its reader in a number of challenges, all of which constitute a call to further thinking and future action.

In *The Domestication of the Savage Mind*, anthropologist Jack Goody helps to unpack the history of lists as a cultural phenomenon. He identifies list-making as associated with some of the earliest functions of writing, predating prose and poetry, because, he notes, in societies with functioning oral cultures, there was little need for those written forms. In this context, list-making arose as a distinctive form. Written lists were a useful and usable means of keeping track of disparate and arbitrary information that could not be remembered orally. But there were many kinds of lists, each serving a different function. A retrospective list might record events, observe situations, or provide an inventory or accounting of people or things. Distinct from this type of list were lists that established future plans and action—for example, in addition to the shopping or the to-do list, the itinerary, a document that mapped out pilgrimages and other movement or travel. A third kind of list, associated with the early emergence of lists, is the lexical list, which served as a kind of inventory of concepts; Goody describes these as protodictionaries or encyclopedias. His point in returning to the early origins of the list is to insist that list-making was not only a form of writing that fulfilled a certain need; throughout history, it has also been a significant mode of thought. Goody details some of the distinct characteristics of lists that make them, as he terms it, "technologies of the intellect." He writes,

> The list relies on discontinuity rather than continuity; it depends on physical placement, on location; it can be read in different directions, both sideways and downwards, up and down; it has a clear cut beginning and a precise end, that is, a boundary, an edge, like a piece of cloth. Most importantly it encourages the ordering of the items, by number, by initial sound, by category, etc. And the existence of boundaries, external and internal, brings greater visibility to categories, at the same time as making them more abstract.[2]

As Goody explains, lists become meaningful in part because of their disrupted, unfinished quality. They are opposed, for instance, to the "continuity, the flux, the connectedness of the usual speech forms," like conversation or oratory.[3] Unlike prose, they are not grammatically finished texts—but herein lies much of their promise and possibility.

In this chapter I consider the complex qualities of the public lists African Americans at the turn of the century created of books and other printed forms that were eventually crafted more formally into bibliographies. While lists are, as Paul Tankard notes, disruptive to a "reading regime" because they can be "entered anywhere" and "read in any sequence," the lists I examine here reveal how a list can also less arbitrarily construct something like a "reading regime."[4] These lists of African American texts served an important purpose: they constituted scaffolding to establish the scope and parameters of Negro authorship and writing about race. They were, I argue, not simply about enumerating books or documenting literary achievements, although this was certainly one of their functions. They were also generative devices, listing books and other printed texts in a particular order, by a particular system, in particular contexts, and under particular category headings as a way of establishing a framework of ideas that were central to the process of mapping out Black letters. Even so, even as they document African American literary tradition in the making, the lists do make visible the instability of the very idea of Negro literature in the historical fold between the nineteenth and twentieth centuries.

While inquiries into scenes of reading have become commonplace in literary scholarship, we have yet to turn our attention to the less visible systems of access used by readers to both locate texts and to understand them as a part of a larger collection or field of knowledge. This chapter works to illuminate the cluster of lists on Black literature that found their way into print around the turn of the century. Read in isolation, these documents are important print artifacts of African American authorship and literature that should reorient our twenty-first-century understanding of the texts that shaped literary understanding at the turn from the nineteenth to the twentieth century. Taken together, they emerge and cohere as modes of practical, collective criticism, helping us to see bibliography as a practice of knowledge production.

My focus in this chapter is primarily on the early twentieth-century bibliographic work of two African American men, Daniel Murray and W. E. B. Du Bois. But I begin by looking at a list from 1894 generated by Gertrude Bustill Mossell for *The Work of the Afro-American Woman*. Embedded in prose, this list effectively illustrates the generative, definitional possibilities inherent in list-making; it embodies the sort of organizational activities that were undertaken in the 1890s to save, manage, and process information. Placed in conversation with other lists generated during this time, Mossell's list points to the necessity of studying the various lists constructed by African Americans around the turn of the twentieth century, the very years in which bibliography was being shaped into an organized and professionalized field in the United States. I then turn to Daniel Murray's 1900 bibliography project, conducted under the auspices of the Library of Congress for display at the 1900 Paris Exposition. In examining the way that he went about compiling and composing the bibliography, first for the exhibition itself and then as a part of a quest to document Black letters, I expose the evolution of his thinking about Black authorship and Negro literature and the ways that it should be known. His sense of the never-ending nature of that project is telling, for it illuminates both the problems as well as the productivity of bibliographies. Finally, the last part of the chapter takes up three bibliographies by W. E. B. Du Bois, published as components of the Atlanta University Studies in 1900, 1901, and 1905, respectively. In these bibliographies, Du Bois makes visible the discursive conversations that are an element of all lists and bibliographies, articulating for his readers how to use their reading by showing them how to put texts in conversation with other texts.

"Send Us the Names of Omitted Volumes"

Scholars have long wondered how to position and make sense of texts from the late nineteenth century whose mode of address is primarily enumerative. Laura Helton has recently identified "acts of enumeration and organization" as "urgent and endemic to black thought in the first half of the twentieth century."[5] Her work to establish the importance of list-making and cataloging as it emerged from the efforts of librarians and archivists intent on laying an infrastructure for African American studies helps us to see the ways that Black intellectuals turned to these structures as a means of defining, preserving, and ensuring access to the materials by which African Americans might be known. It also underscores the extent to which Black women were central to this effort. Helton chronicles the pioneering work of librarians and archivists such as Dorothy Porter and Vivian Harsh, whose "infrastructural agenda" (84) was carried out at least in part through the production of lists. As Helton documents, their labor and that of other information workers has been generally overlooked, and the systems that they authored to preserve and organize information and ensure that it could be accessed have remained invisible. This is at least in part because of what Helton calls the "gendered framework of intellectual history," which has led not only to the neglect of women's contributions to literary and intellectual history, but also to a disregard of certain "*types* of labor" that "are associated with women's domestic work" (100). Recovering the history of list-making, then, is a part of the process of recovering a long history of African American information workers who were both male and female, the roots of whose efforts can be seen in the late nineteenth century, when Black women's work to define literature by and about African Americans and to ensure its accessibility is particularly notable. Their lists, which existed, in Helton's words, "at the formal and gendered edge of authorship" (84), are embedded in the addresses and multigeneric volumes of essays that are representative of the intellectual work done by African American women across the "Woman's Era." These lists respond to the writer and educator Anna Julia Cooper's 1892 call, in *A Voice from the South*, for African American women to "address ourselves to the task of casting up our account and carefully overhauling our books."[6] Black women quite literally overhauled the books of African American history by authoring lists, making bibliographic information public as a way of establishing a framework of knowledge about their race and accounting for its achievements.

Just how lists proved useful in this effort is nowhere more visible than in Gertrude Bustill Mossell's *The Work of the Afro-American Woman*, published in 1894 under her married name, Mrs. N. F. Mossell. As Elizabeth Alexander notes, Mossell's book is "a compendium that seems to be attempting to list everyone, not to miss a soul."[7] Her writing can best be described as enumerative: Mossell composes, in prose form, lists that are both explicit and exhaustive. Her systematic naming—of educators, writers, journalists, medical practitioners, missionary workers, businesswomen, farmers, and inventors—functions as both recuperative and forward-looking: by recording the past, she wishes to inspire future generations of African Americans and command respect and recognition for the race. The listing of names is a way of gathering together and making visible the breadth of African American achievements, in particular those of Black women. Mossell is particularly interested in documenting African American intellectual labor, asserting that the "intellectual history of a people or nation constitutes . . . the very heart of its life."[8] It is for this reason that she devotes a significant chapter of her book to what she calls "Afro-American Literature." In passionate prose, Mossell begins the chapter by heralding the writing of Phillis Wheatley; she goes on to discuss the literary contributions of Frances E. W. Harper and contemporaries Anna Julia Cooper and Victoria Earle Matthews, as well as other Black authors, the quality of whose writing she judges as effective because it gives "inspiration to the youth of the race" while at the same time winning "the hearts of the enemy."[9] Mossell's writing in this chapter is both eloquent and cogent. But it is when she breaks out of this essayistic mode that her effort to document and mount an argument about Afro-American writing becomes most pointedly articulated. She ends the chapter not in narrative prose, but with a list of seventy-two titles by "Afro-American" writers.

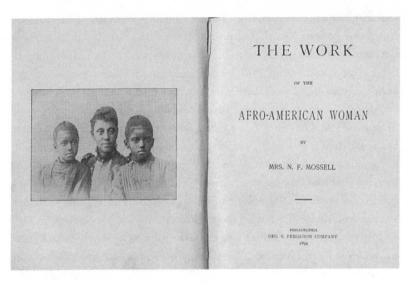

THE WORK

OF THE

AFRO-AMERICAN WOMAN

BY

MRS. N. F. MOSSELL

———

PHILADELPHIA
GEO. S. FERGUSON COMPANY
1894

2.1 Title page and frontispiece, *The Work of the Afro-American Woman*, by Mrs. N. F. [Gertrude Bustill] Mossell (1894).

Mossell's "List of Afro-American Publications" jumps out at the reader in part because of its obvious difference from the prose that surrounds it. It interrupts her narrative exposition on the history of the hard-won intellectual achievements of African Americans that forms the bulk of the chapter's contents. In this context, the list constitutes a substitute for writing: it takes the place of a prose essay on African American authors and their publications. But the "List of Afro-American Publications" does something different from the prose around it; arresting our attention, for a moment it suspends what Tankard calls the "relentlessness of prose and rescues the reader from the subjection to the grammar and syntax of an authorial voice." This is the effect, Tankard argues, of lists embedded in literary prose where "a list shows (in some clearly defined area, large or small) the list-maker's summative power." As a summary, the list is differently usable than the prose: among other things, Tankard notes, it "stops us reading and starts us counting."[10] This is the effect of the "List of Afro-American Publications": even though its entries are not numbered, the list confirms in raw data unembellished by narrative prose Mossell's argument about the abundance of Black writing.

What Mossell draws on here is the list's authority: its straightforwardness implies factuality. The list is, for the most part, limited to titles and authors and is unadorned with the sort of publication information we associate with formal bibliography. We nevertheless learn from this list a tremendous amount about the ways that Mossell was thinking about Black literature. First, it is notable that Mossell's list, which predates Victoria Earle Matthews's 1895 call for an expansive definition of "Race Literature," includes every category of publication that Matthews cites in her famous address "The Value of Race Literature." The "List of Afro-American Publications" includes works of poetry and prose, but also religious, journalistic, and scientific writing. It even includes an "Elementary Text Book": William S. Scarborough's *First Lessons in Greek*, published in 1881. In this, Mossell anticipates Matthews's assertion that all of these kinds of print sources counted as "Race Literature," even if they did not specifically concern "race matter."[11] Second, by including "two volumes written by whites, yet containing personal writings by the Negro Race," Mossell's list implicitly makes an observation about the complexity of recovering the archives of Black writing: accounting for African American publications required some sleuthing, because the writing done by members of the race was sometimes buried in print sources that bore the names of white authors. Finally, Mossell's attention to the work of Black women lays the groundwork for their inclusion in subsequent lists compiled by those less attentive to Black women's contributions to literature. Mossell's list of "Afro-American Publications"—as well as the essay in which it is embedded, a chapter that lists contributions to "Afro-American Literature" that in turn sits within a book that lists Black achievements—is not focused exclusively on Black women's authorship. Yet the presence of so many titles by them, beginning with Wheatley's 1773 poems and including less-familiar publications like Mrs. Julia A. J. Foote's *A Brand Plucked from the Fire*, Mrs. Harvey Johnson's *Corinne*, and Mrs. Josephine Heard's collection of poems, *Morning Glories*, insists that the authorship of Black women be recognized and that their contributions be included in the historical record.

Why were African American literary practitioners drawn to the form and quality of the list, whether written in prose form or as a freestanding element embedded in a prose text, as was the "List of Afro-American Publications"? One reason was clearly for its enumerative quality: lists illustrated the sheer quantity of intellectual activity to which African Americans could lay claim, their visual tally refuting charges that Black people were intellectually inferior and unaccomplished. But there are other reasons that list-making was such a vibrant form of writing as the nineteenth century drew to a close. Again and again in *The Work of the Afro-American Woman*, Mossell suggests that she was drawn to lists at least in part because of their discursive quality. In the book's preface, she invites readers to talk back to her lists: "The author would be grateful to her readers," she writes, "if, by personal communication, they would make any correction or suggestion looking toward a more extended and revised edition of this work in the near future."[12] Mossell's inclusion of her home address—1432 Lombard Street, in Philadelphia—ensures that readers could offer their feedback on the various lists she assembled, supplementing or suggesting amendments or corrections to them and, in doing so, contributing to what must be an ongoing effort to make Black history more visible, more accurate, and more accessible. What she offered her readers was not presented as complete: rather, the list's unfinished quality acknowledged the difficulty of tracking down and reassembling an archive of Black accomplishment. This was particularly true of Black writing. In a note that follows the list, Mossell issues a similar invitation to take action to add to or correct the historical record, telling readers that "we would be glad if authors would send us the names of omitted volumes to be used in a possible future addition."[13] This invitation to participate in the "making" of African American literary history signals the open-endedness that the genre of the list both announces and represents. Mossell reinforces the ongoing nature of her project a third time at the end of *The Work of the Afro-American Woman*, where she includes an "appendix" made up of snippets of information that arrived "too late to be Classified."[14] The eight added items enumerated in the appendix underscore the generative nature of list-making. They also explain the preponderance of lists around the turn from the nineteenth to the twentieth century: lists inspired more lists, each one documenting, framing, and preserving its subject in a distinct way.

As Shirley Moody-Turner notes, the value of Mossell's project in *The Work of the Afro-American Woman* "has been largely erased in the larger public discourse."[15] But by attending to the plethora of lists that appear in works from the late nineteenth century, we are able to see its importance. Consider three examples. The first, Robert Mara Adger's "Subjects Relating to the Past Condition of the Colored Race and the Slavery Agitation in This Country" (1984), is an inventory, both metaphorically and literally, since it both offers a broadly defined archive of Blackness, but it also offers that archive for sale.[16] A second example is the U. S. Bureau of Education's *Report* for 1893–1894, which includes "Works by Negro Authors." This list was assembled by a member of the bureau's staff, but it was "compiled from data" furnished by African American educational and religious leaders. It highlights texts first delivered orally as addresses as well as part of conference proceedings, emphasizing the ways that what might have been ephemeral events become enduringly printed texts.[17] A third and final example is the list of "Colored Authors and Names of Publications" that concludes the long "Noted Personages of the Afro-American Race" prose chapter in *Progress of a Race*. At the chapter's end, the authors offer a six-page itemized list that reveals the literary products of those "personages" they had designated as the "forerunners of liberty."[18] We can get a sense of the authors' purpose by examining how the chapter and the list were to work in tandem. In the case of Frances Ellen Watkins Harper, for instance, we see how they identified her, first, as an abolitionist activist in the prose section entitled "Forerunners of Liberty," and then a second time as an "author" in the prose section "Authors and Literary Workers," and finally a third time in the list of "Colored Authors and Names of Publications."[19] The repeated references to Harper, in different forms (list, prose), and in terms of the different kinds of work she has performed (lecturer, activist, author), reveal some of the key bibliographical imperatives of *Progress of a Race*: to arrest the reader by shifting visual formats (from prose to list to prose) and to distinguish the range of diverse kinds of literary work that have led to "progress."

Individually and as a group, the lists produced in the last decade of the nineteenth century illustrate the kinds of dilemmas and questions at stake in sorting through and defining Black authorship and Negro literature, a task that the sheer proliferation of lists in the 1890s suggests was a pressing concern that was aligned with general interest in Negro education. One of the particular challenges was that African American writing was scattered and its authors difficult to identify. The problem of how to identify and group authors, how to define what counted as the work of Negro authors, and how to move past partial or incomplete bibliographic data would continue to plague African American list-makers into the twentieth century. As we will see, more formal efforts to establish partnerships, not only among African Americans, but also across racial lines, would be essential to the collection and formal documentation of Negro authors and Black letters.

Daniel Murray's Bibliographic Project

The leader of this effort was Daniel Murray. Working under the auspices of the Library of Congress, with the clear goal of presenting a complete list of "Books and Pamphlets by Negro Authors" for display at the Paris Exposition in 1900, Murray strategically made use of earlier lists of books such as that published as a part of the Bureau of Education's report. He also engaged the help of collaborators within both the Black community and the community of bibliophiles and librarians, and he did so at a time when bibliography as a discipline and, indeed, as a profession was taking shape in the United States. At the end of the nineteenth century, everything about how books were perceived and valued was changing. Most significantly, bibliography emerged as an urgent responsibility as the need to define the parameters of all that was American—including the parameters of American literature—was felt acutely. Murray's 1900 bibliography must be located amid this effort, for doing so explains the urgency of his project, not only as a means of establishing African American letters, but as a part of a bibliographic imperative that promised to solve the problem of identity as well.

At the very moment when African Americans were creating lists of "colored authors and publications," bibliography was rapidly taking on important meaning and legitimacy in the United States, where it was being imagined as a critical tool in establishing and articulating the parameters of American literature and in making texts known and accessible to readers. As the nineteenth century drew to a close, bibliography was becoming recognized as a crucial form of intellectual leadership in uncertain, unstable, and seemingly threatening times. Nowhere is this transition seen more clearly than in conversations surrounding the 1899 formation of the Bibliographical Society of Chicago. The society identified its work as distinct from the kind of antiquarian book-collecting that they felt Chicago's Caxton Club and New York's Grolier Club represented, as well as distinct from "library associations."[20] Their work was serious. "To spend our time largely in amusing ourselves, in gratifying our taste for the aesthetic, and our vanity, by cultivating exclusively the old, the queer, and the select in bibliography," the first president of the Bibliographical Society of Chicago, Charles H. Hastings, proclaimed, "would . . . be dodging 'the white man's burden' which the times have laid upon us."[21]

The work of bibliography, then, was as critical as the work of colonization celebrated in the Kipling poem he quoted. Organizing the knowledge available about books was akin to organizing a newly expanded polity that the previous year had come to include Puerto Rico, Guam, the Philippines, and Cuba. Hastings reiterated this point when he commented in his inaugural address that "there is a bibliographical problem, just as there is a social problem, which will worry us all until it is solved."[22] At the dawn of a new century, in the wake of American global expansion, the Bibliographical Society of Chicago exhibited an anxious nationalism that they attempted to allay by bibliographically mapping the nation's literature. In the pursuit of that goal, the society sought both to provide a sense of continuity, both temporally and territorially. One aspect of their work was local: to assemble a list of the contents of "private libraries in Chicago" whose owners were willing to open their libraries to scholars; to complete "a list of all English books printed before 1640 to be found in Chicago libraries, private and public"; and to make "a list of incunabula [or texts printed, not handwritten, before the year 1501] in Chicago libraries, private and public." But their mission was also national. In cataloging the incunabula in Chicago libraries, they expected to contribute to "the work of Mr. John Thomson, of the Free Public Library of Philadelphia, who is compiling a list of incunabula in the United States." By establishing national networks, they would be able to make known a national literature. One project they imagined was to produce a "bibliography of first editions of American authors."[23]

Two things stand out in the mission the Bibliographical Society of Chicago set for itself. The first was a focus on use value. The society believed that bibliographies of "all the written records of the world" would make these texts "more easily available to students."[24] It saw its members as a crucial "class of middlemen" who would facilitate contact between "the literary worker, and the idea of which he is in search."[25] They recognized bibliography to be a powerful instrument of investigation and a means of thinking intellectually, which would lead to the formation of new perspectives on various bodies of literature. Practically speaking, bibliographies would organize and make visible particular constellations or sets of texts, but they would also be a way to conceptualize, structure, and revise new understandings or bodies of knowledge about the past out of its literary remnants.

The second thing was the issue of scope and method. The work of constructing bibliographies needed to become an organized, collective, and professional endeavor. The society considered bibliographies as opportunities to create maps, which could not be constructed individually or in isolation. Bibliographers needed to work together, across the membership of the society, across institutions, across the nation, or across national lines. The new society stressed collaborative projects and the coordination of individual efforts; their aim was not to promote themselves or their own collections but to promote authority. This understanding was at the core of the Bibliographical Society of Chicago's view of itself as a provisional entity. From the moment of its inception, the society's leadership began to work toward the establishment of a national organization that would make the Chicago society obsolete. Within a year, it would boast of "eighty resident and nineteen non-resident" members, a balance that was a sign of the society's success.[26] The membership wished that their organization would "lead to the founding of a national bibliographical society." "We will find our most important task," said one of the founders, "in bibliography proper, and here a national society would be able to do much more than a society confined in membership to one locality."[27]

The professional association most relevant to the Bibliographical Society of Chicago's work was the American Library Association (ALA), which had been founded in 1876 to "provide leadership for the development, promotion, and improvement of library and information services and the profession of librarianship in order to enhance learning and ensure access of information for all."[28] The ALA staked its claim to professional status on the librarians' responsibility to build institutions that would preserve knowledge and make it accessible to the people. They were determined to disabuse the public of the idea that anyone with a love of books was qualified to serve as a librarian and sought to establish standards for training people in library work. Although some worried that standardizing practices would detract from the intimate, informal feel of a local library, others believed that bringing a businesslike efficiency to library services and some basic uniformity to systems of cataloging books would ensure that large collections could be sustained without the resulting chaos that many rapidly growing libraries were experiencing by the turn of the century. By forming an association to discuss the broad needs of libraries, library professionals committed to debating questions about the shape libraries would take in the new century. There was much their membership didn't agree on, but they did agree that the central role of the librarian lay in developing collections and guiding users to the literature they wished to read.

The Bibliographical Society of Chicago was particularly attentive to what the ALA represented. The society's members compared themselves to the association of library professionals when they articulated their wish to perform the "same pioneer work at the humdrum problems of bibliography" as that "accomplished in library economy" by the ALA.[29] They too sought professionalization and a wider association at the national level. Moreover, unlike those professional organizations that were organized around creating a uniform methodology (as, for instance, the American Historical Association sought to do), the Bibliographical Society of Chicago wished to define and set the boundaries of the field of study.[30] They believed that a "national bibliographical society might accomplish . . . without great difficulty, a complete bibliography of American literature."[31] Where the other groups were trying to create uniformity in practice, the bibliographers were trying to establish comprehensiveness and definitiveness. What they identified as "American literature," in the lists they generated and published, would thereafter for them be what "American literature" was.

Although Daniel Murray's introduction to this professional world came through none of the formal channels or associations that I have just reviewed, the professional vision of these associations is everywhere visible in his effort to compile a "Preliminary List of Books and Pamphlets by Negro Authors for [the] Paris Exposition and Library of Congress" in 1900. It is likely that, as an African American, Murray would not ever have been welcomed by the members of the Bibliographical Society of Chicago, but I argue that Murray's success as a bibliographer was informed by the movement to establish bibliography as a key method of literature's organization and an essential mode of literary practice. Likewise, Murray was not formally educated to be a library professional. But his career as a librarian took place amid the drive to promote access as a key feature of the library and to make the Library of Congress specifically a premiere site for research and scholarly production.

Murray began his working life as a waiter for his brother, who oversaw the day-to-day operations of the restaurant on the Senate wing of the ground floor of the Capitol. At the time, the Library of Congress was located on the Capitol's main floor, and it's likely that the restaurant was where Murray first encountered Ainsworth Rand Spofford, then the head librarian. Details of exactly how Murray came to work in the library are unknown, but he assumed a part-time position there on January 1, 1871, most likely as a member of the custodial staff.[32] This was a period of rapid growth for the Library of Congress: Spofford envisioned the library as a "national repository of knowledge," and his rate of acquisition of books and other materials underscored his mission. "Let other libraries be exclusive," Spofford said, "but let the library of the nation be inclusive."[33] This tremendous ambition for the Library of Congress resulted in near chaos, as his acquisitions—not only of books and pamphlets, but also of newspapers, magazines, maps, charts, graphs, and engravings—rapidly overwhelmed the small space in the Capitol dedicated to the library. For Murray, this state of chaos was fortuitous, as it surely would have provided him with increased opportunities to be helpful beyond his janitorial duties. In fact, Murray proved proficient at one of the things that Spofford, in his role as head librarian, valued most: quickly locating books and other library materials.[34] This was no small feat in the ever-increasing mess of the library space. Spofford recognized in Murray a talent for library work and hired him as a full-time assistant in 1874.

In taking Murray under his wing, Spofford trained him in all aspects of library work. Murray would come to be described in relationship to his mentor as "second only in his knowledge of books and authors to that incomparable bookworm and erudite scholar, A. R. Spofford, under whom he has

2.2 The chaos of the original Library of Congress is best captured in the image *Scene from the Old Congressional Library, Washington, DC, Showing Present Congested Condition, 1897*, which originally appeared in *Harper's Weekly* 41 (February 27, 1897). Prints and Photographs Division, Library of Congress, Washington, DC.

trained for . . . many years."[35] Spofford was himself largely self-educated and appeared to have no qualms about the possibility that others could excel with only informal education as well. In addition to teaching him how to efficiently use and work in a library, Spofford also tutored Murray in historical inquiry and encouraged his study of foreign languages. To this Murray added his own intellectual activities and pursuits. Described as one who "burned the midnight oil to make of himself a man of no ordinary intelligence and of book learning," he was a member of the Negro Society, one of the many smaller organizations that might be considered forerunners of the better-known American Negro Academy, where he served on the "Lectures Committee."[36] In this context, he interacted socially and intellectually with the likes of John Cromwell and Alexander Crummell, as well as T. Thomas Fortune, who was, in 1877, a student at Howard University. All of these men would become important intellectual activists dedicated to bringing civil rights and educational opportunities to the Black community.

As an assistant librarian at the Library of Congress, Murray's job was broadly defined as library service; this meant that his days were filled with locating and supplying books and information to government officials and library patrons and replacing books that were no longer needed. Murray was also responsible for retrieving the mail from the post office and distributing it each day. It was not until 1896, as the Supreme Court was deciding the *Plessy v. Ferguson* case in the Capitol building and as the Library of Congress was preparing to move into its new, larger space across the street, that the library and its staff was organized—or reorganized—into divisions. Then, a reading room, an art gallery, a hall of maps and charts, a periodicals department, a music department, and a law library were established, each with a divisional chief in charge of its operation. In 1897, Murray was promoted to chief of the periodicals department, and he supervised the move of this, the most widely used division of the library, to the new building. It was a post he would hold for less than two months. In his own words, Murray was "summarily reduced," not only in position but also in pay grade, because of what one biographical essay published in the *Colored American Magazine* in 1902 delicately labeled "the friction incident to caste."[37] It was uncomfortable, it seemed, for the white attendants who were assigned to work under the department chiefs, of which in Murray's periodicals department there were three, to report to a Black supervisor. When the new Library of Congress opened to the public on November 1, 1897, Murray had been reassigned to the catalog department, where he was one of the sixteen assistants working under the division's supervisor. In 1898, he was reassigned again, this time to the Smithsonian Collection, and in 1899 he was assigned to the general reading room service. That same year the decision was made to reduce the term "assistant librarian," which Murray had proudly used since he joined the library staff, to "assistant." It was a title he refused to adopt. He would continue to present himself as an "assistant librarian" at the Library of Congress for the rest of his life.[38]

I chronicle these details of Murray's employment at the Library of Congress because this disheartening series of events, which mirrored the deteriorating status of African Americans throughout the nation as they became subject to greater and greater segregation and discrimination across the 1890s, must have left Murray hungry for some means of asserting his place at the library, as well as the place of African Americans more broadly. In July 1899, Murray published his own "Bill of Grievances" in the *Colored American*, which included the lack of Black representation on the National Industrial Commission and in the military, as well as the denial of Black participation in government in Washington, DC. Overall, he was furious at the assumption that Black men would unquestioningly support Republicans, given that party's demonstrated lack of respect for African Americans. His disappointment with President McKinley, and with the overall reluctance to recognize Black people as responsible and capable citizens but also as human beings, was palpable.[39]

This frame of mind must have made him particularly eager to accept the challenge brought to him in January 1900 by his superior, superintendent of the reading room David Hutcheson, to build a bibliography of Negro literature that would appear as a part of the Exhibit of American Negroes at the 1900 Paris Exposition. African Americans had found it necessary to lobby hard for the right to be represented in Paris. Their bid for representation was initially rejected by Ferdinand W. Peck, who had been appointed commissioner general for the United States for the Paris Exposition Universelle and was therefore responsible for the composition of the nation's exhibit. It was Thomas J. Calloway, a graduate of Fisk University, who in the end sent a letter to over one hundred race activists to gain their support for a Negro exhibit in Paris. "We owe it to ourselves to go before the world as Negroes," he said. "The Europeans think of us as a mass of rapists, ready to attack every white woman exposed, and a drug in a civilized society. This information has come to them through the horrible libels that have gone abroad. . . . How shall we answer these slanders?" The best way to counter these ideas and images, he recommended, was through the display of a "well selected and prepared exhibit representing the Negro's development" in Paris. "Thousands and thousands would view such a collection," he indicated. Perceptively, he noted how important a showcase of African American achievement would be, both domestically and abroad. "Not only will foreigners be impressed, but hundreds of white Americans will be [too]," he wrote.[40] Peck was unmoved by this petition, but Booker T. Washington's personal appeal to President McKinley to intervene led to a decision by Congress that the United States would sponsor a Negro exhibit and that Calloway himself would be in charge of it.

At the center of Calloway's vision of the Exhibit of American Negroes was a display of Negro literature. His request that the Library of Congress help with the process of "making a collection of books by Negro authors to form a part of the Negro exhibit at the Paris Exposition 1900" went first to the Library of Congress's new head librarian, Herbert Putnam.[41] Putnam had left his position as the head of the Boston Public Library to assume leadership of the nation's national library in 1899. His influence on the Boston

Public library had been extensive and decisive. When he assumed control of that library in 1895, the board of trustees, who had appointed him, preferred to make the decisions about the library by itself. But Putnam was a professional librarian who believed that a library should be under the primary control of library professionals. His priorities lay in professionalizing and modernizing the library system. In his first position, at the Minneapolis Public Library, Putnam had hired his own staff, established a network of branch libraries, and designed avenues for the libraries to enter into collaborative work with teachers and in schools. He had also instituted modern systems for cataloging and classifying books and for checking them out. He insisted that library patrons should have direct access to the collections through open stacks and shelving. He would bring these same initiatives to the Boston Public Library, where he was praised for pursuing his "conception of what the Public Library should be to the people of Boston."[42] First and foremost, his actions as a librarian insisted, was maintaining the clear understanding that libraries and their texts ought to be easily accessible. His priority in every instance was to expand and facilitate access to library collections.

These same priorities were behind Putnam's leadership of the Library of Congress, and at the heart of the bibliography project undertaken early in 1900 by Daniel Murray. Calloway met with Putnam in person on December 18, 1899, to discuss the "Negro Book Exhibit" and elicit the Library of Congress's help; two weeks later, Putnam confirmed the library's support of the project in a letter that assured Calloway that library service superintendent David Hutcheson would give such "assistance as may be practicable." He is "apt to assign the work to Daniel Murray," Putnam predicted. He went on to qualify the time Murray could dedicate to the project. "We cannot specifically detail him for any given period for work so special, but will assign to it such portion of his time as is not required by routine duties," Putnam wrote.[43] In fact, the bulk of the work for the project was completed after hours: Calloway would note that Murray "labored late at night, and with great expense of time."[44]

After receiving the assignment, Murray spent two weeks preparing a list of 270 titles, which he then sent out with a cover letter requesting "the co-operation of men of literary knowledge in several cities" (2). As a starting place, he used the list of "Works by Negro Authors" included in the Bureau of Education's Report of 1893–1894. To that list he added 117 titles. Calling this set of 270 titles "A Preliminary List," he had it professionally printed (2). Murray knew that "many more [texts] existed, by reason of the imperfect recollection of individuals, who said, they had seen or heard of a book written and

WASHINGTON, D. C.,

January 22d, 1900.

The object in this effort is to secure a copy of every book and pamphlet in existence, by a Negro Author, the same to be used in connection with the Exhibit of Negro Authorship at the Paris Exposition of 1900, and later placed in the Library of Congress. Any persons able to furnish books or pamphlets on this list, or having knowledge of such as are not on this list, will greatly aid this effort by interesting themselves to make certain that all books or pamphlets are duly represented in the collection.

The undersigned will furnish, upon application, penalty labels which, when attached to a package, will insure its free transmission through the mail.

DANIEL MURRAY,

Library of Congress,

Washington, D. C.

2.3 Daniel Murray included this solicitation letter in the pamphlet he produced to advertise his project and its objective, "Preliminary List of Books and Pamphlets by Negro Authors: For Paris Exposition and Library of Congress," U.S. Commission to the Paris Exposition (1900). Daniel Murray Pamphlet Collection, Library of Congress, Washington, DC.

published by a colored author and that copies had been in circulation in their neighborhood years ago" (4–5). His objective in printing the preliminary list was to spur people's interest in the project and their participation, in order to "test and trace to a finality every rumor or inkling in this regard" (5). Accompanied by a circular meant to "acquaint the public with the purpose of this Library to compile a bibliography of all books and pamphlets which Colored authors had at anytime published" (3), the list was sent out by mail on January 22, 1900. "My dear Sir," the circular began. "The Librarian of Congress (now Herbert Putnam), at the request of the Commissioner-General [Ferdinand W.] Peck, has undertaken to cooperate in the work of making a collection of books by Negro authors to form a part of the Negro exhibit at the Paris Exposition of 1900 . . . and has detailed the undersigned to take charge of the same," Murray wrote, clearly articulating his understanding of the importance of this display on the world stage and for the development of Black literary and intellectual history. "I need not dilate upon the importance of having such an exhibit at Paris and the value of such a collection to future investigators of the bibliography of Negro Authorship etc." (3). To ensure that the circular received as wide a distribution as possible, he asked "each one receiving the circular of information . . . to secure its publication in the local news-paper" (4). This way, his request traveled beyond the reach of the immediate circle of his mailing. Murray's understanding of the importance of the project was twofold. First, it was crucial for African Americans to make a good showing on the public stage of the Paris Exposition. But he also understood that the nation's national library needed an accounting of Negro literature for its own benefit and use. "At the close of the Exposition," he told those who received his request for assistance, "the whole collection will be installed in the Magnificent Library of Congress, to be on exhibit and for consultation for all time" (3–4).

The confidence Murray expressed in the circular, that "a work appealing so strongly to every Colored man and woman in the land would enlist their active cooperation" (4), underscores the extent to which he believed that the Black community would be crucial in naming and locating the texts that would fill out his bibliography. To this end, his first impulse was to send copies of the preliminary list, the circular, and prepaid return envelopes to "the one hundred and eighty educational institutions devoted to Negro youth, located in the South"; from these schools he hoped to receive "contributions and titles or information that would lead to obtaining" more entries for his bibliography" (6). But the initial response was disappointing. "From the whole number twelve answers were received"; a full five of these were from "white men presiding over Colored schools" (7). Murray's report to his supervisor at the Library of Congress, David Hutcheson, written at the completion of the project in October 1900, voiced his frustration. He wrote,

> After a month's effort and fully a thousand circulars sent out, I was rather discouraged and disappointed. I had pictured the race, eager, anxious and appreciative of such a golden opportunity. Certainly one might be justified in supposing, that when an opportunity presented itself to put in evidence proof that the Negro race possessed high intellectual capacity and had produced literary works of an exalted character, the opportunity for such proof would have been eagerly seized. Either there had been a general misapprehension of what was sought, or lack of definitiveness in the method of disseminating the information through the circulars sent out. (7)

Murray admitted that this second reason—that the circulars had not communicated effectively what he was asking for—was "the more cheerful to entertain"; but, he said, it was "not sustained by the other evidence gathered." In comparison, he noted, "white people took hold of the matter with an enthusiasm to me truly astonishing" (7). He pointed to the "large number of unsolicited letters [he] received proffering books and pamphlets, and information in regard to the same" (8).

There are several important factors at play here that Murray doesn't directly address or acknowledge. One is that the institutional priorities of Black colleges and universities had not been focused on the preservation or collection of Negro writing, nor did they have the resources to do so. In most cases, this had not been a priority of any white college, university, or institution, either. And yet the fact that these texts ended up in their collections speaks to the extent to which Black writing had nevertheless come into the possession of and under the control of whites. It was Murray's good fortune that extant copies of African American literature had found their way to institutions that valued print culture generally, even if they did not particularly value Black writing. His timing was also fortuitous: many of these institutions were in the process of taking stock of their own collections, and his requests, coming as they did from the Library of Congress, bestowed a sense of legitimacy and importance to the project. But, as he acknowledged, the task of gathering up the scattered remains of Black print culture into one recognized entity would prove more difficult than he had initially imagined. His real success began from a shift in tactics. It was only after embarking on two trips, "at the expense of the Commission," which "yielded most gratifying results," that Murray became convinced that "suc-

NEGRO BOOKS FOR PARIS EXPOSITION.

Where a book or pamphlet is found, and the owner will not donate the same, take a description by filling out this blank and return to DANIEL MURRAY, Library of Congress, Washington, D. C.

Author *N. C. Cannon* Rev

Title *"The Rock of Wisdom. Portrait of author*

Size, *Quarto . . . (144 pages),* 8°, 12°, : 16° or 18°.

Place of Publication *Albany, New York*

Name of Publisher *not given*

Date of Title Page *1833*

Edition *First*

Private Collection of J. E. Bruce

2.4 While assembling books for the Paris exhibit, Daniel Murray used printed forms to register titles that came to his attention. This slip is for Noah Caldwell Cannon's *The Rock of Wisdom* (1833), which Murray located in the private collection of John Edward Bruce. Confirmation of Cannon's race came from the author's portrait in the book. Daniel Murray Papers, Wisconsin Historical Society, Madison, WI.

cess lay in a personal appeal." He wrote "with [his] own hand, and sent out four thousand personal letters, each worded in a form to suit the case in hand" (9). His personal communications went to distinguished bookmen such as Wilberforce Eames of the Lenox Library, later to become part of the New York Public Library; by March of 1900, Eames has sent fifty-four titles that Murray added to his list (16). He also wrote specifically to Edmund M. Barton, the American Antiquarian Society's head librarian from 1881 to 1908, to appeal for that institution's support. "Mr. Edwin C. Goodwin [U. S. Senate Librarian] gave me your name and urged me to write," Murray began his letter. "No doubt many rare pamphlets are now in the collection of your Society and it is to have a list of them for bibliographic purposes that I address you." His hope was that Barton would scour the American Antiquarian Society's formal collection for titles he could add to his list, but also solicit them informally from African Americans residing in and around his local community. Murray makes clear in his letter to the librarian that a list of titles that might be added to his growing bibliographic list would be appreciated, but he also hoped that Barton would send him copies of any texts he had available or could secure. "I enclose penalty envelope for your reply," Murray optimistically told Barton, "and label for any package you could collect from your duplicates, or from some of the colored people in the vicinity."[45]

No records remain to indicate whether Barton was able to successfully solicit titles or texts from the African American community of Worcester, Massachusetts, but he did supply Murray with "Benjamin Banneker and Phillis Wheatley titles, and many very helpful suggestions" (16). Neither of these authors had been included on the Bureau of Education list that Murray had initially consulted. Barton was one of the librarians singled out by Murray in his final report on the project as especially helpful; he clearly appreciated his effort and wished to reciprocate. In an undated letter to the Honorable George F. Hoar, U.S. senator from Massachusetts, an elected member of the American Antiquarian Society since 1853 and its president from 1884 to 1887, Murray asked Hoar for his assistance in "transmission to the Worcester Antiquarian Society" a biographical sketch of Paul Jennings, whom Murray described as "a colored man who sustained an intimate [c]onfidential relationship to President Madison." His gesture was "animated," Murray wrote, "first by a desire that a knowledge of [Jennings] may be brought to the attention of the eminent literary men of the Antiquarian Society." Secondly, Murray wanted to "attest [his] gratitude to Mr. E. M. Barton[,] the Librarian, for valuable assistance afforded me in the work of compiling a bibliography of books and pamphlets by African Americans and Afro European authors."[46]

Murray was surprised to find that "our own library"—meaning the Library of Congress itself—was "well supplied in the matter of Negro books and pamphlets, far more so than any other Library" (8). The process of assembling the bibliography enabled him to make critical observations about the geographical distribution of African American print materials, which were related to patterns of the development of and access to Black print culture: "In Philadelphia," he reported, "can be found . . . more of the early books and pamphlets by this class of author, than any other place" (8). He identified where the bibliographic collections of some of the nineteenth century's Black elite were held, and he located various collections of print that were ripe to be pursued by repositories such as the Library of Congress. "The University of Pennsylvania," Murray reported, had "received by bequest the valuable collection of Mr. Robert Purvis" (8). "The collection of Mr. Jacob C. White," he would note, "will probably come to this Library [the Library of Congress], if his expressed intention is carried out" (8). Because Murray could promise that the texts he was given would have a future after the Paris Exposition, in the Library of Congress as a part of its permanent collection and available "for consultation for all time" (10), donors were themselves more willing to contribute. In fact, Murray's project lay the groundwork for some key acquisitions: "Several parties who have collections of very rare books and pamphlets by Negro authors," he noted in his final report, "have expressed a willingness to present them" to the Library of Congress (10). The library itself was clearly committed to the project and to the inclusion of literature by African American authors in their collection. Murray felt supported in his work, noting that the "helpful interest by suggestions, shown by Mr. Putnam," had given him confidence that the collection would indeed be valued and find a permanent home at the Library of Congress. Indeed, "upon the suggestion of Mr. Putnam," the process of cataloging the print artifacts that Murray received was immediately undertaken. "Mr. Hanson of the Catalogue Dept. ha[s] made a classified Catalogue of the several subjects represented by the 980 titles in hand by March 31st 1900," Murray wrote in his report (10). Additionally, Murray was provided with "the means to rebind and repair all books needing such attention" (10): by the time he wrote his report, 60 books and about 175 pamphlets had been repaired or bound (10). This and other actions gave "full satisfaction to the donors of the books and pamphlets" that their contributions to the Library of Congress were respected, making the solicitation of future donations easier (10). Murray's work, then, was not only effective as a way to establish his own bibliography of Negro authors, but also paved the way for the expansion and preservation of the Library of Congress's collection of Black print culture.[47]

One irony of Murray's effort is that we know more about the trajectory of the process by which he put together the list of Negro authors than we do about the final bibliography he assembled. While he noted the growth of the project in his correspondence—saying in a March letter that he had nine hundred titles, and twelve hundred at the end of April—he seems to have sent off, in May, what he described as "214 vols.[,] the engrossed sheets, and two bound volumes of Miscellaneous news-papers," and a bibliography, apparently, of "980 titles . . . arranged under the subject head on sixteen large sheets, 18 × 24 encased in a frame under glass and attached by hinges to a stationary post" (11). By all accounts, the display in Paris was impressive. It was hailed as "perhaps the most unique and striking" part of the Exhibit of American Negroes. "There are many who have scarcely heard of a Negro book, much less read one," wrote W. E. B. Du Bois, in proclaiming the importance of this collection of texts. "Here is a bibliography made by the Library of Congress containing 1,400 titles written by Negroes; 200 of these books are exhibited on the shelves."[48] Calloway, who had spearheaded the display, voiced his belief that "the most credible showing in the exhibit is by Negro

2.5 *Exhibit of American Negroes at the Paris Exposition* (1900).
Prints and Photographs Division, Library of Congress, Washington, DC.

authors collected by Mr. Daniel Murray."[49] Newspapers in the United States and around the globe specifically took notice of the literary display, with the *New York Times* pronouncing that it was "perhaps not an exaggeration to say that no one would have believed that the colored race in this country was so prolific in the production of literature."[50]

Murray did not accompany the collection to Paris, and this perhaps points to one of the reasons why there is not a final list of the titles that were arranged for viewers to see at the exposition. Another reason might be that, in Murray's own mind, the list was never fixed or completed. He was clearly addicted to the project and continued to work on it long after the materials he compiled left for Paris. By the end of eight months, he claimed to have "gathered the necessary data to establish fully fourteen hundred titles" (9). We are left with rich information about how Murray thought about what he hoped would become a burgeoning field of inquiry into Negro authors and their writing, but little concrete ability to piece together the list as it grew and developed. It's quite possible that the list shifted during the process of compiling it, as Murray came to think more about Black authorship and the category of Black letters and to refine his sense of who and what, exactly, should be included in it. An analysis of Murray's "Preliminary List of Books and Pamphlet by Negro Authors" offers some sense of the initial ways he was thinking about Black literature and begins to suggest how he used the bibliography as an intellectual workspace through which to grapple with the challenges of finding, defining, and framing African American literature at the beginning of the twentieth century. The list is organized alphabetically by author, and its formatting includes three columns, one for the text's author, one for its title, and one for its place and date of publication. This last column is frequently left blank, indicating that this information, although desirable, often remained a mystery. This and other "holes" in the bibliography, coupled with Murray's general sense of the status of the bibliography—incomplete and constantly in need of revision, ever on the way to fulfilling his objective to one day compose a "complete Negro bibliography"—effectively underscores the difficulty of bibliographically recovering the multiple genres and formats of early African American print, a fact that remains true of efforts to recover the historical and textual specificities of early Black print culture in our own time.[51]

Like the lists of "Negro authors" that had preceded it, Murray's bibliography offered a scaffold for thinking about Negro authorship and what should be included as Negro literature. This bibliography included Ida D. Bailey's *Atlanta Souvenir Cookbook*, published in 1895 (one of the many print relics

PRELIMINARY LIST

OF

BOOKS AND PAMPHLETS BY NEGRO AUTHORS

FOR

PARIS EXPOSITION AND LIBRARY OF CONGRESS.

COMPILED BY

DANIEL MURRAY, LIBRARY OF CONGRESS,

WASHINGTON, D. C.

2.6 Title page of "Preliminary List of Books and Pamphlets by Negro Authors: For Paris Exposition and Library of Congress," U.S. Commission to the Paris Exposition (1900). Daniel Murray Pamphlet Collection, Library of Congress, Washington, DC. This is the list that Murray initially sent to "men of literary knowledge in several cities" to spur interest and participation in his project.

of the Atlanta Exposition, but published in Washington, DC), as well as Margaret Brown's *French Cook Book*, or *French Cookery Book*, also published in Washington, DC, in 1886 and compellingly described by the author in the preface as "dictated by me, and carefully written down by my friend, Louise A. Smith."[52] These appear alongside texts that remain well known to scholars of African American literary history, such as Linda Brent's *Incidents in the Life of a Slave Girl* (a text listed under the name of its fictional persona rather than its author, Harriet Jacobs, and whose publication date and location remained unknown to Murray at the time of the bibliography's printing) and Solomon Northup's *Twelve Years a Slave* (1853). William Wells Brown's *Clotelle* appears on Murray's list, but in its final 1867 edition, which was published in Boston; neither the novel's original publication as *Clotel* (published in London in 1853), nor its repackaged 1864 version, is listed. Interestingly, while Charles Chesnutt is included as the author of the short story "The Wife of his Youth" (published in the *Atlantic* in 1898) and the story collection *The Conjure Woman*, published in 1899 by Houghton Mifflin, Murray identified neither text by date or place of publication. Murray's 1900 preliminary bibliography includes David Walker's *Appeal*, a text omitted by all of the lists I referred to in the first part of this chapter except Mossell's 1894 list of "Afro-American Publications" from *The Work of the Afro-American Woman*. It also includes two texts that Murray identifies as anonymously authored: "Joshua" and "Fifty Years." There is an argument inherent in the decision to include these texts without knowing who, exactly, authored them—not only about the difficulty of recovering the African American past, particularly given its sparse traces and its erasure from the very sorts of documentary traditions in which Murray worked, but also about the necessity of doing so, even if it results in a record of African American writing and authorship that remains incomplete.

There are certainly questions that can be asked about Murray's methods and about the texts he included in his list. In at least one instance during the process of compiling the Paris list, Murray appealed to his friend George Myers, asking him if he had "some printed pamphlet bearing your name that I can have so as to include your name in the bibliography[?] If it's a campaign pamphlet and issued in your name, that will give me something."[53] Myers was indeed an important if now largely unrecognized Black intellectual whose career as a barber in Cleveland, Ohio, brought him into close contact with the nation's Black social, political, and intellectual elite. He maintained a prolific correspondence on matters spanning politics and literature, and Murray clearly respected him and thought him worthy of inclusion on the list. But Murray's request has the air of a fishing expedition, raising the question of whether he reached a point in his project where his interest in expanding the list led him to pad it by seeking out friends and acquaintances to send their writing in for inclusion. Still, his desire to include Myers's writing on the list is more effectively considered as a part of Murray's attempts to work out in his own mind what "counted" as Negro literature, a term and an ideal that he embraced more and more fully as his project expanded and his research interests shifted. Murray's preliminary list was clearly preliminary not only in terms of the titles that it included, but also in terms of the very ways that he was thinking about how Black print culture should be considered. It documents a moment when Murray himself was grappling with the questions he wished to raise about Negro authorship: Who were Negro authors? How much was available to know about their texts and the location of their publication? In what contexts should their publications be viewed and valued?

As might be expected, some of the response to Murray's work was dismissive, but even the most negative reviewers at times began to appreciate what African American writers had indeed accomplished. The *Washington Bee* review of an exhibit of the collection Murray mounted after the Paris Exposition, for instance, began with a stock indictment: "We may as well be entirely frank in the appraisal," the reviewer begins. "Much of it is rubbish. There has been no negro Homer, Shakespeare, or Dumas—no American counterpart of the great French mulatto." Yet, after this wholesale dismissal, the reviewer seemed to acknowledge that there were some impressive things in Murray's exhibit. A "great deal of the work has better qualities than the world has reason to expect, when it remembers the condition of its origin." While this writer claims early in the review that the "chief value" of the collection has "no concern with the graces of literary form," he goes on to offer a substantive critique of Negro literature, while raising important questions about how it should be read and the contexts in which it should be valued. His assessment of the poet George Marion McClellan, for instance, the author of a book of poetry published in Nashville in 1895, speaks of the "high lyric quality" of the poetry, which, he determined, "present[s] a true poetic interpretation of nature and of life." McClellan's work, he argues, "should be known to students on the subject." The reviewer recognized the contributions of Black writers to historical fiction, a genre described as "fiction founded on fact," pointing to Pauline Hopkins's recently published *Contending Forces* and T. G. (Theophilus Gould) Stewart's "A Charleston Love Story," published in 1899 by the publisher F. Tennyson Neely. The authors of these texts, the reviewer implied, had the "literary discernment" to tell his or her story "as simply as possible, and not dilute it with trash in a vain effort to achieve a great novel."[54]

In cases where the dismissal was not attended by any growing appreciation for what African American authors had accomplished, Murray intervened. The New York *Mail and Express*, for instance, confidently claimed "there is no such thing as Negro literature." It was not that African American life was uninteresting, since the reviewer knew it to be an important aspect of American literature, as long as that literature was written by white American authors. The "Negro has furnished inspiration rather than found it," the reviewer concluded. That reviewer, the *Mail and Express*'s literary editor Richard Stoddard, was also the editor of the *Cyclopedia of American Literature*, so his dismissal was not trivial. Murray began an exchange with Stoddard, in which he first informed him of the growing list he was compiling: the original list of "270 titles," he told him, had now become a list of "fully eleven hundred titles of books and pamphlets by Negro authors, many of them excelling in a literary sense, of the highest order." By showing that the field of "Negro literature" was growing so quickly because it was finally being cataloged, Murray was alerting Stoddard to the danger of his hasty negative judgment. He then went on to suggest that Stoddard might include some African American writers in any future edition of his book, since, as he tellingly wrote, any "'Cyclopedia of American Literature' that omitted to notice so large a number of American books as are described in the Bibliography prepared by me, cannot justly lay claim to completion."[55] Murray appreciated the bibliographer's striving for "completion," and he used this potent weapon to show that there were several ways a bibliography could be incomplete: sometimes by inadequate research or omission, but also by active and willed ignorance.

Here Murray advances an argument about Negro literature as an integral but heretofore overlooked component of American literature. That recognition, he asserted, was slowly coming. Murray cited as evidence of that fact the extent to which his project and its products were being heralded by the press, citing recent articles in the Harrisburg *Telegraph*, the *Washington Post*, and the "Chicago papers and the press generally." But he also argued that evidence of the native Americanness of African American writing lay in the fact that the texts he had identified by Negro authors were being processed to become part of the catalog of the Library of Congress "by direction of Herbert Putnam, Librarian" and thus, officially recognized by and entering the permanent collection of the nation's library. This was, for Murray, sound judgment that this body of writing was indeed "American literature." "I shall be greatly indebted," Murray wrote to Stoddard, "if you will see to it that the literary world is informed, that the Negro may have justly accorded to him, all that is rightfully his due."[56]

Critical reading of the collection must have pleased Murray, who, by the end of 1900, showed no signs of stopping his work on expanding the bibliography project. Yet even as he continued to compile the bibliography, Murray turned his attention to a related but different project. In July 1900, he wrote to George Meyers, explaining his vision of "giving the world a history of Negro literature" in book form.[57] This idea of writing a book-length history of African American literature became the root of Murray's ambitious but forever-unfinished encyclopedia project, which exists in many draft versions in Murray's papers. Murray's title for that book, "A Bibliography of Negro Literature," already suggests a significant distance from the preliminary bibliography's focus on assembling a set of "books and pamphlets by Negro authors." Although it is unclear exactly when Murray made the semantic shift from "Negro authorship" to "Negro literature," it seems apparent that in the very process of assembling books and pamphlets by Negro authors, he came to recognize that a body of Negro literature existed and that, as opposed to listing this literature in column format as he had in the preliminary list, which highlighted in an easily readable way the titles and authors of which it was comprised, a larger history of Negro literature needed to be recorded in narrative prose.

By December 1900, he described the book as "probably somewhat more than half-finished."[58] This project would remain unfinished—but at the forefront of his work—for the rest of his life. It's possible that one reason he became determined to recast his bibliography in narrative form was to move the project forward: as I have already noted, a list is in some ways an eternally unfinished form, always begging to be altered through addition, subtraction, and revision. Still bearing the label "bibliography," prose drafts of his work highlighted the biographies of the African Americans whose printed texts he had listed bibliographically. This was itself an act of African American literary criticism, one that underscored his belief that Negro literature had to be seen and understood biographically and, more fundamentally, historically. Only by examining the "conditions under which [Negro authors] labored" could one "estimat[e] the place and rank belonging to Negro authors," Murray wrote, in an incomplete draft of the prose bibliography.[59] Looking at authors in this way also revealed to Murray important nuances about the history of African Americans generally. For instance, by knowing where writers came from, Murray was able to establish patterns "showing which states exhibited liberal human tendencies, by the state of literature among the Negroes within their borders."[60] Evidence that Murray continued to work on the book can be found in various artifacts from 1901, including letters to printers inquiring about terms of publication. There is even an advertisement for the book that, according to at least one prospective printer, Harper and Brothers, was to be sold by subscription; it ran in the *Twentieth Century Union League Directory* for 1901. "Daniel Murray is preparing a very valuable book for publication, *Bibliographia Africana, or History of Afro-American Literature*, with sketches of 125 distinguished writers allied with the Negro race, to which will be appended a bibliography of 1600 books and pamphlets by Afro-American writers," reads the advertisement's copy.[61]

Although Murray's papers include letters from people who had seen advertisements for or heard of "The Literary History of the Colored Race" and wished to buy it, one reason that the manuscript was never published may have been that Murray found himself unable to get the required number of buyers lined up to meet the minimum number set by a press to print the book. But the various drafts of the book in his manuscript collection also underscore that the work of constructing a bibliography of Negro literature such as the one Murray envisioned was indeed a task "of herculean proportions," one that kept getting larger and larger in scope.[62] As the term "literature" and the idea of literary work evolved in meaning, Murray would move away from the pursuit of African American literary figures and literary history, focusing instead more broadly on creating an "Encyclopedia of the Colored Race." The project would grow to include an imagined six volumes of eight hundred pages each. His papers include quotations for printing the work, as well as inquiries from publishers about its progress, but Murray never seemed ready to let the project go.[63] By 1922, when Du Bois asked Murray about drawing an excerpt from his manuscript to include as an article about Alonzo or Alexander Hamilton in the *Crisis*, he did so with two concerns in mind. The first was to help Murray think about avenues to publication for his now gargantuan project. The "only feasible way of getting a larger work printed," he suggested to Murray, "would be to print parts of it [in periodicals like the *Crisis*] so that people could see its interest." This was practical advice. "It is quite possible that i[f] three or four essays of this sort did appear, some material aid might be forthcoming to you for the printing of your work," he added.[64] His second concern was more to the point: that Murray would die before the work found a publisher, and that it would be lost. "Practically," Du Bois told Murray, "you have got to face these facts: You have reached the allotted span of human life in the ordinary course of events. You cannot hope for much further time to work. If you should die before the publication of any part of your work, what would become of it?" Du Bois here lamented what he tenderly described as "the practical loss to the world of [Murray's] long and arduous labors," which, he said "would be a calamity to the Negro race."[65] His words proved prescient. Murray retired from the Library of Congress in 1923; although he continued to work on the project into his retirement, he died in 1925 with the encyclopedia unpublished.

Bibliographies for the "General Reader"

Although the Exhibit of American Negroes at the 1900 Paris Exposition Universelle was a collaborative effort, "planned and executed by Negroes, and collected and installed under the direction of a Negro special agent, Mr. Thomas J. Calloway," it has come to be associated predominantly with W. E. B. Du Bois.[66] Du Bois went to Paris only because he determined that his contribution to the exhibit—in particular the elaborate set of in-fographics on the Black population composed by students and alumni of Du Bois's sociological laboratory at Atlanta University—"would fail unless I was there."[67] He wrote compellingly about the Exhibit of American Negroes during and after the exposition. Calling it "an honest, straightforward exhibit of a small nation of people, picturing their life and development without apology or gloss," Du Bois considered it a way to bring into focus the social advances and intellectual accomplishments of African Americans.[68] Murray's bibliography of Negro authors and the variety of printed texts included in the exhibit were central to this mission. Du Bois's appreciation for Murray's accomplishment is well documented. But his own bibliography from the same year is suggestive of the different ways he experimented with the genre as a medium through which to critique and revise the avenues through which "the Negro" could be approached and studied in print. Whereas Murray's list seemed intent on providing an index of African American print culture, Du Bois used bibliography to illustrate the discursive extension of print sources by and about African Americans. That is, he was interested in the use value of print by and about African Americans, as they initiated and extended a network of conversations about race and Black identity in the United States.

Du Bois taught history and the then-new discipline of sociology at Atlanta University from 1897 to 1910. One of his chief responsibilities was directing the Atlanta University Studies, a program inaugurated in 1896 "in an effort to study carefully and thoroughly certain definite aspects of the Negro problem."[69] It resulted in annual conferences and publications from

1896 to 1914. Bibliographies formed a significant part of the publications in 1900, 1901, and 1905. Here, I look first at the bibliography that Du Bois published in 1900, which corresponds chronologically to Murray's bibliography for the Paris Exposition. But I am mostly interested in the three successive Atlanta University Studies bibliographies. Their importance lies not in the fact that each is longer and more fully developed than the one before it, although this is one thing that becomes apparent in their analysis. Rather, Du Bois's repeated return to the form of bibliography insists that bibliographies were central to his work and to his scholarly practice. Du Bois had a specific agenda for bibliography, one that centered on helping readers to manage print sources as they used them to educate themselves about African Americans, and their history, culture, and condition. He is ultimately interested in using bibliography not to index a cumulative count of African American literary or historical sources, but managerially, to help readers to move efficiently from a curated list of print sources to the work of study and learning.

Published in 1900, the proceedings of the Fifth Annual Conference, titled *The College-Bred Negro*, illustrates this in its structure and organization and through its instructions for the bibliography's use. "A Select Bibliography of the American Negro for General Readers" is in essence a part of *The College-Bred Negro*'s introduction, and one of the most fundamental questions about the bibliography is raised by its very title: Who were, in Du Bois's mind, the "general readers" toward whom the bibliography was aimed? The Atlanta University Studies were publicized and reviewed in many periodicals that would have primarily reached white readers: in 1903, for instance, they were heralded by *Outlook*, a top-ranked magazine of news and opinion, which wrote that "no student of the race problem, no person who would either think or speak upon it intelligently, can afford to be ignorant of the facts brought out in the Atlanta series."[70] But the studies, printed in pamphlet form, were also likely to have been read by a professional and intellectual class of African Americans eager to learn about the advancements of their race, or by those who aspired to such an identity. It is worth noting that a key aspect of the Atlanta University Studies was the dissemination of information: it employed a secretary to "furnish correspondents with information upon any phase of the Negro problem, so far as he is able" and to "[point] out such sources as exist from which accurate data may be obtained." Yearly, requests for information on "the Negro" were addressed to the secretary, from "the United States Government, professors in several northern and southern institutions, students of sociology, philanthropic societies and workers, and many private persons."[71] From 1899 to 1900, the list of those requesting information ranged from Black intellectuals that made up the membership of the American Negro Academy to students from largely white institutions like Harvard University, Columbia University, Catholic University, the University of Chicago, Wellesley College, and the University of Texas.[72]

So who was the general reader? I argue that one objective of the 1900 bibliography was to call into being a set of general readers with an interest in African American studies that did not yet exist. If, as Du Bois believed, deep knowledge about the Black community—their "current conditions and current needs," as he put it—was key to resolving what Du Bois called "Negro problems," the Atlanta University Studies and the bibliographies that they contained were a valuable means of bringing this knowledge to light by showing where, practically speaking, it could be found. The expressed point of these studies was not improving the *condition* of African Americans, though this would be an important by-product. It was to facilitate *study* of the social, economic, and physical condition of African Americans as they moved from slavery to freedom and, in particular, as they made the transition from rural to urban living. A set of general readers had to be engendered, and their study of "the greatest group of social problems that has ever faced the nation" directed and supported. As Du Bois noted in the introduction to the 1901 report, studies of African Americans "do not naturally appeal to the general public, but rather, to the interested few and to students." With the Atlanta University Studies he hoped to change this by transforming a general public into general readers. "There ought to be growing in this land a general conviction that a careful study of the conditions and needs of the Negro population—a study conducted with scientific calm and accuracy, and removed so far as possible from prejudice or partisan bias . . . is necessary," Du Bois believed. "Americans must learn that in social reform as well as in other rational endeavors, wish and prejudice must be sternly guided by knowledge, else it is bound to blunder, if not to fail."[73] The bibliographies in the Atlanta University Studies were, then, an "appeal" or invitation to study Blackness and its history in the United States; they were deliberately constructed to guide readers to and through the knowledge that was available on African Americans and to teach them how to effectively approach, process, and digest it.

In the introductions to the Atlanta University Studies reports, Du Bois returns again and again to the word "study," animating it as a mode of consciousness and precursor to the sort of action necessary for African Americans, whom he considered "destined to be part and parcel of the Nation for many a day if not forever," to be truly seen and to see themselves.[74] As students, all Americans, white or Black, would require direction in how to approach this study, not only in terms of how to find the print sources of information they should consult, but also how to organize their pursuit of this knowledge. Just as the pamphlets and other print materials issued by the Atlanta University Studies were meant to serve as educational resources on the so-called Negro problem, then the "Select Bibliography of the American Negro for General Readers" was intended to offer a textual basis for approaching Black studies generally. As such, Du Bois's 1900 bibliography is not focused on Black authorship, but mixes texts written by Black and white authors without identifying them racially. The bibliography appears quite informal: with few exceptions, entries are limited to authors' last names and the titles of works, suggesting that Du Bois had confidence that the body of general readers he wished to congregate through the bibliography could find these texts for themselves. Likewise, placing the texts historically, chronologically, or in terms of publication details was not a priority. What that general reader did need, Du Bois makes clear in the structure of his bibliography, was guidance of an intellectual type. The list of pertinent titles is broken down by each text's focus, as well as by genre. Sections included "History," "Present Social Condition," "Biography," "Literature and Art," and "Bibliography, Methods of Study, etc." The section on history is helpfully divided further into subsections that specify several historical subjects that the general reader might wish to better understand, be it the history of the Negro generally, "Slave Codes," the "Character of Slavery," the "Economics of Slavery," "Emancipation," "Reconstruction," or the history of "Negro Soldiers."[75]

While this breakdown may seem overly simplistic to twenty-first-century eyes, what is interesting here is the way that Du Bois insists on the complexity of Black history by asserting that, as a classification, it demanded subsections. All texts on "the Negro problem," he insisted, were not the same; understanding "the Negro" and Negro history warranted complex delineation. The structure of Du Bois's bibliography insisted that there were multiple avenues through which to access Black history, and it began the process of distinguishing them. The effect here may seem trivial, but in bibliographies, as in libraries, "a certain vision of the world is imposed upon the reader through its categories."[76] Classification in this case reflected Du Bois's wish to expand the known world of the Negro by insisting on its multiple points of entry. In this, Du Bois disrupted readers' assumptions about the nature of Black people and their history, expanding what was narrowly advanced in other sources as authorized knowledge. In insisting that in the very structure and organization of the bibliography general readers see a constellation of subjects associated with the Negro, Du Bois laid the groundwork for the ways its readers would approach and think about what they read and the kinds of questions they would ask of the material. Consider Du Bois's entries under "Slavery," for example. He includes five subsections that distinguish books on the "Slave-trade," "Slave Codes," "Character of Slavery," and "Economies of Slavery" from the books on slavery in general. Certainly the texts in all of these sections address the history of slavery, but their arrangement points to Du Bois's refusal to collapse all texts on this aspect of the Black past into a single category. Here, Du Bois expands and complicates the subject of slavery by naming different categories through which slavery must be explored. In doing so, he frames inquiry into the subject as something much more complex than acknowledged by most turn-of-the-century filing systems. The history of slavery, he insists, was not a single, universal story; his arrangement of the materials in the bibliography instead makes the argument that studying it required nuanced analysis, as it was deeply intertwined with questions of legal maneuvers, economics, and empire.

Du Bois's most interesting gesture in the 1900 bibliography comes in its section on "Present Social Conditions," which appears as a list of 20 numbered texts and is followed by a systematic breakdown of those texts into various reading lists. If readers were interested in books on "Health and Mortality," for instance, they were directed to look at the following texts: numbers 4, 6a, 7, 8, 10, and 18. Du Bois's recommended set of texts on "Amalgamation" included number 1 (which was the U.S. Census and included both the 1860 and 1890 reports), 3, 6b, 10, and 16. Each of these numerical clusters outlined represented courses of study, intended to provide a curriculum for the broader and deeper understanding of their subjects. The texts could also be approached through more general "courses of reading," which were also mapped out; a "short course of reading" included 7 texts (16, 19, 20, 12, 11, 6, and 5), while a "longer course of reading" included these texts as well as 11 others from across the "Present Social Condition" section of the bibliography. These lists, or courses of study, form the core of the bibliography: although they are, in some ways, paratextual to the texts named in the bibliography, they are central to articulating the bibliography's use and value for general readers. Du Bois's intention here is to manage both the field of Black studies and the way his readers approach its study. The bibliography communicates his sense of the imperative of guiding readers to various aspects of Black history and culture and showing them how to learn it. In this case, Du Bois is intent on putting a variety of texts in conversation with one another. It is notable that, particularly against the backdrop of Daniel Murray's monumental attempt to gather all writing by Black authors in one list, Du Bois's 1900 bibliography appears diminutive: it does not include all that many titles. But this abbreviation was entirely related to its purpose. The point of Du Bois's bibliography is to manage access to Black studies, reducing it to a set of key texts that might profitably be read as discursive extensions of one another by readers who might not otherwise find or figure out how to appreciate it. Du Bois's presentation of a relatively small network of pertinent texts in the bibliography aims to make a large subject knowable by effectively limiting and managing its sources.

The bibliography can be read, then, as an effort to promote Black studies as a necessary curriculum and as the subject of scholarship; it served as an invitation to embrace a radical concept of careful and sustained study of Black life. This challenge was taken up in a number of settings. The bibliography was of value, for instance, to Mary Roberts Smith, an associate professor of sociology who in the winter of 1903 wrote to Du Bois to request the bibliography for assistance in putting together a "short course on Race Problems" she would use to teach sophomores at her home institution, Stanford University. In the same year, John H. Gray wrote on behalf of Northwestern University to inquire about purchasing all of the Atlanta University Publications for the university's library.[77] Du Bois's numerical courses of study would be a useful resource for Northwestern University's students, even without the direction of a teacher or the context of a formal class. Indeed, the value of Du Bois's bibliography lay in its ability to serve as a course of study for those not enrolled in programs of higher education: his general readers could study alone or in self-made, informal communities. Although produced in the context of the highest levels of academic research, the orchestrated reading guides that structure Du Bois's bibliographies provided the means for Black and white people outside of academia to participate, in an intellectually robust way, in thinking about African Americans, racial history, and racial politics.

Du Bois ends his 1900 bibliography with the category of "Bibliography, Methods of Study, etc.," a section that underscores his conviction in the importance of thinking bibliographically and through bibliographies, as intellectual practice: it was for him a means of conserving information, but also a means of criticism, revision, and change. Not everything he advised his readers to read was recommended because it was praiseworthy. Du Bois also used bibliography to keep account of textual material that showed poor scholarship, faulty logic, or damaging bias; this too, he believed, should be studied, if only as objects of critique that put into perspective sound approaches to the topics at hand. Du Bois would turn to bibliography as a genre again and again in the first years of the twentieth century, carefully crafting and recrafting bibliographic documents according to his perception of the needs of the set of general readers he wished to see develop among the American people and his sense of bibliography's potential as a structure for communicating the ways Black studies might be approached.

When "A Select Bibliography of the American Negro for General Readers" appeared in the 1901 edition of the Atlanta University Publications— a volume focused on "The Negro Common School"—the bibliography had changed significantly from its original form. It was not only considerably longer, having been expanded from a modest four pages to a more robust nine; it was also revised in important ways. Du Bois adds texts to the list that show the expansion of his thinking about African Americans specifically and Blackness generally as a field of study. But he also increases the bibliography's complexity in ways that illustrate his own shifting sense of both the development of the field of African American studies and the kind of guidance his general reader needed.

The 1901 bibliography is proceeded by a note that explicitly explains its origins and purpose: it was created "for the benefit of numerous inquirers after the best literature on the Negro problems."[78] Du Bois remains true to the 1900 bibliography by beginning with a section of titles on history. But he has added two important subsections to help readers further understand and appreciate the global nuances of Black history. The first, on "Colonization," directs readers toward the reports of the American Colonization Society, Alexander Crummell's *Africa and America*, and J. H. T. McPherson's study of Liberia. The second entirely new subsection is on abolition. It includes nine entries, including Lydia Maria Child's *The Oasis*, F. B. Sanborn's *Life and Letters of John Brown*, F. J. May's *Recollections of Our Anti-Slavery Conflict*, and the reports of the Anti-Slavery Society. The other historical fields designated in the 1900 bibliography remain the same, but Du Bois has revisited the recommended texts and made some changes. Gone is W. O. Blake's *History of Slavery and the Slave Trade*, Thomas Fowell Buxton's *The African Slave Trade and Its Remedy*, George H. Moore's *Notes on Slavery in Massachusetts*, Philip Alexander Bruce's *Economic History of Virginia*, and John J. Lalor's *Cyclopædia of Political Science*.[79] What he has added to the list may at first glance seem like less appropriate titles than the ones he has taken away. George Bancroft's *History of the United States*, for instance, is a multi-volume work that appeared in multiple editions between 1854 and 1878; as its title indicates, its coverage of American history is broad, stretching "From the Discovery of the American Continent." So too is Herrmann von Holst's *Constitutional History of the United States*, a two-volume set on American history and politics. Both of these texts suggest Du Bois's belief that studying "the Negro problem" was inseparable from the study of the history of the United States generally. They also represent the sort of scholarship that Du Bois himself practiced and the scholarly standards he brought with him to Atlanta University. Bancroft was a serious and accomplished educator who had been trained, as had Du Bois, in the German universities. Although much of his scholarship is focused on the United States, von Holst was a native of Germany and had received his doctorate under the supervision of Ludwig Hausser, a German historian known for the scientific study of archival sources. Von Holst's career was spent moving back and forth between American and German universities, but in 1892 he became head of the Department of History at the University of Chicago. In including these scholars in his bibliography, Du Bois pushed even those he acknowledged to be general readers (rather than those with scholarly credentials) to align their standards for inquiry into the condition of African Americans in the United States with the philosophies of the German universities, whose academic curricula and emphasis on science and research were beginning to influence the structure and curricula of American universities.

Even as it adds titles and swaps out some titles for others, Du Bois's 1901 list maintains his balanced approach to reviewing the history of race relations in the United States. This means including in the bibliography authors and works whose perspectives Du Bois surely found reprehensible—for instance, Thomas Reade Rootes Cobb, whose 1858 book on slave laws was the most comprehensive restatement of the laws of slavery written during the antebellum period. Cobb's book is a decidedly proslavery treatise: its opening premise is that the "negro race" was "peculiarly fitted for a laborious class," because their "mental capacity renders them incapable of successful self-development."[80] But it was included on Du Bois's list because he rightly recognized Cobb's text as a vital resource for scholars of slavery and legal historians who sought to understand how laws were interpreted to support American slavery and the logic used to justify it.

The most significant changes to the 1901 bibliography come in the section listing the "best Sources of Information" on the present social condition of the Negro. Here Du Bois not only expands the number of texts he offers to readers, but also refines the information he gives about them as well. In increasing this list from twenty to thirty-three sources, Du Bois recognizes important works of scholarship by women writers such as Anna Julia Cooper and Gertrude Bustill Mossell, whose texts would expand readers' understanding of Black women's experience and deepen their knowledge of race and gender as intersecting categories. He also identifies important avenues of research into Black life and culture that he had only superficially noted in the 1900 bibliography, such as the AME Church and the Black press. Whereas in the 1900 bibliography Du Bois assumed that readers could locate recommended texts on their own, here he offers much more assistance: he specifies particular issues of reports, points to indexes that will help readers locate "sections on Negroes," and identifies specific titles. For instance, in the first bibliography Du Bois refers readers to "Proceedings and Occasional Papers of the Slater Fund"; in the 1901 bibliography, however, he specifies the proceedings by date (1882–1901) and lists ten occasional papers by author and title. He even helps readers to locate them, telling them that "Nos. 1–6 are reprinted in Report of U.S. Commissioner of Education, 1894–1895." He also lists by author and title seven publications of the American Negro Academy, telling readers of the bibliography that, to obtain these, "address the Secretary, 1439 Pierce Place, Washington, D.C." This is one example of the way that Du Bois sought in the 1901 bibliography to create a document that more fully provided general readers with the core elements needed to gain access to the textual resources he recommended. By 1901, Du Bois was much more purposeful in speaking to his reader through the form of bibliography, adding details to the titles of texts he recommended, filling in key pieces of bibliographic information—such as a text's publisher or hints as to where to find it—that might help readers to locate these sources physically as well as intellectually.

By more fully citing and, in many cases, repeating the titles to which he referred readers, Du Bois increases the authority of the 1901 list, offering in specific terms the texts that would augment the depth of their knowledge of Black history and culture. An important difference in this bibliography is that Du Bois is intent on including more Black-authored materials in his list. While, in the 1900 bibliography, Du Bois pointed to an "endless number of discussions of the Negro in periodicals," all of which, he argued, have "degrees of value," he cited only three periodicals in which articles of the "greatest permanent value" were located: the *Atlantic Monthly*, the *Nation*, and the *North American Review*. In the 1901 version Du Bois downplays periodicals such as these that were aimed most directly at white readers. His focus here is instead on the section "Chief Negro Periodicals," in which he lists sixteen African American periodicals by name and frequency of publication. In addition, he steers readers to I. Garland Penn's path-breaking study *The Afro-American Press* and to *The Negro in Business*, the report of the 1899 Atlanta University Study, as sources of information on Black periodicals and journalism.

Another important development in the 1901 bibliography is his introduction, for the first time, of a new section on "The Negro in Fiction." In doing so, Du Bois stands by his assertion that fictional texts might be considered important as historical points of reference, leaving Harriet Beecher Stowe's *Uncle Tom's Cabin*, for instance, in the "Character of Slavery" section. But he reasserts its importance as a category of historical and cultural concern by designating "The Negro in Fiction" as its own section in the 1901 bibliography, where he lists fifteen titles. Particularly notable is Du Bois's listing of three of Charles Chesnutt's recent publications: *The Conjure Woman*, *The Wife of His Youth*, and *House behind the Cedars*. Equally notable is his inclusion of Paul Laurence Dunbar's novel *The Sport of the Gods* on this list: by 1901, Dunbar was renowned as a poet (and is listed by Du Bois in the 1900 bibliography as the author of "Poems") but largely unrecognized as a writer of fictional prose. Du Bois's recognition of Dunbar's novel anticipates the importance this genre would take for African American writers later in the twentieth century. It may also have been his way of steering readers away from Dunbar's dialect poems, which were embraced by whites in part because they reinforced racist stereotypes of African Americans, and toward a text by the same familiar author that stepped—at least to some extent—out of that mode to depict Black migration from the rural South to the industrial North and the pursuit of economic and social opportunities.

This section of the bibliography reflects Du Bois's own search for the best formats and genres in which to investigate and reflect on race; it merges what he described in the introduction to the 1901 Atlanta University Studies publication as a "study conducted with scientific calm and accuracy" with his own tentative and deeply experimental efforts to move into the fictional mode in his own writing.[81] Even during the heyday of his belief in the Atlanta University Studies, with their emphasis on the efficacy of empirical social science and academic historiography, he also showed deep interest in and appreciation for the value of the imaginative. In a world where the need to take action against racial prejudice and discrimination was everywhere apparent, it was crucial to think critically about the best approaches to spreading knowledge and to taking political action. His conscious decisions in the 1901 bibliography to draw on both scholarly and imaginative practices offer a context for a better understanding of his most canonical work,

The Souls of Black Folk (1903), as well as the fictional and semifictional forms that Du Bois would turn to again and again in his writing. It's interesting to note, though, that his list is primarily composed of historical fiction by white authors. In addition to Stowe's *Uncle Tom's Cabin*, her 1856 novel *Dred* is also listed. Albion Tourgee's *Bricks without Straw* (1880), a fictionalized account of how Reconstruction was sabotaged told from the perspective of the emancipated, is included, as is Harriet Martineau's 1840 novel, *The Hour and the Man*, which is based on the career of Toussaint Louverture and the slave uprising in St. Domingo at the end of the eighteenth century. South African writer Olive Schreiner's *Trooper Peter Halket of Mashonaland* (1897) is included, a text that fictionally depicts the racial violence and massacres that had just taken place in South Africa. Schreiner was a feminist and a socialist whose writing illustrates the interrelationship between the concerns of women and questions about race and colonization; her critique of race and racism in southern Africa would prove to be among the most prescient of her time. What these books have in common is their merging of fact and fictional devices to tell the story of racial relations and racial injustice. In the case of *Trooper Peter*, for instance, Schreiner's fictional story is preceded by a photograph showing three Black Africans hanging from a tree, surrounded by a group of whites surveying their handiwork. The event it represents is cast in the story as fiction, but the photograph reinforces its factual nature, visually confirming its truth.[82]

Du Bois was surely influenced by Daniel Murray's work on Negro authors in his definitive expansion and reorganization of the "Literature of American Negroes" section of the 1901 bibliography, which replaces the short "Literature and Art" section of the 1900 version. He officially acknowledges Murray's work by citing his bibliography in the "Bibliography, Methods of Study, etc." section of the 1901 bibliography, but the fullness of Du Bois's bibliographic data on Black authors is another tribute to Murray's project. Like the "Literature and Art" section of the 1900 bibliography, Du Bois's section on "Literature of American Negroes" in the 1901 bibliography maintains its broad understanding of literature, preserving subsections on folklore and music. These subsections remain both slim and virtually unchanged from the 1900 bibliography; they nevertheless underscore Du Bois's interest in what might be considered the literary arts generally and in Black folk cultures as communicated specifically in music and story. But it is literature that he highlights here, setting it next to but aside from art in a way he had not done in the earlier bibliography. Du Bois lists titles, according to publication date and then author, under the subheading "Distinctive

Works," as if to emphasize that these are some, but by no means all, of the texts attributable to "American Negroes." Du Bois's list runs from the 1773 publication of Phillis Wheatley's "Poems" to Charles Chesnutt's *The Marrow of Tradition*, published in 1901, which is the only Chesnutt text to appear in this section. Du Bois recognized the significance of Booker T. Washington's literary achievement in *Up from Slavery* (1901), but he also recognized texts with far less recognizable authors, like William Douglass, whose 1862 *Annals of St. Thomas* made Du Bois's list, as did the 1838 entry *Appeal of 40,000 Colored Citizens*, for which Du Bois did not list an author. The list comes with no accompanying commentary to help us understand how Du Bois selected for inclusion the texts that he did. In what ways and for which set of reasons, for instance, did he consider the *Appeal of 40,000 Colored Citizens* to be "distinctive," either for its original antebellum audience or for the "general readers" Du Bois wished to engender? It does, however, effectively suggest that African Americans consistently produced works of literature across the nineteenth century, production that increased dramatically around the middle of the century, particularly after the Civil War. The cluster of books that Du Bois attributes to the years 1890–1900, which include Anna Julia Cooper's *A Voice from the South*, William Crogman's *Talks for the Times*, Archibald H. Grimké's biography of Charles Sumner, Paul Laurence Dunbar's *Lyrics of a Lowly Life*, Booker T. Washington's *Up from Slavery*, and Charles Chesnutt's *The Marrow of Tradition*, are grouped in such a way as to indicate their rapid-fire publication. In doing so, Du Bois effectively brings the bibliography up to date and signals that such abundance is representative of the current state of African American literary production.

Du Bois would continue to introduce the Atlanta University Studies annual publication with a bibliography, but for the next three years these were less general and focused on the topic of the subject of the volume of that year. Between 1902 and 1904, each volume contained a bibliography on the subjects of the Negro artisan, the Negro church, and Negro crime, respectively. Though all brief, these bibliographies were uniformly complete in giving full bibliographical details of the texts. His return, in the 1905 publication, to a fuller and more general bibliography of the American Negro was both cautious and deliberate. In fact, unlike the previous placement of the bibliographies as introductory to the reports, the bibliography makes up the entire report of the tenth Atlanta University Study, the subject of which was "Methods and Results of Ten Years' Study of the American Negro." Du Bois purposefully reflected on the decision to issue the report in the form of a bibliography, as well as on the nature of bibliography itself. He considered

Literature of American Negroes.

Distinctive Works:
1773—Phillis Wheatley: Poems. London.
1793—Richard Allen: Life. Philadelphia, 8vo, 69 pp.
1810—Act of Incorporation, Causes and Motives of the African Episcopal Church. Philadelphia.
1829—David Walker: An Appeal, etc. Boston.
1838—Appeal of 40,000 Colored Citizens. Philadelphia.
1852—M. R. Delaney: Condition * * * of the Colored People. Philadelphia.
W. C. Nell: Services of Colored Americans in the Wars of 1776, 1812. Boston.
1854—F. E. W. Harper: Miscellaneous Poems. Boston.
1855—Frederick Douglass: My Bondage and Freedom. New York, 464 pp.
1862—William Douglass: Annals of St. Thomas. Philadelphia.
1863—W. W. Brown: The Black Man. New York, 310 pp.
1867—B. T. Tanner: Apology for African Methodism. Philadelphia, 468 pp.
1875—Sojourner Truth: Narrative. Boston, 320 pp.
1831—W. S. Scarborough: First Greek Lessons. New York, 150 pp.
1878—J. M. Trotter: Music and Some Highly Musical People. Boston, 505 pp.
1883—J. M. Langston: Freedom and Citizenship. Washington, 286 pp.
1883—W. Still: Underground Railroad. Philadelphia, 780 pp.
1884—T. T. Fortune: White and Black. New York, 310 pp.
1885—D. A. Payne: Domestic Education. Cincinnati, 184 pp.
1837—W. J. Simmons: Men of Mark.
1890-1900—A. J. Cooper: Voice From the South. Xenia, O., 304 pp.
W. H. Crogman: Talks For the Times. Atlanta, 330 pp.
A. Grimke: Charles Sumner. New York, 515 pp.
P. L. Dunbar: Lyrics of Lowly Life.
B. T. Washington: Up From Slavery.
C. W. Chesnutt: The Marrow of Tradition.

Folk Lore.
Cf. Southern Workman.
Cf. Journal of American Folk Lore.
Harris: Uncle Remus.

Music.
Jubilee Songs as Published by Fisk, Hampton and Calhoun.
Also, 31.

Bibliography, Methods of Study, Etc.

Publications of the American Academy of Political and Social Science, No. 219.
American Society for Extension of University Teaching: Brief on Negro. Philadelphia.
Report U. S. Commissioner of Education, 1893-1894.
Bibliography of Negro Authors, Library of Congress (Ms.)
Correspondence Bureau, Atlanta University, Atlanta, Ca.

2.7 The "Literature of American Negroes" section from "A Select Bibliography of the American Negro for General Readers," which was published in W. E. B. Du Bois's *The Negro Common School* (1901), replaced the short "Literature and Art" section of the 1900 bibliography and suggests the growth of Du Bois's thinking on "Negro literature."

the bibliography to be the culmination of the first ten years of the Atlanta University Studies project, but he criticized it, telling his readers that "as a bibliography, the present report is very imperfect."[83] One thing that Du Bois laments here is the necessary incompleteness of the bibliographic enterprise, which he considered to be the chief dilemma of the bibliographer, who attempts to give a comprehensive account of texts written on a particular subject. He records his concern over "whether this should have been attempted at all or not," but tells readers "it seemed to the editor better to print a poor bibliography of this great subject, in the hope of bettering it in future editions, than to wait for those better situated to do the work" (5). Even as he ruefully acknowledges the provisional nature of bibliography as a genre and laments that it could not do more, DuBois nonetheless offers it to the public as a building block and as an essential means of furthering research on African Americans, their history, and their culture. His preface underscores the extent to which Du Bois found the project of bibliography to be a collective one, a list to which people would add, subtract, revise and critique his work as forever preliminary: "The editor would welcome specific criticism especially on omissions and the inclusion of improper titles," he wrote (5).

Du Bois recognized the 1905 bibliography, which was expanded and enlarged to seventy-one pages, to be the "third edition of this bibliography" (5), which had grown out of his initial 1900 bibliography as well as the one published in 1901. Although the 1905 bibliography looks very different from the earlier, more informal bibliographies, it remained a document that bears the marks of his efforts to define the parameters of a field in terms of its most relevant lines of inquiry and printed texts. Exactly what field or fields he was trying to define over the course of the three bibliographies becomes paradoxically more uncertain in this longer, more formal bibliography, which begins with a very brief category titled "A Bibliography of Bibliographies of the American Negro." Here he includes the 1900 and 1901 bibliographies from the Atlanta University Studies publications, as well the short bibliography that was included in *The Philadelphia Negro*, his pioneering study of race that had been published in 1899. The bulk of the 1905 bibliography is broken down into two sections, the first titled "A Select Bibliography of the Negro American" and the second "Periodical Literature." The distinction between these sections is located in their place of publication: texts on the second list appeared in the periodical press and are organized by the periodicals' titles followed by a listing of the relevant articles that they included, whereas those on the first list were published in different venues and arranged alphabetically by author. This means of organization does away with Du Bois's earlier effort to suggest useful boundaries between historical texts and their various areas of focus, as well as his tentative steps taken up in the 1901 bibliography toward establishing boundaries between texts on the subject of Negroes and literature by Negroes. Here, works by Black and white authors, on all aspects of Black history, whether fictional or factual, are merged together into the same list.

As is evident in the titles of the sections of the 1905 bibliography, Du Bois effectively creates a structure of nesting bibliographies here, with bibliographies emerging from—and in fact merging into—one another in a way that is reminiscent of Russian Matryoshka dolls. But the sheer number of layers at work here, and the presence of minimal subcategories to help organize the lists, suggest that bibliography, for Du Bois, had become at once an idealized and an unwieldy form. The 1905 bibliography is more in keeping with standard bibliographic form, but it's a much harder document to read and to critically unpack. Whereas the earlier bibliographies had carefully managed the list, orienting its readers' attention in various directions in part by limiting the amount of material it included, the 1905 list establishes few usable boundaries, and those that are established don't clearly articulate their purpose or how they should be used. It is unclear, for instance, how Du Bois assigned texts to the final section of the bibliography, which he lists as an "addenda." One use of the addenda was clearly supplemental: although five titles by Alexander Crummell, for instance, were included in the main body of the bibliography, Du Bois added two more to the addenda that had perhaps been initially overlooked. But the second part of the addenda includes a variety of texts centrally and definitively placed in earlier versions of the bibliography, including the American Negro Academy's *Occasional Papers* and the Slater Fund's *Proceedings and Occasional Papers*. Even more curiously, all of Charles Chesnutt's writing appears in part 1 of the addenda, as does other writing that we know Du Bois found to be critically important and influential by Harriet Beecher Stowe, Albion Tourgee, and Phillis Wheatley. While creative writing is not excluded from the main body of the bibliography—part 1 includes Pauline Hopkins's *Contending Forces*, for instance, and two books of poetry by Frances E. W. Harper, as well as her novel *Iola Leroy*—the fact that the bibliography does not specifically advance Du Bois's earlier, tentative foray into setting apart Black literature and art as a distinct category is curious. Du Bois dedicates the 1905 volume to those he calls the "dead Pioneers," a group that includes Phillis Wheatley, David Walker, Frederick Douglass, William Wells Brown, and Paul Laurence Dunbar, whose status as writers of "Literature of American Negroes" he had distinguished in a separate section of the bibliography in 1901. In the 1905 version, after acknowledging them in the dedication, they are relegated to the addenda, leaving the very writers that Du Bois pays tribute to as launching African American literature a mere afterthought, to be added to an enormous list of publications in which their names and works were likely to be lost.

Crucially, the 1905 bibliography no longer carried the specific "courses of study" recommendations that had been staples of the 1900 and 1901 bibliographies and had contributed to them an intimate quality. This was submersed or overwhelmed in the 1905 bibliography by the sheer size of the list of resources, which appears to have been motivated by the desire to represent an exhaustive tabulation of the culmination of a decade's worth of studies. Du Bois reflected openly in the bibliography about the difficulty of deciding what to include in a bibliography of the Negro American and what should be excluded: "The selection of titles in this bibliography was especially difficult on account of the large number of works on slavery which bear more or less on the Negro and yet do not properly come within the scope of this list" (5). He clearly recognized the tentative nature of his decisions, saying: "In the attempt to separate from the mass of American slavery literature those works which deal especially with the slave rather than the system, many mistakes have been made both through ignorance and inadvertence" (5). Even as he lamented the mistakes that he himself knew were inherent in all of the bibliographies he compiled, he expressed his understanding of the connection between the shortcomings of the bibliography and a problem of access. Some of the "imperfections" of the bibliography, he believed, were "due to the fact that it has been compiled at a distance from all the great collections of *Americana*" (5). Whether he was referring to this as a personal problem or one more widely shared by those of African descent throughout the United States is left ambiguous. Du Bois made no secret of his dissatisfaction with living in Atlanta, where he was confronted on a daily basis by racism and disrespect; he would later come to describe the horrific "situations" he encountered, situations "that called—shrieked—for action," even as they were paralyzing in their audacity.[84] His frustration with living under the injustice and violence of Jim Crow was exacerbated by the isolation from the literary and intellectual culture of the major universities of the Northeast, and the sense of being peripheral to the work of these academic communities was further complicated by the fact that his research could not get the funding it needed. He had made this overall dissatisfaction readily apparent in turning down a job at Tuskegee offered by Booker T. Washington in 1900. After considering Washington's offer—which included, in addition to a salary of $1,400, "a comfortable and convenient house," the "opportunity to conduct sociological studies that will prove helpful to our people," and Tuskegee's printing press "wholly at your service"—Du Bois wrote to Washington, "I have decided not to accept your very generous offer." It was not, he indicated, that he was unwilling to move from Atlanta University or that he did not wish to entertain other job offers. "The only opening that would attract me now," he told Washington, "would be one that brought me nearer to the centres of culture & learning and thus gave me larger literary activity."[85] In saying this, Du Bois may have been conceitedly expressing his own sense that his scholarship was too good for what he considered the provincial intellectual atmosphere of the South. But he also seems to mourn here what racial animosity made largely inaccessible to the Black scholar in the early twentieth century, which he describes as "all the great collections of *Americana*." The distance between African American intellectuals and those collections almost certainly left important works by and about African Americans inaccessible to the very scholars who cared most deeply about their recovery.

Paradoxically, the bibliographies that Du Bois deemed "imperfect" would open the door to the larger literary activity he aspired to, not only for Du Bois himself but for generations that came after him, whether scholars or general readers. The publication of the 1905 bibliography in many ways marked both the end and the beginning of an era, as Du Bois began to venture away from Atlanta University and his work in its classrooms and laboratories to test the efficacy of different forums and modes of activism. The most visible sign of this movement was his effort to organize, in 1905, the Niagara Movement, a Black civil rights organization that would stand in opposition to Booker T. Washington by condemning racial segregation and disenfranchisement. But, as I mentioned in the introduction to this book, he also bought a job-printing business, which he used to quietly pursue another important venture that would be rooted in education but take shape outside of the academic world. As in his first two bibliographies, he used the *Moon Illustrated Weekly* to distribute reading lists that would guide readers as they negotiated the world of racial scholarship; these reading lists would also become a staple of Du Bois's later journalistic efforts, the *Horizon* and the *Crisis*. But the audience for these publications would be specifically African American, and his interest would lie in disseminating the logic of literary activity as a mode of social action for African Americans outside of formal educational venues. In this, he would fulfill one goal of the bibliographies that were a part of the Atlanta University Studies: he had envisioned them reaching a broad audience beyond the world of the academy. Indeed, one way to achieve this goal was to sell the 1901 "Select Bibliography of the American Negro" as a separately printed document for ten cents, making it accessible to those who might not be able to afford the entire report, which cost twenty-five cents. But journalism would provide Du Bois with a venue through which to further expand his efforts to provide access to important reading materials and study guides to a broader set of those interested in learning about what he called "the greatest group of social problems that has ever faced the nation" (6).

The *Moon Illustrated Weekly*, as well as his later newspaper, the *Horizon*, would not replace Du Bois's bibliographies, but they would offer a means of distributing bibliographic information to a wider audience. Bibliography would remain an important workspace in which to organize his thinking about racial matters and aesthetic practices.[86] Like Murray, Du Bois found that bibliographies necessitated other bibliographies, enabling their readers as well as their creators to *think bibliographically*. It is telling that, scribbled at the top of his "Bibliography of Negro Folk Song in America," drafted around 1903, is a note in Du Bois's handwriting, presumably to an assistant but perhaps to himself, which reads: "Can you give me a bibliography of Negro Melodies?"[87] Ever rethinking and expanding the scope and subjects that made up the terrain of Black inquiry, Du Bois believed that a bibliography of Negro folk songs and Negro melodies would lead not only to recognition but, more important, to the systematic study of these forms. He was all too familiar with what happened in the absence of this sort of systematic attention.

When Du Bois proposed to Dodd, Mead & Co. that he write a biography of the poet Paul Laurence Dunbar in 1906, he was informed by the publishers that they did not "believe that a life of him would sell sufficiently well to warrant its publication." Whatever logic Dodd, Mead & Co. used to assess the financial viability of the proposed biography, what they specifically told Du Bois was that "we have no ... bibliography ... made up of Mr. Dunbar's works."[88] Here was one more clear example for Du Bois—who needed no new ones—of the importance of the bibliographic imperative. Without a bibliography, the life of an author, the subject of a study, the exploration of the history and culture of a whole people could not begin. It was this same bibliographic imperative that animated Mossell's "List of Afro-American Publications" (1894), *Progress of a Race's* list of "Colored Authors and Names of Publications" (1898), and Murray's list of "Negro authors" (1900), even as these bibliographies worked in different ways. In *The Work of the Afro-American Woman* and *Progress of a Race*, the list existed to arrest the reader within the prose, in order to demonstrate quantitatively what the prose is describing. Murray's list was intended to impress the reader (it was, after all, part of an exposition), while Du Bois's lists worked to *engender* the reader. All of these efforts nevertheless fall into place as a part of a complicated impulse to sort through, order, and present Black print culture and the categories of Black authorship and Negro literature and to consider their relationship to Black history and other valued elements of culture. In making visible how structures of knowledge and categories of thought were arranged, considered, and rearranged, these texts have much to tell us about how the subjects of Blackness were being mapped, aesthetically imagined, and politically mobilized at the very beginning of the twentieth century.

CHAPTER THREE

WASHINGTON'S GOOD FORTUNE

WRITING & AUTHORSHIP IN PRACTICE

SO FAR IN THIS BOOK I HAVE LOOKED AT TWO WAYS THAT LITERACY was supported and a sense of a literary presence advanced by African Americans at the end of the nineteenth and into the first years of the twentieth century. Both the enormous volumes like *Progress of a Race* that I consider as informal schoolbooks in the first chapter, and the series of lists and bibliographies that I explore in the second chapter, served as *scaffolding* for Black literary culture, lending both focus and definition to thinking about African American literature and literary study. They constituted a means of increasing the visibility of African American engagement with literature, both in and of itself and as a means of fortifying Black identity. But even as they show the underpinnings of literary culture, these chapters also provide insight into Black authorship as it was practiced around the turn from the nineteenth to the twentieth century. Rather than originality or creativity, the authorship modeled in *Progress of a Race* was based on locating and excerpting from texts and arranging them in ways that communicated information clearly and efficiently; the job of the author was to identify important sources of information on African American history and identity and break them down as a way of facilitating their wider dissemination. In the second chapter, I show the presumed authority embodied in lists while also exploring the ways in which a model of authorship that is tentative and investigative is inherent in their making. Authorship here is advanced as dependent on constant revision and demanding the participation of others: the very form in which these authors worked implied that the lists' readers themselves become authors by adding to, subtracting from, and offering challenges to the basis of these lists' organization or means of categorization.

We turn now from those two models of authorship—the first curatorial, the second collocative—to a third model based on *managed construction.* Whereas the two earlier models were focused on providing scaffolding for African American literary presence, this third model provides both framing and substance. It is not based on offering information, or making information accessible, but rather on claiming authority itself. The prime exemplar of this model is the relationship between Booker T. Washington—who, at the end of the nineteenth century, assumed authority over his college, over Black educational aspirations, and over African American political hopes— and T. Thomas Fortune, the writer who largely "authored" Washington's literary career. Fortune, as we will see, worked with the idea that Washington could *center* African American writing, giving it a coherence, a visibility, and a degree of power that Fortune believed it desperately needed.

Between 1899 and 1901, Booker T. Washington published four books: *The Future of the American Negro* (1899), *The Story of My Life and Work* (1900), *Up from Slavery* (1901), and *Sowing and Reaping* (1901). All four were written not by Washington, but by a series of friends, aides, editors, and ghostwriters, who cobbled together Washington's words and ideas, gave them form, and made them publishable. Authorship for Washington was not an individual enterprise, but a concerted effort by a series of literary workers whose collective labor on his behalf maneuvered his identity as an author into being. T. Thomas Fortune was the most important of these literary workers. He worked alongside and most often in the absence of Washington to *write* text that would appear with Washington as *author.* In this chapter, I will explore the dynamics of that relationship, discerning the meaning of that distinction between "writer" and "author" and examining how Fortune undertook a calculated, painstaking effort to steer Washington into the space of authorship around the turn of the century; we will see, in other words, how Washington's authorship was *constructed.* We will also see how it was *managed:* how Fortune advised Washington on particular authorial practices, counseled him on seeking out specific publication venues, and attempted to reveal to him the significance of the uses of the "literary." Finally, we will see how this writer and this author fared in their foray into the literary marketplace: how Washington worked his way into it by using his political wiles and business savvy, manipulating, negotiating, and at times strategically deceiving publishers in his efforts, and how Fortune sacrificed his own literary aspirations to further Washington's, as he was himself sometimes manipulated, always ill-compensated, and generally underappreciated. Fortune, as we will see, is a hidden but significant figure in African American literary history, and his career illuminates some of the biggest hazards and costs for African Americans at the turn of the century as they tried to capitalize on the literary marketplace to advance racial politics.

The success of the partnership between Washington and Fortune was dependent on Fortune's sense that Black writing needed a literary center and on his belief that Washington could fill that role. Even though Washington's politics significantly differed from his own, Fortune believed that Washington represented the best hopes for the future of the Black South and the advancement of African American writing. By focusing on Fortune's commitment to Washington's publishing career, we will discover the details of how Washington emerged as a writer at the beginning of the twentieth century and observe specifically the ways in which Fortune monitored the quality, the look, the sites of publication, and the value of his writing. Their relationship raises questions about the place of both ghostwriters and book editors in the culture of African American letters.[1] How does literary history address those who were devoted to the publishing careers of others? How, exactly, did Fortune work alongside Washington, showing him the priorities of writing and successful authorship? What did it mean for Fortune to lend Washington his talents as a writer, and how did he think of writing, whether his own or that done on Washington's behalf? In outlining the conditions of Washington's centering as a figure specifically associated with books, I am able to distinguish between Washington's authorship as a public posture and Fortune's writing, which was labor-intensive and poorly compensated, and which took place largely in solitude. Whereas Washington has been characterized as an author who distanced himself from his writing, this chapter examines that distance from a literal perspective by examining Fortune's behind-the-scenes work to make Washington into an author. It also considers the cost of Washington's authorship, which was, in many respects, achieved at the expense of Fortune's own.

Fortune's early life reveals the sources both of his later political sensibilities and his sense of the importance of African American writing. Born into slavery in 1856 in Marianna, Florida, Fortune came of age during early Reconstruction.[2] As a child, he watched his father, Emanuel Fortune, venture into politics, first as a representative at the Florida Constitutional Convention of 1868 and then as a member of the Florida House of Representatives. The elder Fortune's political activities would eventually result in threats of violence by those resentful of Black political participation; to protect themselves, the Fortune family was forced to leave Marianna, giving up their farm and relocating to Jacksonville in 1869. As a teenager, Fortune served as a page in the Florida state senate, which provided him with further exposure to the tumultuous world of Reconstruction politics and legislation. He left after four sessions, with the overwhelming sense that Reconstruction politics was a fraud, governed by unscrupulous whites who duped and exploited African Americans while professing to be their friends. Although his formal education was sporadic, the family's move to Jacksonville allowed Fortune for a short time to attend Stanton Institute, one of the best schools established by the Freedman's Bureau. Fortune was an avid reader, and working as a "printer's devil," or apprentice, in various printing and newspaper offices, including the weekly *Marianna Courier*, gave him plenty of material with which to expand his knowledge. With the help of an acquaintance from his days as a senate page, Fortune left the South in the fall of 1875 in order to take a job in Delaware as a customs inspector. Within days of starting he would be ordered to leave that position; the proprietor had not realized Fortune was Black. He once again fell back on his experience as a printer, quickly securing another job at a local weekly paper. But his time in Delaware was brief. He left a few months later, in time to enroll at Howard University in Washington, DC, in the winter of 1876. There he pursued the university's preparatory program of study, which had been designed to reinforce skills of those students like Fortune whose primary school education had been incomplete.

Fortune intended to study law at Howard, and he did take some classes toward that degree, but financial need propelled him back into the world of printing and journalism. He took a job in the print shop of the African American newspaper the *People's Advocate*, initially working part time. But when the paper's editor, John Wesley Cromwell, moved the *People's Advocate* from Alexandria, Virginia, to Washington, DC, in 1877, Fortune took charge of the mechanical process of printing the paper. He would also write a column for the *People's Advocate* under the name "Gustafus Bert," an activity that perhaps initiated his transition from the work of a printer to that of a full-fledged journalist. Catapulted into the literary and intellectual company of a range of Washington's most distinguished and scholarly African Americans, including Frederick Douglass, Alexander Crummell, and Richard Greener, who had been the first African American graduate of Harvard College, he abandoned the idea of becoming a lawyer. In Washington, he met and formed lifelong relationships with two other young African American journalists who, along with Fortune, would shape the Negro press at the turn of the century: John E. Bruce, who never succeeded in starting a successful paper of his own but would come to write under the pen name "Bruce Grit," and W. Calvin Chase, whose Washington newspaper, the *Washington Bee*, relentlessly criticized racial injustice, racial violence, and segregation from 1882 to 1921. These relationships were influential for Fortune, shaping his intellectual development and his skills as a journalist as well as his outlook on the state of race relations in the United States.

Newly married, expecting his first child, and perhaps sentimental about making a home in the South, Fortune left Washington to return to Florida around 1878. After a brief foray into teaching, he returned to employment as a printer in the office of the *Jacksonville Daily Union*, a newspaper he had worked for before moving north. By this point, however, the rote work of printing did not satisfy him, and his life in Florida failed to bring with it the same sort of intellectual stimulation and political vitality he had found in Washington. Furthermore, after living in the North, Fortune found life as a Black man in the South to be unbearable. He had faced discrimination and the limitations placed on African Americans in the North, but the degradation of racism of the South was overwhelming. "It feels like a dagger against the heart," he would say of the atmosphere he and his wife encountered in Florida, "and we felt like using dagger against dagger. Instead of doing this, we moved out."[3] Surrounded by restrictive Jim Crow laws, mob violence, and the constant threat of lynching, Fortune described feeling more like a "revolutionist than a patriot," a stance that he knew from his father's experience would prove emotionally destructive if not physically fatal in the racially violent climate of the post-Reconstruction South.[4] Fortune's decision to "move out" was not a bid to abandon racial politics, but to engage in it more fully from a location in which his voice would be more audible and more effective. He left the South again in 1879, this time for New York City, where he had been offered a job as a compositor in the print shop of a religious paper called the *Weekly Witness*. In 1881, he would join other Negro journalists in

3.1 An engraved portrait of *T. Thomas Fortune*, the writer whose words became Booker T. Washington's as he orchestrated the beginning of Washington's career as an author, in 1891. Schomburg Center for Research in Black Culture, Manuscripts, Archives, and Rare Books Division, New York Public Library, New York, NY.

T. THOMAS FORTUNE.

producing the *Globe*, which by 1883 claimed six thousand subscribers. One thing that distinguished the *Globe* from other Negro newspapers was a column devoted to reviews of books as well as of articles that had recently appeared in leading literary journals.[5] In 1884, the *Globe* evolved into the *Freeman*, with Fortune listed as the newspaper's sole proprietor, editor, and printer. He would remain in this role when, in 1887, the *Freeman* was reorganized as the *New York Age*, the newspaper with which Fortune is most commonly associated.

In his career as a job printer, an editor, and a writer for the Negro press, Fortune focused on putting Black voices and political perspectives into print and, subsequently, into motion. As a journalist, he vowed to fight "the battle for justice and fair play for the race."[6] Writing was, for Fortune, a means of agitation, which he defined as "constant protesting, always standing up to be counted, to be heard, or to be knocked down."[7] It was a way of being seen that, for Fortune, could not be contained in journalism alone. In 1884, he published *Black and White: Land, Labor and Politics in the South*, a book that opens with an assessment of and argument about the importance of Black textual representation, specifically in book form. "The books which have been written in this country—the books which have molded and controlled public opinion—during the past one hundred and fifty years have been written by white men, in justification of the white man's domineering selfishness, cruelty and tyranny," Fortune lamented. "The white man's story has been told over and over again, until the reader actually tires of the monotonous repetition." His comments constituted a call to African Americans to take it upon themselves to write and publish, in book form, a "glimpse of the other side of the picture so studiously turned to the wall."[8] In 1883, Fortune had praised George Washington Williams for doing just that, actively promoting his *History of the Negro Race in America, 1619–1880* in the pages of the *Globe* on multiple occasions.[9] The importance of producing literature and seeing it into publication was a message he would communicate repeatedly in his writing, including in a two-part article published in the *Age*, in June 1889, where he called upon African Americans to write their own history and literature.[10] Writing was, to Fortune, a responsibility. It was also a craft that was for him flexible enough to take on several different generic iterations across his lifetime.

In the 1880s, Fortune used writing as a weapon against racism and injustice. In his journalism, he spoke out to indict civil rights violations, to endorse economic fairness, and to organize African Americans to stand up against racial injustice. Fortune's writing was passionate and unforgiving in its criticism of racism. One review described his 1884 book *Black and White* as "[giving] notice that the Negro is here to stay—an American and not an African, and an American citizen who is biding his time and intends to be counted."[11] After its publication, Fortune was heralded as "*the most prominent and brilliant young Negro in America.*"[12] He was, as historian Tameka Bradley Hobbs notes, the definition of "what a committed public intellectual could and should be."[13] In 1887, Fortune formed the Afro-American League, a political organization that had over twenty local branches by the time it held its first national convention in 1890. The league was meant to bring together what Fortune proudly called "Afro-American Agitators," who would sound the "death knell of the shuffling, cringing creature in black who for two centuries and a half had given the right of way to white men."[14] Fortune's politics, then, in both his writing and in his affiliation and organization, were militant. He was critical of those who did not directly confront racism, and utterly dismissive of those who gave "the right of way to white men."

It was while he held this mindset, and this set of commitments, that Fortune met Booker T. Washington. In the 1880s, when they began their friendship, both were at the start of their careers, with Washington just beginning to build Tuskegee Institute after the Hampton model and Fortune launching a career as a New York newspaperman. They certainly didn't form a friendship from any political agreement. Fortune was deeply critical of precisely the kind of accommodation to the South's racial conditions that Washington represented and would make his platform in the 1895 Atlanta Exposition address. Given the difference in their political stances, one wonders what the basis of their relationship could have been. One might expect that, over time, Fortune and Washington would have become rivals instead of friends. But Fortune's newspapers covered the growth and development of Tuskegee and, as Washington's visits to the North to seek funding for the school became more frequent, the *Freeman* and the *Age* covered his speeches. In 1890, Fortune traveled to Tuskegee to deliver two lectures, a trip that seems to have marked a new stage in his relationship to Washington. From this point forward, Fortune wrote about Tuskegee and about Washington with increasing frequency. Correspondence between the two men tells us that many of the articles and editorials Fortune wrote were requested or their content directed by Washington, in keeping with the messages he wished to project. Fortune became, as Washington's biographer Louis R. Harlan calls him, "Washington's most important black friend . . . and the most paradoxical one."[15]

Harlan speculates that Fortune and Washington's relationship was based on mutual need, that "each had some quality or insight the other lacked."[16] Fortune was a valuable asset to Washington: his facility with words and his access to print extended the reach of Washington's ideas, and his reputation for radical thought surely also meant that Fortune could give voice to what Washington's political stance would not allow him to say. Additionally, Washington had little contact with and therefore limited insight into Northern Black leadership, and Fortune gradually became a conduit to this world. In turn, Fortune relied on Washington's "steadiness," which balanced out his own fiery temperament. Fortune had a propensity to drink heavily, and Washington was often able to steer him out of the sticky situations in which he found himself. Fortune's instability was not limited to his excessive drinking: he also often found himself in financial difficulties, for which he also turned to Washington for assistance. As early as 1891, Fortune felt close enough to Washington to ask him the favor of loaning him two hundred dollars. Washington wasn't able to extend him credit at that time.[17] But Fortune's need established a dynamic between the two men that put an unspoken price tag on their friendship.

There were at least two other elements of their friendship that drew the men together despite their differences. First, Fortune saw in Washington a fellow Southerner of his own generation who, to some extent, shared his experience, and whose leadership was in keeping with his own vision of the practical questions at stake in the future of the Black South. Both men were born into slavery at about the same time; their knowledge of Southern Black life came not from distanced accounts of it but from experience. Although Fortune moved to the North, his attention to the precarious situation of African Americans in the South never wavered, even as he grew disenchanted by his own prospects there. When he recounted the corruption of Reconstruction politics, the exploitation of Black workers, or the threats and violence to which African Americans had been subjected, he spoke from personal experience. He was all too familiar with the ways so-called race leaders had deserted the Negro masses, "selling out" to white leaders. He recognized that the African American educated elite in the North had a detached understanding of the lives of African Americans in the South, their perspectives theoretical rather than practical and their distance emotional as well as geographical. The second thing that bound Washington and Fortune was perhaps more sensitive: both men lacked a formal college-level education. In this, they both differed from the rising Black leadership that would increasingly speak out against Washington's politics and his philosophy. Washington would come to label this group—which he rightly identified as for the most part educated in colleges and universities in the North and who made their homes there—"the intellectuals." He believed them to be wholly unfit to speak for African Americans in the South: "The intellectuals know books but they do not know men," he would come to say. While college-educated men could "quote a phrase or a sentiment from Shakespeare, Milton, Cicero, or some other great writer," Washington's "life in the South and years of study and effort in connection with actual and concrete problems of Southern life" made him more equipped to be the leader of the African American people.[18] Washington considered his informal education and insights superior to those of the formally educated. But that doesn't mean he wasn't sensitive to their criticism and judgment, or unaware that he was an outsider in their world.

Fortune's formal education had also been minimal, and yet his professional trajectory left him firmly entrenched in the world of the Northern intellectual and cultural elite, and he recognized that this was the very world in which Washington needed to operate. He was more widely read than Washington, and he clearly valued literary and intellectual work differently. But, like Washington's, Fortune's education had been practical: it was mainly located in exposure to politics and his work in printing offices, where he was surrounded by a diversity of opinion, copious reading materials, and endless examples of Black leadership. He himself credited his development as a thinker to the intellectually and politically vibrant conditions of his youth in Jacksonville and Tallahassee, Florida, rather than his formal schooling. Looking back over his life, he would downplay the two years he spent at Jacksonville's Stanton Institute. As a student entering Howard University's preparatory program he would retrospectively describe himself as both "very illiterate" and someone who had "read a great deal and learned much in printing offices and by contact with intelligent people."[19] Fortune's prominence as a journalist ensured that he moved in the same Northern, activist circles as "the intellectuals" and was widely respected by them. But in working with Washington to make him an author, he seems to have recognized Washington's culturally and intellectually marginal position and found it to be undeserved. Recognition as an author would lend Washington a degree of intellectual credibility, allowing him to speak in the same register as Northern intellectuals, Black or white. These "reading people" would determine Black leadership and, with it, the future of African Americans in the United States. Recognition as an author would serve Washington as a sort of stepping stone to an intellectual center that was intent on excluding him.[20]

By 1895, Fortune appears to have made peace with, or was at least resigned to, Washington's conciliatory politics. While he did not agree with Washington that African American leaders should forego striving for civil rights—Fortune wrote that it "is not necessary to give [a]way the *whole* political case in order to propagate the industrial idea"—he accepted the value of industrial education and Washington's economic principles.[21] In the end, he believed that Washington was the best hope for what Fortune felt were three key imperatives in African American politics at that moment: first, that the race be unified behind one leader ("*We must have a head*" who will be "the single figure ahead of the procession," he argued); second, that the leader ought to originate from and be situated "in the South"; and, finally, that the lacuna created by the death of Frederick Douglass be immediately filled. "It looks as if you are our Douglass," Fortune wrote to Washington shortly after the Atlanta Exposition speech.[22] Accepting these needs, and yet not entirely comfortable with them, Fortune took on the task of making Washington into an "author." That literary alliance began with a notable moment when Washington was decisively rejected by the American literary establishment. Fortune would pick up the pieces of this rejection, redirecting Washington's attention to different avenues of publication and literary

3.2 *Booker T. Washington, Half-Length Portrait,* by Frances Benjamin Johnston (ca. 1895). Library of Congress, Prints and Photographs Division, Washington, DC.

possibilities that he believed would lead to the same end point. His was a scrappy sort of back-door strategy through which he would use his own creativity, intellect, sensitivity, talent, and knowledge to propel Washington to a place where he could claim authorship and its authority.

Centering the "Literary Talent of the Race"

The crusade to make Washington into an author had an inauspicious beginning. In the spring of 1896, Fortune wrote to Washington with a proposition: he wished to make Tuskegee a "literary center" for African American writing. Tuskegee had not been his first choice for such a center. One year earlier, he had discussed a similar arrangement with Hollis Frissell, then the president of the Hampton Institute, proposing that he transform the school and its journal, the *Southern Workman*, into the physical and material sites around which African American literary efforts might be organized. Frissell had "thought mighty well of the idea," Fortune told Washington, but "the old barnacles who control affairs [at Hampton] were averse to change, and so we dropped the matter." It's unclear exactly what "changes" Fortune had proposed, to either the school or its journal, but Fortune clearly imagined his own employment to be part of the proposal. Undeterred by Frissell's response, Fortune turned to Washington one year later, extending his idea to Tuskegee, whose *Black Belt Magazine* Fortune saw as equally well suited to becoming a first-rate journal that would represent "the literary talent of the race." With the support of other literary activists, among them Victoria Earle Matthews, with whom Fortune worked as a New York journalist, Fortune believed that he could "command the cream of the literary talent of the race." By extension, Fortune believed that Washington's standing and reputation would be enhanced if Tuskegee and its *Black Belt Magazine* were the focal point of Black literary culture and exchange. "You would be a great power in it," Fortune told Washington, speaking of the literary nexus he imagined forming as a means of organizing African American literary culture, refining its shape and enhancing the means of its distribution. "We could easily make Tuskegee the center of the literary thought of the Southern educational work."[23]

Fortune's proposal to Washington was indicative of a personal and professional crossroads: he was weighing in his own mind whether he would be of greater value to the race working in the North or in his native South.[24] A spring 1890 trip to Tuskegee had left Fortune a great admirer of the school, and the idea of a permanent position there was tempting. In his letter Fortune outlined other "routine things" he could do at Tuskegee to round out a full-time job: he suggested, for instance, that, in addition to forging a literary center, he could deliver "lectures once a week on fiscal, economic and social subjects, in line with the literary studies necessary to a proper editing of the magazine."[25] The proposal wasn't, however, entirely self-serving. It represented Fortune's understanding of the importance of Black writing, not only as it addressed matters of African American education but also more broadly as a means of consolidating African American leadership and showcasing Black thought. It underscored Fortune's mounting concern that African American literary efforts lacked coherence, a fact that, to a newspaperman, was especially evident in the emerging colossus of mass journalism. By the last decade of the nineteenth century, the sheer proliferation of African American newspapers across the nation was remarkable, but it was also unsustainable.[26] The publications were of uneven quality and at times produced an unproductive cacophony that scattered Black views and voices. Fortune himself was a co-owner and served as the editor of one of the most stable, influential, and long-lasting African American newspapers, the *New York Age*. But as his interest in fiction and other expressive forms shows, he considered writing to also be an important means of creative expression that, Fortune increasingly considered, would play a crucial role in the struggle for racial justice. By organizing the literary around a single geographical and textual space, Fortune believed its impact would be concentrated and enhanced. Additionally, it was a plan that would allow the Tuskegee president to heighten his own visibility and that of his educational agenda by fixing it in print. Such a project, Fortune told Washington, "would be of great service to you and Tuskegee and the race at large."[27]

Fortune's plan to transform Tuskegee and its magazine into a center for literary productivity, turning Washington into a leader in the literary arena, turned out to be beyond the immediate scope of Washington's understanding of the importance of the literary and his agenda for the school. Tuskegee did not have the money to successfully undertake the venture, Washington wrote. Fortune reluctantly accepted Washington's reasoning—"I understand fully what the cost of such a venture would be and I know how tight the money market is"—but implied that he still had hopes for eventually winning him over: "Some other time we shall talk it over."[28]

Fortune's response here—a combination of acquiescence and deferral—is typical in their epistolary relationship, which unfolded as a series of advances and retreats, collaborations and quarrels. They were good friends, but each was headstrong in his own way, and, despite the alliance that formed between them, their dispositions and priorities differed significantly. In this case, Fortune put his idea of transforming Tuskegee and its magazine into a literary center for African American writing on hold, and yet he would not altogether abandon the belief that African American literary efforts needed centering, or that he should take the lead in promoting the visibility and coherence of Black writing in the United States. Rather than a physical location like Tuskegee or the textual space of a journal or newspaper, Fortune would turn his attention to making Booker T. Washington himself a "literary center" by orchestrating his emergence as an author. Washington was prolific as an orator, and it was in this spoken medium that he felt the most comfortable. His name appeared regularly as the writer of essays and articles in newspapers and magazines, but Fortune knew these to be diffuse and ephemeral sources that, in the hierarchy of print, carried less prestige, impact, and authority than bound books; he recognized that the authorship of books was crucial to gaining a more solid foothold in the intellectual landscape in which Washington needed to be recognized and respected. Washington's Southernness and his lack of college-level education defined his leadership, but it also marginalized him, labeling him as an outsider, fundamentally disconnected from the literary and intellectual center of the United States, the urban North. Authoring books was one way to connect him to this world. Book authorship would amplify Washington's voice— for African Americans and whites alike—to better spread his educational philosophy and his political agenda. Significantly, it would also give his ideas mobility, moving them quite literally out of the geography of slavery, of Tuskegee, and of the South and onto a more visible national and intellectual domain. Greater visibility in this domain would certainly lead to greater support for Tuskegee from the North's philanthropic base; it might also lead to greater respect from the North's rising Black leadership class that was increasingly speaking out against Washington's educational philosophy and challenging his leadership. Finally, Fortune predicted, Washington's authorship might bring with it money. Although Fortune's own career as a writer was defined by financial hardship, he predicted that Washington's writing could have commercial value, if only he could cultivate an effective literary voice and effectively leverage his publishing options. In addition to funding Tuskegee and Washington's educational agenda, Fortune perhaps believed that the money from Washington's authorship might find its way into his own pocket, effectively offsetting the cost of his own career as a writer.

Washington's career as an author of books began with his decisive rejection from the American literary establishment. In 1896, Walter Hines Page suggested to Washington that he submit a manuscript for consideration by the Boston publishing firm Houghton, Mifflin. At the time, Page was an editor of the prestigious *Atlantic Monthly*, but he also served as a literary advisor to Houghton, Mifflin. Page's correspondence with Washington in July 1896 was initially regarding editorial changes to an article Page wished to print in the *Atlantic*. The letter downplayed his criticism of the technical aspect of Washington's writing, highlighting instead revisions to the article's trajectory and its scope. He proposed that Washington expand the article's argument about the efficacy of the Tuskegee model of education to include a sense of its usefulness outside of that institution. Washington should "strike out from the shoulder," Page recommended, by "broadening the application of the principle you have worked out so as to show in the next part of your article that this principle which has made a success of Tuskegee is really the proper principle for education in the whole south without reference to race."[29] This directive was in keeping with Page's belief in the promise of the post-Reconstruction South and the importance of education to its rebuilding; it also suggested his desire to promote Washington's philosophy and his leadership beyond Tuskegee. Print was a way of doing so. Revised according to his instructions, Page believed the article would not only be well received; it would also serve to "throw [Washington's] work where it properly belongs, among the great forces of our time and not simply the force of the work done at a single institution."[30] The *Atlantic Monthly* was widely recognized as a distinguished literary and cultural commentary magazine that published only the nation's leading writers. Publication in this particular magazine was an opportunity for Washington to animate his ideas and his leadership for a new and previously inaccessible audience. Page's offer to sponsor Washington's admission to these hallowed pages—"I wish it to serve you to the very best advantage," Page told Washington—was effectively an invitation into a world of mainstream publishing that was largely inaccessible to African Americans. Page communicated this to Washington when he wrote: "The ATLANTIC is . . . as important a platform as a man can stand on."[31]

Recognizing Washington's potential as a literary commodity, Page flattered Washington and laid the groundwork for a future relationship. He not only promised to give Washington's article "a place of distinction" in the journal, but also to compensate him "at the rate at which most of the best articles in the Atlantic are paid for."[32] Washington must have felt warmed at such attention. Just three months earlier, he had been awarded an honorary master of arts degree at Harvard University, a tribute he would later describe as "the greatest surprise that ever came to me."[33] And now he was being offered another gesture of belonging by the Northern literary set: prime positioning for his writing in one of the nation's leading intellectual forums. Having laid the groundwork, Page reiterated his interest in furthering Washington's career as an author, requesting "the manuscript of your addresses about which we wrote you some time ago" and stating his own desire "to read" the book.[34]

Washington's article, titled "The Awakening of the Negro," appeared in the *Atlantic*'s September 1896 issue, and Washington sent a manuscript drawn from his addresses to Houghton, Mifflin soon after. It proved not to be quite what Page expected, and he sent a formal letter of rejection to Washington on October 13, 1896. The next day, Page sent a personal note to Washington explaining that even though "H. M. & Co. is not the natural or the best channel for a book so made up," he nonetheless hoped to publish what he described as "a possible book in a different form—not speeches but a history or narrative, with some familiar features—about Tuskegee."[35]

Given the sheer volume of Washington's correspondence, it's curious that there are no letters that illuminate Washington's reaction to the rejection of his book of speeches by Houghton, Mifflin. That the manuscript had been solicited by Page and then turned down must have confused Washington, or even angered him. Coming on the heels of his triumphant acceptance of the honorary degree from Harvard, and amid his overall rise in stature that followed his address in Atlanta, there is little doubt that Washington found inconsistency in the fact that his ideas, communicated in the form in which he excelled, were unpalatable to the white book buyers that formed the basis of the literary establishment's clientele. Page and Washington would eventually come together again, with Page returning, in 1898, to the idea of Washington writing a narrative based on Tuskegee and featuring Washington speaking about his own life. For the time being, however, Washington seemed to withdraw from Page's guidance. Instead, he turned to Fortune as a literary mentor.

The book that Fortune and Washington first came together to produce was in fact a collection of speeches much like what Washington had offered Houghton, Mifflin. During a trip through the South in 1896, Victoria Earle Matthews had stopped in to visit Booker T. Washington and his wife, Margaret Murray Washington, at Tuskegee. While there, she spoke to Washington about her own idea to cull from his addresses to make a book. Washington was enthusiastic and gave her copies of some of his speeches before she left Tuskegee. Matthews was an established journalist and political activist with strong ties to literature; she would be described in her obituary as "a great reader and thinker, one of the best read women in the country," and "a writer of considerable ability."[36] Her journalistic work had appeared in white and Black newspapers, both under her own name and under various noms de plume. Matthews's most well-known piece of imaginative writing, the short story "Aunt Lindy," was published in the AME *Church Review* in 1889. In 1895, she distinguished herself as an insightful theorist of and authority on African American literature when she delivered the address "The Value of Race Literature" at the first Congress of Colored Women of the United States, held in Boston, Massachusetts. It was a forceful speech in which she spoke both practically and critically on the importance of literature authored by African Americans to challenging racial stereotypes and promoting racial progress that exhibited a nuanced understanding of the intertwined future of Black art and politics. Matthews believed that producing race literature was a key to the successful future of Black Americans, not only because it would prove to whites that African Americans were a literary people, but also because literature was a means of providing African Americans with a window onto their own talents and histories. She regularly taught classes in racial history and literature at the White Rose Mission, a settlement house in Brooklyn, New York, that, in 1897, Matthews founded along with Maritcha Lyons to help African American women from the South acclimate to life in Northern cities and prepare for the employment opportunities available there. As a teacher of classes offered to the mission's clientele, her coworker Frances Keyser would note, Matthews "eagerly, almost impetuously" labored to instill in her students "the knowledge of the work and worth of the men and women of their race—knowledge with which she was completely saturated."[37]

Given her perspective on race literature, Matthews found the task of assembling a collection of Booker T. Washington's quotes and sayings appealing.[38] She shared Washington's vision of the importance of practical education and had firsthand experience with the young people who might benefit the most from his inspirational sayings. Washington's words, collected and issued in book form, would serve as what Matthews termed "counter-irritants" to the debasing stereotypes perpetuated in other literatures.[39] It would also raise his visibility in a way that would benefit his stature and leadership. For Fortune, Matthews's project to collect Washington's "words of wisdom" and print them in the form of a book presented itself as an opportunity to garner

3.3 Victoria Earle Matthews was a literary activist, a journalist, and the founder of the White Rose Mission, the first settlement house for Black women in New York City. She is pictured here in 1903. Schomburg Center for Research in Black Culture, Manuscripts, Archives, and Rare Books Division, New York Public Library.

just the sort of literary recognition he believed Washington needed to receive. Washington would have to share the title page with Matthews, as the compiler of the collection, but his name would be the one primarily associated with the book's contents. Fortune respected Matthews as a writer and as an activist; he employed her as a writer for both the *New York Age* and its predecessor, the *Globe*, and he supported her efforts to found the Federation of Afro-American Women, which would, in 1896, merge with the National League of Colored Women to form the National Association of Colored Women's Clubs. Matthews was the potential coworker Fortune had referred to when he pitched to Washington his idea of transforming Tuskegee into a literary center. He saw her as an "estimable woman," not least because she was, like him, "active along literary lines."[40]

Fortune would come to take a greater interest in—and, in fact, commandeer the production of—Matthews's book as soon as it presented itself as a potential gateway to a prestigious New York publisher who might give Washington entry to the literary establishment. Matthews's work on what would become the collection *Black-Belt Diamonds* was slow: at least once it was significantly delayed because of illness, and then it was again delayed by the opening of the White Rose Mission. An active writer, she was also busy with other literary projects with deadlines that kept her from the Washington project. One of these caused Fortune to pay Matthews a visit in the spring of 1898. "I had to stop by Mrs. Matthews on the way over yesterday about a current publication for today," he wrote to Washington. "She said she wanted 9000 words out of your Sunday talks to complete her collection which she says the Putnams are to consider."[41] Fortune implied that Matthews had command of something essential to Fortune's literary agenda for Washington: a relationship with a reputable New York trade publisher. The expansive ramifications of Matthews's book project were suddenly apparent—in addition to providing the public with a taste of Washington's words, Fortune saw Matthews's book as an opportunity to cultivate a relationship with a major New York publishing venue. Fortune was well aware of the high stakes of Northern publishing and, in particular, of Washington's earlier, failed effort to interest Houghton, Mifflin in his book manuscript. Putnam's interest in Matthews's project made that manuscript a potential vehicle through which to advance Washington as an author. This was especially attractive to Fortune as he contemplated the growth of Washington's literary career and the kind of future publishing opportunities that he imagined. "The publication of hers by Putnam will certainly affect the sale of ours," Fortune told Washington.[42]

It's unclear exactly what publication Fortune had in mind when he referred to "ours": as we will see, by 1898, when work on what would become *Black-Belt Diamonds* intensified, Washington had a considerable number of writing projects in progress, all intended to result in a book-length publication, and any of these might have proven attractive to a publishing house already interested in Washington as a literary figure. Fortune's enthusiasm lay in his belief that Washington could take advantage of Matthews's connections with a major New York publisher, piggybacking a book of his own on the one Matthews was compiling. His use of the plural here—"ours"—is telling, as it begins to give voice to the extent to which Fortune had, by 1898, bound himself to Washington's efforts to become an author. His sense of Washington's pursuit of authorship as a joint effort is evident in the way he immediately took charge of Matthews's publication, both to ensure that it was finished in a timely fashion and to guarantee that it would serve as an appropriate introduction to Washington as a figure of literary authority. In fact, Fortune initially found Matthews's book to be in relatively good shape, but he nevertheless insisted that the manuscript pass under his critical eye before publication. Fortune would assume the role of literary middleman. With her, he had gone "over all the points of the publication canvassed by you and me," but a last edit of the manuscript he would do himself.[43] After he finished what he called the final "critical reading and correction" of the manuscript, he acknowledged the "excellence of the collection." He recognized the importance of the book and assured Washington that it would "contribute permanently to your reputation as a philosopher, as a wise and safe leader."[44]

Fortune's praise for Matthews's role in completing the manuscript was abundant. "When the work is in print you will appreciate more than now the thoroughness with which Mrs. Matthews has done her part of the work," he told Washington.[45] And yet he did not hesitate to indicate that his own part of the work had been arduous and extensive, as well as necessary to wrangle the manuscript into the sort of shape that would do justice to and enhance Washington's standing as a literary man. As a partner in Washington's pursuit of authorship, Fortune was detail-oriented and meticulously aware of how important it was that every aspect of a book set in print be carefully considered. He was confident in his own literary abilities and, as Washington's primary mentor on literary matters, felt it his responsibility to fully articulate his judgment on issues of literary quality. Nowhere is this more apparent than in his pronouncement of the mediocrity of the title that Washington and Matthews had conceived of together. "I am agonizing over a title," he wrote to Washington in May 1898, "as the one you and she hit upon will not do at all." He remarked, "The title of a book makes half the sale of it."[46] In the end, Matthews and Washington left the decision to Fortune, who chose *Black-Belt Diamonds* over Matthews's preferred title, "Gems from Booker T. Washington." Fortune's rationale here is important: in his opinion, *Black-Belt Diamonds* was the better title not only because it was catchier, or because the title could be typeset to fit in a single line on the page, allowing it to be quickly captured by the reader's eye. These were important features of the title he selected. But Fortune was also interested in what it signified. The title that Matthews preferred promoted Washington, to be sure, but Fortune's title more broadly embraces the South as a source of verbal diamonds, positioning it as a place associated with the richness of Black thought and wisdom rather than characterized by violence, inferiority, poverty, or lack of opportunity. His insightful opinion on the title serves as a reminder not only of his perceptiveness as a reader, but also the breadth of his knowledge of printing and the publishing industry. He labored over things like the book's title and its typeface because these elements were essential to promoting Washington as a literary figure. His report to Washington on the manuscript as it went into print—he was "charmed with the beauty of it"—suggests something of Fortune's appreciation of the aesthetic details of literary work, and the finesse with which he believed it should be handled, even down to the choice of type.[47] This keen understanding of literary craft and his printer's attention to detail made Fortune invaluable to Washington. This was the beginning of Fortune's tireless work as Washington's literary advisor, in which he dedicated his own literary skill to ensuring that Washington be recognized for his.

Fortune took great pride in writing the introduction to *Black-Belt Diamonds*, which was intended to make a bold statement about literature and politics. Matthews found it likely "to provoke antagonism among Southern white men," Fortune informed Washington, primarily because Fortune insisted on casting Washington as a safer and more sound intellectual leader than Henry W. Grady, the journalist who used the Atlanta *Constitution* to promote a "New South" that remained founded on white supremacy and what he called "the domination of the negro."[48] Fortune feared that Washington would agree with Matthews about the tone and tenor of the introduction and was pleased when Washington expressed no reservations about it. "I am delighted in your estimation of the Introduction," Fortune wrote to Washington. "I was conscious that it had plenty of masculinity, and from the business point I thought it would do good in the South by provoking the white papers to take notice of your broad humanity and Americanism." What the language of Fortune's literary criticism sums up here is the difference he saw between his own writing and that of Matthews: his willingness to show "plenty of masculinity," to take risks, to be bold. This was certainly in line with the image of Washington as an author Fortune wished to cultivate. In communicating his ambition for *Black-Belt Diamond*'s introduction and for the book, he articulated the bravado that for Fortune was ever associated with writing: "It is for us to give our men their proper place *in books*."[49]

Fortune's words here make visible some of the gendered processes by which Black women's literary output became lost in the historical record: the work Matthews performed in conceiving, collecting, selecting, editing and arranging the volume's content fades into the background, eclipsed by Fortune's focus on textual "masculinity" and his public-facing voice as the author of the introduction. I will return to Matthews's authorship at the end of the chapter, for, notwithstanding Fortune's gendered understanding of powerful, effective writing, his fate as a literary practitioner was not dissimilar to her own. Both made important contributions to the making of

African American literature—perhaps most significantly through editorial work—that stand at odds with the androcentrism that has traditionally been associated with literary authorship, and both are destined to remain largely invisible until we learn to read literary acts and modes of authorship, like collecting, arranging, or editing that have long been considered feminine alongside more familiar forms of authorship that display, to use Fortune's words, "plenty of masculinity." In the case of *Black-Belt Diamonds*, writing for Washington did give Fortune the chance to author his own text and to complicate Washington's public message with his own, nudging it in subtle rhetorical ways. And yet the sort of piggybacking of writing and of rhetoric embodied in *Black-Belt Diamonds* was rare. Their literary alliance was not about Fortune's writing or his opinions, but about using printed books to embody Washington's authority as a leader. Fortune believed that the book would present Washington as "the man, the tower of strength, who has taken the place so worthily filled by Frederick Douglass, as 'the guide, philosopher and friend' of the ten million Afro-American citizens of the republic."[50] It was not only that Washington should assume Douglass's leadership role in the Black community; Fortune intended that Washington would assume Douglass's literary presence as well. Supporters and critics alike would be transformed through the common experience of reading Washington's printed words into believers and followers. In this way, the print volume, itself a permanent, stable representation of his views, would communicate Washington's reputation as a wise man, securing his status as the nation's leading spokesperson for a reasoned approach to the "problem" of its African American people.

"No Reason Why We Should Make a Present of It"

In the end, "the Putnams" did not publish *Black-Belt Diamonds*; it would instead bear Fortune's own name as the publisher. As he made decisions about the book's cover, its typesetting, and its illustrations, he would also negotiate the costs with the printer, explaining to Washington the particulars. "The book will make 150 to 185 pages," Fortune told him, "and the estimated cost, exclusive of dies for cover and half tone cut and changes in proof, is $250, so I put the whole probable cost at $300. We shall not know the exact cost until the work is finished, which will be about the 15th [of June 1898], as they have promised to rush it."[51] In July the book was ready and had Washington's approval. "I like 'Black Belt Diamonds' very much, I hardly see how it could have been better," Washington wrote to his personal secretary, Emmett Scott.[52] Fortune was also relatively upbeat about the success of the publication. "Black Diamonds are getting a fair share of newspaper notice, but the sales are slow," he reported to Washington, assuring him that this was "no disappointment at all. They are going slowly but sure right along because they [the "Diamonds"] are good."[53] But Washington had clearly become apprehensive. His inquiries about the different venues through which the book was being marketed and distributed suggest that he questioned whether they might achieve better sales. Fortune detailed the various marketing practices that were underway. "Referring to your reference to booksellers I have to say when they have calls for books they either send direct to publishers or order through their New York agents," Fortune said.[54] "This is being done in the matter of 'Black Belt Diamonds'. The orders are not very numerous, but some are coming in." When Washington wondered whether different pricing—the book was being sold for one dollar—or possible revisions might lead to better sales, Fortune answered defensively, "As to the price of the book, I wanted to make it 60 or 75 cents but was overruled by Mrs. Matthews. I shall consider the matter of reducing the price. Mrs. Matthews wants me to rearrange the book, leaving out the division into Parts, and I can't see how I can do it." His exasperation with the doubts expressed about the book, coupled with his confidence in the quality of his initial work on the volume and his disinclination to tinker with it, is apparent in the letter's testy closing line: "I may turn the whole thing over to her and let her murder it, if she keeps bothering me about it."[55]

Fortune's correspondence with Washington here offers rare insight into the business aspect of African American literary production at the turn of the century, serving as a reminder that Fortune's literary alliance with Washington cast him as both a man of letters and a man of business. But Washington and Fortune's differing priorities are telling. Whereas Washington's questions about the book's success revolved around money, Fortune's priorities remained consistently focused on casting Washington as a literary authority. Washington's name had been given priority on the book's title page, placed above and significantly larger than that of Matthews, who was credited with selecting and arranging the contents, or Fortune, who was listed as the author of the introduction. Catalogs such as the *Publishers' Weekly* listed the book under Washington's name. In this, Fortune remained adamant that the book had "served [Washington] well, which was one of my main desires in the publication."[56] Yet he understood establishing Washington as an author to be a part of a long-game strategy: *Black-Belt Diamonds* was but one of a series of needed publications that would all together give Washington the literary identity he needed to communicate his agenda and enhance his authority as a leader. "The Diamonds are good," he wrote to Washington on July 27, 1898, "but do not sufficiently unfold your system and philosophy."[57]

Throughout 1898, Fortune encouraged Washington to move forward to new writing ventures. Fortune employed an interesting strategy of sometimes suggesting some projects he knew Washington would reject because of his politics at the same time as he proposed others that would be more palatable. In July 1998, for instance, he proposed that the "best service you and I could render the race would be a judicial history by me on the attitude of the Supreme Court on the question of Civil and Political Rights from the foundation of the Government." Fortune believed that the "Supreme Court [was] the storm center in our system of government"; by exposing the "bias and inconsistency and autocratic character of the Court" in print, Fortune believed, "the American people might be aroused to the dangerous position which the Supreme Court holds in our system of Government." Fortune knew that a book of this sort would require "a year of hard study at Washington and the expenditure of $2,500." But he was ready to take on the assignment: the "results of the work," he told Washington, "would justify the expenditure." Even as he presented the idea, Fortune was aware that this was not a battle Washington would be willing to wage at all, much less in print. The same letter returns to what for Washington would have been more familiar, safer ground, with the suggestion that he aim to publish more of his addresses. Washington could gather the series of inspirational talks given to Tuskegee students, Fortune said, and publish them as a book "within the next six months." With this advice, he returned their conversation to a literary agenda that was far less radical, much more in keeping with Washington's own preferred genre, the safe space of his own oratorical performances, recast in written form. But in proposing ideas that promoted agitation for civil rights rather than accommodation, Fortune challenged Washington to expand his position and extend his voice in print. He also kept Washington to a strict timetable that would allow future books to build on previous ones. It was, he argued, the only way to ensure the growth of Washington's "work and reputation."[58]

Washington did branch out to embrace different genres, most significantly signing on to write an autobiography strikingly similar to what Page had suggested in 1896. Given Page's expressed interest in that kind of manuscript, it is curious that Washington did not contact him about the prospect of Houghton, Mifflin's publishing it. Instead, sometime around the middle of 1897, he sent a prospectus for an autobiography to the J. L. Nichols Company, in Naperville, Illinois, the same firm that was preparing *Progress of a Race* for subscription publication. Washington received a response from the Nichols Company's representative John Hertel late in 1897. The publisher was very interested in the manuscript, which Hertel referred to as "your prospective book entitled 'Story of your life.'" But, he explained, they could not take on the book immediately. "You understand that we are at present pushing our new book 'Progress of a Race' extensively," Hertel wrote to Washington. He explained the Nichols Company's marketing strategy: "It has been our method of handling a few articles at a time and then put on more energy." Given this practice, Hertel felt that they could not publish Washington's autobiography immediately. "We do not think it would be advisable to put on another book short of one year," he told Washington.[59] Aside from this necessary delay, the Nichols Company was ready to make a commitment to publish the autobiography. He closed the letter with a list of concrete terms to be worked through on the way to establishing a formal contract.

Washington accepted the publisher's terms with no apparent reservations. Just six weeks later, however, Page reiterated his suggestion that Washington write an autobiography, recommending that he commit to paper "certain life sketches which might illustrate in a vivid and personal way the social and race conditions down South, and particularly the interesting work you are doing for the uplifting of the race."[60] Washington did not share with Page that he had agreed to do just that, for another press. Given the determination with which, with Fortune's help, Washington pursued authorship around the turn of the century, why he did not return to Page to take advantage of his interest in Washington's authorship remains one of the biggest mysteries about the start of Washington's career as an author. I suspect that one reason might be because Page had been critical of Washington's writing. Even in accepting "The Awakening of the Negro" for publication in the *Atlantic* in 1896, Page had been the one to correspond with Washington about some necessary revisions. Coupled with Houghton, Mifflin's rejection of a book that Page had seemed to ask for on their behalf, this may have caused Washington to be wary of Page's advice. And while by 1898 it was no secret that Washington did little of his own writing, or that much of the literary work that bore his name was produced by Fortune, few acknowledged this or challenged Washington to write for himself. But Page did, in the same letter in which he inquired again about Washington's interest in doing some autobiographical writing, by somewhat awkwardly suggesting to Washington that the book he proposed Washington write could really only be produced by him. Washington generally did not like awkward situations, preferring to have someone else face them on his behalf. He may therefore have been embarrassed and humiliated to be directly confronted by Page on his propensity to farm out the writing that appeared under his name. In this case, Page directly named Fortune as the person responsible for too much of Washington's writing. "I have great respect for the work that Mr. Fortune has done," he said, adding that Fortune would be welcome to submit his own writing to the *Atlantic* to be considered for possible publication under his own name. But Page pushed Washington to write for himself: "I am looking forward with great interest to *your own effort* at this interesting task which you were good enough to say some time ago that you might make."[61] Washington talked openly about his use of ghostwriters in his correspondence with his most trusted advisors, never evincing any embarrassment or sensitivity about receiving credit for work that was substantially written by others. But it is telling that he does not seem to have responded to Page on this issue. Page would not learn of Washington's agreement with the Nichols Company to publish his autobiography until 1900, when the Nichols autobiography was almost complete. Only then would Washington take Page's advice and try to move the autobiography from the Illinois-based subscription publishing company to the New York publisher Doubleday, Page.

I will return to Washington's autobiography later in the chapter, for this was just one of his many writing projects that came to a head in the final year of the nineteenth century. Indeed, 1898 and, in particular, 1899 were the busiest years of Fortune's literary alliance with Washington. During these years Fortune continued to monitor requests for Washington's writing and to help him distinguish between opportunities that might be worthwhile and those that could detract from his literary reputation. In some cases, this meant getting Washington out of projects to which he had already committed. In the spring of 1899, for instance, Fortune advised Washington not to provide an introduction to the proposed "National Biographical Cyclopedia of Eminent and Progressive Colored Men," edited by Edward Elder Cooper, a prominent Black journalist and editor of the *Indianapolis Freeman* and *The Colored American*, whom Fortune dismissed as someone who "can't parse a simple sentence," and the kind of race man who "thinks every humbug at a cross roads who can write his name is a great negro." To work with Cooper, Fortune concluded, would be to place Washington in "bad company."[62] Washington needed to pick and choose his literary projects with great care, for his name should only be associated with literary people and productions of the highest quality.

Fortune labored conscientiously to make the writing that appeared under Washington's name of the highest possible quality itself. As multiple writing projects came together in 1899 and, particularly, in 1900, this became increasingly hard to do. In the spring of 1899, Fortune began what he expected to be a relatively small project: Washington's contribution to the collection *A New Negro for a New Century*, which was to be published by a subscription firm in Chicago called the American Publishing House. The work appeared to be relatively straightforward. Fortune's description of the project gives us a concrete sense of his work habits. "I came home this afternoon and pinned down the War business and at 8 o/clock I am able to forward the first chapter," he wrote to Emmett Scott on May 22. "Go ahead and typewrite it," he instructed, referring to his usual practice of writing in longhand and sending those pages to be typewritten at Tuskegee, then sent out under Washington's name.[63] But Fortune's work on this project would prove more time-consuming than he had first thought, and in his correspondence he would come to alternate between generating ambitious deadlines for himself in order to move the work forward and acknowledging its unexpected difficulty. "I am off for home to try to finish the Soldier business for you by mail time tonight," he told Scott, with whom Fortune began to correspond regularly, perhaps finding him at times a more receptive and sympathetic epistolary listener than Washington himself.[64] Hours later he seemed to have accomplished this goal, but he acknowledged that the work was challenging: "I draw a long sigh of relief and satisfaction in writing Finis to the 4th and last installment of the War matter. It has been four days of hard steady grind."[65] One problem was that the project kept expanding, as Fortune was asked to write on more topics.

As he would increasingly have to do, Fortune was writing for Washington under pressure—in this case, "the Chicago people were howling for it"— and he found it exhausting. The "job did me up badly!" he told Washington of the pieces for *A New Negro for a New Century*. "I am glad it is done," he wrote on June 1.[66] Yet it turned out not to be done, as the publishers wanted more. Fortune was annoyed, because the "more" they wanted required research, in this instance on the Treaty of Paris. Additionally, the work was ballooning far beyond what Washington had committed to contribute. Although the original agreement was for 33 pages, Fortune complained, "I have furnished them about 61 pages."[67]

In doing this work, Fortune saw himself and Washington as partners, and he described the work of authorship in collective terms. When raising the issue of the financial relationship with the publisher, he told Washington that he saw "no reason why we should make a present" of the work they did, although it was Fortune who was doing the research and writing the essays.[68] There is little to suggest that Washington experienced authorship with the same degree of collectivity. We can get a better sense of how each thought about the work of writing and authoring by seeing how they differed in their focus on compensation. Fortune largely thought of himself as a foot soldier altruistically serving a greater cause. "I am fighting your battles as the occasion requires," he would tell Washington.[69] But Fortune was also keenly aware of what his labor was worth. He repeatedly tabulated the value of his time and his writing. In one letter, with the intelligence of someone who had been a printing compositor, he carefully calculated the value of word to printed page: "15,504 words = 272 words to printed page = 57 printed pages @$3 = $171.00." Adding the last section on the Treaty of Paris—"1500 words or 6 printed pages"—he concluded that they were owed $189.[70] In a different letter, he used a different metric of the amount of time he invested to make it clear to Washington what he was worth. He had spent 30 days on a research trip in DC, and 10 more in writing the essay, and the value of those "40 days taken from other work" (at a rate of "five dollars a day for such work") came to $200.[71] Such accountings were pressing for Fortune because the state of his own finances was dire. He told Scott that he had "a settlement of an account of mine that can't wait."[72]

While Fortune calculated the cost of his labor, and stewed at the Press's attempts to lowball them—"*They accepted 62 pages* and want to square up for the whole by paying for half or $96"—Washington seemed unconcerned, his attention elsewhere.[73] He does not appear to have written to the publisher regarding the matter of fair payment for the work. Instead, he was pursuing another publishing venture with the small and relatively new Boston firm of Small, Maynard & Co., which had expressed interest in a collection of his addresses and magazine articles. While Fortune was still trying to get fair recompense for work already done for the American Publishing House, Washington was contemplating the "rather generous offer" made by Small, Maynard. With no slight insensitivity, he told Fortune, "I need the money that I think will come from such a publication."[74]

With perhaps equal disregard, he informed Fortune that Small, Maynard would supply Washington with what he called their own "wide-awake and experienced book man" to help work on the manuscript.[75] Still, Washington was anxious that Fortune go over it before he turned it in to the publishers. Perhaps sensing the toll that working on Washington's writing in isolation was taking on Fortune's stamina, Washington promised that either he or Emmett Scott would travel to New York. However, when the manuscript arrived, both men were needed at Tuskegee, and Fortune was once again left to go through the manuscript alone, without the benefit of guidance or feedback from its apparent author. This tested his loyalty: still reeling from the paltry sum he had received from the last project, Fortune clearly felt used, his effort disrespected. And yet, he told Washington, there were two reasons he would "do the Monograph for you." Both reasons offer insight into Fortune's understanding of his literary partnership with Washington. First, Fortune believed that Washington's literary "work ought to be done properly"; although Washington had other people besides Fortune writing for him, Fortune didn't trust them to bring to Washington's writing a combination of literary skill and editorial rigor that matched his own. Distinct from this was Fortune's understanding of the larger stakes to Washington's authorship. Fortune's willingness to write for Washington, and, more broadly, to oversee the literary aspect of his career, was justified by his belief that Washington "ought to have the honor and credit of the work, as you are our representative."[76] Here, Fortune explains his vision of Washington's authorship, which, as the race's representative, would attest to the quality of African American literary work generally. In an environment where the shortcomings of individual African Americans were seen as indicative of the failings of the race, Fortune believed Washington's distinction in the literary arena would help to produce the conditions necessary to advance Black writing as a whole. In shaping Washington's thoughts and his educational and political agenda into words that would endure in books, Fortune understood himself as a crucial part of a crusade to enhance Washington's literary reputation, but he also believed that the race as a whole would benefit from Washington's literary acclaim.

The Future of the American Negro

Washington would come to describe The Future of the American Negro, published in 1899 by Small, Maynard, as a response to the "oft-repeated requests that I put in some more definite and permanent form the ideas regarding the Negro and his future which I have expressed many times on the public platform and through the public press and magazines."[77] Before sending the manuscript to Fortune, Washington expressed confidence in its shape and overall condition: "The manuscript I think has been reasonably well arranged and I think is going to present a pretty respectable appearance in book form." Even so, Washington had some questions about it that he relied on Fortune's literary expertise to answer. One was the volume's title, "which the publishers and I have not agreed upon . . . they are inclined to call it 'The Future of the Negro,'" Washington wrote to Fortune. He was characteristically nervous that it expressed the very bravado with which Fortune was widely associated.

"I have had a little fear that that will be misleading and seem like biting off a little more than one can chew," he wrote. Although Scott had already weighed in on the title, deeming "The Future of the Negro" appropriate, Washington remained uncertain, telling Fortune he would "leave the whole matter of the title undecided until you have had an opportunity to go through the manuscript." Fortune must have been pleased to see that Washington had finally become concerned with such details, and generally with the importance of getting things right in the book. Washington's comments to Fortune on the matter are reminiscent of Fortune's own concerns around Washington's authorship: "While of course I want to get some financial returns from the book, I am determined to do nothing that will in any way sacrifice the good of our case or my reputation for the mere matter of dollars and cents."[78]

Interestingly, although the content of *The Future of the American Negro* was drawn from addresses that Washington had already delivered, and although he had worked on it with Small, Maynard's "wide-awake bookman," it is through this manuscript that we gain the greatest sense of what Fortune saw as Washington's shortcomings as a writer and the sort of work that he considered necessary to enhance Washington's reputation as a writer and as a leader. Fortune was particularly critical of this manuscript, telling Scott in a private communication, "*I am appalled at the literary execution of the work.*" Speaking collectively, he continued, "It will ruin us to go as it stands."[79] As he worked to rewrite, revise, and edit the manuscript, Fortune "had to use the blue pencil very freely."[80] This heavy editorial hand provided no shortage of opportunities to offer Washington lessons in literary craft and style. Fortune found Washington to be inexperienced as a writer, in need of basic lessons in style and composition. "Your propensity to cut sentences short and to leave out qualifying clauses in subordinate sentences cannot be tolerated in a book," he told him, reminding Washington that "clearness of thought and lucidity of diction in a book are indispensable."[81] It was not only that Washington seemed indifferent to the difference between shorter writing, such as might appear in an article, and the length and development of a book; he appeared unable to make the transition between the oral styles in which he expressed himself most comfortably and the sophisticated forms of writing associated with the literary. "You have ideas to burn," Fortune told him, "but your style of expression is more oratorical than literary, and in the written word the oratorical must be used most sparingly."[82] Even as he said this, Fortune did focus on the *ideas* expressed by Washington as much as did on the style of composition. In *The Future of the American Negro*, Fortune took it upon himself to revise the nuances of those ideas, in ways that suggested the limits of his support of Washington's political positions and leadership style. One thing that he would not tolerate was Washington's conciliatory manner, particularly on what he tellingly called Washington's "unconscious habit of apologizing for the shortcomings of white men" during "Reconstruction deviltry."[83] It was a subject that Fortune knew about from his own experience and about which he felt strongly.

Worse than readers' disagreement with Washington's controversial ideas or timid mode of address, Fortune feared, would be their recognition of his weak writing and undistinguished literary style. The whole point of producing books—as distinct from giving speeches, or even publishing shorter journalistic articles—was for Washington to become known for his literary talent. Quality writing and its elegant presentation in book form would define Washington and his theories of race relations as learned, cultured, and intellectually sound. Shoddy work would convey the opposite impression and, in Fortune's words, "it would ruin us." To avoid this, Fortune worked to refine Washington's writing in *The Future of the American Negro* until he was "tired to death."[84] In addition to strengthening its prose and tone, it is clear that Fortune also undertook research to both ground Washington's writing in fact and bolster his observations and arguments. This was onerous work, the difficulty of which Fortune increasingly withheld from Washington, sharing it only in his private correspondence with Emmett Scott. It was "hell," he told him, to have to read a "hundred different reports" to "chase the facts and figures" of how governments racially discriminated in their funding of public education in the South after 1870.[85] But Fortune knew these facts and figures to be essential to buttressing Washington's assertions and reputation and so had to be woven into the manuscript. Working with a mishmash of material that included handwritten pages, typewritten sheets, and scraps of paper, and sending this material back and forth by mail between New York, Tuskegee, and, in this case, the publishers in Boston, presented its own challenges. Fortune would often indicate to Washington's Tuskegee staff where to insert new pages and bits of material by pinning them to the manuscript with dressmaker's pins, the best way he found to make sense of the manuscript's layers of additions and alterations. It must have been maddening to receive these, along with instructions for their insertion, after the manuscript had been typewritten, but Fortune insisted that they were "indispensible."[86] Instructions of this sort certainly did not add to Fortune's popularity as an editor. In his own words, his thoroughness often resulted in copy that was so marked up it looked as if "a cyclone had struck it."[87] He regularly predicted that printers and publishers would "howl murder" upon receiving extensive edits and revisions in the final stages of production.[88] But Fortune believed it crucial that Washington's books showed well: as Fortune would remind him from time to time, they needed to "make a credible exposition of your opinions and enhance your reputation."[89]

In late October 1899, Fortune expressed satisfaction and even pride in the shape *The Future of the American Negro* was in, telling Washington that in his final reading of the manuscript "text looks well booked off and it reads smoothly and in many parts eloquently." In all, it had been a frenetic six weeks of work to get the manuscript in shape. "In the form 'we' have corrected it I am sure you will have a credible book," he wrote to Washington— his quotes around the word "we" displaying a touch of resentment at the imbalance between the one who did the writing and the one who would receive the credit. Fortune's comments here and his incessant drive to make Washington a better writer serve as a reminder that his interest was not only in the commercial viability of Washington's authorship, but also in the critical appreciation of his writing. This would be a book, Fortune wrote, that would be "a success with readers and critics" both for its "substance and manner of treatment." What he was "most concerned" about in his revisions, he added, was "the literary point."[90]

In referring here to the "literary point," Fortune meant the quality of the prose in *The Future of the American Negro*. He had a strong sense that a certain kind of writing was essential for African American progress—for the "future" of the Negro literally, and in letters. This point is clear in his discussions with Washington about contemporary literature, which he encouraged Washington to read. When Washington mentioned Joel Chandler Harris's *The Chronicles of Aunt Minervy Ann*, for instance, Fortune expressed disgust with Harris's stock stereotypical characters and, especially, his trivial and uncritical treatment of the Reconstruction violence that Fortune's own family had suffered; he recognized the danger this type of storytelling posed to the popular imagination. Powerful accounts that pitched racist narratives as fact would become more and more prevalent and compelling in the first decades of the twentieth century, their racial configurations replicated in blackface minstrelsy, in historical romances like Thomas Dixon's *The Leopard's Spots* (1902) and, eventually, in motion pictures like D. W. Griffith's *The Birth of a Nation* (1915). Against these narratives, Fortune knew journalism to be ineffective. "The only way we can meet this sort of thing is to go into fiction and do it," Fortune told Washington. It was, in fact, Fortune's aspiration: "I shall go in and do my share if possible," he told Washington, sharing with him his plan to write a novel.[91]

The years Fortune worked most diligently to promote Washington as an author were the very years during which racism and realism were inextricably linked in American letters, forming what Gene Jarrett describes as a "marriage, of caricature and American literary realism."[92] This context helps us to understand Fortune's determination to write creatively around the turn of the century; he had at least two projects on which he was working in the fall of 1899. Even in the midst of his intense literary efforts for Washington, Fortune reported that he had "begun work on a novel, 'After War Times.'" He also told Washington that he had finished and "submitted my collection of verse to F. Tennyson Neely this morning."[93] He wasn't optimistic that the poems would be accepted for publication. Even as he secured additional publishing opportunities for Washington, his lack of success in placing his own creative writing gave him opportunities to see firsthand the ways in which writing by any African American without Washington's stature or story (and without a full-time agent to refine and promote it) found few avenues to publication. Fortune also knew from experience that there were other, more immediate reasons that Black writers achieved limited success: for the most part, they lacked both money and time. His own finances were perpetually in a dismal state, and although Washington recognized *The Future of the American Negro* to be a lucrative publication, very little money seemed to trickle down to Fortune. He continued to write for the *New York Age*, but, as he told Washington, "the Age only yields one $20 a week, and my fixed charges are $40." From time to time, Fortune addressed payment directly with Washington. "I am in the position of being unable to do the work *without the pay in advance*," he confessed in one letter. He was having trouble making "ends meet," as "the pay is miserly." It wasn't just that Fortune could not pay his bills or support his family; without time to dedicate to his writing, his own literary aspirations were at stake. Alongside Fortune's work for Washington and his journalism, Fortune was always trying to carve out the time and space to dedicate to his own creative writing, setting for himself the same agenda he was pursuing for Washington, to become recognized as an author. He pursued this goal with what he termed a "settled determination to break through the difficulty in literary lives." Fortune knew he needed to attend to his own career with the sort of forcefulness, attention, and diligence he was giving to Washington's bid for authorship. He clearly articulated his determination to do just this: "I am going to bull the publishers of books, and with the work and sacrifice of the next six months in that line I hope to *create* some permanent results," he told Washington.[94] But he also knew that "permanent results" would require the investment of time—something his financial situation would not allow. "If I only had four months away off in a corner to finish ['After War Times'] and 'The Man without a race' I could hope for substantial results."[95]

His hopes for "permanent results" and "substantial" ones were frustrated, however, even in the moments when they seemed most possible. When the publisher F. Tennyson Neely accepted his book of poems, on the condition that Fortune "stand half the cost of production, $200, taking 234 copies of the book to cover it," Fortune sought and received funding, only to have the publisher declare bankruptcy ten days after he made his payment.[96] "I guess my $200 has gone glimmering up salt lake," Fortune would tell Washington. "I am as blue as indigo. There *seems to be no success for me*."[97] For Fortune, who was subject to depression, this sort of hopeless despair was not unfamiliar; the gloom that would settle on him as he contemplated the dismal state of his affairs often lasted for weeks at a time. But his defeated stance here also speaks volumes about how hard it was to become recognized as an author, even for someone whose talents as a writer had been recognized.

Manipulating the "Western Publishers"

In the fall of 1899, as Fortune sank more deeply into depression at his inability to launch his own literary career, Washington was on the verge of tremendous and unprecedented literary success. Most critics cite Washington's 1900 contract with the publisher Doubleday, Page for what would become the autobiography *Up from Slavery*, or William Dean Howells's recognition of that work in the *North American Review* in August 1901, as signs that heralded Washington's arrival as an author. Indeed, both the contract and the review reveal that Washington had gained full entry to the white-dominated literary marketplace. There were, however, two other critical milestones—literary crises, as it were,—that effectively show the evolution of Washington's authorship between 1896 and 1900, and, by extension, Fortune's success as a literary coordinator. The first is Washington's effort to manipulate, and then manage, his agreement with the Nichols Company, the subscription publisher that had enthusiastically accepted his autobiography for publication in 1897, when Doubleday, Page expressed interest in publishing his autobiography in 1899. The second crisis involved the false claim that Washington was the author of *A New Negro for a New Century* when the collection appeared in 1900. Both incidents illustrate the extent to which Washington was successful at occupying the space of authorship, a position he assumed largely without writing.

As we will see, however, while becoming an author was one thing, managing and controlling Washington's authorship amid rising confidence in its commercial viability would be another. As publishers embraced the image Washington projected in print as culturally and intellectually palatable to their readers, the literary marketplace proved a difficult place for Fortune and Washington to successfully navigate. In this shifting literary environment, Fortune would struggle to negotiate the business side of Washington's success, fighting to ensure that he exploited every possible opportunity for publication without himself being exploited. This would result in a new set of dilemmas and a complex tangle of situations that underscore both Washington and Fortune's fundamentally uneasy relationship to the world of print.

The first of these situations began to unfold in November 1899, when Emmett Scott wrote to tell Washington that "Mr. Henry Wysham Lanier, who is connected with the Doubleday and McClure Company" had visited Tuskegee in Washington's absence and expressed interest in publishing "a forty or fifty thousand word book."[98] This pronouncement, alongside the fact that the publisher had sent someone all the way to Tuskegee to deliver the message in person, was itself a sign of Washington's success as an author. But Scott immediately perceived the impending dilemma: "I am very certain," he told Washington, "that what he wants is such a work as you are doing for Nicholls and Company [sic]." Here was a publisher, Scott wistfully thought, with "a prestige so much greater and a vaster amount of money to push their publications," than the Nichols Company. In 1897, when Washington made the agreement with them, no prestigious trade publisher had believed Washington's writing would sell. In two short years this situation had changed: not only was Doubleday, McClure interested in publishing Washington's autobiography, but their representative had told Scott they were interested in publishing "anything at all that [he] could give them."[99]

Scott wisely protected Washington's options. He said "nothing to Mr. Lanier about the Nichols' book, only speaking to him about the Small, Maynard publication [*The Future of the American Negro*] of which they know."[100] Like Scott, Washington recognized immediately that his agreement with the Nichols Company compromised his ability to freely accept other, more attractive, and potentially more lucrative publishing opportunities. Unhindered, though, Washington quietly pursued the inquiry from Doubleday, McClure. The publisher planned "to have me write my life running it first through McClure's Magazine and after putting it into book form," he told Scott. Washington's life story would have the advantage of attracting a readership in a prestigious magazine before being published in book form by a major trade press. It was, Washington told Scott, "a very generous proposition" that he hoped to get himself "into a position to accept."[101]

Washington seems to have at first believed he could get out of the Nichols contract, or that, by rushing the project along and trying to finish it in the short time before the end of 1899, he could avoid the perception of conflict between the two works. But, given the intermittent progress that had been made on the manuscript over the previous two years, and the overall disorganized state of that project, finishing the autobiography for the Nichols Company would not be a quick or an easy job. As usual, Washington turned to Fortune for counsel. Fortune's advice clearly shows his concern that Washington not jeopardize his reputation by producing a shoddy product, if he could not get out of that contract; he had good information that the Nichols Company had a reputation for doing inferior work. "If you are going to run that book in I am [anxious?] it should be watched closely at every stage," Fortune advised. "You can't afford to rush into print anymore."[102] Washington could no longer be associated with anything but exceptional literary efforts; Fortune understood Washington's stature to have shifted, and his status as an author could only be maintained by ensuring the high quality of his literary work.

Washington delayed making a decision about the Doubleday, McClure offer, leaving Fortune in the dark about the status of the contract with the Nichols Company. Celebrating for a moment Washington's wealth of opportunities, and their lucrative nature, Fortune wrote, "If you could fire all the orders in hand for autobiographies you could easily retire to a farm and live on your interest." Still, the letter's finale returned to the question for which Fortune really needed an answer: "By the way, what has become of the Naperville book?"[103] Fortune continued to be concerned about the quality of the production; if the Nichols autobiography was moving forward, they would need to take the time to ensure that it was properly shepherded into print. Three days later, Washington's intention was clear: they would move forward with the Nichols autobiography. Fortune had received some part of the manuscript and wrote to tell Washington he was "working on it."[104] One week later, he was deep into the process of reviewing it.

Fortune would continue to devote his full attention to the manuscript throughout the winter and spring of 1900. As he had predicted, it was a mess, requiring nothing less than a complete rewriting. Some of the responsibility for this lay with Edgar Webber, the man hired two years earlier to help Washington: he did not have the experience needed to work on a project of the autobiography's size or scope. But Webber had received little supervision from Washington, and it had proved difficult to make progress on the manuscript without consistent input from the man whose life was its subject and who was its purported writer. Webber described the process of composition to Fortune: "I went over the work and made an outline for it before anything was written, making at the same time a memorandum of all authorities, documents, newspaper clippings, magazine articles, etc. that have been used either directly or indirectly." Working from this outline and detailed memorandum, Washington had apparently been loosely involved in filling in the wording of the manuscript itself, talking Webber and others through some of what he wished to say. After that, as Webber told Fortune, the "work of grouping into chapters, choosing a name for each chapter, and making the table of contents which appears at the beginning of each chapter also fell to me, besides the duty of correcting the MS when it came to me from the typewriter to whom it was dictated."[105] This method resulted in considerable disorganization, which was reflected in the text Fortune received. Rather than give it a final, cursory reading, Fortune was left to piece the book together from odd and disorganized pages that arrived on his doorstep with apologetic notes from Webber.[106] Fortune's task was to fix the manuscript, making its various fragmented and largely unfinished parts cohere. Like Washington, Webber counted on Fortune to make the manuscript presentable to both publisher and readers alike.

Fortune was exasperated with these demands, and he recognized how the series of inefficiencies could produce a book that would not enhance, but endanger, Washington's reputation as an author. The Nichols Company was impatient to get the book out, and, in Fortune's opinion, was altogether too willing to compromise on its quality. Because he insisted on correcting mistakes—which was costly after the book had been typeset—the Nichols Company, in the end, simply bypassed him and told him that they would read the proofs. Fortune's attempt to get the book "on the market *as nearly correct as possible*" was thwarted by publishers who wanted to "rush" to meet the orders, they told Fortune, that "are pouring in on us for this book."[107]

As Fortune dedicated his time to fixing *The Story of My Life and Work*, Washington's attention during the first three months of 1900 was devoted to the second autobiography project. Walter Hines Page, who had resigned as editor of the *Atlantic* and bought a stake in what would in early 1900 become Doubleday, Page, proposed that Washington pursue that project, which he had first broached in 1896. This time, impressed by the quality and success of *The Future of the American Negro* as a trade publication, Page suggested that the manuscript be published serially in the *Outlook*, which would stimulate interest in the book and also attract what he described to

Washington as a "somewhat more serious minded class of readers" than *Mc-Clure's* would have provided.[108] Page guaranteed Washington a solid contract, "on terms which I have no hesitancy in assuring you now will be satisfactory to you." He expressed confidence that the book would not only be a boon to "the good cause" Washington represented, but would also achieve "a very considerable financial success."[109]

As promised, Page outlined and solidified the terms of the book publication in late January 1900, telling Washington that "it seems to us that a fair rate for the book publication would be a 10% royalty on the first 2500 copies, and 12½% on the second 2500 and 15% on all copies sold thereafter. Does this strike you favorably?"[110] Page posed this question again and again, trying to confirm Washington's agreement while Washington delayed, quietly weighing the question of whether he could get out of his commitment to the Nichols Company, or whether moving forward on both fronts would be seen by either of the parties involved as a breach of contract. It is clear that Page knew from the beginning of their discussions at least something about the Nichols situation, but he appears not to have held the company or their contract with Washington in high enough regard to believe it presented a real obstacle to Washington's entering into an agreement with Doubleday, Page. While he recognized that the "situation" with what he derisively termed the "western publishers" complicated Doubleday, Page's deal with Washington, he did not see it as insurmountable. Indeed, he dismissed Washington's contract with the Nichols Company ("the people in Chicago," as Page called them) as a mere "technical obligation."[111]

Washington too was determined that the Doubleday, Page project would go forward. But by the time *The Story of My Life and Work* was published in late May 1900, he had still not mentioned to the Nichols Company his intention to write a second autobiography for Doubleday, Page. The book's publication would bring with it more reasons for Washington to regret having made a decision to publish with the Nichols Company in the first place. Despite Fortune's considerable labors to wrestle it into shape in the winter and into the spring of 1900, the finished book was, as Fortune had predicted it would be, a mess. On June 1, 1900, Fortune wrote to Washington to express his indignation over the state of *The Story of My Life and Work*; it did not come close to meeting the standards he had set for Washington's writing. The book was filled with inadvertently blank pages, printed on what he termed "execrable white paper" and was "chock full of typographical and aesthetic blemishes." However, flawed as it was, Fortune still saw an opportunity to make it part of a larger public record. He advised Washington to send a copy to Thomas Calloway, the prominent African American lawyer and educator who, together with Daniel Murray and W. E. B. Du Bois, was organizing the Exhibit of American Negroes at the 1900 World's Fair in Paris. Having Washington's book in the "Paris collection" would help it become part of the "literary" record of African American accomplishments. He was also touched that Washington publicly acknowledged their friendship in the book.[112]

Washington agreed with Fortune's assessment of *The Story of My Life and Work*; but by this point, he was less interested in that book's quality than he was in figuring out what he would say to the Nichols Company when they discovered he had entered into an agreement with another publisher to simultaneously market what was to be conceptually a strikingly similar book. By September, Washington had spent considerable time working on talking points for conversations with the Nichols Company about the Doubleday, Page autobiography, which was well underway. These points illuminate the various strategies he came up with to lessen the perception of a conflict between the two books, or at least to make things right by proposing compensation for the damage done. An undated memo, most likely not shared directly with the Nichols Company but used internally by Washington and his staff to think through how to approach the publishers about the situation, offers a sense of his thinking on the matter.

1   Book will not interfere with the other as it is different and will be sold only in stores, etc.
2   Permitted the increase in price which reduced revenue without objection.
3   Will take special pains to assist in circulating book.
4   The two classes of readers are wholly separate and the territory is different.
5   Wish to do it for the benefit of school and cannot ruin chance. In proportion as the school is a success there will be demand for Nichols book.
6   As a matter of last resort will write a new book on some subject without cost.[113]

Overall, the list confirms that Washington knew that, in committing to the second autobiography, he had disregarded the terms of his contract with the Nichols Company. He was now intent on manipulating the Nichols Company into seeing this violation as minor or irrelevant, or that it was something done only after the Nichols Company had changed the terms of their agreement. The list's second item—that Washington had permitted the Nichols Company to change the price of the book without complaint— had indeed been flagged by Fortune as a major infraction of the company's agreement with Washington. Fortune was, of course, particularly sensitive to money matters, and the change in pricing, which had not been discussed, left him inclined to argue that Washington owed nothing to the publishers of *The Story of My Life and Work*, leaving him free to make whatever arrangements he pleased with Doubleday, Page.[114]

Washington wanted to set up a tit-for-tat situation, where his sly commitment to do a second autobiography with another publisher simply balanced out the Nichols Company's covert alteration of the price of the book. For Washington, this was not a matter to be taken to the courts, but one to use strategically to mitigate any problems that might arise once the first publisher learned of the second autobiography. He was not interested in suing the Nichols Company, but he thought "it will help matters to scare them a little."[115] Fortune agreed: because the Nichols people were what he called "hard fisted money men who are looking to the dollar always and not to the sentiment of the thing," Washington could get "substantial" concessions from them by a threat to their bottom line.[116]

The principal concession Washington sought was, of course, the Nichols Company's approval of the Doubleday, Page autobiography. Early in September, Washington sent a barrage of representatives to confer with the publisher and present a rationale for the coexistence of both autobiographies; this group included Scott and Washington's Chicago-based attorney, S. Laing Williams. Unsurprisingly, they found Hertel reluctant to approve of the publication of the second autobiography. By the end of the meeting he would insist that he didn't even have the power, as a mere employee of the firm, to give such permission without a full consultation of the board. Washington did not meet with Hertel in person, but he addressed the matter in a letter to him in which he cast his bid for the company's approval as a courtesy rather than a requirement: "So far as the mere letter of the law is concerned I feel quite sure I could go ahead and publish the Reminiscences and be sustained in doing so, but it has been my rule to deal frankly and sympathetically with my publishers." He asserted that the two texts would not conflict because they were "to be on different lines and to be sold in an almost wholly different section of the country and to be sold by the trade instead of by subscription." He went so far as to tell Hertel that, in fact, the second autobiography would actually help the sales of the first, assuring him that "what I have planned to do for the other people will help your book since you know that anything that keeps my name before the public will assist in increasing the sale of your book."[117]

Washington was astute to articulate his understanding of the different geographies and audiences reached by the different publishers, and he also understood the value of the Nichols Company. More than once in the short letter, Washington expressed his desire to remain on friendly terms with the firm, insisting that he wanted to work "with [Hertel and the Nichols Company] and not in opposition to [them]." He wrote, "I shall hope in the future to do more business with you in regard to publishing books," insisting that he was at the beginning of his career as an author, and that he neither wanted nor could afford to burn bridges. "I don't want this to be the last by any means," he told Hertel. Washington's sentimental insistence that he wished to "keep in close and sympathetic touch" with Hertel, coupled with his assurance that the other book was to be "on different lines" than *The Story of My Life and Work*, most likely helped to soften Hertel's stance.[118] By early October, Hertel wrote to say that the Nichols Company would not object to the publication of the other book.

It was not until the new autobiography began to appear in the *Outlook* in November of 1900 that Hertel knew he had been duped. He was "really surprised" to discover that the new book was to be "an autobiography pure and simple," he complained to Washington, since Washington had misled the Nichols people to believe their concern about it was "making a howl out of nothing." Now they fully appreciated the situation. "This is doing us a great injustice," Hertel wanted Washington to know. "When this question came up . . . we hesitated considerably, but when we were assured that you were going to write a series of sketches entitled 'Reminiscences' and that the subject matter and the *title* was to be entirely different from that of our book we consented. We stated very specifically that the title should be such that this book could not be confused with your Autobiography, 'The Story of My Life.'" Hertel knew that, at this point, Washington would do nothing about the infraction, but he wanted Washington to understand the potential damage done to sales of the first autobiography by a second's entering the market. Booksellers would be loath to sell a book that was simultaneously being reprinted "in a monthly newspaper." The Nichols Company had put "lots of money and energy" into the book, he wrote and, in a thinly veiled threat, were "planning to get out another 10,000 edition which we shall do unless the Autobiography in the 'Outlook' interferes materially."[119]

In the end, the Nichols Company did put out another edition, and they had tremendous success with the book. By 1903, they had sold 75,000 copies, while the Doubleday, Page book had sold only 30,000. Even though modern scholars tend to embrace *Up from Slavery* as Washington's quintessential autobiography, it was *The Story of My Life and Work* that was, as Anthony Bly notes, the "bestseller in its day."[120] Sales of *The Story of My Life and Work* don't seem to have been damaged by the nearly simultaneous appearance of a second autobiography on the market. The reason is because the Nichols Company's target audience and their sales methods differed significantly from those of Doubleday, Page. Not until late in 1905 did the Nichols Company believe the principal "territory for the book (the South)" had been "pretty well worked over." They still thought that the region had potential buyers, though, since, as they noted, the cotton crop was good that year, "the colored people are employed" and therefore had money to spend on a book as widely valued as Washington's life story.[121] The publisher's intention to sell "between four and five thousand books between [October of 1905] and the New Year" seems ambitious, but by November they reported having sold 562 books, with the goal to average 500 copies a month "for another year or two."[122]

As Washington expanded the circle of his travel, sales of the book expanded as well. Late in 1905, for instance, he went to Arkansas, Oklahoma, and what he described as the "Indian Territories"; he followed up with the Nichols Company after this trip, asking them to make a special effort to market his book in these areas.[123] Anywhere Washington traveled to speak, the Nichols Company would "immediately advertise in the large dailies of those cities."[124] They also offered gifts upon the purchase of their books, like a free "Bird's Eye View of Tuskegee," or a "large portrait" of the author himself.[125] All of these worked to ensure that *The Story of My Life and Work* was consistently visible and attractive to potential buyers. Washington himself was surprised at the book's success, not only in terms of its sales but also its impact. "Everywhere I go I am constantly surprised to meet the large number of colored men and women who tell me that they have been helped in many directions by reading this book," he wrote to Hertel in the fall of 1905.[126] The Nichols Company also reported to him that they likewise received letters from customers who had "been greatly helped reading [Washington's] book." These letters, they confirmed, came not only from Black readers; by 1905, they had "received many similar letters from white people." The book, wrote a company representative, was "exercising an influence for good that can never be properly estimated."[127] In this light, it becomes evident that Washington was right to do everything he could to preserve his relationship with the Nichols Company, which marketed books differently than the New York trade publishers. Doubleday, Page allowed him access to an elite, Northern, highly educated market while the Nichols Company enabled him to tap into an altogether different audience, in a different region of the nation, through which he would also both magnify the sphere of his authorship and make money.

"Mr. Washington Has Been Imposed Upon"

If Washington had not already put himself in hot water with regard to the Nichols Company's fury over the publication of the second autobiography, the brouhaha over his authorship of the collection *A New Negro for a New Century* might not have appeared to him and to his closest advisors as the crisis it did. But, arising in the midst of the development of a strategy that would mitigate his contract dispute with the Nichols Company, Washington's apparent authorship of the collection *A New Negro for a New Century* became his second literary crisis in 1900. The book appeared in July, reviving Fortune's anger at what he saw as the injustice of his low payment for the work he did on Washington's behalf. "I have a copy of 'The New Negro of the New Century'—the first 100 pages of which are ours," he wrote to Scott on July 13, 1900. "I cuss every time I [think of] the $100 they swindled us out of. There is [a] good $200 worth of work in that contribution and that is what they stipulated to pay." Written in longhand, the missing words in this letter are indicative of Fortune's fury at the situation, which had not ebbed but was intensified by the fact that he had also not received what he considered fair payment for the work he did on *The Story of My Life and Work*. By the fall of 1900, he remained so enraged with both the Nichols Company and the American Publishing House, the publisher for *A New Negro for a New Century*, that he initiated a conversation with Washington's lawyer, S. Laing Williams, about both issues.[128]

The problem with the American Publishing House would exceed the matter of Fortune's compensation, in part because it further jeopardized Washington's relationship with the Nichols Company. The American Publishing House had misrepresented Washington's role in the book's production; in Washington's words, he found himself "represented as the author of [*A New Negro for a New Century*] . . . when of course this is not true."[129] Washington was indeed not the author of the book. Although Fortune's writing for this volume had exceeded what had been requested, in the end it had been fewer than one hundred pages of a book of over four hundred pages. In fact, much of the book was a reworking of an earlier collection, *The White Side of a Black Subject*, by the Reverend Norman B. Wood, which the

American Publishing House originally published in 1897. In that volume, Wood was listed as the sole author and the holder of the book's copyright; his name remained on the title page of *A New Negro for a New Century*, alongside that of another contributor, Fannie Barrier Williams. But the publisher had taken advantage of Washington's popularity and renown, placing his name most prominently on the title page in a way that suggested his overarching responsibility for the book's content. The image of Washington on the book's cover reinforced this impression: taken by Elmer Chickering, a white studio photographer with a reputation for his portraits of the famous and the elite, it had first appeared on the cover of *Munsey's Magazine* in 1899 and quickly became the most widely reproduced and distributed of Washington's portraits. It was, in fact, the same image that the Nichols Company had selected for use on the cover of their most expensive binding of *The Story of My Life and Work*, a book published in the same month as *A New Negro for a New Century*.

Although Washington had contributed to *A New Negro for a New Century*, submitting the two essays Fortune had worked up on Negro soldiers and Negro education, the driving force behind the compilation was J. E. MacBrady, the president of the American Publishing House; he is plainly listed in the book as both the holder of its copyright and the author of its preface.[130] It is no surprise that Washington was perceived to be the book's author. MacBrady's purpose in his prominent positioning of Washington's name and his image in *A New Negro for a New Century* was to help market the book; the visual and textual cues pointing to Washington's authorship would ensure steady sales. It's likely that the company also pushed Fortune to keep expanding the scope of the essays he wrote on Washington's behalf for *A New Negro for a New Century* as a part of a calculated effort to increase the size and, therefore, the apparent significance of Washington's contributions to the volume. By 1900, there were many collections of writing geared toward African Americans, all of them similar books that presented Black history alongside visual and verbal portraits of accomplished African Americans as a way of promoting racial identity and pride. The American Publishing House's decision to revamp its 1897 volume, with some changes, under a new, inspirational title that called attention to the shift in Black identity promised by the new century, was a shrewd attempt to capitalize on the historical moment and Washington's prominence by manufacturing a fiction of his authorship. Given what we know about Washington's efforts to promote himself in print and, in particular, his desire to be seen as a book author in the years leading up to 1900, his disavowal of authorship

3.4 Cover of Booker T. Washington's *A New Negro for a New Century* (1900).

may seem odd. As the presumed author of the collection, he would have received gratuitous recognition for a book that even he admitted, in a letter written to MacBrady in July 1900, "shows up well."[131] But he was adamant about setting the record straight that he had not authored *A New Negro for a New Century*. Washington expressed his displeasure forcefully in a letter to Emmett Scott, whom he had asked to look into the matter: "Please let me know what answer you have received from the American Publishing House in Chicago. The fraud which they have perpetrated is outrage[ou]s." Washington's determination to take action to disassociate himself from *A New Negro for a New Century*—to find the means to "have the circulation of the book stopped, at least, in its present form"—offers a window through which to see the precarious nature of Washington's authorship.[132] Just as it had required extensive management to make Washington into an author, it was an identity that, by 1900, would require extensive management to control.

While Fortune remained incensed because he felt swindled out of the full payment he deserved for the writing he had done on Washington's behalf for *A New Negro for a New Century*, Washington's concerns were broader, and they return us to the terms of his contract with the Nichols Company for *The Story of My Life and Work*. The agreement had stipulated that Washington was forbidden to write on Negro-related subjects "for any other subscription book publisher during the life of his contract with us." That this clause was included in the contract suggests the Nichols Company's awareness of the potentially lucrative niche they had uncovered in marketing books on "Negro-related subjects"; it also implies their consciousness of the potential for competition in this arena, which would dilute the market and jeopardize the sales of their books. The American Publishing House's *A New Negro for a New Century* was just the kind of subscription book that the terms of the contract with the Nichols Company had anticipated; it was clearly a book on race-related subjects, and its publication and marketing would most likely place it in competition with *Progress of a Race*. In fact, the Nichols Company feared that *A New Negro for a New Century* would compete not only with *Progress of a Race*, but also with Washington's autobiography, even though the two books represented completely different genres. Already dealing with the repercussions of his decision to publish a second autobiography with Doubleday, Page in violation of his agreement with the Nichols Company, Washington worried that his apparent authorship of *A New Negro for a New Century* would cause more problems with the firm, who would perceive his authorship of that text to be a further violation of their contract.

The situation was made murkier by the fact that, although he was not the volume's author, Washington *had* been involved in *A New Negro for a New Century*, at least to some extent. He admitted this much in his letter to MacBrady, in July 1900. But, he continued, "I do not remember to have authorized you to use my picture on the front page or cover nor to publish my name in connection with the matter which I wrote for you." On the contrary, he continued, "my remembrance is that I advised that it would not be possible for me to grant" this permission.[133] It's interesting to note here that Washington appears to have agreed to contribute to the book only if his name was not used in connection with it; he intended his writing— really Fortune's writing on his behalf—to appear in the collection without his being identified as its author. Given this, the promotion of Washington as the book's most prominent author ran counter to his initial determination that his role in the project be entirely anonymous.

Washington's lawyer was left in the awkward position of trying to appease the Nichols Company as he worked to coerce the American Publishing House to make changes to subsequent printings of *A New Negro for a New Century*. After he reviewed the existing correspondence between "author" and publisher, he determined that it was not realistic for Washington to try to "have the circulation of the book stopped," as Washington had wished.[134] Instead, the publisher agreed to identify precisely where Washington's "contribution begins and ends," so that it was clear that he was not the sole contributor to the volume.[135] These changes would then permit him to "disclaim responsibility of authorship" for *A New Negro for a New Century*.[136] The other factor that made it seem that Washington was the author of the book was the photograph on the cover, and on this point the lawyer found himself with no grounds for objection, since, as the lawyer told his client, Washington had granted them "the use of your picture 'in' the book." In the end, Williams told Washington, that was the best outcome they could expect: "I believe you have gained all that it would be possible to get by a lawsuit."[137]

The fact that Washington had in fact had *some* involvement in *A New Negro for a New Century* made Williams's conversations with the Nichols Company particularly sensitive. Washington's impulse was to show them his correspondence with the American Publishing House as a way of proving his limited role in the production of *A New Negro for a New Century*. But Williams thought this unwise. While he had forwarded one letter to the Nichols Company for their review, "I did not think it advisable to show him all of your correspondence," he told Washington. He reasoned that the "letters to the American Publishing House dated Nov. 29th—1899 and Jan. 16th—1899 might be construed by them as not sufficiently regardful of your contract with them." To lessen the damage they predicted *A New Negro for a New Century* would do to sales of *Progress of a Race* on the subscription market, the Nichols Company asked Washington to write up a document for selling agents downplaying his connection with *A New Negro for a New Century*; this document, they hoped, would give them some way to distinguish between the Nichols Company's books and *A New Negro for a New Century*. Williams did not try to dissuade Washington from writing the letter, but he did issue a warning. "Permit me to further advise you," he wrote, "that if you write a letter which may be used by the Nichols Co. with their agents, that it is so worded as to show just the facts of your connection with 'The New Negro For A New Century.' The use of such terms as 'To deceive the public' and criticisms of their [the American Publishing House's] method of publishing the book after changes have been made may involve you in some difficulties." Williams identified the tightrope Washington walked as he manipulated his agreement with both publishing venues in a way that would serve his interests and antagonize neither of theirs. Whereas Washington had wanted a lawsuit, Williams seemed to recognize the layers of exploitation that had been mobilized around Washington's authorship, both by the publishing firms and by Washington himself. He was intent on quashing protests from both parties, going so far as to say that he would caution Hertel in the same way he cautioned Washington, to avoid inciting the American Publishing House to any further confrontation. "I have already told Mr. Hertel to be careful about this [using the phrase or implying the company's intention to 'to deceive the public,' and criticizing their methods of publishing], for your protection," he wrote to Washington, "and I shall further caution him."[138]

No one was happy with the American Publishing House's response to the situation. Washington felt the publisher had deceived him, and Fortune felt he had not been paid for the work that he did. The Nichols Company believed that they had been dealt with in bad faith. Williams continued to insist that Washington would have been ill-advised to attempt to pursue a resolution through any "legal process," which, he told Washington, "would have been quite expensive and annoying, with perhaps unsatisfactory results."[139] He told his client that he hoped to persuade the American Publishing House to change the cover for the next edition, but the revised edition issued a year later foiled that plan by stating that the book was "by Booker T. Washington and Others."[140] Because it was "a matter of fact" that the book had been written by "Mr. Washington and Others," Williams determined, "the publisher puts himself beyond our reach."[141]

For the lawyer, the lesson in all this is that an author required a firm contract instead of informal terms established through unofficial correspondence. As Williams told Scott in confidence, "Mr. Washington has been imposed upon, but the fact is he did not sufficiently protect himself in his original agreement."[142] In the case of *A New Negro for a New Century*, Washington had indeed been imposed upon, but what the lawyer was perhaps less willing or able to admit is that Washington freely imposed upon others as well in an effort to capitalize on all the publishing opportunities that came his way. In negotiating the world of authorship, Washington and his entourage were taken advantage of, but they also took advantage of others, practicing their own form of deception by carefully cultivating and maintaining relationships with publishers in a way that provided both the financial reward and the cultural and intellectual capital that Washington needed.

"We Are out of Harmony and Should Separate"

As publishing opportunities became more and more accessible, Washington would continue to depend on Fortune. In addition to *The Future of the American Negro* and the two autobiographies, Fortune would prepare a fourth publication for Washington in the spring of 1900: *Sowing and Reaping*, a collection published by Boston's L. C. Page & Co. for their series "A Day's Work." The slim volumes that made up this series, which consisted on average of thirty-five pages and measured 5¼ × 7¾ inches, were small enough for readers to tuck into a pocket and featured what one reviewer described as "a distinctive message which is given with force or interest."[143] Washington had instructed Scott to "set some good careful person at work on it and let them decide what subject will be covered by any portion of the manuscript," noting his willingness to "pay the individual for his work."[144] This was perhaps a pro forma request, as Washington likely knew that Fortune would step in himself. Soon after, Fortune wrote to Washington, explaining that, after being delayed by the task of completing *The Story of My Life and Work*, he was hard at work on *Sowing and Reaping*. He had fully taken over the project, explaining to Washington that he had picked a focus for the collection and "made the text read as far as possible for the book reading public instead of for the Tuskegee students." While Fortune was pleased with the results, he was perhaps even more pleased by the fact that the *Sowing and Reaping* project had inspired him to conceive of yet another, future project, in which more of Washington's words and ideas "should be carefully edited for preservation in book form." By this point, Fortune knew that finding a publisher would not be difficult: the goal of crafting for Washington a literary presence had been achieved. "Any publisher would take the book for the Fall or Winter trade," Fortune predicted, acknowledging that Washington was a hot commodity in the literary world. He closed by volunteering his own services for what he hoped would be a well-paying manuscript. It was a rare moment when Fortune would name the price that he felt was fair compensation for the work: "I would like to go off in a quiet corner in the Summer time and do the work. I think it could be properly done for $250 and the manuscript should be worth at least $2000 to you outright, or a possibly larger return in royalty arrangements." [145] The ratio he indicates here, where he would get a mere one-eighth of Washington's earnings, offers significant insight into the difference between the value of Fortune's writing and of Washington's authorship.

Emmett Scott would call *Sowing and Reaping* "a splendid little publication." When Washington gave him a copy of the book as a gift, Scott sent a quick note reflecting on the great year of Washington's authorship: "Have you thought of how much literary work you have done within the past 12 months. . . . You have abundant reason to be proud of it all." Washington, he concluded, had made a deeply impressive "showing" in "a literary way."[146] Washington clearly embraced his identity as an author, performing it more and more frequently, not only by continuing to embark on book projects but also by visually inhabiting the role. When Doubleday, Page published *Working with the Hands*, a sequel to *Up from Slavery*, in 1904, the title page would be preceded by an image of Washington sitting at his desk, pen in hand, ink at the ready, seemingly caught while writing. In Frances Benjamin Johnston's photograph, Washington has assumed a pose that, as Shawn Michelle Smith rightly notes, is "a classic way of suggesting his intellect, power, and importance."[147] Positioned as if poised to add more words to the paper in front of him, flanked by stacks of books, Washington presents himself as a consummate man of letters. Tellingly, he industrializes but also romanticizes writing in *Working with the Hands*, identifying it as a useful "tool of close, accurate thinking." His description of it as such suggests the extent to which he embraced writing as a part of his identity and found ways to speak of it as in keeping with Tuskegee's vision: "There is something, I think, in the handling of a tool that has the same relation to close, accurate thinking that writing with a pen has in the preparation of a manuscript. Nearly all persons who write much will agree, I think, that one can produce much more

3.5 *Mr. Washington in His Office at Tuskegee,* by Frances Benjamin Johnston (1904), the frontispiece to Booker T. Washington's *Working with the Hands.*

satisfactory work by using the pen than by dictation."[148] The irony, of course, was that Washington was prone to dictating and had a reputation for doing so. He saw, however, the value of presenting himself as someone who, as the title of his book put it, works with his "hands." It was as an author, not an orator, that Washington staked his claim to leadership in the new century.

The carefully composed image of solitary authorship projected in this photograph obviously belies the collective effort that stood behind Washington's literary pursuits, as well as the difficulty of writing and publishing for African Americans at the turn of the century. Washington was the author—indeed, he had become a literary center. But others made that identity possible by writing for him and by developing the early strategies by which his books found their way into publication. The human and the literary costs of this calculated effort were considerable, and they were assumed most directly and most concretely by T. Thomas Fortune. Fortune's efforts to make Washington into a literary center for Black writing had all but consumed him. Fortune believed in the necessity of his effort; it was a form of patriotism to his race and to Washington's leadership. But it cost him dearly. Fortune at times enjoyed the exalted feeling of being Washington's literary partner, but he also at times suffered the depressing reality of being so exploited by him that he had no time for his own literary pursuits. At the height of their literary partnership, the years between the publication of *Black-Belt Diamonds* and *Up from Slavery*, Fortune was obsessive in his correspondence with Washington, creating a sort of intimacy with him that must have seemed to obliterate the distance that existed between them, which was both physical and, increasingly, related to the differences in their stature. These letters reveal that he was often left feeling neglected and underappreciated as he waited for Washington's responses and his validation. "I seek always to satisfy you in the quality of the work I turn out on your orders to me," he would write to Washington on May 17, 1900, in response to the news that the manuscript of *Sowing and Reaping* had met with the publisher's approval. And yet it sometimes seemed that his commitment to writing for Washington had no limits. He reflected on it as a form of addiction that left his own life in shambles. "*I shall have to reform*," he said, in an exchange with Emmett Scott on the time spent with and working for Washington, "as my affairs are going to _____."[149] Fortune's letters to Scott frequently echo this one: "I am worked off my heels with book proof, monograph, Age et al. ad nauseum. Bah." The final line of this letter—"O, for a lodge in some vast wilderness"—is indicative of his propensity to dramatically use literary references to relay his own fluctuating emotions. [150] But, tellingly, the poem from which he quotes, William Cowper's "Slavery," also suggests the degree to which Fortune sometimes felt himself inescapably bound by literary responsibilities that were not his own, in a power arrangement that left him feeling powerless. As Washington's primary writer, he did not himself feel entirely "up from slavery."

The most significant casualty of Fortune's promotion of Washington as an author was that it left him little time or energy for his own writing. Hard work for Washington left him exhausted. Coupled with that, he was plagued by health problems that limited his productivity. Excessive drinking became more and more problematic for Fortune, and even though from time to time he reported that he had "stopped lushing and shall not begin again," he continued to show a weakness for alcohol.[151] All of these things combined to limit Fortune's energy for his own writing, to which he could never find the time to return. His determination to "pin down to the novel," for instance, made on April 17, 1901, is followed a month later by a report that the "novel is at a standstill, on account of my eyes."[152] His correspondence with Washington shows that he was constantly in the process of trying to finish his own writing projects; when he did complete some, these manuscripts faced the formidable task of finding a publisher. Despite his close proximity to and knowledge of the world of publishing, Fortune was unable to attract publishers for his own work. Self-publication was a viable option, and yet he always lacked the money to finance the venture.[153] Even his close association with Washington did not provide the "opening wedge" into the literary world that Fortune had hoped it would.[154] In the spring of 1901, for instance, Fortune submitted a book of poetry to Walter Hines Page, in hopes that he would be interested in publishing the collection under the imprint of Doubleday, Page. Page's rejection letter was full of praise for the work: "Your poetry is good; much of it, I think, very good, and our readers agree with me in this." Yet there was "no practical way to make a success with it in the market." As Page dismally informed him, "It is not the kind of excellence that is popular."[155] Fortune's initial reaction was to remain optimistic; he told Washington he was "disappointed; but shall try again."[156] One week later, this optimism had given way to anger and frustration. Page's judgment of his writing had clearly struck a nerve. My "poetry has merit all right," he wrote to Washington, "and I don't see why Page did not take it."[157]

As savvy as Fortune was in terms of promoting Washington's writing, he was naïve to think that Washington's success as a writer would serve as a segue to his own. Page's observation—that Fortune's poetry was "not the kind of excellence that is popular"—reeks of a publishing industry driven by popular expectations of Blackness and its appropriate subject matter and literary forms. Washington's "rags to riches" story as told in *Up from Slavery* was palatable to white readers, its conciliatory tone easily embraced as an acceptable rendering of Black leadership. Similarly, Paul Laurence Dunbar's dialect writing, which was also commercially successful around the turn of the century, reinforced racial stereotypes of African Americans and romanticized the Old South and plantation tradition, which were in keeping with how white readers wished to see African Americans. In Gene Jarrett's words, Dunbar's dialect poetry was considered by the literary establishment to be an "artistic manifestation of black authenticity."[158] But Fortune's writing did not fit into either of these molds, making it, according to trade publishing standards, not "Black enough" to be popular or commercially viable for Northern presses. Subscription publishers would also have been hard pressed to find a market for Fortune's work, which would not have appeared "valuable" in the terms appreciated by their consumers. Written in formal—or what critics of the time called "literary"—English, Fortune was committed to Western, classical poetic forms and their conventional diction, metrical structure, and rhyme schemes. For the most part, he addressed universal rather than racial themes in his poetry. Dunbar's formal, "literary English" poems were also criticized by the literary establishment, but his popularity and his professional success had been driven by his dialect poems, which Fortune condemned as "pure niggerism from the white man's point of view hashed up by a black man."[159] For himself, Dunbar had figured out what sort of writing he needed to do to find a publisher. "I didn't start as a dialect poet," he would tell James Weldon Johnson. "I simply came to the conclusion that I could write it as well, if not better, than anybody else I knew of, and that by doing so I should gain a hearing."[160] Fortune had figured out how to "gain a hearing" for Washington, and yet his own writing, which gravitated between fiery statements condemning racial injustice and sentimental poetry, was considered neither critically nor commercially viable by the publishers with whom Fortune aspired to work.[161]

The irony of the situation—that Washington won praise for writing he did not do, while Fortune's writing, deemed "very good" by the literary establishment, could not find a publisher—could not have been lost on Fortune. He would continue to serve as Washington's primary literary advisor, checking in with him about Washington's ongoing projects but also ensuring that Washington was conscious of the larger African American literary landscape in which Fortune saw both of their writing to be situated. In June 1901, for instance, Fortune guided Washington to *Overshadowed*, a new novel by Sutton E. Griggs. He deemed the novel "good work in some respects," but criticized Griggs's "fearful pessimism" as "almost as demoralizing as Dunbar's realism in 'The Sport of the Gods.'"[162] Washington's responses to these gestures were spotty, and he never seemed to register Fortune's effort to engage in conversation about literature as a means of thinking deeply about its efficacy and value, or in terms of the emergence of a Black aesthetic. Fortune appeared to grow tired of his behind-the-scenes role in Washington's affairs. This was exacerbated by the fact that, more and more often, he found Washington monitoring him and limiting what he could say, either directly or indirectly. In September 1901, for example, Fortune was furious at being told by one of Washington's colleagues that he "should say nothing about lynching and the like" at a Chicago convention.[163] Perhaps finally realizing the depth of their political difference, or maybe seeing an opportunity to escape this stifling work environment, he telegrammed Washington this short message: "We are out of harmony and should separate."[164] Washington, unwilling to lose his preeminent literary counsel, quickly patched up the rift. But this pattern became increasingly characteristic of the dynamic of their friendship.

Whereas Washington sought political control and power, Fortune's desires and his aspirations always revolved around and returned to literary work. "I want to make enough money to pay my debts and start fresh in purely literary work," he told Washington in November 1902.[165] He seemed incapable of starting fresh, however, and even the literary work he proposed seemed unlikely to be taken seriously. In 1903, for instance, Fortune wrote to Scott to say, "I am thinking of writing a philippic on the Negro question, naming it 'An Appeal from Caesar,' a book of some 200 pages, in which I shall rip the hide off the American people, in about fifteen chapters. I want to know what you think of it. I can have the ms. in shape by Oct. 1." Fortune's description of this work makes it appear to be a text he is offering to write for Washington. But from the subject matter of the book, and its aggressive promise to "rip the hide off the American people," it was unlikely to result in a book that Washington would want to claim as his own, or one for which Fortune would find a publisher with himself as author. Given this, Fortune's inquiry appears to be more of a plea for a sounding board. In asking, "Which would be the best title for the proposed book?," Fortune appears to be looking for someone to engage him in his own literary work as a way of gaining traction on his own writing.[166] It is telling that this person was not Washington, but his assistant, Emmett Scott, to whom, in Washington's perpetual absence, Fortune had grown close through the frequency of their communications.[167] In a fundamental way, Washington grew increasingly inaccessible to Fortune, their literary relationship a one-way street that was based on Fortune's literary prowess and his facilitation of Washington's career as an author. Once Washington was inside that world, Fortune's services became less valuable.

Despite Fortune's tremendous accomplishments as a writer and a literary mentor to Washington, he grew increasingly disappointed in what he himself had accomplished. By 1903, he had lost the respect of his colleagues in journalism, many of whom agreed he had become a "weak man." An editorial in the *Chicago Conservator* summed up this perspective:

> Twenty years ago every intelligent Negro in this country regarded Mr. Fortune as the coming national leader of the new-born citizens that needed only to labor and wait for the mantle of the great Fred Douglass to fall upon him. Then Mr. Fortune was known all over the country as the most fearless advocate of the manhood rights of the Negro in this country, Fred Douglass not excepted. . . . Had any Negro then, great or small, rose up and started to canvass the country with a view of spreading the sentiment that the Negro as a race should be trained for good servants and laborers only, that disenfranchisement of the Negro was a blessing rather than a curse. . . . We say, if any Negro in the days when Fortune was regarded as race loving and brave, had started out advocating these things, Tom Fortune would have met him on every corner and crossed swords with him and openly and loudly denounced him as an enemy to his race.[168]

This criticism must have stung, particularly as it suggested that Fortune had been poised to himself become the next "Fred Douglass," a mantle that for Fortune was so meaningful that he dedicated his literary career to ensuring it was assumed by Washington. Fortune would come to believe he had given Washington too much, telling Scott in 1904 that "other men look out for themselves exclusively."[169] But, by this point, he could neither recover his work as a respected journalist nor create for himself the literary career to which he aspired. His own work continued to be rejected, regardless of the directions he took to revise it. He continued to submit writing to publishers; in October 1903, he sent a collection of poems to the Century Publishing Company, telling Washington that he had "worked very hard on the revision of the work." He anticipated that there was a readership for his poetry, if only it could find a publisher willing to take a chance on it. "I am sure that it is in good shape for publication and that it would have a large sale if published," he said, "if the resistance of publishers to publish new verse could be overcome." His letter included this prescient prediction: "I would not be surprised if [I] should not have to pay for the publication of it myself some day."[170] That day would come in 1905, when Fortune privately published *Dreams of Life: Miscellaneous Poems.*

Other literary projects—the novels "The Man without a Race," about which Fortune spoke of finishing in 1899, and "After War Times," a book that he said would be an "eye-opener" about the reality of Reconstruction—appear not to have been completed. Fortune described "After War Times" as a novel about Reconstruction, centered in his home state of Florida. In 1901, he had completed eight chapters.[171] When it was finally published, however, it was not in the form of a novel, but as a sort of semiautobiographical retrospective that was serialized weekly in the *Norfolk Journal & Guide* and the *Philadelphia Tribune*, beginning in July 1927. Although the text as printed in these journals was written from a third-person perspective, it bears little resemblance to the fictional literary effort to which Fortune aspired three decades earlier and that he believed in 1899 was essential if Black writers were to combat the ridiculous caricatures and the nostalgia for a static sense of racial hierarchy embodied in works of popular fiction.[172] There is very little evidence to suggest the subject matter of "The Man without a Race," but its title hints that the text may have foreshadowed some aspects of James Weldon Johnson's *The Autobiography of an Ex-Colored Man*, originally published in 1912, a novel that tells the story of a young biracial man whose appearance allows him to "neither disclaim the black race nor claim the white race," but "let the world take [him] for what it would." In the case of Johnson's fictional protagonist, the world takes him for an "ordinarily successful white man," and, as such, the Ex-Colored Man marries, has two children, and prospers financially. The novel ends on his lasting regret, however, that he did not have the courage or the stamina to pursue his dream of being an African American musician. His "fast yellowing manuscripts," evidence of his engagement with Black culture and its musical forms, he keeps in a drawer and takes out only occasionally; they are a reminder of what he has given up, not only in terms of racial identity, but also in terms of unproduced Negro art. The loss that Johnson outlines in the novel is palpable and serves as a reminder that the sum total of African American literary history is not only what has been written but also those literary attempts that were imagined but never completed, or written but never published. Fortune's letters to Washington insist that his manuscripts, unfinished, abandoned, and lost, like those of the Ex-Colored Man, are "the only tangible remnants" of a "vanished dream, a dead ambition, a sacrificed talent."[173]

Whereas Johnson found the freedom and support to write the story of the Ex-Colored Man, Fortune's "Man without a Race" would remain unwritten. In this case, Fortune's talent was not sacrificed but channeled in a direction he believed at the time was necessary. His opportunity for individual literary success was compromised by his prioritizing of Washington's authorship above his own. Fortune recognized the importance of his role as a crucial agent in advancing the fiction of Washington's authorship, but, by 1905, this recognition was punctuated by bitterness, pessimism, and a vivid sense of personal loss. "I have reached the conclusion that the Fates have the cards stacked against me, and that all that is left to me is to plod on in the effort to make a fair living and to die decently at the psychological moment," he wrote to Scott, early in 1905. Fortune went on to sum up his life in this way: "*All the way I have shaken the trees and others have gathered the fruit.*"[174] This final observation speaks volumes about the nature of Fortune's literary alliance with Washington and the depths of his disappointment at the fate of his own writing, a disappointment that certainly contributed to Fortune's excessive drinking and to what was then described as a mental breakdown that, by 1907, had debilitated him.

To date, Fortune's presence in Washington's writing has been grossly overlooked. We read what Washington did not write and fail to recognize the force and strategy of the writer behind the texts. Fortune's ability to harness the power and authority of writing and give it to Washington is instructive, for it highlights the distinction between authorship and writing, between the author as a public identity or performed role and the writer as a person who grapples with words. It also highlights the way that Fortune's words *became* Washington's through the process of commodification by which they were published and became known. It is the nature of the commodity to conceal what Antonio Negri has called the "living labour" that makes it possible.[175] What was obscured, then, as Washington's books became a commodity, is Fortune's writing and his intellectual labor on Washington's behalf. But Washington's authorship was the result of an elaborate dynamic process: it involved borrowing and lending of status, including the status of writing itself. The story of Washington's authorship and Fortune's writing reveals profoundly what was involved and at stake in the handling of these exchanges. Fortune called on the status of writing to elevate Washington's own status as a leader, believing at the same time that the increased visibility of Washington as an author would lead to the increased visibility of Black writing in general. The transactions in their relationship are important, for they suggest that authorship was almost entirely severable from the acts of composing and writing: Washington became an author without being someone who wrote.[176]

In contrast to the image of an author embraced by Washington and reproduced in images of him at work at his desk, pen in hand, Fortune emerges as the embodied laborer behind Washington's name, the writer who wrote constantly but never achieved the status of authorship. Fortune's writing and his literary savvy served Washington well at a moment when commercial opportunities for Black authorship were just beginning to open up, but whereas Washington's authorship is easily accounted for in the tally of books published around the turn of the century, Fortune's labor is far less readily perceptible or appreciated. His job as a writer was bringing Washington as an author into being: an effort that, as we have seen, involved labor on multiple levels, which included engaging Washington in literary conversation; mentoring him on the craft of writing; negotiating various publishing venues and the details of print; and writing, revising, and editing the writing that went out under his name. The alliance forged between Washington and Fortune illuminates competing definitions of the author and different concepts of authorship. For Washington, claiming authorship was about gaining the writer's power, prestige and legitimacy; for Fortune, the historical value of his writing is located in the extent to which he gave these things away, by subordinating his presence as a writer to the power of his words. By doing this, Fortune took part in reanimating the place of Black writing and made way for possibilities of African American authorship beyond any imaginable in the nineteenth century.

The story of Fortune's writing for Washington suggests the wisdom of thinking about Black authorship as a network of what Eric Gardner has recently called "literary presences"; this is one way to recover the nuances of African American literary history at the very moment of its capitalist modernization.[177] A more complete investigation of the various "presences" at work in Washington's authorship would include not only the story of T. Thomas Fortune, but also those of the many other unrecognized or underacknowledged literary practitioners who wrote, edited, or otherwise contributed to Washington's emergence as a writer and to the ways in which he performed and sustained that identity into the twentieth century. Chief among the figures that lurk in the shadows of Washington's authorship is Victoria Earle Matthews. Matthews's name appears on the title page of *Black-Belt Diamonds*, leaving a permanent record of her involvement in the book's production. But, as my own abbreviated inclusion of her in this chapter suggests, a fuller account of that involvement—including the ways in which it was curtailed by discourses of masculinity and gendered expectations of women's literary work as fundamentally supportive rather than generative—will augment our knowledge of the conditions under which she performed the range of activities that for her constituted literary activism. Matthews's slipping status as the authority in the project she herself initiated brings to the fore the precarious nature of Black women's attempts to publish, whether as authors or editors. As we will see in the next chapter, that precarity becomes even more apparent when their publication projects were intended to center their own experience and that of other Black women in the larger public discourse. Their efforts shed light on a less visible but no less pertinent history of Black print culture, one that makes evident the innovative ways Black women performed literary work in their pursuit of a public voice.

CHAPTER FOUR

THE CASE OF MARY CHURCH TERRELL

❦

IN FEBRUARY 1924, MARY CHURCH TERRELL WROTE TO AGNES REP-
plier, "Your essay on the Happiness of Writing an Autobiography is most
interesting, instructive and entertaining," Terrell said. "I have enjoyed every
syllable of it and have read it twice." Repplier was a white writer, well known
and well respected for the quality of her essays, which regularly appeared in
the *Atlantic Monthly*, among other prestigious literary magazines.[1] In addition to praising Repplier's work, Terrell wished to elicit her advice. "My
friends have been urging me for a long time to write an autobiography," she
said. "I am wondering whether you will have the time or the inclination to
advise me how to write [it]." Taken on its own, Terrell's request is straightforward: she hoped to glean from an experienced woman writer tips for
composing a memoir. However, Terrell was also signaling the complexity
of her own literary positioning. "I have been unable to place my article[s] in
American magazines," she admitted to Repplier, "because I have written on
various phases of the Race Problem. I did succeed in placing my article on
Lynching from a Negro's point of view in the North American Review for

June, 1904," Terrell wrote, pointing to a publishing achievement some two decades in the past. She lamented that the articles in which she most firmly believed, with titles such as "The Convict Lease System in the United States" and "A Plea for the White South by a Colored Woman" were "rejected by every magazine in this country," even those "which print matter like that." Her experience trying to publish short stories and other works of fiction was all the more discouraging. Even when these texts addressed the so-called "Race Problem" only indirectly, they were still rejected. Terrell believed that the story of what she termed in her letter to Repplier her own "unusual experience in this country" was worth recording.[2] And yet how could this be done in a manner that would successfully see its way into print?

Born in 1863, Terrell was sixty-one years of age when she initially contacted Repplier; her autobiography, A Colored Woman in a White World, would not be published for another sixteen years. In the end, she turned to a vanity press, the Ransdell Company of Washington, DC, after her manuscript was rejected by publisher after publisher. It is in fact not Terrell's difficulty in publishing the autobiography that interests me here, but the experiences that motivated her to contact Repplier in the first place, to admit her frustration, and to ask for advice. What were the literary conditions that led to her discouragement and necessitated her query? To what must we credit Terrell's lack of confidence in her ability to tell her own story and see it into print? What happened between the successful 1904 publication of "Lynching from a Negro's Point of View" and her disheartened appeal to Repplier in 1924? And how can the story of this apparently marginal aspiring writer help us to better understand African American literary history and, more specifically, the conditions of early twentieth-century authorship in African American contexts?

Terrell casts herself, in her letter to Repplier, as a failed author, and that is precisely how she would be considered under a conventional understanding of what makes for the "success" of an author. But, as she makes clear, it isn't that she didn't write in the interval between 1904 and 1924. Rather, she had little success in publishing her writing. Terrell is quick to tell Repplier about her struggle to place her nonfiction articles, but what she doesn't address in detail is that it was the writing that mattered to her the most—her fiction— that was the most consistently and the most roundly rejected. This apparent "failure" has rendered Terrell's career as a writer of short stories invisible. Indeed, the stories themselves exist only in the archives: the Mary Church Terrell Collection at the Library of Congress is filled with the manuscripts she wrote and sought to publish. It is also filled with correspondence that proves she successfully shared these stories with friends, advisors, writing instructors, and editors. And yet, despite evidence of her prolific literary production, Terrell would be considered a failed writer because her short fiction did not get past the gatekeepers of "official" literary culture. While she submitted her stories again and again, they were never accepted.

My aim in this chapter is not to "rediscover" Terrell as an accomplished writer of short fiction, or to establish a place for her in the canon of early twentieth-century African American literature. Rather, I want to think critically about the terms and conditions of her "failure" and, by doing so, to gain a greater appreciation for what labeling Terrell a "failed writer" means and what it masks. It bears reiterating here that "success" and "failure" for Black authors around the turn of the century often hinged on their willingness to concede to publishers' and to the public's demands for writing that reinforced and perpetuated racist stereotypes. As I outlined in the introduction to this book, the "successful" writing of both Paul Laurence Dunbar and Charles Chesnutt was scrutinized and, indeed, tightly regulated by the white literary marketplace according to these demands, and both authors found their greatest publishing success when their writing fell in line with images of Blackness that white readers expected and approved of. Each author in the end recognized their literary accommodations as a necessary, if limiting, element of their publishing success. Terrell refused to make these accommodations, and her failure to publish her short stories is a sign of this refusal.

How does literary history account for writers that "opted out" or otherwise refused to make the sort of compromises in their writing that were expected of them? In this context, it's helpful to see the case of Mary Church Terrell as an example of the sort of queer failure that José Esteban Muñoz explains as "not so much a failure to succeed as it is a failure to participate in a system of valuation that is predicated on exploitation and conformity."[3] She refused to adhere to the white literary establishment's limited and limiting definitions of Blackness, which were intended to reinforce and maintain a racial hierarchy in which African Americans were understood to be inferior. What was deemed "acceptable" specifically excluded depictions of the lives and aspirations of the educated, cultured, economically stable Black middle and upper classes, the population that was the subject of Terrell's stories. Her failure can be read as queer in that it is defined not by an aesthetic shortcoming but, rather, by the political refusal her stories embody. By repeatedly submitting her fiction for publication in the nation's most highly respected magazines, Terrell registered her opposition to these demeaning institutions and to the demand that Black writers contribute to the never-ending stream of negative, racist depictions of African Americans if they wanted to be included in their pages. The fact that Terrell continued to write short stories that cut across the grain of white expectations of Blackness, coupled with the meticulous way in which she saved these rejected pieces as well as the letters that documented her inability to publish them, signals a critical practice that demands recognition.

Terrell had her own compelling theory for why her work was deemed unacceptable to the literary establishment: a "conspiracy of silence," she believed, existed among the editors of the most widely read American magazines, which ensured that Black writers whose stories did not reinforce popular racist stereotypes would not be published in these venues.[4] This theory, which I will explore at length in this chapter, helps to further elucidate the conditions of authorship for African American authors at the beginning of the twentieth century. As we saw in the previous chapter, T. Thomas Fortune made his way as a writer by authoring Booker T. Washington's career, and his story makes visible the anonymity that was one condition of Black authorship during the nadir. Inquiry into Terrell's career as a writer of short stories illuminates something different: the fate of her fiction was to languish in her archives, circulated only among a relatively small public sphere. Her short stories were denied the mass public venue of print publication, but the very fact that her unpublished fiction was read by friends, professional acquaintances, publishers and editors, and writing instructors reveals that Terrell cultivated what I consider a limited and relatively private reading public. Attention to her private authorship, then, and to the body of work that resulted from it—an assortment of unpublished short stories—suggests another way of understanding African American authorship and literary history, one that recognizes literary production, even when that production did not culminate in publication. It insists we move away from acknowledging only the most obvious and public forms and sites of literary accomplishment and pushes us to think more carefully about literary *acts*—not only those that were successful in the conventional sense, but also those that failed or were only partially achieved. What we might find, I argue, is that texts that exist only in manuscript form are even more important than printed, published ones for examinations of African American literary culture in the early twentieth century.[5]

Terrell's private authorship suggests the importance of showing greater appreciation for the different kinds of literary access and audiences that different writers, at different times, have had or worked toward. By doing so, we can more fully appreciate Terrell's "failure" as an author less as a judgment on her career and more a sign of the impediments she had to overcome to create a readership for her stories. Try as she might, she could not get her stories published in the public print venues where she thought they would do the most good. But, denied access to these venues, Terrell deliberately sought other, less orthodox ways of insisting her stories be noticed, read, and appreciated. By submitting her fiction again and again to the nation's most prominent literary magazines despite knowing that they would not be accepted for publication, Terrell insisted that those whose objective it was to deny her a readership take notice of her authorship. She came to understand that her short stories would not be published in traditional ways, yet she insisted that they be made public, albeit to a limited and relatively private audience. This private audience may not have been the readership to which she initially aspired, but it has a lot to tell us about an author who lived at a time in which she was denied more visible venues of publication.

My argument in this chapter is that Mary Church Terrell's unpublished short stories and her correspondence with a limited reading public of editors and advisors encourages us to rethink what success, failure, and even publication meant in the historical moment in which she lived. The chapter unfolds in four parts. I begin biographically, by looking at Terrell's life and her upbringing. Here I am most interested in the way that she came to understand writing as central to her aspirations and to the expression of her identity as a woman and as an African American as she studied and traveled in Europe, even as she remained uncertain about the kind of writing that she wished to do. The second part of the chapter looks at Terrell's most widely acclaimed publication, the 1904 *North American Review* article "Lynching from a Negro's Point of View," which, in her letter to Agnes Repplier, Terrell points to as her one publishing success. I argue that it was through this publication that Terrell came face-to-face with the power and efficacy of fictional narrative, against which her own fact-based nonfiction writing on the subject of lynching was no match. The third part of the chapter looks closely at Terrell's short stories themselves, as they exist in the archive. I put into context the historical moment at which Terrell turned to writing short stories, a moment that saw the short story teeter in status between a commercial and a literary genre and the advent of handbooks and correspondence classes that communicated the ease with which stories were written and marketed. Like most of Terrell's stories, the two on which I focus in this chapter emerge directly from her own experience and resonate with the experience of those of her race and class. They demonstrate the ways that her short fiction was controversial and propagandistic in that it was intended to critique ideologies that were both unspoken and widely accepted. Finally, in the last part of the chapter, I consider both the feedback Terrell received on her short stories and her correspondence, in particular with the editors of some of the most popular and widely read American magazines, about the publication prospects for African American fiction. By unpacking Terrell's understanding of the "literary atmosphere" in which she lived and, especially, the "conspiracy of silence" that effectively prevented her writing from appearing in the pages of American magazines, I am able to illuminate her resolve to protest that treatment and open up these avenues of publication for future generations of African American writers.

"I Want to Write and I Cannot Begin Any Younger"

Born in in Memphis, Tennessee, in 1863, Mary Eliza Church Terrell belongs to that first generation of African Americans freed from slavery. Unlike her parents, both of whom had been enslaved, Terrell, as she notes in her autobiography, "did not have to go through life as a slave."[6] Both her parents were of mixed race, and both were successful entrepreneurs: her mother established a freestanding hairdressing establishment in the most "exclusive business district" in Memphis, and her father became a millionaire (perhaps the first African American from the South to do so) through his real estate investments (cw 9). Her childhood was not especially happy, however, as her mother, who had attempted suicide just months before she gave birth to her daughter, and her father, who was subject to explosive, violent episodes of rage, divorced when she was very young. This Terrell remembered as both painful and embarrassing.

Although neither parent had much formal schooling, they prioritized education for their daughter. Believing that the local schools for African Americans would not give her the kind of education she needed, they sent Terrell north at the age of eight to be educated. In Yellow Springs, Ohio, she boarded with a family and began her studies at the Model School, a division of Antioch College focused on elementary education. She would eventually move to the Yellow Springs public school, where she was the only African American in her grade and one of only a few African American girls in the school. It was in the context of these two schools that Terrell came to understand her racial identity. Classmates would repeatedly emphasize her difference and define her in terms of racial stereotypes. Terrell would come to describe these incidents as filled with great embarrassment, humiliation, and hurt. In her words, they "indelibly impressed my racial identity upon me" (cw 22). Her early education in Yellow Springs was also the place where she began to question stereotypes of Blackness and find ways to reject the hurtful comments of classmates that were intended to make her "the object of ridicule" (cw 22). She also credits Yellow Springs for raising her awareness of both women's activism and politics. A hotbed of the Temperance Movement, Yellow Springs was where Terrell first saw women band together to speak out for their beliefs; it was a place where candidates for office and other political speakers drew large crowds to make their platforms known. Terrell's own public speaking during this time was limited to the recitations of poems she memorized and performed "to anyone [she] could induce to listen" (cw 25). But even these juvenile performances laid the groundwork for her career as an activist, a lecturer, and a writer.

These were skills she honed in Oberlin, Ohio, first as a student in the public schools, where she completed what would now be considered high school, and then at Oberlin College. It was in high school that she began writing poetry, and she took great pride in her classmates' admiration of her literary skills. This may have given her the confidence to reject the course of study usually pursued by "ladies" at Oberlin College, which involved some study of literature but did not award a bachelor's degree. She instead enrolled in what was commonly considered the "gentleman's course of study," a program that took two years longer to complete and necessitated the study of Latin and Greek. Terrell excelled at these languages and in every way received an exceptional education at Oberlin. She also took algebra and trigonometry and continued to improve her critical writing and oratorical expression through the study of British and American literature. The essays from her college years show the wide range of topics she was asked to address, and the rigor with which her writing was critiqued, not only by teachers but by fellow students as well. It was at Oberlin that Terrell first saw her name in print in the *Oberlin Review*, for which she served as an editor. She was also asked to join a prestigious women's literary society, the Aelioian. It was a haven for Terrell, who in her autobiography generally downplays episodes of racism but nevertheless relays incidents that acknowledge the difficulty of the predominantly white environments in which she received her education. At Oberlin College, where she was one of only three Black women to graduate in 1884, racist incidents were not uncommon. But Terrell recalled the literary society as one of the spaces in which she felt most at home: the "members of my society," she recalled, "did not discriminate against me on account of my race" (cw 45).

Eager to put her education to use and serve her race, Terrell became a teacher after graduating from Oberlin in 1884. She was first employed at Wilberforce University, where she taught everything from French to miner-

4.1 Mary Church Terrell at Oberlin College (1884). Photo courtesy of the Oberlin College Archives, Oberlin, OH.

alogy, before accepting a job in 1887 at the prestigious M Street High School in Washington, DC, where she joined fellow Oberlin classmate Anna Julia Cooper and a cohort of other Black college graduates. She was appointed assistant to the head of the Latin program, Robert Heberton Terrell, her future husband. After a first successful year at the M Street High School, Terrell took a trip to Europe to see its sights, imbibe its culture, and learn its languages. Over the course of two years in Europe she learned French and German, and she kept a personal journal written in each language.

Much of what we know about Terrell's early life comes from her own auto-biographical reminiscences in *A Colored Woman in a White World*. There, from the perspective of her highly successful career as a lecturer and a racial activist, Terrell offers a public representation of her life story, fitting together its pieces into a seamless narrative. She portrays herself as a highly capable and determined woman who from the start had an understanding of her duty to her race. But to understand the nuances of her early life, including its difficulties, we must turn to the journals she kept on her trip. It is in these personal volumes that we discover that Terrell arrived in Europe with a second agenda: her desperate desire to become a writer.

This aspiration is particularly visible in the journal written in French and kept between August 26, 1888, and February 11, 1889. The journal paints a portrait of a young woman far more uncertain of herself and her future than that reflected in *A Colored Woman in a White World*. As Jennifer M. Wilks has noted, the French journal reveals the woman that was Mary Eliza Church, before she became Mary Church Terrell, a wife and mother whose renown was based on these roles and on her public performances as a clubwoman, a lecturer, and a civil rights activist.[7] From the journal, it is evident that Terrell corresponded regularly with both her future husband and her colleagues at the M Street High School, but in the moment captured by this journal, theirs is not the life that she longs to assume. Alongside the record of Terrell's daily activities is a record of her conviction that she must begin her career as a writer. Just two weeks after saying goodbye to her father, for whom a career as a writer would surely have been unimaginable, Terrell notes the urgency of her pursuit: "I want to write and I cannot begin any younger."[8] One week later Terrell sought out a mentor she hoped could advise her on literary matters. In a surprisingly intimate conversation with John Chapman, the owner of the radical British journal the *Westminster Review*, "I revealed my great desire to be a good writer to him and asked him to tell me his opinion." Chapman offered her both encouragement and direction, pushing her to think harder about what, specifically, she wanted to write about. "One has to be full of a subject before trying to write," Chapman told her. Chapman also instructed Terrell to think about the purpose of her writing, telling her that "one must have, as the goal of writing, the advancement of society." Terrell used the journal itself to ponder what, exactly, she wished to write about, saying "there are so many [things] which interest me." She isolates two of them as examples of a broader field of concerns she wished to address in her writing: "My gender, my race."[9] These were difficult topics that she had lived—subjects she was "full of"—and writing about them, she believed, would be of great service to the "advancement of society."

Despite this apparent confidence, however, Terrell alternates in the journal between expressing her desire to write and her fear of it. In lines such as "Je veux écrire. Je dois écrire" (I want to write, I must write), Terrell communicated the urgency of her desire to be a writer, one that, I argue, was sustained throughout her life.[10] But she also speaks of the "courage" it takes to write, an act that had the potential to expose personal and racial truths that contradicted the polished reserve and scrupulous refinement long associated with the Black middle and upper classes of Memphis and Washington. Writing on what she knew best—her gender, her race—threatened to unmask her deepest thoughts and feelings, including the racial humiliations and injustices that she kept discursively contained and tended to gloss over in her public life. The courage to write was something that Terrell tried, on a daily basis, to muster, in part through the act of writing in the safe space of her journal. There she expresses her concerns vividly, even as she dances around their exact nature. One mounting anxiety was that she would never actually do anything: she recognizes and laments that "there are a lot of people who have had good intentions, but they have never made any progress."[11] She speaks of writing as "my calling, my sacred duty."[12] But in the pages of the journal, writing is also exposed as something Terrell was terrifically frightened of: in addition to the vulnerability it introduced, it was hard work. Terrell would come to describe writing as a terrifying activity: "If ever a human being wrote with fear and trembling, it was surely I" (cw 221).

Terrell's journal's juxtaposition of her determination and her uncertainty reflects the struggle that was likely playing out in her own mind, between the writing life she so desperately wanted and the ridicule that might result from her pursuit of something so out of line with expectations of what an African American woman's career choices at the end of the nineteenth century might be. That this struggle took place in Europe and not the United States serves as a reminder of the international and cosmopolitan history of the construction of African American authorship. In a two-day span, Terrell visited a Paris library to learn the addresses of publishing houses, recording the names of nine London establishments in her journal; she also visited a Paris publishing house, speaking there to an "English Gentleman" who supplied her with the addresses of "other publishers that publish novels."[13] That she did this within the first month of her stay in Paris suggests an awareness that African Americans had historically looked to Europe for publishing opportunities. Terrell showed great confidence in taking the initiative to learn about various publishing options. But this confidence was easily undermined. It is contradicted again and again in the journal, which animates Terrell's overall uncertainty about her writing. At the heart of this uncertainty was the very question of what she wanted to write. It is unclear what, exactly, Terrell wrote during her sojourn in Europe, but her journal suggests that she worked on what she called "her pieces" continually during the time she spent in France and Switzerland.[14] This ambiguous designation intimates that Terrell herself didn't have a name for what she was writing, but it may also indicate that she saw her writing as falling between existing forms and genres, or that she was working in innovative ways that were difficult to categorize. Terrell aspired to do some translations, and some of her pieces were journalistic. But she bristled under Robert Terrell's suggestion that she write for newspapers.[15] This uncertainty—over form, audience, and potential publishing possibilities—surely contributed to what Terrell perceived as a lack of productivity. She continually asks in the journal, "Why am I not writing?" Her answer was a further reflection of her unsettledness: "It's procrastination or surely lack of time. The two I think." This entry ends on the positive while shedding more light on her aspirations as a writer. "Let's hope it will happen," she wrote. "I intend to write something original."[16]

One reason writing something original was elusive was because of the pressure Terrell placed on herself to have "as the goal of writing, the advancement of society."[17] The dilemma of how to do something "substantial" without exceeding traditional ideas about women's nature and their role in the world threatened to derail her momentum at every turn.[18] In the midst of what appeared to be a fairly productive period during which Terrell seemed to gain traction in her writing, she also weighed the value of the opinion of someone named in the journal only by the initials "M. G.," who "made fun of women who would want to get mixed up in politics because they should be busy darning stockings and also lack the mind to grasp the issues of politics."[19] This perspective she rejected. But it was, in a cruel way, the perspective most prominently held by the world for which she seemed in training. Her father had expected her to remain in Memphis, to marry, and to assume the life of a respected member of that city's Black elite. Her mother had sent her for her college graduation a fancy dress and a pair of opera glasses, both items that exemplified similar expectations. Even by herself in Europe, with the expressed desire to dedicate herself to writing, Terrell could not maintain distance between her own aspirations and those expectations that had always driven her progress. "I am a little dissatisfied with my narrow-minded life to a certain extent," she would write, "and with its atmosphere lacking intellectual vigor." But in the same entry she would lament her appearance in a photograph, criticizing the visible wrinkles in her dress and the fact that "the photographer only took one side of my face."[20] This would not do as a picture to send Robert Terrell, who had asked for one and whose

4.2 Mary Church Terrell as a young woman. Prints and Photographs Collection, Library of Congress, Washington, DC. The photograph is likely to have been taken around the time that Terrell began keeping her European diaries, in 1888.

letters clearly implied that he saw himself as a potential suitor. Did she dare to ignore the state of her dress in addition to the affection (and the promise of a good marriage, to a man as highly educated as she) that his letters to her communicated, in order to pursue her own goal as a writer? Or was she, as she sometimes speculated in the pages of her journal, someone who "lacked the courage to really do it"?[21] The tensions inherent in her own desire to write creatively left her paralyzed, and the journal is punctuated with signs of her fluctuating emotions. On one day, the promise of becoming a writer seemed to be firmly within reach; on the next, it would not. This was the case in late November 1888, when she wrote in her journal, "I still have not written anything. Unhappy 'procrastination.'"[22]

In the end, Terrell returned to the United States and, after a visit to see family in Memphis, she resumed her job in Washington, at the M Street High School. Here she became the Mrs. Mary Church Terrell most often represented by history. She married Robert Terrell and, according to social custom, gave up her career as a teacher. She had a daughter she named Phyllis, after the eighteenth-century poet Phillis Wheatley, and adopted another, making her the mother of two girls. With her husband's support she settled into a second career as a clubwoman, a role that was in keeping with her class privilege but nevertheless transformed her into an activist, a lecturer, and a public reformer.

She was the first president of the National Association of Colored Women, formed in 1896, and an early proponent of the NAACP. In addition to being an active clubwoman, she was a suffragist and a race spokeswoman who used writing, public speeches, and refined protest to speak to her own position and that of Black women in the United States, who faced discrimination because of both their race and their sex. As a lecturer, an educator, and an activist who traveled widely, Terrell did find ways to courageously speak out for members of her sex and race. She considered herself a "meddler," a term she knew was aligned with gender stereotypes that associate women with interfering in the affairs of others or intruding in spaces and conversations in ways that are unwelcome. Terrell nevertheless embraced this moniker, transforming its negative implications in her 1905 essay, "The Mission of Meddlers," into a badge of pride and courage for African Americans seeking racial justice. She defined a "meddler" as someone who investigates and exposes injustice and oppression. By concluding that there was "an imperative need of meddlers today," she armed herself and other middle-class Black women with a way to assume public and political voices.[23]

Terrell's career as an activist might not have advanced as it did were it not for two important things. The first is that, early in her marriage, she lost three babies in five years. All of the babies she carried to term, and all three died within days of their birth. Terrell describes in her autobiography the "depths of despair" into which she fell after the death of the third child, whose loss she felt the most keenly: the infant was placed in an "improvised incubator" after birth, and Terrell was haunted by the thought that "if the genuine article had been used, its little life might have been spared" (CW 107). The suspicion that this child might have lived were it not for the fact that African Americans received inadequate hospital care surely sharpened Terrell's sense of racial injustice and drove her to fight harder for social and political equality. More specifically, in the wake of these losses, her activist work proved to be a welcome distraction and gave her a much-needed sense of purpose. As Terrell wrote in her autobiography, "I had to get on with it. . . . Obliged to be interested in the troubles and trials of others, I had little time to think of my own aching heart" (cw 152). Her daughter Phyllis was born in 1898 in a New York hospital, where Terrell believed both mother and baby would have access to proper equipment and receive better care than they would in Washington. There is no doubt that Terrell poured her life into motherhood, and her diaries illustrate that she was actively involved in every aspect of Phyllis's care and upbringing. She nevertheless began, in the first years of the twentieth century, to spend more and more time on the road, pursuing public work in the form of lecture tours that kept her away from home for weeks at a time. It is likely that this was not only because she enjoyed her work. Around the turn of the century, Robert Terrell suffered great losses in several real estate and commercial dealings; this marked the beginning of a period of financial strain that would force him to ask his father-in-law for a loan to repay money he owed to the Capital Savings Bank, a Black-owned business in which he was a director.[24] In her autobiography Terrell says she did not take up her work on the lecture circuit for the money, and yet the modest payments she received did help the family through what was a difficult period financially.

As an activist, Terrell mustered the courage that had eluded her as a young woman in Europe. One of the most daring things she did was to criticize Booker T. Washington, whose philosophy of higher education for African Americans ran contrary to her own belief in the importance of intellectual aspirations. She was not against industrial education, and she was full of respect for Washington's efforts to prepare the "masses to earn a living." But she did not believe that this had to be done through the "total exclusion of academic education." She herself advocated for an educational approach that fused Washington's interest in vocational training with W. E. B. Du Bois's concern that Black children also engage in math, science, and the liberal arts. Terrell publicly criticized Washington for his propensity to "make colored people, who had acquired an education, appear as ridiculous as he could"; it was, she asserted, both "unwise and unfair" (cw 191). In August 1906, Terrell again went against Washington when she supported the Constitutional League's petition to President Roosevelt to reinstate Black soldiers who had been dishonorably discharged from the army because of their alleged involvement in the riot in Brownsville, Texas.

She would continue to dwell on the injustice of this situation, sketching the soldiers' mistreatment and suffering more fully in her 1907 *Voice of the Negro* article, "A Sketch of Mingo Saunders." Terrell's criticism of Washington was especially daring since it jeopardized her husband's job and his reputation. In 1901, Washington had secured for Robert Terrell an appointment as the first African American federal judge, and with that position came the assumption that he was and would be a loyal cog in the "Tuskegee Machine." That loyalty was tested again and again by Mary Church Terrell, who was candid in voicing her disagreements with Washington. In 1906, Washington had written to Robert Terrell, condemning one of his wife's speeches as "radical."[25] Washington would also question her support of the Black soldiers, accurately viewing it as a criticism of his support of Roosevelt's decision. It was not until 1909, when Terrell was involved in the organization of the NAACP, that Washington would directly express his anger and embarrassment over Mary Church Terrell's vocal criticism of his policies and leadership. "Of course," Washington wrote to Robert Terrell, "I am not seeking to control anyone's activities, but I simply want to know where we stand."[26] Washington never broke his ties with Robert Terrell, nor does he appear to have spoken disparagingly about him or about Mary Church Terrell in public settings, but his wife's independence surely caused tension in Robert Terrell's relationship with Washington. Despite this, he does not seem to have censured his wife, or limited the scope of what she was "allowed" to address.

Amid her speeches and organizational work, and alongside her role as a mother and as a wife, Terrell did find her way to becoming a writer. The bulk of Terrell's writing in the early twentieth century is best described as pedagogic in nature. One way to promote interracial understanding, Terrell believed, was through publicizing the achievements of the race, and she set out in all of her race essays to introduce to both Black and white audiences the prominent African Americans she felt they most needed to know. To this end, Terrell wrote numerous articles on Phillis Wheatley, extolling her poetry and prowess in the world of letters. The skill of English musician and composer Samuel Coleridge-Taylor was the subject of one of her essays after his U. S. debut in Washington, DC; she praised his work, pointing to him as proof that "no musical Parnassus [is] too lofty or too steep for colored people to scale."[27] Numerous other Black pioneers, such as scientists George Washington Carver and Ernest Just, poet Paul Laurence Dunbar, and spokesperson Frederick Douglass, also became the focus of biographical sketches. In most cases Terrell told stories of the successes of these rep-

4.3 This Central Lyceum Bureau brochure from 1904 advertises Mary Church Terrell's various lectures, and documents her popularity as an invited speaker. Redpath Chautauqua Bureau Records, Special Collections Department, University of Iowa Libraries, Iowa City.

resentative individuals and their rise from difficult circumstances to great heights. She believed that publicizing their contributions in print would be transformative, inspiring African Americans throughout the country to develop pride in their people and become exemplary citizens while also correcting misinformation about African Americans and their habits and values that had been communicated to whites. She therefore placed the bulk of her writing in African American journals, which circulated widely among the nation's Black middle class. Such writing, for Terrell, was a part of an uplift ideology in which she was firmly invested: her articles were meant to inspire the Black middle class to claim images and racial personalities that would counter racial stereotypes, ultimately improving conditions for themselves and for the Black masses on whose behalf they worked.

Terrell's 1904 essay, "Lynching from a Negro's Point of View," stands apart from these inspirational essays, in part because of the place of its publication, the *North American Review*. Along with *Harper's*, *Century*, *Atlantic Monthly*, and *Forum*, the *North American Review* was one of the leading magazines of culture and opinion in the United States. With the exception of Walter Hines Page, editor of the *Forum* from 1886 to 1895, and of the *Atlantic* after 1896, all the editors of these magazines were Northerners, as was the majority of their readership. In general, the magazines mirrored the refined tastes of the established middle and upper classes; their style was genteel, and, for the most part, they avoided vulgarities. The exception to this rule was in their treatment of African Americans. Scholars have questioned the extent to which these publications, written for and read by Northerners who were themselves "devotees to the Genteel Tradition[,] found such evident delight in the lampooning of Negroes."[28] In his story of the portrayal of African Americans in the leading literary magazines at the turn of the century, historian Rayford Logan describes the derisive terms, the exaggerated dialect, the ridicule, and the stereotyping of African Americans in their pages. Reinforced by cartoons, creative art forms such as fiction and poetry, as well as journalistic pieces reporting on crime, the journals were consistently designed to support ideas of white superiority and Black inferiority. Images that might compete with these rarely appeared in their pages. Only the *Forum* regularly accepted essays from Black Americans, and those who published in this journal were generally accommodationist Bookerites; even the famous Frederick Douglass appeared there only once.

On matters as extreme as lynching these magazines tried to avoid controversy; one way to do this was to "balance" the publication of perspectives on the subject, and this may have been behind the *North American Review*'s decision to publish Terrell's article in June 1904. In January of that year, it had published an essay by Thomas Nelson Page, "The Lynching of Negroes: Its Causes and Its Prevention." Page, a Southerner whose father had lost everything in the Civil War, had given up a career in the law to focus on writing fiction, which presented itself to him as an effective medium through which to recreate romanticized versions of the antebellum South and its lifestyles and institutions. His stories and novels idealize that place and time, as well as the New South of the early twentieth century, where racial segregation and white supremacy were being reestablished. Page's fictionalized version of the South was finer than any real place could ever be, but his stories satisfied the nostalgia of his readers for the South as it might have been—a place where heroic men and women adhered to a code of perfect honor. The plantation imagery and rape fantasies he created and perpetuated in "The Lynching of Negroes" would be fully realized and embraced by the public in the coming decades, in the form of novels like Thomas F. Dixon Jr.'s *The Clansman* (1905) and films such as *Birth of a Nation* (1915) and, later, *Gone with the Wind* (1939). The coarse caricatures from these works have continued to define stereotypes of Blackness into the twenty-first century, as well as those of gender and class.

In the *North American Review* article, Page drew on his own nostalgic descriptions of Southern life to frame his discussion of and arguments about the causes of lynching in the United States. Although he began the essay with a short introduction in which he cited substantial statistics on lynching gathered from the *Chicago Tribune*, he quickly moved past these statistics and what they suggested, preferring to advance a narrative of Black bestiality and white victimization that was in keeping with the images of African Americans commonly circulated in the media. He described a dire state of affairs in the post-Reconstruction South that was particularly dangerous to Southern white women, who were the prime subjects of Negro interest and the target of their violent tendencies. "To-day no white woman, or girl, or female child, goes alone out of sight of the house except on necessity; and no man leaves his wife alone in his house, if he can help it," wrote Page, vividly constructing a scene intended to instill fear even in the most liberal-minded of Northern reformers. "Cases have occurred of assault and murder in broad day, within sight and sound of the victim's home," he wrote. "The white population is sparse, the forests are extensive, the officers of the law distant and difficult to reach."[29] Page counted on the fact that the impact of the narrative he evoked would overwhelm any statistical data he presented at the essay's beginning. As he rightly calculated, under the power of the dramatic scenario of Southern life that he presented, one that portrayed white women as the frail and frightened victims of brutish Black male sexual aggression, fiction became irrefutable by fact. In addition to defending the practice of lynching, Page drew on this dramatic scenario to argue that any effort to help African Americans pursue civil rights was directly damaging to white women. "To the ignorant and brutal young Negro," he wrote, social equality "signifies but one thing: the opportunity to enjoy, equally with white men, the privilege of cohabitating with white women."[30] The effect of this narrative was to reorient the mindset of even those readers sympathetic to African American interests, releasing them from the moral obligation to repair the injustice of slavery.

Magazines like the *North American Review* often packaged the work of authors presenting different points of view on the same topic in successive issues, creating the effect of a debate forum. This is most likely the reason they decided to print Terrell's essay. She was accustomed to seeing her work in journals published within and for the Black community, but acceptance by *North American Review*—one of the handful of elite, quality monthlies that functioned as gatekeepers of European American literary culture—and exposure to its broad readership were surely among the reasons she would come to describe seeing "Lynching from a Negro's Point of View" in print for the first time as a "thrill which comes once in a lifetime" (CW 226). Indeed, the publication of this article was among her most daring achievements, but it must also have been, in some respects, a disheartening literary event, one through which she began to understand the impotence of nonfiction when compared to the power of the dramatic scenario that pervaded most writing about race in the United States. Page's extreme portrayal of Southern women as frail, frightened, and fragile victims who needed to be protected by Southern white chivalry was precisely the sort of dramatic fictional narrative that made fear of rape so widespread in the South as to be irrefutable, regardless of widely publicized facts. As feminist critics like Jacqueline Dowd Hall have illustrated, rape and rumors of rape became a sort of acceptable "folk pornography" in the South, and details of stories of sexual assault took on epic proportions in the literary imagination.[31] In the hands of authors like Page, the elements of the crime and its cast of characters became fixed: the attacker was not just a Black man but a ravenous brute, and the victim a beautiful, pale, frail young virgin. By the turn of the century, descriptions of both the attacker and victim were rendered in ever-more embellished, minute detail, until both characters became part of a public fantasy that implied a kind of group participation in the rape of the woman that was almost as cathartic as the subsequent lynching of the alleged attacker.

In attempting to refute Page's claims in her own essay, Terrell faced numerous challenges. Simply put, Page had the upper hand. He had defined the terms of the argument, and try as she might to subtly shift its focus to issues that were of more pressing interest to the African American community, the topics Page initiated and his perspectives were inescapable. Page had centered the discussion around the issue of lynching, not the disenfranchisement of freed slaves or the laws and policies adopted by Southern states to reduce them to sharecroppers. The question he raised was how to stop lynching, not what needed to be done to guarantee the civil and political rights of African Americans. Terrell wished to move beyond the narrow range of topics that Page introduced as relevant to the subject, such as whether lynching was the result of the rape of white women, or whether or not freed slaves understood equality to mean miscegenation. However, in her fact-based assault she found no effective means of shifting the focus to broader issues, like how mob violence could be eliminated, and what means of protection and support African Americans would need to ensure their own progress. As she understood it, lynching had nothing to do with rape: rather, it was indicative of the lengths to which whites were willing to go to maintain the status quo of white superiority and economic control in the South.

To appreciate better Terrell's strategy, as well as its limitations, we can turn to the assault on lynching culture her contemporary Ida B. Wells had made a decade earlier. Following the 1892 Memphis lynching of her friend Thomas Moss and his two business partners, who were killed for opening a grocery store in competition with a white grocer, Wells wrote *Southern Horrors: Lynch Law in All Its Phases* in order to "give the world a true, unvarnished account of the causes of lynch law in the South."[32] The "causes," as Wells emphatically put it, had nothing to do with the myth that Black men desired or raped white women. Lynching, as she argued, was an instrument of control and punishment for those African Americans who dared to "protect [themselves] against the white man or become his rival."[33] What was described as "rape" by pro-lynching advocates like Page were more often consensual relationships or pure fabrications, as she showed by extracting testimonials from respected white newspapers. In her next anti-lynching tract, 1895's *A Red Record: Tabulated Statistics and Alleged Causes of Lynching in the United States*, Wells explained that she cited white sources of information, like Memphis's *Public Ledger* and the *Chicago Tribune*, so that she could not be accused of "exaggeration." Out "of their own mouths," that is, in the reports "made by white men . . . or sent over the world by white men in the South," she insisted, would come the testimony revealing the true causes of lynching.[34]

Terrell followed Wells's example of exposing the mythology that lynching was a result of rape by drawing on facts, and facts drawn directly from what Wells called "white men in the South." For Terrell, the Southern white man was Page, whose data—"vouched for" by Page himself—gave her the ammunition she needed to expose the fallacy of his reasoning. While Terrell never once mentions Page's argument or positions her article as a direct rebuttal of his, she is nonetheless able to craft the piece in such a way that it constitutes a point-by-point response to his argument. Like Wells, though, she discovered the limitations of her strategy: that facts are no match for a pervasive white supremacist mythology that took the form of the fictionalized narrative Page had developed in his essay.

Terrell's cold, factual account could not compete with Page's absorbing scenes of sexual promiscuity, bestiality, and brutality: facts could not outdo his fiction. This "debate" provides an example of the ways that "a fictional scenario comes to be accepted as truth, becomes part of 'common sense,' and is virtually impervious to evidence and argument," as Karlyn Kohrs Campbell describes it.[35] Moreover, in trying to be balanced in a way Page wasn't, Terrell ends up accepting a class-based distinction between law-abiding African American men and those she considers criminals, whom she describes in terms uncomfortably similar to Page's: "Ignorant, repulsive in appearance and as near the brute creation as it is possible for a human being to be."[36] These, then, are the limitations to the strategy of rebuttal Terrell chose. One final point is worth noting, which involves the extent to which her very identity was controlled and defined by the editors of the *North American Review*, who edited Terrell's essay in only one way: they delete two words from her original title—Colored Woman—and replaced them with one: Negro. With this seemingly simple alteration Terrell's efforts and her authority were immediately undermined, her voice reinserted into the largely disrespected collective voice of Black America.

Terrell's *North American Review* article, then, placed her in a larger community of African American writers of nonfiction who all relatively failed to stem the tide of lynching through their factual exposition of what was wholly wrong about the kinds of defenses of lynching that Page offered. Statistics- and fact-based writing was important, for it drew attention to lynching and the issue of racial violence in the South. But the fact that, by the beginning of the twentieth century, lynching and racial violence remained prevalent in the United States, reveals that it was not effectual in the long run. Ida B. Wells knew this when, in 1902, she summarized the previous year's work for Chicago's Afro-American League's Anti-Lynching Bureau, for which she served as the chair. "Time was when the country resounded with denunciation and horror of burning a human being by so called Christian and civilized people," she began. But, she noted, the "last time a human being was made fuel for flames it was scarcely noticed in the papers editorially."[37] Although Wells continued to believe that facts would move people to action against lynching, she knew that, despite the efficacy of this tactic, lynching continued. Indeed, by the beginning of the twentieth century, the facts about lynching—the sheer numbers of Black men lynched and the gruesome details of their murders—seemed to shock even African

Americans that Wells had imagined to be her greatest allies in the crusade against racial violence into a state of traumatized paralysis. Her journalistic methods did challenge professed ignorance about lynching, and they were considered so effective as to be adopted by other organizations like the NAACP. But her mode of writing was unable to "loosen lynching's fit within modernity," as Jacqueline Goldsby puts it.[38] Fact-based journalistic writing was also unable to curb the public's enthusiasm for the myth- and stereotype-filled narratives used to vilify Black men, dehumanize African Americans, and romanticize white supremacy; these would continue to drive a seemingly insatiable desire to kill and mutilate Black bodies well into the twentieth century. "Lynchings continued . . . with unabated fury," the NAACP would state in 1919 in a disheartening report titled "Thirty Years of Lynching in the United States."[39] Despite that association's efforts to cultivate public support for antilynching legislation, it would repeatedly be struck down in Congress due to both Southern resistance and Northern indifference. Although the number of lynchings declined, it has remained a means of maintaining white supremacy in the United States.[40]

The "Instrumentality of the Story"

In this context, while there is no doubt that Terrell's publication in the *North American Review* served as a lesson in literary empowerment, it may also have played a part in her emerging belief that her greatest effectiveness as a writer lay in the cultivation of fictional forms more in keeping with those used so effectively by Page in his article and in the fiction that he continued to publish, all of which contributed to the development of a literary genre that celebrated in a common, authoritative narrative the lost golden age of slavery and the Black and white caricatures and social roles associated with it. These stories were *attractive* in a way that facts and figures alone were not. Not that facts and figures were to be ignored—but Terrell came to understand that African American writers needed to develop the means to "present facts in a forceful, tactful, attractive manner, so that sentiment may be created in behalf of the race."[41] In an address delivered in 1913, Terrell instructed her audience to "learn to express their thoughts as forcibly and clearly as possible."[42] Whereas statistics were forceful and precise, they were not attractive: they lacked a compelling narrative animated by alluring characters, captivating plots, and titillating scenes. The attractiveness of these elements is what drew Terrell to turn factual episodes into fictional forms, specifically the short-story format. Increasingly, she saw fiction as a powerful way to bring to life the racial landscape in which she lived. She came to believe that "the Race Problem could be solved more swiftly and more surely through the instrumentality of the story or novel than in any other way" (CW 234).

At first glance, there is a certain irony in the fact that Terrell considered fiction as the most effective vehicle for disclosing the truth, but she was not alone in this understanding, or in her devotion to the short story genre. Studies in the American short story suggest an uptick in story writing around the turn of the century that can be attributed in large part to the tremendous social changes brought about by industrial capitalism, immigration, and urbanization. Reformers of the progressive era came together in what Susan M. Ryan has called a "nexus of social movements," all of which were concerned with marginalized groups and each of which had their own social and political priorities.[43] These reform movements drew on the social utility of literature, which was seen as one way of activating the urgency of social change. Terrell's preference for the short story was in keeping with that of many of the era's reform journalists, who turned to works of fiction that thinly disguised accounts of factual circumstances as a mode of activist engagement. It is not coincidental that this period also saw a tremendous surge in the production of magazines, in which short fiction was a popular feature and, for an expanding magazine industry, commercially successful. The fact that readers were eager for short stories ensured that opportunities to publish them were widely available and potentially lucrative—as long as their authors gave readers what they wanted. What Edgar Allan Poe noted about the efficacy of short stories in 1844—that the "energetic, busy spirit of the age tended wholly" to literature that was "curt," "terse," "well-timed," and "readily-diffused"—applies as well to the beginning of the twentieth century.[44] Short stories were not a new kind of literature, but at that time they were shaped, packaged, and mobilized for a readership that found new appreciation for the form, which provided glimpses into the lives of the marginalized characters that made up America's rapidly diversifying population.[45]

Surely the brevity of short stories contributed to the impression of their accessibility to readers. But equally important to understanding Terrell's choice of the genre is the extent to which short stories were marketed as straightforward to write and simple to sell. As Andrew Levy has argued, the first decade of the twentieth century saw a proliferation of "how-to-write-a-story" handbooks and correspondence school courses, all of which communicated the perception that creative writing in general and the craft of the short story in particular was readily teachable.[46] These texts were designed to appeal to a broad swath of the American public, offering would-be writers what appeared to be a formula for success by advertising themselves as practical guides to the "structure, writing, and sale of the modern short story," to quote the subtitle of one the books on short story writing that Terrell herself consulted: J. Berg Esenwein's *Writing the Short-Story*. Published in 1908, it was one of the most popular books of this genre. In the book's introduction, Esenwein articulated his pedagogical objective: to convey the "practical principles of short story structure as recognized by American and British magazine editors, and as practised by authors whose products are judged to be of the first order."[47] His was a guide to writing the "popular and marketable short story," designed to "inspire and guide the individual writer, amateur or professional," in composing stories that were commercially successful (wss xi). *Writing the Short-Story* included a significant chapter on the use of "Fact in Fiction," as well as instructions on both "The Themes Sought Out" by magazine editors and readers, and those deemed "Improper," "Polemic," or "Themes Barred" (wss 44–49). It also included specific instructions for "Selling the Story" and an appendix that compiled the names and addresses of the most noteworthy publishing companies. In the first decades of the twentieth century, handbooks like Esenwein's set down rules and gave out models for what short stories should look like, and they surely influenced Terrell as she sought instruction outside of a formal academic setting on how to write a short story.

In 1901, Terrell succeeded in getting a short story published: "Venus and the Night Doctors" appeared in the *Washington Post* on April 7, 1901.[48] The title character, Venus, is an African American woman who works as a domestic for a white family in Washington, DC. The story's opening paragraph establishes two things. The first is Venus's respectability: although she is a maid, she works for a well-regarded family and has gained from "daily contact and association" with upper-class whites what she lacked in "book larnin." The second is that she is utterly terrified of "night doctors," a kind of doctor that, rather than healing, lurks around silently at night to capture and kill African Americans. On the one hand, the story casts the night doctors that Venus describes as figments of her superstitious mind, which remains captivated by the folk beliefs that Terrell herself most likely associated disparagingly with the intellectual inferiority of the uneducated. But what Venus imagines as "a living, breathing, terrible reality" bears striking resemblance to two very real threats faced by African Americans at the turn of the century, from both the so-called Night Riders, or members of the Ku Klux Klan, whose nighttime escapades were a means of racial terrorism, and from those medical doctors, both licensed and unlicensed, who performed cruel and inhumane experiments and procedures on African Americans, either as punishment or to advance theories of racial pseudoscience. In Terrell's story, Venus's fear of the night doctors is designed to entertain, but it also advanced the narrative's romantic plot: a male suitor who knows of her fear devises an elaborate scheme to save her from what she believes to be an attack by night doctors in order to lure her into marriage. Because Terrell never makes an explicit connection between the night doctors that plague her fictional character and the all-too-real night doctors that, in 1901, terrorized the South's African American population, what stands out most vividly in "Venus and the Night Doctors" is Terrell's use of dialect. In keeping with African American writing that was both "popular" and also successful in terms of finding its way into publication, the speech of both Venus and her suitor, Brownie, is distinguished from that of their white employer and thereby identifies both characters as honest and morally good while not terribly intelligent or sophisticated.

It is unclear whether Terrell understood at the time of publication that her story might have been accepted precisely because her characters did speak in dialect, but she later came to that realization. The story "was probably accepted . . . because it made the Colored cook appear ridiculous," as she wrote to one correspondent.[49] For the most part, Terrell eschewed and abandoned this style of writing. "Venus and the Night Doctors" did not reflect the advice she was given as a young woman in Europe: "One has to be *full of* a subject before trying to write about it."[50] As a clubwoman, Terrell was focused on elevating those African Americans in the lower classes, whose speech patterns often differed from her own, but what she was "full of" were stories of the injustices and discrimination experienced by her own sex and social class, many of which were determined by her privileged upbringing, her solidly upper-middle-class status, and the light color of her skin. These were often the experiences that Terrell kept most private, recording them even in her journal with a brevity and indirection that belies their importance and their impact. That they appear again and again in Terrell's stories suggests that one reason she wished to write fiction was that it allowed her to reflect upon and make sense of her own experience of the three things that most readily defined her identity: her race, her gender, and her class privilege.

Terrell's best stories allow her to do this, through characters and plots that emerge from her own experiences as both a woman and an African American. A small but significant incident that Terrell recorded in her 1906 address to the United Women's Club, which was later printed in the *Independent* as "What It Means to Be Colored in the Capital of the United States," became the basis of one of her most polished short stories, "Did Jeff Jackson Hear Caruso?" The essay tells of a light-skinned Black man who wished to take a group of girls to the theater one night, where African Americans were not permitted. Three were sisters, two of the siblings very fair and one brown-skinned. This child attracted the attention of the theater's ticket taker, who protested her admittance. The Black man silenced the ticket taker with this response: "Do you mean to tell me that I must go clear to the Philippine Islands to bring this child to the United States, and then I can't take her to the theatre in the National Capital?"[51] This episode exemplified the absurdity of race relations in the city of Washington and, indeed, in the United States generally. Terrell recognized that "Indians, Chinamen, Filipinos, Japanese, and representatives of any other dark race" were welcome in theaters and any other social spaces in the nation's capital, "if they can pay for them." The African American was the only person of color "thrust out of the hotels [and most other public spaces] of the national capital like a leper."[52]

"Did Jeff Jackson Hear Caruso?" fictionally recasts this situation. The story takes place in a Southern town, where Caruso, a popular musician likely inspired by the renowned tenor Enrico Caruso, was to perform. Jeff Jackson loved the singer: he "would have given five-sevenths of his chances to reach Heaven, if he could only hear Caruso sing," but the theater would not admit African Americans.[53] "Crazy to hear Caruso sing," Jeff enlists the assistance of Robert Reaves, the son of white parents who has recently returned to the South from a university in Massachusetts (JJ 5). Robert, who shares Jeff's love for music, devises a plan whereby they will both be able to see the show. Dismissing the danger for himself if he is discovered to be involved in the deception, Robert calls Jeff to his room late at night. There, he gives Jeff a "nifty fez" and a cape, telling Jeff he need "be a Turk for one night only" (JJ 7). The disguise is not at all sophisticated; both boys know that the object is simply to make Jeff look "different from the rest" (JJ 7). He is instructed to "speak little or no English," and "if . . . obliged to speak at all, "[to] break the English language into a thousand bits and throw it away" (JJ 7). Robert's disguise works; no one bothers the two boys as they enter the theater. Disguised as a "foreigner," Jeff is palatable to his Southern neighbors, despite his dark skin.

Crafting a story that condones such trickery may seem radical for Terrell, whose belief in agitation had its limits: she did not, for instance, approve of breaking the law. Yet she believed that "people who are discriminated against solely on account of race, color, or creed are justified in resorting to any subterfuge, using any disguise, playing any trick, provided they do not actually break the law, if it will enable them to secure the advantages and secure the rights to which they are entitled by outwitting their prejudice-ridden foes" (cw 115). This was precisely the upper hand Terrell portrayed through her fiction. Preferring simple plots that allowed her to draw on popular fictional formulas, Terrell's stories enacted contemporary moments that were shaped by the racial situation in the United States. Situated securely within the middle-class society that Terrell herself knew best, the characters Terrell creates are well educated and lead respectable lives, and their desires— attending the theater, riding on a train in safety—are modest. These features alone contradicted most contemporary depictions of African Americans, where Black characters were predominantly cast as criminals or servants who were minimally educated, enveloped in poverty, and distinguished by their lack of opportunity. In stories of light-skinned African Americans who might pass as white or as "foreigners," Terrell employed a fictional mechanism that enabled her to represent the absurdity of Black-white relations, as well as the maneuvers to which African Americans resorted in order to gain basic access to the nation's institutions and services. Narratives of passing allowed her to draw on conventional and formulaic strategies such as the use of disguise; with this narrative technique, Terrell portrays Blackness as both a source of victimization and a platform of cunning. It also allows her to celebrate her characters' small victories over racial oppression and discrimination. In the wake of their successful effort to pass Jeff off as a Turk instead of an African American, both Jeff and his friend Robert are described as "so convulsed with laughter [that they] could hardly speak" (jj 9). It is a victory for Terrell, and a significant development in African American literature as well. Popular fictional formulas that appeared at the turn of the century allowed white characters to darken up their skin and move into and out of Black communities, and "blacking up" offered white characters entry into Black culture in vaudeville and minstrel shows.[54] Yet American literature and culture at the turn of the century offered no equivalent convention that would allow Black characters access to fictional white society.

While "Did Jeff Jackson Hear Caruso Sing?" is a story about racial passing, it is also a story about the right of African Americans to buy tickets to a musical concert and, more generally, to forge a relationship with culture. This was something denied to African Americans, not only by the white owners of theaters or white ticket collectors, but also by some factions of African American leadership, who deemed music, literature, and the arts unnecessary for the race. Booker T. Washington famously claimed in his 1895 Atlanta Compromise speech that the "opportunity to earn a dollar in a factory just now is worth infinitely more than the opportunity to spend a dollar in an opera-house."[55] The story of Jeff Jackson challenges this belief, as did Terrell's own life and experiences. You will remember that for graduation from Oberlin College, Terrell's mother sent her two gifts. The first was an elegant dress. The second was a pair of opera glasses. As Terrell remarked in her autobiography, she would have preferred her parents' presence at her graduation to the presents she received. Still, Terrell loved music and the theater. As her French journal makes readily apparent, as a young woman her dedication to these cultural forms was second only to her desire to be a writer. In France and Switzerland, she vowed to practice the piano for two hours each day.[56] In Berlin she made good use of the opera glasses, attending the opera "twice and sometimes three times a week" (cw 76). Not only was this a good way to attune her ear to the German language; it was also a passion that Terrell could enjoy without regard to race. The concert halls were open to her in Europe in ways they would not be in the United States. Having experienced this was a feature of the extraordinary privilege that enveloped Terrell's life. And yet it led her to believe that culture should be available to all. Accepting segregation because it offered greater spending power was a decision made at the expense of the opera, among other cultural opportunities to which African Americans needed and deserved exposure.

As I have already suggested, Terrell found ways to speak out against Booker T. Washington's leadership and to criticize his theories about the place of African Americans, and this unpublished short fictional story is certainly one of them. Whereas, for her husband, Washington represented an opportunity, he was for Terrell an obstacle, not only professionally, in terms of the ways he could limit her voice and political leadership, but also personally, because his vision of the place of culture in African American lives threatened to further limit its place in her own life. In fictional terms, Jeff Jackson's ability to see Caruso depended not only on desegregating public spaces, but also on embracing the right of African Americans to become consumers of culture. The story is therefore an implicit response to Washington, and a testimony of the importance of cultural opportunity in the lives of African Americans.

Like "Did Jeff Jackson Hear Caruso Sing?," the story "Betsy's Borrowed Baby" allows Terrell to address her own particular vulnerabilities and, at the same time, condemn one of the men who had represented an obstacle to her career. It is about train travel in the South, a subject that Terrell would return to again and again in her short fiction. Telling of a young girl's trip home to a Southern town from a midwestern college, the story chronicles the dangers of train travel for African Americans, regardless of their wealth, educational status, or exposure to high culture. Betsy's dread of the leg of the trip from Cincinnati to her hometown in the South is evident from the story's beginning: she described the journey, three days and two nights in the Jim Crow car, as a "hideous nightmare."[57] "In spite of all the courage she could muster . . . it was very hard for Betsy to board the Jim Crow car at Cincinnati," Terrell writes of Betsy, whom she describes as "well-groomed, dignified and prepossessing" (BBB 4). It was not, Terrell insisted, that Betsy "objected to riding with members of her own race" (BBB 3). Rather, it "wounded her feelings and crushed her pride to be thrust into the car solely on account of her color. Moreover, she rebelled against the dishonesty and the unfairness of the railroads, which sold her a first class ticket but forced her to ride in a second or third class seat" (BBB 3).

In fact, Betsy identifies a distinctive warmth with the Jim Crow car, which is described as so small as to "invite [a] sort of familiarity among passengers" (BBB 5). It is when the car is empty of other African Americans—specifically, overnight—that Betsy is afraid. Her concerns are well warranted. "Say Bob, there's some good looker in the Jim," Betsy overhears one white man saying to another as soon as she is alone. His friend responds, "I'll come and give her the once over myself" (BBB 5). Try as she might to stay awake to guard against these men's approaches, Betsy falls asleep and is awakened to "find herself in the arms" of one of the men (BBB 6). While running his hands up and down her body, the man underscores her peril by meaningfully saying "it will be a long time, before we reach another station" and telling her that her screams will be lost in the racket made by the train (BBB 7). Betsy's struggle to free herself is met with more threats: "If you make yourself too disagreeable," he tells her, "I'll take you to the platform out yonder behind the baggage car, throw you off the train, break your sassy neck" (BBB 7).

Only a sudden lurching of the train as it rounds a bend saves Betsy from her attacker. While he is off-balance, she runs toward the smoker; before she reaches it, he grabs her arm, "twist[s] it brutally, thr[o]w[s] her into the seat and pass[es] into the smoker himself" (BBB 8). Betsy knows that she has no recourse against her attacker, since "white men below the Mason and Dixon line very rarely punish, defy, or rebuke one of their race from offenses committed against a colored woman" (BBB 8). She tells the conductor what has happened, but his response is in keeping with her expectations: "That man didn't mean no harm," he tells her. "He just wanted to see what kind of stuff you're made of" (BBB 8). Like the attacker, who tells Betsy "I've had a heap of fun . . . monkeying with you girls coming home from school" (BBB 7), the

Written by Mary Church Terrell
1615 S St., N.W.
Washington, D.C.

Betsy's Borrowed Baby.

Never in her life had Betsy longed to do anything quite so much as she wanted to spend the summer with Narka Davis. The two girls had entered Ralston, a college of the middle West, on the same day- the very same day - as they always said with great emphasis and zest, whenever they mentioned it. They were juniors now and had been fast friends ever since their freshman year. As a student at Ralston Betsy had made an enviable record for herself and there was little doubt that she would be the proud possessor of a Phi Beta Kappa pin, when she graduated the following year.

Narka lived in Maine and had frequently urged Betsy to spend the summer vacation with her. She had rhapsodized again and again over the good times she and Betsy might have taking ocean dips near Portland and had expatiated eloquently on the beneficial effects which salt water would have on her friend's health.

As Betsy sat in her room that afternoon thinking about this, there was a certain, brooding wistfulness in her large, dark-brown eyes which seemed on the verge of tears. But suddenly with a distinct effort at self control she raised her head and smoothed the jet black hair from her forehead, as though she were trying to brush away the gloom. The deep-red flush which every now and then shone through the rich bronze of her swarthy complexion was indisputable evidence of great agitation of mind.

It was not solely because of the prospect of having a good time nor on account of the virtue in salt water that Betsy wanted very much to go to Maine. There was another reason. In the midst of her reverie she heard a group of girls pass through the dormitory hall near her door. They were all gleefully talking about going home. One had counted the exact number of minutes and seconds which would elapse between the time she was then speaking till she would actually board the train for home. The conversation of these girls stabbed Betsy's heart like a knife. It reproached and rebuked her, so that she felt ashamed of herself. Here she was worried to death, because she was forced to go home,

4.4 First page of Mary Church Terrell's short story "Betsy's Borrowed Baby." Mary Church Terrell Papers, Library of Congress, Washington, DC. Terrell meticulously saved the typewritten manuscripts of her stories, as if to insist that ample evidence of the kind of writing that was to her most important be included in her archive.

conductor is amused by Betsy's situation. Indeed, he recognizes, as does her attacker, that the "spunk" she has acquired as an element of her Northern education makes her more attractive as a target of sexual harassment than she would otherwise be. To find safety, Betsy has to look outside of herself. She returns to school at the end of the summer in the comfort of a Pullman car and enjoys three meals a day in the train's dining room, but only because she has agreed to serve as the nurse of a small white child going to stay with her grandmother. Despite her education and refinement, Betsy needs the white child to make her introduction, as it were, to others. Initially, Betsy "did not want the passengers to discover she was well-educated, for fear they would assume a hostile attitude toward her" (BBB 14). But in the company of a white child for whom Betsy is responsible, she is seen as a "comely, dignified, intelligent" young woman (BBB 14).

"Betsy's Borrowed Baby" is another of Terrell's short stories deeply rooted in her own experience. As a young child traveling with her father, a conductor tried to relocate her from the first class car to the Jim Crow car "'where [she] belonged'" (CW 16). Only her father's return from the smoking car and the ferocity of his protests ended the incident: they stayed where they were. But for Terrell this experience was nevertheless jarring. She reviewed with her mother her deportment and dress on the train, assuming she had done something wrong that had signaled to the conductor that she belonged in an inferior space. She would come to learn that it did not matter how well-dressed a woman was or how dignified her demeanor: if she were African American, she would be relegated to the Jim Crow car upon reaching the South. Terrell does not reflect in her autobiography on her experience traveling back and forth from her father's home in Memphis to school in Ohio as a teenager, or to work as a young woman in Washington, DC. But she does effectively communicate the principal danger of that journey: being alone in the Jim Crow car and "at the mercy of the conductor or any man who entered" (CW 337). This was a situation that occurred again and again in the South, resulting in what Terrell called "awful tragedies which had overtaken colored girls who had been obliged to travel alone on these cars at night" (CW 337). As an adult woman and a paid lecturer, Terrell was not immune to this menace. She traveled extensively in the first decade of the twentieth century and had no shortage of stories about the perils of the Jim Crow car; these she did reflect on in her autobiography, albeit in a veiled and generalized way. It was not only that these cars were dirty and lacked ventilation and food service; they also left her feeling unsafe. Her own experience trying to protect herself from the sexual advances of white men in a

Jim Crow car of an overnight train was, like Betsy's, harrowing, leading her to assess the necessity of spending the night on a train in the South as a "real peril for a colored girl" (cw 298).

Even in Terrell's journals—from which she clearly drew in her crafting of short stories—the details of this threat remain largely unspoken, in part because it is impossible to put into words for a woman of Terrell's social class, who prided herself on her moral standing, her dignity, and her decorum. In her diaries and journals, she documents the way she was treated in the South, both at various speaking engagements and in the hotels where she stayed, in the restaurants where she ate, and on the trains that carried her between locations. Yet she speaks in shorthand, revealing a tension, as Terrell's biographer Alison M. Parker notes, between disclosure and secrecy.[58] About an overnight train trip between Atlanta and Savannah, she would observe, "Had a restful night considering the kind of car in which I rode."[59] So frightening were some of these experiences that Terrell took to passing as white when she traveled deep into the South. This was often an equally frightening disguise and, importantly, it did not further her ultimate goal of advancing social and political change; nevertheless, it provided a layer of protection that she sometimes embraced as necessary. Her dramatization of the attack on Betsy was a way for her to face and publicize Black women's vulnerability to sexual assault, a topic that she could not speak about openly in other forums. Long-standing stereotypes left Black women's sexuality a particularly precarious subject. Female slaves had been branded as sexually promiscuous and morally void, and these labels ensured that white men would continue to see African American women as their playthings long after Emancipation. But Terrell knew that even to raise the issue was to risk unwanted attention. She therefore adopts an old strategy of fugitives from slavery, whose most devastating experiences remain shrouded in silence in their narratives. "No pen can describe and no tongue portray the indignities, insults and assaults to which colored women and girls have been subjected in Jim Crow cars," she observes in her autobiography. "If I should dare relate some of the things which have happened, many would not believe me, and very serious objections to publishing them in a book would probably be raised" (cw 229).

In this case, the unpublished story "Betsy's Borrowed Baby" speaks up for Terrell, by making visible both Betsy's assault and her attacker's purpose: he wishes to rape her. The form of the short story gave Terrell a way to express herself about experiences that she was not able to speak about even in the privacy of her journals. It also allows her to respond to Thomas

Nelson Page, whose article on lynching in the *North American Review* had demonized Black men for raping white women. As we have seen, Terrell's response to Page dismissed the rape of white women by Black men as an effective justification of lynching, since in most cases this was not even the crime allegedly committed. In that article she does touch on the rape of Black women and girls, pointing out that "throughout the entire period of bondage colored women were debauched by their masters."[60] But it was not the purpose of her article to dwell on this, nor was it a subject she wanted to draw attention to in the *North American Review*. What she must gloss over in that forum as well as in her autobiography the guise of fiction allows her to address more directly. Here, she says in no uncertain terms who is really endangered by rape in America: not white women at the hands of Black men, as Page had claimed, but Black women at the hands of white men. In doing so, Terrell draws on the appeal of narrative to craft a story that is compelling in part because Betsy is not anonymous or based in statistics. Throughout much of the first half of the twentieth century, sexual assault remained an open secret in American literature. In her fiction, Terrell unveils this secret, exposing us to those memories seared into her own mind and those of countless other Black women. Her aim is to replace what had long been relegated to silence or presented as tales of Black women's promiscuity and immorality with narratives that detail their refinement, their tenacity, and their cunning.

"Nobody Wants to Know a Colored Woman's Opinion"

For the most part, Terrell's short stories exist only in the archives. But while it would be easy enough to therefore declare that both Terrell's voice and that of her fictional character, Betsy, remain unheard, this would be inaccurate. It is true that "Betsy's Borrowed Baby" never found an audience in the conventional manner, but this does not mean that the story found no readership. On the contrary, Terrell's short fiction was submitted to, circulated among, and read by editors that she hoped would accept it for publication. For the most part, they were rejected. But, by submitting them again and again, Terrell insisted that they be read and acknowledged, and that these readers acknowledge the real reason for their rejection. She also established a trail of correspondence between herself and various friends, editors, and writing instructors that documents both her avowed aspirations as a short story writer and her understanding that these goals could not be met in the historical moment in which she lived—perhaps not even in her lifetime. Her greatest disappointment, according to her autobiography, was that she did not succeed as a short story writer, and yet her own assessment of this failure was that she did not live in a "literary atmosphere" (CW 237). In this final section of the chapter, I look to Terrell's exchanges with literary professionals to see how she came to know and understand the atmosphere of the early twentieth century as it pertained to African American fiction; how, through her correspondence, she created a role in it for herself and her stories; and how she worked to change the "literary atmosphere" for African American writers. Here I am most interested in the sort of work she performed in and through her correspondence as she identified the reasons for and came to terms with her own failure as a short story writer, and how she used this correspondence to ensure that future failures by Black writers were less likely. Terrell's "failed" authorship, I argue, has much to tell us about the historical moment in which she "failed," as well as what kind of work she nonetheless performed to ensure that the fictional writing of future Black writers would not languish in the archives as hers did.

Terrell dedicated an entire chapter of *A Colored Woman in a White World* to recounting her efforts to succeed as a writer, a chapter that generally ignores the very real successes she had as a nonfiction writer and journalist and focuses instead on her lack of success in becoming a published writer of short stories. As she tells it, there are several reasons for this. First, she points to the difficulty of finding the time amid her personal and professional responsibilities to dedicate to fiction. Even as she felt the urgency to write it, it was always the kind of writing pushed to the margins of her days, prioritized after the nonfiction articles she chose or was asked to write and the work of preparing the addresses she was paid to deliver on the lecture circuit. Second, she indicates that her role as a mother ate into time she might have used for creative writing, as did the household duties she felt compelled to complete. Juggling these responsibilities also took a toll on her energy: as she puts it in her autobiography, before she knew it, the "minutes I had at my disposal for literary composition had been consumed, to say nothing of my patience, strength and inspiration" (CW 236). Terrell returns again and again in her memoir to the intellectual space, the "concentration and peace of mind" required of the kind of writing to which she aspired (CW 235). Finally, as she had in her European journals, Terrell also dwells in the memoir on the bravery required to be a creative writer: her lack of it was something she also blamed for the failure of her career as a writer of short stories, admitting to her readers that she "could not generate the courage" required for this kind of writing (CW 235).

But these were not the only reasons Terrell did not succeed in her aim. Indeed, as the many short stories that exist in manuscript form in the archives attest, Terrell did find the time, the energy, and the courage to write, but those stories were not published, in part because she insisted that her short fiction should be published in a different venue from her nonfiction articles or journalistic writing. As I have said, the bulk of her nonfiction writing appeared in the popular African American journals of the early twentieth century, including the AME *Church Review*, the *Voice of the Negro*, and the *Southern Workman*. Terrell recognized these periodicals, edited by African Americans and addressed to a Black audience, to be instrumental in providing a forum through which African Americans could both craft a group identity based on a shared past and work toward the achievement of full national citizenship. But she made a conscious decision not to pursue them as venues for her literary fiction. Instead, she insisted on submitting her short fiction to the "quality monthlies" that were marketed to a newly emergent leisured white readership. This decision illustrated the extent to which she sought to situate herself as a writer of fiction within the nation's community of primarily white writers. And yet it was not an elitist gesture but an effort based in her determination that her fiction reach as wide and as interracial a readership as possible, in order to have the greatest possible impact.[61] Fiction, Terrell believed, could promote understanding and effect change in a way that nonfiction writing could not.

One of the writers that Terrell admired most was Harriet Beecher Stowe, whose *Uncle Tom's Cabin* served as a model of the sort of literature Terrell wished to write. It was a work of fiction that was credited with influencing public opinion about the institution of slavery and leading to its abolition. Equally important, *Uncle Tom's Cabin* was the work through which Terrell herself had come to know slavery, which for many middle-class African Americans who came of age during Reconstruction was shrouded in secrecy, as it was a topic that their parents and grandparents wished to forget. Even Terrell's maternal grandmother, who from time to time did tell Terrell "tales of brutality perpetrated upon slaves who belonged to cruel masters," found these stories so distressing that she would "stop abruptly and refuse to go on," leaving Terrell deeply affected by but infinitely curious about the unknown, unspoken past (cw 11). Untold at home and untaught in schools, the history of slavery was often accessible to those of Terrell's generation only in fictional sources. It is no wonder, then, that Terrell aspired to emulate Stowe, and write a "modern version of *Uncle Tom's Cabin*" that would expose "the injustice commonly perpetuated upon colored people all over the United States[,] . . . as the original *Uncle Tom's Cabin* exposed the cruelties and barbarities of slavery" (CW 233).[62] To do so would be to educate white readers in particular, who might be moved to a better understanding of African Americans through an account of their lives and conditions. This, in turn, Terrell believed, would motivate them to take action to oppose and end racial discrimination, segregation, and violence.

Terrell knew that the leading journals, the oldest of which was the *North American Review*, effectively functioned as the gatekeepers of the nation's highest cultural literary domain. Magazines like *Harper's*, the *Independent*, and the *Century* followed political currents but were known primarily for fiction, and they competed with one another for the best literature by the most popular writers. Many of these magazines had their roots in the abolitionist past, but in the post-Reconstruction period they had emerged as distinctly ambivalent about racial politics. By the beginning of the twentieth century, the quality literary magazines appeared to champion the racist contributions of Southern writers. Their embrace of the popular genre of plantation fiction like that written by Thomas Nelson Page, in which racism ranged in tone from condescending to virulent, helped to spread racial hatred by establishing widespread romantic notions about the Old South, reinforcing anxieties about the dangers of the present, and fortifying in the American imagination popular caricatures of African Americans that served to escalate racism and racial violence. As Page himself observed in 1891, "The great monthly magazines which had become the vehicle of transmission of literary work were not only open as never before to Southern contributors, but welcomed them as a new and valuable acquisition."[63] Page's most famous plantation stories from the end of the nineteenth century, "Mars Chan" and "Meh Lady," had been published in the *Century*. These and similar works of fiction went largely unanswered in the pages of the nation's most prestigious literary magazines. Terrell's objective was to meet these stories in the same publication venues as they appeared and counter their images and messages with her own.

But Terrell would have to do battle with the editors of these publications to get her fiction accepted. Over at least two decades, she continuously submitted stories for publication, filing away the letters of rejection she received in return, deeming them valuable enough to preserve. In the beginning, Terrell understood her writing to be rejected because of its quality. This was the reason cited by Howard B. Wells, editor for Harper and Brothers Publishers, whose letter to Terrell in the summer of 1907 was apologetic, but firm: "I wish I could tell you that we liked [the story], but it is part of the editor's function to be brutal and I can't say that the story has appealed very strongly. In the first place, the subject seems to us a little trivial, offering good material for an anecdote, rather than a story of some length. Then, too, the handling does not seem to be quite as good as it should be." Wells's sense that her fiction writing was "nothing like as good as the handling of your articles which I have read" might have sent her back to the more familiar mode of journalistic writing and the publication venues in which she had excelled, but she persevered nevertheless, submitting more stories to the same magazines associated with the "highest literary standards."[64] Again and again, the editors of those magazines found reasons to reject her writing. Over time, the reasons they offered for turning down her work became more and more ambiguous, each an echo of the broad yet imprecise criticism articulated by Hamilton Holt, the managing editor of the *Independent*, in 1909: "This is a pretty good story," he wrote to her, "and yet not quite 'irresistible.' I am reluctantly returning it to you."[65] The wording of these responses at first led Terrell to believe that manuscripts were "returned to [her] because they fell too far below the required standard to be accepted" (cw 224). But, more and more often, the terms with which Terrell's writing was praised contradicted its rejection. "You have an excellent literary form," she was told in 1910, for instance, by William English Walling, a journalist in his own right and a founder of the naacp. But to "interest our magazines, a given piece of work must either have very exceptional literary merits, or else it must be 'cooked up' in exactly the manner to which the American public is accustomed."[66] Perhaps, she began to speculate, her writing wasn't "cooked up" in the way that pleased the American public.

Terrell continued to work on the quality of her writing, seeking the feedback of "reputable critics" (cw 224), reading handbooks like Esenwein's *Writing the Short-Story* and *Writing the Photoplay* (1913), and enrolling in writing classes offered by the Home Correspondence School, a distance-learning program located in Springfield, Massachusetts.[67] But even as she endeavored to improve her craft, she gradually began to suspect that the reason her short stories were being dismissed by the editors of American magazines had nothing to do with their quality. Terrell privately voiced her mounting conviction in a 1909 journal entry: "No one wants a story about a Negro."[68] By 1916, she had refined this suspicion into a full-fledged theory, which she laid out in a letter to F. Arthur Metcalf, president of the Home Correspondence School. With exasperation, Terrell explained her reason for withdrawing from the school's literary department. "My Dear Mr. Metcalf," she began. "A few years ago I joined the Home Correspondence

School. . . . But, after thinking about the matter I decided that it would do me personally no good to continue, for the reason that the only subject in which I am deeply interested is one which the American publications will not consider for a minute. If I had all the talent of all the short story writers put together, it would avail me nothing in this country, provided I should try to write anything which would present the Colored-American's side of the question." It was not, she had determined, that her stories were poorly written: it was that the editors of these magazines were not interested in the way she handled her subject matter. She had come to believe that only authors who make African Americans look "ridiculous or criminal can get a hearing in the press, but [their] trials and struggles and heart aches are tabooed." Terrell related to Metcalf what she had been told by countless editors to whom she submitted her short stories: if they were "on the Race Problem," there was "no use sending them [to American magazines], for they would not accept them, no matter how well written they might be." Terrell knew the impact of fiction and, increasingly, the new technology of "photo-plays" on reinforcing racial stereotypes and increasing animosity between Blacks and whites. She believed that her stories could counter this. But, as she told Metcalf, she had reached the conclusion that there was no reason "for a Colored woman who wants to make an appeal for justice and equality of opportunity thru the medium of the short story . . . to make the effort." Terrell's closing was bitter and to the point: "The advice, therefore to writers . . . should be write mainly of characters who arouse the spectators [sic] sympathy, provided those characters are white. Be sure to let your brothers and sisters of a darker hue alone, unless you make them monkeys or criminals."[69]

Metcalf replied promptly to Terrell's letter, encouraging her to persevere with her work in the school, but his response entirely validated her suspicion that American publishing was inhospitable to the writing that she wished to do. "It seems to me that a great deal might be accomplished for the colored race through fiction," he acknowledged, "but of course . . . [the material] would have to be very wisely handled. Anything that would give offense or that would serve to rekindle the fires of old prejudices would be most unfortunate."[70] Metcalf's words confirmed Terrell's impression that African American writing was monitored for its "acceptability," with little regard for artistic merit. It also confirmed for Terrell that her hopes and aspirations as a writer could not be met at this historical moment. The writing career that she desired was beyond her reach because of a publishing industry that allowed only those images of African Americans that were "popularly and generally accepted" to appear in print (cw 224). The stories she wished to write,

about the daily lives lived and injustices faced by well-educated and economically successful middle-class African Americans, held no interest for
the editors of American literary magazines or, presumably, for their readers.
She would come to express this understanding in no uncertain terms in her
autobiography: "Nobody wants to know a colored woman's opinion about
her own status or that of her group. When she dares express it, no matter
how mild or tactful it may be, it is called 'propaganda,' or is labeled 'controversial'" (CW 264).

These key terms haunted Terrell, and they speak volumes about the kind
of writing that was acceptable to American publishers. Terrell's stories, largely
about the injustices faced by the Black middle class, were considered "controversial" and labeled "propaganda" because they failed to reinforce the image
of Black authorship—and, indeed, the image of Black people themselves—
lodged in the American imagination. More specifically, they failed to conform
to what white Americans thought a Black woman writer should say, what
she should sound like, and what kind of demeanor was appropriate for her.
Terrell's stories were not "cooked up right" because they failed to depict African Americans as uneducated, criminal, or consumed by poverty; they "gave
offense" because they illustrated the lives of middle- and upper-class African Americans who wished to enjoy the same rights and privileges as white
people and were often able to subversively claim these because of the color of
their skin. In this, both Terrell and her stories were accurately judged by the
literary establishment to be "controversial," in that they contradicted popular, accepted images of African Americans, replacing these with images that
threatened to upset the status quo. The stories were considered "propaganda"
only because they served as a critique of prejudice and racial injustice.

Terrell believed that African Americans had been inadequately depicted
in literature, and she set out in her fiction to correct this by telling stories
that capture the complexity of race, particularly as it intersected with class
and gender. As we have seen, she came to disdain the simplistic manner in
which she had drawn on dialect and stereotype in "Venus and the Night
Doctors." The bulk of her stories reject this familiar and popular means of
identifying African Americans and, in doing so, invert plantation fiction's
understanding of the knowable Black subject. Indeed, the characters she
creates are defined by their complexity, a fundamental departure from the
stock Black characters and formulaic characteristics of Blackness that circulated in early twentieth-century literature. In this, Terrell challenges her
readers—in this case, the editors to whom she sent her stories—to expand
their own understanding, as well as that of their readership, of African

American literature and authorship, just as her characters challenge the very social order and racial hierarchy of the South.

Terrell's stories were seen as both "propaganda" and "controversial," then, because they are peopled with characters that find ways around discriminatory practices to attend the opera or ride in the first class car of the train. They are able to access these segregated spaces not only because of their economic privilege; as in the story of Jeff Jackson, they are also often light enough to pose as white or as a "foreigner." Other writers in the early twentieth century had addressed miscegenation and its aftermath, creating characters in the tradition of the tragic mulatto/a, such as Sappho in Pauline Hopkins's *Contending Forces* or Rena in Charles Chesnutt's *The House behind the Cedars*. But replicating these characters was not Terrell's intent. Her fair-skinned characters don't dwell on, question, or regret their racial affiliation, nor does it bring on for them a crisis of identity. Like Terrell, they do not consider themselves to be of mixed race, and we do not learn about them through detailed flashbacks of their paternity or ancestry. Rather, they are proudly African American, posing as something different not out of shame or as a way to deny their racial identity but as a matter of opportunity: as a means of obtaining the privileges, the experiences, and the levels of comfort that they deserve. In her stories, Terrell is quick to show how African Americans have manipulated systematic oppression in ways that not only underscore the senselessness of definitions of racial identity and difference, but that will also eventually result in their demise.

Metcalf was not alone in confirming Terrell's suspicion that a "conspiracy of silence" effectively prevented stories about African Americans that were not "wisely handled" from appearing in American magazines. Terrell also approached Ray Stannard Baker, one of the founders and an editor of the *American Magazine*, to ask his opinion of the fate of fiction about African Americans in the hands of American publishers. She asked him "if he thought his or any other publication would accept a modern version of *Uncle Tom's Cabin*" that "depicted the injustice commonly perpetrated upon colored people all over the United States." Baker discussed her question with colleagues before delivering his conclusion: "No periodical in the country would publish any such story at that time" (CW 233). In her autobiography Terrell would write of the devastating impact of this exchange, claiming that Baker's response "confirmed my own views on the subject and sounded my literary death knell. I knew full well that the kind of story I would be able to write would not appeal to the average editor of an American magazine. I was sure it would be interpreted as 'propaganda' of the deepest dye, and would be voted controversial and 'inartistic' to the nth degree. Right there," she claimed, "I gave up my literary ghost" (CW 233–34).

What Terrell casts as a moment of resignation, in which she accepts both the fact that her stories had no chance of being accepted for publication in the nation's most prominent magazines and her fate as a short story writer, was at least partially this. She writes in her autobiography of the "bitter disappointment" she felt at not succeeding as a short story writer (CW 234). But out of this resignation came an inner resolve to continue both writing short stories and, most significantly, submitting them to the same set of elite magazines for publication. She did this not because she believed that they might eventually find their way to an editor who would accept them, but because she saw it as a way to both protest the silencing of Black writers and work toward opening up those avenues of publication for future generations. In this context, the cover letters that Terrell submitted to editors along with her short stories are important evidence of the campaign she mounted against American magazines that refused to publish literature by or about African Americans that contradicted popular stereotypes. They are evidence of her failure only in that they illustrate her refusal to accept the stale and static modes of representing Blackness deemed "acceptable" by the American public and her rejection of the policies put in place by the white publishing industry to monitor and control the voices of African Americans. Within what looks like failure, then, is what José Esteban Muñoz calls "a kernel of potentiality": for Terrell, failure became a platform of criticism and dissent.[71]

Although Terrell's archives indicate that she sent her writing to a number of the nation's leading literary magazines, no publisher presented itself as a more significant target of her criticism and wrath than *Harper's Magazine*. Known for its reprints of the fiction of popular British authors in the nineteenth century, *Harper's New Monthly Magazine*, as it was called when first launched in 1850, remained a popular journal with a reputation for publishing short fiction. While it included in its pages stories about African Americans, these were typically in the tradition of plantation fiction, which were written exclusively by white authors, romanticized slavery, and depicted African Americans as happy-go-lucky "darkies" themselves nostalgic for the well-ordered world of the antebellum era. By the time Terrell submitted "Betsy's Borrowed Baby" to the editor of *Harper's*, she did so without any faith that the magazine would actually accept the story. She nevertheless opened her cover letter very traditionally. "Inclosed [*sic*] is a story entitled 'Betsy's Borrowed Baby', which I hope you will accept," she wrote. "If, however, you do not please return it to me, for which I inclose [*sic*] stamps." But what follows is not

(Copy of letter to the editor of
Harper's Magazine   March '22)

To The Editor of Harper's Magazine:

     Inclosed is a story entitled "Betsy's Borrowed Baby", which I hope
you will accept. If, however, you do not please return it to me, for which
I inclose stamps.

     Will you be kind enough to tell me whether you would consider any
story in which difficulties confronting colored people are set forth? I know
you would not take an appeal in their behalf. As I understand it, that is not
a magazine's business. But, there are a great many conditions confronting
colored people about which comparatively few white people in this country
know any thing at all. If you really want something new, it can be found in
the life the life which colored Americans lead. It seems to me that the American press has entered into a conspiracy of silence, so far as letting the
world know any thing about the colored man's point of view is concerned. Editors will accept anything which make colored people appear ridiculous , criminal, or undesirable, but they will reject anything which shows the obstacles
against which they are obliged to contend, The thousand and one humiliations
to which they are subjected every minute in the day and the injustices of
which they are the victims at the white man's hands. Anything showing that up
is taboo with a vengeance. White people say they are superior, and yet they do
every thing they can to keep the so called inferior race down. There are many
generous hearted, broad minded, justice loving white people in this country
who are willing to assist colored/in every way they can. Many of them would be
shocked, if they knew the blighting, blasting conditions under which colored
people live all over this country, But particularly in the South. If they knew
these conditions they would be willing to try to improve them. I have always
beleived that much could be done to solve the race problem thru the medium of
the short story. But. unless a short story ridicules colored people, depicts
them as criminals or shows up thier defects, american magazines will not accept
them. How long, Oh! Lord How long? Personally, I would be ashamed to make
the life of any human being less favored than myself any harder than it is by
refusing to let the world know the deplorable conditions under which he lives,
if it were in my power to do so. And yet, that is what many editors do by re-
jecting everything which would reveal the truth about the injustices of various
kinds of which colored people are victims in this greatest republic on earth.

     My dear Mr. Editor, open up your coumns, so that the colored man's
point of view may shine forth every now and then. Your magazine is strong and
can afford to take any stand it wants to take. I am not pleading for myself.
of course I wish you would accept my story. That goes without saying, but I
have very little hope. If If it were a master piece of literature and told
the story of a colored girl's plight on a Jim-Crow car, I fear it would not
be accepted by Harper's Magazine. It would be against your policy would it
not?

     I hope you will not misunderstand me. I don't mean to be "impudent!"
I do want you to consider your point of view, however.

     With the hope of receiving an early reply, I am yours with the
highest esteem

                 (Mary Church Terrell.)

4.5 This draft of the cover letter that accompanied Mary Church Terrell's short story
"Betsy's Borrowed Baby" when she submitted it to *Harper's Magazine* is an exemplar of
the way Terrell used cover letters as a platform for criticism and dissent. Mary Church
Terrell Papers, Library of Congress, Washington, DC.

typical of the brief cover letter that might traditionally accompany the submission of a story to a magazine. It is instead a scathing criticism of *Harper's* and an indictment of the American publishing industry. Terrell used this letter to give voice to the truth surrounding the magazine's refusal to print her stories and any other fiction that depicted African Americans in positive terms. She knew her story would not find a place in the pages of *Harper's* because its editors refused to print "any story in which difficulties confronting colored people are set forth," she wrote. Here she names the "conspiracy of silence" that she believed existed, whereby the editors of the nation's most widely read and influential magazines effectively stifled Black literary voices. "Editors will accept anything which make [sic] colored people appear ridiculous, criminal, or undesirable," she wrote, "but they will reject anything which shows the obstacles against which they are obliged to contend, [t]he thousand and one humiliations to which they are subjected every minute in the day and the injustices of which they are victims at the white man's hands. Anything showing that up is taboo with a vengeance."[72]

Terrell knew that her stories covered terrain as yet uncharted in American literature and believed this to be just the sort of fiction that *Harper's* should be most eager to publish. "There are a great many conditions confronting colored people about which comparatively few white people in this country know anything at all. If you really want something new, it can be found in the life which colored Americans lead," she told the editor. Terrell remained convinced that Black lives could be opened up through imaginative literature, and that, specifically, "much could be done to solve the race problem thru the medium of the short story." It was a means of revealing the humanity of African Americans to those "generous-hearted, broad-minded, justice-loving white people in this country." This group, Terrell believed, might be moved by short stories that depicted the "blighting, blasting conditions under which colored people live all over this country," just as white readers had been informed and moved to action by Stowe's account of the horrors of slavery in the middle of the nineteenth century.[73] Safely cast in fictional form, what Terrell wished to write about, which she characterized to Arthur F. Metcalf in 1916 as the "conditions under which Colored people actually live today—their inability to secure employment, the assault and battery constantly committed upon their hearts, their sensibilities and their feelings," would reach a wider audience and move that audience more effectively to sympathy than did her nonfiction writing.[74] Narrative fiction was an important medium for African Americans, but she knew that *Harper's* would not accept a story that seemed to be "an appeal in their behalf."[75]

Terrell's letters changed nothing about her own particular circumstances. "Betsy's Borrowed Baby" was rejected by *Harper's* and, it appears, by every other publication to which it was sent, and the bulk of her own stories languished in the archives. She refused the recommendation of the veteran journalist William T. Stead, whose advice was that Terrell submit stories under a pen name, "so that the editors would not know I am colored" (cw 213). Instead, she simply continued to submit her stories for publication, a process that allowed her to expose the racism that lay at the core of the nation's most popular magazines. She did so not because she believed her own stories would eventually see their way into print; that hope had faded into nonexistence. Indeed, she often declared precisely that in her cover letters to editors. Consider the letter she sent to the editor of *Harper's* with her submission of "Betsy's Borrowed Baby": "Of course, I wish you would accept my story. That goes without saying, but I have very little hope." What was at issue, she informed the editor, was not the quality of her writing, but a wholly different thing: "If it were a master piece [*sic*] of literature and told the story of a colored girl on a Jim-Crow car, I fear it would not be accepted by Harper's Magazine. It would be against your policy, would it not?" She was no longer afraid to declare the truth to those whom she had no interest in placating. She stated forthrightly that she had no "hope" that her work would be accepted. What she was intent on doing instead was to issue a challenge to those editors who maintained the "conspiracy of silence" she now had discovered. "Open up your columns, so that the colored man's point of view may shine forth every now and then," she appealed to the editor of *Harper's*. These were journals, she believed, that should establish rather than follow public opinion. "Your magazine is strong and can afford to take any stand it wants to take," she continued. By making her own case an example of what happens when someone attempts to publish in an inhospitable "literary environment," she was striving to alter that environment. She states her case directly to the editor: "I am not pleading for myself."[76] What she was doing, we can see, was engaging in a mode of protest, one she hoped would make it possible for future writers of African descent to have access to those venues that denied her an opportunity. By embracing a politics of failure, she was trying to make future failures by African American authors less likely.

It bears emphasizing that the future Terrell anticipated was not readily foreseeable. Inherent in the queerness of Terrell's failure is the queer temporality it acknowledges and embraces. Terrell knew that the development of African American literature, its widespread publication and its recognition, would not follow a reliably linear, unbroken trajectory.[77] Her letters nevertheless anticipate and insist on the possibility of a future that was neither guaranteed nor yet in view, when a Black writer might pick up where she left off, by building on and realizing her literary aspirations. In retrospect, Terrell's practice of incessantly submitting for publication works of fiction that she knew would be rejected can be seen as a part of an effort to chart a bold new course for Black writers and for African American letters, one that both recognized the imperative of expanding the parameters of Black representation and eliminated the restrictive distinction between Black writers, their literary cultures, and their publishing venues, and those of white Americans. Taken together, the letters articulate her refusal to accept how white editors—and, indeed, the educated American public that formed the readership for their magazines—saw African Americans and how they valued their writing. She refused the limiting and distorted guidelines for acceptable Black representation established and maintained by the white literary establishment, and the hostile ways in which Black writing was read and dismissed. Her cover letters undertook important literary work for the future. Although she had given up her "literary ghost," as she herself put it, she did not stop haunting those editors to change the policies that had killed her aspirations.

Today, Terrell is not recognized as a writer of fiction, and her short stories are unlikely to ever make their way into print. But her practice of submitting her own short stories to American magazines for certain rejection makes visible what a "failed" authorship can successfully tell us about the particular historical moment in which that particular author failed. In the case of Mary Church Terrell, failure was not due to the fact that she did not write, or that her writing was not read: rather, it was inevitable because the political climate in which she found herself was inhospitable to Black writers and to the array of stories about themselves they wished to tell. She nevertheless insisted that her failure be productive, by performing it again and again in her letters. Terrell spoke frankly in her autobiography about the disappointment of not being recognized as an accomplished writer of fiction, and yet her vague conclusion that she did not "live in a literary atmosphere" only begins to get at the truths that are most vividly exposed in her missives to the private readership she established, which consisted of friends, acquaintances, editors and writing instructors who, as we have seen, cast judgment on her writing less for its quality than for its author's identity and handling of its subject matter. Because she chose not to adhere to popular stereotypes that belittled African Americans and reinforced the same offensive, demeaning narratives that, widely circulated in the press, shaped most white Americans' knowledge about and understanding of them, Terrell's career as a writer of short stories was derailed. But her letters successfully preserve a record of her refusal to bring her writing in line with narratives that ridiculed Black people, represented them as one-dimensional, or reinforced a belief in their inferiority. That she meticulously saved them suggests that she understood the importance of creating an archive of her failure and, in doing so, recording an important means of political action that she did not wish to go undocumented.[78]

Failure is a window through which we rarely look to consider literary history and print culture, and yet it constitutes an important lens through which to understand literary practices that might otherwise go unnoticed or unappreciated. In this case, neither Terrell's literary productivity as a writer of short stories, nor the practices through which she deliberately cultivated a private readership despite being denied a more public audience, have been given the attention they deserve. But attention to Terrell's failure to publish her stories and to her theory for why her work was deemed unacceptable helps us to better understand a key moment in African American literary history. Her lack of success in becoming a published short story writer yields meaningful insights into the past by opening up for examination both the ways that the editors of American magazines limited the stories told about African Americans, and how one African American writer launched her own epistolary campaign to protest the restrictions placed on Black narrative and representation. What is important about Terrell's failure to publish is not only that it was the result of a calculated and deliberate effort by literary gatekeepers, but also that her recognition of that fact and her response to it were equally calculated and deliberate and, arguably, took more of what she called "courage" than the fearlessness she thought she lacked as an author of fiction. The case of Mary Church Terrell is, then, a special marker of the particular political and social moment in which she lived; it serves as a reminder that we need to rethink what success, failure, and publication mean in different historical moments. Embedded in the archival remnants of Terrell's failure to become a published writer of short fiction lies a series of significant achievements, including her ability to construct a private readership for her stories in lieu of the more public venues she was denied and her willingness to call out racism where she saw it: in the acceptance policies of the nation's most distinguished literary magazines. Whereas much of her career was spent speaking for the race or serving as its representative in ways that seem relatively conservative, Terrell used her short stories, and in particular the body of correspondence that represented it to editors, to mount a furious and systematic assault on a segment of a publishing institution intent on denying the complexity of racial identity. In this she found the courage to do something important that she felt eluded her as a writer. She also made a significant contribution to the development of African American authorship, albeit one that is critically legible only in the story of her failure to publish.

UNDERGROUND RAILROADS OF MEANING

BY 1922, MARCH CHURCH TERRELL HAD BEEN TRYING TO PUBLISH her stories for the more than two decades since "Venus and the Night Doctors" appeared in the *Washington Post* in 1901. In that year, on the threshold of the Harlem Renaissance, she approached William Stanley Braithwaite, an important African American writer, editor, and anthologizer, to see if he would be able to publish a collection of her stories with the Boston publishing house he had established the previous year, the B. J. Brimmer Company. In the end, this did not work out, because it was not financially feasible for Braithwaite to publish short stories. Poetry, like Georgia Douglas Johnson's collection *Bronze*, which the Brimmer Company published in November 1922, and novels, a stream of which would appear over the next few years, during the heyday of the Harlem Renaissance, were the genres that would sell. Like Terrell, Braithwaite felt constrained; he told her that he too had "tried again and again to get other publishers . . . to do *something*," but it seemed that the writing of "colored authors" was still too great a gamble to be assumed by most publishing companies.[1]

The publishing house established by Braithwaite in 1921 also represented an effort of two decades' duration. In 1902, Braithwaite had written to Charles Chesnutt with what he called an "embryo" of an idea: to start a Negro magazine "of a literary standard." There is a "wealth of material in this country," he wrote, and it required a vehicle for its dissemination. The magazine he had in mind, he stated, would create what he called "a backbone for a school of Negro writers."[2] Twenty years later, the embryo of an idea for a magazine was hatched in the form of a Black-owned publishing house with the same aim of providing infrastructural support for the flourishing of African American literature. Braithwaite might perhaps have reflected on the long journey he had taken as he wrote his letter to Terrell, informing her of what he referred to as "a dream of mine—the recognition of our writers—the becoming of a world force in literature."[3]

The story I have told in *To Make Negro Literature* has focused on what this encounter between Terrell and Braithwaite centers around: failed attempts, and infrastructures. Terrell failed to get her stories published, just as Braithwaite failed to start his literary magazine. But both recognized that they had to create something to house, circulate, and promote the literature they both valued—something institutional, some vehicle. In Terrell's case, that became an archive to record and explain her failure, a repository of her relentless efforts to change the engrained values that kept her from publishing her work and a kind of private epistolary campaign that, she hoped, would make it possible for future writers to succeed. Braithwaite's sense of producing a "backbone" is the biological equivalent of the "scaffolding" metaphor I have used to describe the work done by schoolbooks and bibliographical lists. Both are hidden or largely unseen, and both make it possible for the structure itself to stand: the body of a literary history, the building of a literary tradition. In architectural terms, these infrastructural, interstitial spaces conceal the "guts" of the building, like its mechanical systems, and as such are meant to disappear from view; such is the case with the kinds of literary practices and projects I have examined here. My aim has been to restore these consequential projects and practitioners to the historical record, bringing the internal mechanics of their practices back into view. It is by making visible this series of previously unlinked, largely hidden projects, modes of authorship, and forms of Black writing that emerged at the turn of the century that we can create an alternative way of looking at literary history—that we can see the processes by which Negro literature was "made."

By giving due attention to the anomalous, the discordant, the aborted, and the failed alongside the published and the recognized, we will go far toward creating an account of literary history that more fully addresses the range of literature's locales and its frequencies. It will also create a view of literary history seen not through the expectations of the present, but from the perspective of the past. Rather than looking at completed and published texts, but at the *workspaces* that made them possible—that is, the working conditions, places, and processes rather than final products—we are better able to understand and make legible why certain literary endeavors were undertaken in the first place, what made them important at the time, and what made that importance fade or become obsolete.[4]

In the end, Negro literature was "made" not by the appearance of books like Chesnutt's novels or Dunbar's collections of poetry, but by the events, transmissions, and forms of organization of information that preceded their publication. What we have surveyed here, then, could be described as a series of attempts and failures rather than the flow of a corpus of literature that would cohere into a tradition. If we think of "literature" in the "traditional" sense as single-authored texts of poetry or prose trafficking in public, then the four cases I have discussed here are *not* literature; they might at best and most charitably be described as the epiphenomena of literature, or scaffolding for a later manifestation of that literature. If we expand our definition of the literary, however, then we can see that these four cases outline the subterranean work of literary production—or, maybe better, the structures and strategies that make literature, in the traditional sense, possible. What we have studied here are two cases about attempts to induce the literary and two cases about attempts to produce the literary. The first two cases involve, first, books that endeavored to reproduce the dynamics of schools and the architectonics of public exhibits that would help lead their readers toward the literary, and, second, a series of endlessly incomplete lists that attempted to identify and catalog what was "literary" by and about the "Negro." The next two cases involved an author who was not a writer, and a writer who was never finally an author—or, perhaps, one who was an author only because he was publicly hailed as one, and the other a writer whose literary legacy is a private archive of failure.

In *The Grey Album*, Kevin Young writes about "shadow books" that haunt African American literary history precisely because they make impossible its full recovery.[5] These books are lost or removed, or were never written. Trying to find them, Young suggests, will allow us to reconstruct what he calls the "underground railroads of meaning" that have shaped African American literature and animated Black culture.[6] Our subject of study here has been the underground networks that laid the groundwork for African American literary culture at the turn from the nineteenth to the twentieth century: that emergent network of routes, passages, and intellectual meeting places through which African American literature was made. None of the passageways or spaces addressed in this book were deeply concealed, but whether we find others like them will depend on our willingness to recognize the unfinished, the unsuccessful, and the anomalous as conditions of the literary. Hidden in plain sight like the Underground Railroad itself, these elements of literary culture are waiting for us, ready to contribute important fragments to the literary history that is our collective responsibility to reconstruct.

NOTES

INTRODUCTION: TO MAKE NEGRO LITERATURE

1 *Catalogue of Atlanta University, Atlanta Georgia, With a Statement of Courses of Study, Expenses, Etc., 1901–2* (Atlanta, GA: Atlanta University Press, 1902), 18.

2 W. E. B. Du Bois, "A Proposed Negro Journal," 4, ca. December 1904, W. E. B. Du Bois Collection.

3 Editorial Department, "Falling of the Moon," *Alexander's Magazine* 2, no. 4 (August 15, 1906): 9.

4 Edward L. Simon to Du Bois, December 22, 1906, W. E. B. Du Bois Collection.

5 For the fullest history of the *Moon Illustrated Weekly*, see Parrington, "*Moon Illustrated Weekly*," 206–16 (reprinted, along with three extant issues of the periodical, in Parrington, *Moon Illustrated Weekly*).

6 "Editorial."

7 Gates, "Foreword," ix, encourages readers "to chart the formal specificities of this tradition and to trace its origins."

8 Foster, "It Behooves Us to Struggle," 353.

9 Gates and Jarrett, introduction to *New Negro*, 9.

10 Bruce, *Black American Writing*; McCaskill and Gebhard, *Post-Bellum, Pre-Harlem*, xii; Chakkalakal and Warren, *Jim Crow*, 8; Smethurst, *African American Roots of Modernism*.

11 For an assessment of how African Americans made use of the symbolism of the ending of an old and the beginning the new century, see Gates's now-classic essay "Trope of a New Negro."

12 Muñoz, *Cruising Utopia*, 182.

13 Muñoz, *Cruising Utopia*, 174. Also useful for thinking about failure as a mode of knowledge is Halberstam's *Queer Art of Failure*. In reflecting on the queerness

of Black life and literature during this time, I have also been influenced by Nyongo's *Afro-Fabulations*.

14 Logan, *Negro in American Life*, 52.

15 Jarrett, "What Is Jim Crow?," 388–90, among others, makes the case that we can understand the legal segregation encoded in *Plessy v. Ferguson* as part of a historical and social continuum.

16 "'NEGRO' WITH A CAPITAL 'N,'" *New York Times*, March 7, 1930, 20.

17 Gates and Jarrett, introduction, 3. Examples include the National Afro-American League (1889), the Federation of Afro-American Women (1895), and the Afro-American Council (1902).

18 My assertion here that the word "Negro" was a hallmark feature of turn-of-the-century African American literature has been influenced by Crawford's argument in *Black Post-Blackness* that the word "black" was, "in a radical manner," a hallmark feature of the Black Arts Movement. The embrace of this word was, in Crawford's words, "a profound overturning of the identity category 'Negro'" (3).

19 Chakkalakal and Warren, introduction to *Jim Crow*, 9.

20 Howells, "Life and Letters," 630.

21 Howells, "Charles W. Chesnutt's Stories," 700; Howells, "Psychological Counter-Current," 882.

22 Chesnutt, quoted in Andrews, *Literary Career of Charles W. Chesnutt*, 127.

23 Dunbar, letter of March 15, 1897, reprinted in "Unpublished Letters of Paul Laurence Dunbar to a Friend," *The Crisis* 20 (1920): 73–76, quotation from 73.

24 Jarrett, *Deans and Truants*, 52.

25 Quoted in Cunningham, *Paul Dunbar and His Song*, 24.

26 The writer of the *Manchester Guardian*'s May 18, 1898, review of Dunbar's 1898 novel *The Uncalled* lamented that the "characters are all white people" and criticized Dunbar for his foray into the "habits and feelings of an alien race." Quoted in Jarrett, *Deans and Truants*, 68.

27 Brown, *Pauline Elizabeth Hopkins*, 2; Knight, "Putting Them on the Map."

28 See Chakkalakal, "Reading in Sutton E. Griggs," in Chakkalakal and Warren, *Jim Crow*, 143–56.

29 Graff, *Professing Literature*. See especially the chapters under the heading "The Early Professional Era: 1875–1915," 55–120.

30 The body of Michaël Roy's work on slave narratives is exemplary of this. See Roy, "Slave Narrative Unbound," 259–76; the quote is from 268.

31 Laura E. Helton's work on Dorothy Porter and the ways that Black archives were organized in the first half of the twentieth century exemplifies the growing interest in the information infrastructures of Black studies. See Helton, "On Decimals, Catalogues, and Racial Imaginaries."

32 Gardner, *Black Print Unbound*.

33 Just Teach One: Early African American Print, a project sponsored by *Commonplace: The Journal of Early American Life*, is intended to advance recovery work of early African American print materials and facilitate their teaching by providing access to and contextualization for lesser-known texts. See jtoaa.common-place.org (accessed December 2, 2020).

34 Examples of these projects abound, but two notable ones are the Colored Conventions Project, an effort to collect and digitize the print remnants—including minutes, press coverage, and petitions—of the "Colored Conventions" that took place in Black communities between 1830 and the 1890s; and Book Traces, a project that calls on students and scholars to locate, in their local libraries, books published before 1923 that bear traces of the past, be they inscriptions, handwritten annotations, or signs of alternative uses. Book Traces was organized by Andrew Stauffer, who teaches English at the University of Virginia; the Colored Convention Project was organized by P. Gabrielle Foreman, now in the English Department at Penn State.

35 An openness to speculation is perhaps the most important lesson of all that I list here. Carla Peterson addresses this directly in her reflections on the methodological issues she faced in writing *Doers of the Word*; see her "Subject to Speculation." The example of the importance of asking questions and speculating is everywhere apparent in Frances Smith Foster's body of scholarship. See especially her "Narrative of the Interesting Origins." Saidiya Hartman discusses her scholarly method of working in the archives of Atlantic Slavery, calling the historical writing that results from it "critical fabulation," in "Venus in Two Acts."

36 Rusert, "From Black Lit to Black Print," 996.

37 Moody and Rambsy, "Guest Editors' Introduction," 4.

38 Hager, *Word by Word*, 15.

39 Xiomara Santamarina makes a similar point in "Are We There Yet?," 311.

40 Hager, *Word by Word*, 4, 23.

41 Nishikawa, "Archive on Its Own," 177, 178.

42 Nishikawa, "Archive on Its Own," 180.

43 Du Bois, "A Proposed Negro Journal," 4, ca. December 1904, W. E. B. Du Bois Collection.

44 Du Bois, "Negro in Literature and Art," 236.

CHAPTER ONE. "THE INFORMATION CONTAINED IN THIS BOOK WILL NEVER APPEAR IN SCHOOL HISTORIES"

1 Hopkins, *Contending Forces*, 141, 144.

2 Harper, *Iola Leroy*, 282.

3 For other such stories, see McHenry, *Forgotten Readers*; and Gardner, *Black Print Unbound*. Stephen G. Hall, in *A Faithful Account of the Race*, notes that

the *Christian Recorder*'s "readership included some of the most urbane and well educated among the race" (143).

4 Hager, *Word by Word*.

5 See, for instance, Collins and Margo, "Historical Perspectives on Racial Differences," 1:111. The U.S. Census for 1900 acknowledges the problematic nature of its own data on literacy, telling readers that the "statistics of literacy, as presented in these tables, represent, in all probability, something less than the fact, due to the return, in certain cases, of persons as literate who in reality are illiterate." See "Illiteracy," Twelfth Census of the United States—1900. Census Report Volume II—Population Part II, U.S. Census Bureau, www2.census .gov/prod2/decennial/documents/33405927v2_TOC.pdf, xcvii (accessed December 2, 2020).

6 Du Bois's data portraits are newly available in print in Battle-Baptiste and Rusert, *W. E. B. Du Bois's Data Portraits*. See especially plate 14 ("Illiteracy") and plate 17 ("Number of Negro Students Taking the Various Courses of Study Offered in Georgia Schools"). Also see Provenzo Jr., *W. E. B. Du Bois's Exhibit*, 90.

7 Du Bois, *College-Bred Negro*, 3. Du Bois was skeptical that all enrolled students were "really of college grade" or receiving that level of education (16).

8 Williams, *Marxism and Literature*, 46–47.

9 Williams, *Marxism and Literature*, 46.

10 Williams's assessment of literature as a concept that developed over time serves as a reminder that definitions of literature and of literacy are not static.

11 The *Oxford English Dictionary* traces the first use of the word "literacy" in print to 1880, when, in an article from the *Atlantic Monthly*, it was contrasted with "illiteracy": "It is not illiteracy I want to prevent, but literacy!" (*Atlantic Monthly*, no. 722; quoted in the *Oxford English Dictionary*, www.oed.com [accessed April 24, 2019]). For a helpful unpacking of the history of the word, see Sullivan, "Research on Literacy in Practice," 230–42; see especially 230–32.

12 Gates, "Trope of a New Negro," 136–37.

13 Hall, *Faithful Account of the Race*, 164. Also see Bay, *White Image in the Black Mind*, 193–94.

14 In *Fugitive Science*, Britt Rusert outlines the circulation of scientific writing by Black intellectuals in the antebellum United States, of which Banneker's six almanacs are but one example. In acknowledging its use in the classrooms of the New York African Free Schools, I call the first African American newspaper, *Freedom's Journal*, a "makeshift textbook"; see McHenry, *Forgotten Readers*, 93. Pennington's *Text Book of the Origin and History* is a valuable if understudied early effort to reconstruct Black history; the quotes are from the unpaginated introduction.

15 Rawick, *American Slave*, 149; quoted in Williams, *Self-Taught*, 130. Ezel refers here to Noah Webster's *Elementary Spelling Book*, which was commonly known as the "blue back speller."

16 "The African Civilization Society," *Freedman's Torchlight*, December 1866, 2.

17 "Address to Our Southern Brethren," *Freedman's Torchlight*, December 1866, 2. In "Roads to Travel," Patricia A. Young calls the *Freedman's Torchlight* a "newspaper textbook" (671).

18 All of the quotes in this paragraph are from the front page of the *Freedman's Torchlight*, December 1866.

19 The concepts outlined in this simple set of practice sentences illustrates the way that the African Civilization Society used the *Freedman's Torchlight* to define progress as a project based in the literary. The ability to read—first in terms of acquiring basic literacy skills, then of reading, analyzing, and critiquing increasingly sophisticated texts—was directly connected to knowing how to "be good" as well as to understanding the hard work and morality necessary to receive God's love. Literate people would also receive instruction on how to advance economically and get material rewards.

20 "Appeal," *Freedman's Torchlight*, December 1866, 3.

21 In *Fragile Freedom*, Erica Armstrong Dunbar advances the idea of "protected space" in her discussion of antebellum Black women's friendship albums (122).

22 Quashie, *Sovereignty of Quiet*. Schoolbooks published by the American Tract Society—to which the *Freedman's Torchlight* can be compared—include *The Freedman's Spelling Book*, *The Freedman's Second Reader*, and *The Freedman's Third Reader*.

23 William T. Alexander, *History of the Colored Race*, n.p.

24 Alexander, *History of the Colored Race*, n.p.

25 Alexander, *History of the Colored Race*, 600.

26 According to Edward C. Mitchell, D. D., "In the United States Statistics of 1893 and 1894 it appears that in the 158 private schools designated for the secondary and higher education of colored people in the South, there were 18,595 primary pupils, while only 13,262 belong to the secondary of high school class and 940 were in the collegiate class." These figures offer some suggestion of the limited nature of college education for African Americans in the last decade of the nineteenth century. Mitchell's address, titled "Higher Education and the Negro," was delivered before the American Baptist Home Mission Society at Asbury Park, New Jersey, May 26, 1895: it is included in the *Report of the Commissioner of Education*; the address runs from pages 1360–66, and the quote is from 1364.

27 Frissell, "Progress of Negro Education," 39.

28 Frissell, "Progress of Negro Education," 39.

29 In *Self-Taught*, Williams uses this phrase as the title of her first chapter. It is drawn from a description of locales where lessons in literacy took place among the enslaved (29).

30 Washington, *Up from Slavery*, 122.

31 Du Bois, *Souls of Black Folk*, 38.

32 These words are Frederick Loudin's, from an open letter he addressed "To the Hon. Frederick Douglass and Oppressed Negro in America" and submitted to the *New York Age*, the *Detroit Plaindealer*, and the *Cleveland Gazette*. I have quoted here from "Indorses [*sic*] a Good Idea," *Cleveland Gazette*, February 25, 1893, 2.

33 For a comprehensive study of racial representation at world's fairs in general and the Chicago World's Fair in particular, see Reed, *"All the World Is Here!"*

34 White and Igleheart, *World's Columbian Exposition*, 391.

35 White and Igleheart, *World's Columbian Exposition*, 399. Harvard was listed separately, distinguished because of its "large gallery space, and its cabinets," which were described as "particularly interesting to scientists" (399). The fact that any schools for African Americans were permitted to represent the work of their students is made all the more significant given that space in the building was so limited that a second site had to be found for the display of many of the exhibits included in the Liberal Arts Building. For a detailed explanation of this crisis and the physical layout of the Liberal Arts Building, see R. Johnson, *World's Columbian Exposition*, 248–82. The text briefly mentions the African American presence in the Liberal Arts Building, saying only that "colleges for colored people from Georgia, South Carolina, and Tennessee indicated that much attention is given to shop and trade teaching" (268). *The Official Directory of the World's Columbian Exposition*, edited by Moses P. Handy, which calls itself "a reference book of exhibitors and exhibits" for the Chicago Fair, revealed only that the Liberal Arts Building housed displays from seven colleges and universities "distinctly for the colored race" (336).

36 J. W. P. Jenks to Edward L. Parks, quoted in Parks, "Biographical Sketch of Professor W. H. Crogman, A. M.," in Crogman, *Talks for the Times*, xii. Jenks also "confess[ed] with shame" in his letter that he "could find no boarding place for Crogman, and with difficulty a lodging room, on account of that race prejudice" (xii).

37 Parks, "Biographical Sketch," xiii.

38 Parks, "Biographical Sketch," x.

39 Penn, "Awakening of a Race," 24–25. For a concise but thorough description of the Negro Building and the rush to assemble it, see Wilson, *Negro Building*, 53–83.

40 Butler, "What Is the Negro Doing," 3.

41 See William Crogman to Francis J. Grimké, September 24, 1894, in Woodson, *Works of Francis J. Grimké*, 34.

42 There was divided opinion about the segregated Negro Building, some African American intellectuals believing that having representation constituted a victory for the race, while other "negro artists of good standing refused to allow their works to be placed in a separate negro exhibit," doubting that "a negro exhibition at a fair in the heart of Georgia devised and conducted by southern whites, could prove to be anything but a by-word and a laughing stock." See Bacon, *Negro at the Atlanta Exposition*, 19.

43 Washington, *Up from Slavery*, 240.

44 Bowen, *Appeal to the King*, 7. Subsequent references to Bowen's speech in this and the next three paragraphs will be cited parenthetically.

45 Perdue, *Atlanta Cotton States Exposition*, 33.

46 On the politics and the power of Black study, see Harney and Moten, *Undercommons*.

47 For more on the program of "Negro Day" and its "large audience," see "Negroes' Congress," *Atlanta Constitution*, December 27, 1895, 7.

48 Calloway, "American Negro Exhibit," 74.

49 In statistics similar to those generated by Du Bois's data portraits, the U. S. Census reported 56.8 percent illiteracy for African Americans above the age of ten in 1890, which would decrease to 44.5 percent by 1900. See U.S. Bureau of the Census, *Historical Statistics*, Series H 664–68, 382.

50 Brown, *Book and Job Printing in Chicago*.

51 "Brief Sketch of Our New Company," 2, reel 51, Booker T. Washington Papers, Manuscript Division, Library of Congress, Washington, DC. I have pieced together the story of James L. Nichols, the owner of the J. L. Nichols Company, from three sources, all of which are in manuscript form, bound together and located at the Naperville Public Library in Naperville, Illinois. See *Autobiography of James L. Nichols, as Told to His Wife, Elizabeth Barnard Nichols*; *Story of the Life of J. L. Nichols*, by Elizabeth Barnard Nichols; and *History of Nichols Library*, by Miriam B. Fry, librarian. Nichols was born in Germany and immigrated to the United States as a child, where he was almost immediately orphaned. In a brief autobiography dictated, in 1885, to his wife, Elizabeth Barnard Nichols, Nichols chronicled his efforts to educate himself despite the instability of his life with various families and employers and the constant demands of supporting himself. "By reading and studying nights and Sundays, with very little schooling, during the winter months, at the age of about nineteen years I was enabled to teach school," he wrote (9). He enrolled in a "classical seminary" and eventually become a student at North Western College in Naperville. Upon graduation, Nichols spent a year as the principal of the Naperville Public Schools; he then joined the faculty at North Western College, where he taught for eight years. Although Nichols's dictated autobiography ends with a reminiscence of his years as an educator, his wife's account of his life, *Story of the Life of J. L. Nichols*, includes the story of how he got involved in the publishing business. In connection with his work in the Business College at North Western, Nichols compiled "a handbook of useful business information and forms, called 'The Business Guide'" (15). Sold by subscription, the book was a success, prompting Nichols to write others. Elizabeth Nichols offers this explanation of the success of the company: "It was the first 'hey-day' of the book agent, [and] the farmer and villager, living far from a book store, with no public libraries, welcomed these valuable aids in their everyday life. No slamming the door in the face of the long-suffering book agent in those

days! They were welcomed and often, in the country, asked to stay for dinner!" (15). Nichols's association with North Western College was also crucial to the success of his company: it supplied "a young army of students" to serve as sales agents, who "were able to earn enough in two months summer vacation to support them through the next school year" (15). So successful was the company and "so absorbing" was the business that Nichols "felt compelled to resign from the faculty and devote himself to it exclusively" (15). His commitment to books and learning was not limited to the publishing business. Upon his death, Nichols left the gift of "a Library to Naperville, so that no boy of girl should be without books, as he had been [as a child]." The Nichols Library was established in 1897, and still serves as Naperville's public library today.

52 "Brief Sketch of Our New Company," 5.

53 Tebbel, *History of Book Publishing*, 511.

54 Tebbel, *History of Book Publishing*, 513. Tebbel's brief overview of subscription publishing provides an insufficiently detailed summary of a vibrant nineteenth-century American industry which demands to be examined more fully from the perspective of subscription books, authors, publishers, agents, and readers. To date, the most extensive study of subscription books in the United States remains "Subscription Book Publishing in the United States," a master's thesis written by Marjorie Stafford that was submitted in 1943. Since then, scholars have written a handful of articles on various aspects of subscription publishing, the bulk of which have focused on Mark Twain, who relied on subscription publishing as a way to bolster his sales, and Mason Weems (usually referred to as Parson Weems), who, at the end of the eighteenth century, sold books by subscription for a Philadelphia publisher who considered his book agent a good way to get rid of his "dead stock." Keith Arbour's catalogue of the Michael Zinman collection of subscription canvassing and sample books, published in 1996, includes an excellent introduction that suggests the extensive areas of study connected to subscription books. Lynne Farrington's recent article, "A Very Good Book Indeed," makes good use of the Zinman Collection to argue for the significant role played by subscription publishing in the nineteenth century. Finally, Amy M. Thomas's "There Is Nothing So Effective" is suggestive of the sort of research that becomes possible when records of subscription bookselling, such as book order receipts, correspondence between agents and booksellers, and letters from the bookseller reflecting on the work, are available for review. Notable also is Claire Parfait's scholarship on the publication trajectories of African American historians George Washington Williams and Joseph T. Wilson; see "Grandest Book Ever Written."

55 Hall, *Faithful Account*, 123.

56 For a fuller account of Still's methods, see Hall, *Faithful Account*, 137–49.

57 Hall, *Faithful Account*, 146.

58 Tebbel, *History of Book Publishing*, 512.

59 Tebbel, *History of Book Publishing*, 512.

60 Gaskell, *Gaskell's Compendium of Forms*, n.p.

61 John Hertel to Emmett Scott, August 9, 1900, Booker T. Washington Papers, reel 179, Manuscript Division, Library of Congress, Washington, DC.

62 All quotes in this paragraph are from Haley, *Afro-American Encyclopædia*, n.p.

63 The Statue of Liberty's use in this image suggests its promise as a symbol of liberty, an irony that was not lost on African Americans, as it communicated a message that ran counter to their own experience in the United States. Shortly after its dedication, the African American newspaper the *Cleveland Gazette* ran an editorial suggesting that the statue's torch not be lit until the United States became a free nation for all its citizens. "'Liberty Enlightening the World,' indeed! The expression makes us sick," read the editorial. "Shove the Bartholdi statue, torch and all, into the ocean until the 'liberty' of this country is such as to make it possible for an inoffensive and industrious colored man to earn a respectable living for himself and his family, without being ku-kluxed, perhaps murdered, his daughter and wife outraged, and his property destroyed." See "Postponing Bartholdi's Statue until There Is Liberty for Colored as Well," *Cleveland Gazette*, November 27, 1886, 2.

64 Leah Price, in *How to Do Things with Books*, draws attention to the tension between the "decorative outsides" and "functional insides" of books in the Victorian era (2).

65 Scholarly inquiry into African Americans' engagement with the discourse of progress at the turn from the nineteenth to the twentieth century is extensive. See, for example, Cardon, *Dream of the Future*; Mitchell, *Righteous Propagation*; Summers, *Manliness and Its Discontents*; Gaines, *Uplifting the Race*; and Dorsey, *To Build Our Lives Together*.

66 The first four pages of chapter 1 are followed by the first six pages from chapter 2. Chapter 14, "Personages of the Negro Race," is represented by twelve of the chapter's pages, as compared with the three pages that offer an example of the book's final chapter, on "Statistics."

67 The images on pages 108 and 109 of *Progress of a Race*, both drawings of fugitive slaves in their effort to escape slavery, stand out as unique in the text. Both are from William Still's *The Underground Railroad* and exemplify a rare moment in *Progress of a Race* where the authors include not only the source of their material but also a note indicating it was used "by permission of the Author."

68 "Sales Talk for *Progress of a Race*" is included in the canvassing book for a "revised and enlarged edition of *Progress of a Race*, published by the J. L. Nichols Company in 1920; it is part of the Zinman Collection of Canvassing Books, Kislak Center for Special Collections, Rare Books and Manuscripts, University of Pennsylvania, Philadelphia. Although these instructions accompanied a later version, they are likely to have been consistent with selling tips for earlier volumes.

69 Edwards, *Practice of Diaspora*, 318.

70 "Sales Talk for *Progress of a Race*"

71 "Sales Talk for *Progress of a Race*."

72 "Subscription-Book Publishing Methods," *Publishers' Weekly*, April 2, 1898, 622.

73 "Subscription-Book Publishing Methods."

74 "Subscription-Book Publishing Methods."

75 "Sales Talk for *Progress of a Race*."

76 "Sales Talk for *Progress of a Race*."

77 "Sales Talk for *Progress of a Race*."

78 "Sales Talk for *Progress of a Race*."

79 "Sales Talk for *Progress of a Race*." The page count of the first edition was anticipated to be 600 at the time of the printing of the prospectus, but by the time the agents were soliciting sales of the book, the anticipated page count had risen to 663. In response to this, some agents crossed out the number 600 and wrote the number 663 by hand in its place.

80 "Sales Talk for *Progress of a Race*."

81 Gitelman, *Paper Knowledge*, 21.

82 The implication is that the subscriber would fill out the form (rather than the agent), and by signing their name, they indicated their formal agreement to purchase the book.

83 See Gilgenbach, introduction, ii.

84 The fact that most of the extant copies of the book's first edition are bound in blue cloth rather than in the more expensive red binding suggests that the less expensive binding was the more popular.

85 "Brief Sketch of Our New Company," 5.

86 Given that Kletzing lived until 1910, it is unclear why John William Gibson replaced Kletzing as the coeditor of *Progress of a Race*. For Gibson's views on education, see his *Junior History of the United States*, 3. "We learn to read by reading," he claimed.

87 "Subscription-Book Publishing Methods," 622.

88 Entry for "North Western College," *American College and Public School Directory*, vol. 16 (C. H. Evans, 1893), 124.

89 Information about Kletzing is scarce. See *Herringshaw's Encyclopedia of American Biography*, 561. Information about his role as a member of the faculty at North Western College can be found in the American College and Public School Directory of 1893 and 1896–97. Kletzing was also an Evangelical Association minister and a part owner of the Christian Witness Company, which published the *Christian Witness* from 1901 to 1910. For a time he also had a college in Iowa named after him. See Kostlevy, *A to Z of the Holiness Movement*, 177.

90 Parks, "Biographical Sketch," xxiii.

91 This sort of white authorization of a Black text is reminiscent of the letters of introduction and authenticating prefaces that preceded many texts by African Americans in the nineteenth century, from the narratives of fugitive slaves to novels. It is interesting to note, though, that while William Crogman and Booker T. Washington's portraits are included in the opening pages of the first edition of *Progress of a Race*, Kletzing's is not.

92 Crogman and Kletzing, *Progress of a Race*, n.p. Quotations from this text will subsequently be cited parenthetically.

93 See, for instance, the section "Moral Improvement," in *Progress of a Race's* chapter on "Moral and Social Improvement," which begins: "'Talks for the Times' says . . ." (151).

94 Hall, *Faithful Account of the Race*, explores the development of African American historical writing across the nineteenth century.

95 E. A. Johnson, *School History of the Colored Race*. In 1892, a second edition of the book was printed in Philadelphia by Sherman & Co.

96 In his dissertation "How the School Became Common," Robby Daniel Koehler quotes from this letter and beautifully illuminates its implications. I am indebted to his fourth chapter for pointing me to this correspondence and helping me to think through ideas about schoolbooks; the quote comes from page 166.

97 Garvey, *Writing with Scissors*, 21.

98 Haley, *Afro-American Encyclopædia*, n.p.

99 See, for instance, Washington's "Why Push Industrial Education in the South?" which was originally published in *Public Opinion* 20 (11 June 1896): 750–51; reprinted in *Progress of a Race*, 329–335.

100 Here I refer to "Industrial Education of the Blacks," an address Booker T. Washington delivered in January of 1896.

101 Crummell, "Attitude of the American Mind."

102 See Crogman to Francis J. Grimké, September 24, 1894, in *Works of Francis J. Grimké*, vol. 4, 34–35.

103 Crummell, "Attitude of the American Mind."

104 Du Bois, *Souls of Black Folk*, 176.

105 C. T. Shaffer, "Bishop Payne's Latest Book," *Christian Recorder*, December 13, 1888, 1. See also Bailey, *Race Patriotism*, 37.

106 Crogman, *Talks for the Times*, 41.

CHAPTER TWO. THINKING BIBLIOGRAPHICALLY

1 Tankard, "Reading Lists," 339.

2 Goody, *Domestication of the Savage Mind*, 81.

3 Goody, *Domestication of the Savage Mind*, 81.

4 Tankard, "Reading Lists," 337.

5 Helton, "Making Lists, Keeping Time," 84.

6 Cooper, *Voice from the South*, 229.

7 Alexander, *Black Interior*, 221.

8 Mossell, *Work of the Afro-American Woman*, 48.

9 Mossell, *Work of the Afro-American Woman*, 59–60.

10 Tankard, "Reading Lists," 345.

11 Matthews, "Value of Race Literature," 170.

12 Mossell, *Work of the Afro-American Woman*, 5.

13 Mossell, *Work of the Afro-American Woman*, 66.

14 Mossell, *Work of the Afro-American Woman*, 177.

15 Moody-Turner, "Recovery," 250.

16 Adger, "Portion of a Catalogue," reprinted in Gubert, *Early Black Bibliographies*, 71–74. Gubert's collection is an invaluable resource for research on Black bibliographies.

17 "Works by Negro Authors," in Gubert, *Early Black Bibliographies*, 60–65. This is the third part of a three-part bibliography. The other two bibliographies, the "Bibliography of Negro Education" and the "Bibliography of the Negro in America," are both relevant, as each includes works by African American authors (see Gubert, *Early Black Bibliographies*, 42–65). In 1976, the archivist Dorothy Porter called the bureau's report "the earliest attempt to identify Negro authors." See "Bibliography and Research," 78.

18 Crogman and Kletzing, *Progress of a Race*, 577–82.

19 Crogman and Kletzing, *Progress of a Race*, 460–67, 563–65, 579–80.

20 Josephson, "Introductory Remarks," 7.

21 Hastings, "Some Recent Events," 18.

22 Hastings, "Some Recent Events," 11.

23 All of the quotes in this paragraph are from Josephson, "Introductory Remarks," 8.

24 Hastings, "Some Recent Events," 11.

25 Hastings, "Some Recent Events," 15.

26 Preface to *Year-Book of the Bibliographical Society of Chicago, 1899–1900*, 5.

27 Josephson, "Introductory Remarks," 9.

28 See mission A.1.2, American Library Association, www.ala.org/aboutala /governance/policymanual/updatedpolicymanual/section1/1mission (accessed November 13, 2020).

29 Hastings, "Some Recent Events," 16.

30 John Hingham offers an overview of the consolidation of historical practice in *History*, 6–11. Stephen Hall discusses this transition as it took place in African American contexts in *Faithful Account of the Race*, 188–90.

31 Josephson, "Introductory Remarks," 9.

32 Lee, "Daniel Murray," 436. Lee's sketch of Murray includes a host of stories about his close relationship with Spofford. Elizabeth Dowling Taylor's recent monograph on Daniel Murray, *Original Black Elite*, adds much to our understanding of Murray's life, his work at the Library of Congress, and the culture in which he lived. Her meticulous research into Murray's work at the Library of Congress has been invaluable to giving me a nuanced sense of his duties at the library and the trajectory of his career there.

33 "The Government Library at Washington," in Spofford, *American Almanac and Treasury*, 357.

34 A popular story about Murray was that he "remembered the contents of all the books in the Library of Congress, more than nine hundred thousand, and could tell the shelf location of more than half of them, his associates relieving themselves of the work of hunting out the shelf markers, a very laborious task, but contenting themselves by asking [Daniel Murray], who nine times out of ten could give the exact shelf number, and this in regard to the varied books called for by the hundreds of readers during a busy day." See Lee, "Daniel Murray," 434.

35 "Daniel Murray, Esq.," *Colored American*, April 28, 1900, 1. Anna E. Murray, Murray's wife, confirms that Ainsworth Spofford took what she described as "a fatherly interest in [Murray's] welfare and . . . made Murray his personal assistant." See Anna E. Murray, "On the Life of Daniel Murray, March 24, 1926," W. E. B. Du Bois Collection.

36 Quoted in Taylor, *Original Black Elite*, 28. Taylor notes that Murray participated in a German language course from 1886 to 1887 at the Lincoln Memorial Church, and that he was also familiar with French (94).

37 Lee, "Daniel Murray," 436.

38 See Taylor, *Original Black Elite*, 159. Murray's promotion to chief of the periodicals division was widely publicized, with announcements appearing in such journals as the *Washington Bee*, the *Cleveland Gazette*, and the *Indianapolis Freeman*. He was demoted less than two months later: not only was his title taken away but his salary was also substantially reduced, below the level it had been before his promotion. The demotion was both professionally insulting and personally embarrassing. Despite his protests and appeals, Murray never again received either a promotion or a raise in salary from the Library of Congress.

39 Daniel Murray, "Negro Vote Is Doubtful: Mr. Daniel Murray, Assistant Librarian of Congress, Presents a Bill of Grievances," *Colored American*, July 15, 1899, 1–4.

40 Calloway included the text of his letter in "The American Negro Exhibit at the Paris Exposition," an article published in the *Colored American* that chronicles the "complete story of the American Negro Exhibit" (2).

41 Murray to Hutcheson, October 3, 1900, Daniel Murray Papers, reel 1, frame 86, Wisconsin Historical Society, Madison, Wisconsin. Much of what we know about the process of compiling the Paris Exposition bibliography comes from this text; written in the form of a letter, it constitutes Murray's final report to his supervisor on the project. The letter runs from frame 84 to frame 100. I have subsequently cited it parenthetically in the text, using the pagination of the document itself. This quote is from page 3.

42 "A Year of the Public Library under Mr. Putnam," *Boston Herald*, April 6, 1896, 6.

43 Herbert Putnam, Librarian of Congress, Washington, DC, to Thomas J. Calloway, January 5, 1900, Daniel Murray Miscellaneous Personnel Files, Library of Congress Archives, Manuscript Division, Library of Congress, Washington, DC.

44 Calloway, "American Negro Exhibit" (*Colored American*), 2.

45 Daniel Murray to Edmund M. Barton, January 20, 1900. Barton printed the letter as a part of his "Report of the Librarian," 364–65.

46 Murray to George F. Hoar, undated, Daniel Murray Papers, reel 1, frames 650–51, Wisconsin Historical Society. Murray's letter was written some time after the Paris Exposition opened, as in it he reports: "When the Exposition opened I was able to place on exhibition a list showing a little over nine hundred titles and more than 200 books and this in a field of literary endeavor, where, ordinarily, little might be expected."

47 At the end of his report to Hutcheson, Murray includes a list of people and publishing firms whose efforts on behalf of the project he was most grateful. See Murray to Hutcheson, October 3, 1900, 16–17.

48 Du Bois, "American Negro at Paris," 577.

49 Calloway, "American Negro Exhibit" (*Hampton Negro Conference*), 78.

50 "Topics of the Week," *New York Times: Saturday Review of Books and Art*, May 12, 1900, 305.

51 Murray strove to get full bibliographic information on each and every title he collected. He claimed that, of the 1400 titles in his collection by the fall of 1900, "I was able in almost every case, to get, [*sic*] size, place and year of publication, authors full name, portrait—if present, and number of pages." He clearly wanted to be able to defend the presence of each of the titles he had obtained, telling his supervisor that he had taken "copious notes from letters of information so that [he could] prove the identity of every title in the bibliography." See Murray to Hutcheson, October 3, 1900, 15.

52 Preface to *Margaret Brown's French Cookery Book*, n.p. According to an advertisement, the complete title of the *Atlanta Souvenir Cook Book* is *Atlanta Exposition Souvenir Cook Book: A Safe Guide to Ordering and Cooking* (Washington, C: R. L. Pendleton, 1895). It was "Compiled by Mrs. Ida D. Bailey, Under the Direction of Women's Domestic Science Committee."

53 Murray to Myer, May 6, 1900, George A. Myers Papers, box 8, folder 3, Archive Library, Ohio History Connection.

54 "Progress of Negro Authors," *Washington Bee*, September 28, 1901, 1. When the Paris Exposition closed on November 12, 1900, the American Negro Exhibit was transferred to the Pan-American Exposition in Buffalo, New York. Murray added to the literature display about eighty books that had come into his possession too late to be sent to Paris. It was this exhibit to which the review published in the *Washington Bee* referred.

55 Murray to Stoddard, in response to Stoddard's article in the New York *Mail and Express*, the *Colored American*, March 31, 1900, 11. The letter, which Murray had written on March 22, 1900, appears in a column called "Our Literature."

56 Murray to Stoddard, March 31, 1900.

57　Murray to Myers, July 6, 1900, George A. Myers Papers, box 8, folder 5, Archive Library, Ohio History Connection. This letter suggests that Murray was contemplating changing jobs in order to have "at command the money necessary to bring out such a book."

58　Murray to Myers, December 2, 1900, George A. Myers Papers, box 8, folder 6, Archive Library, Ohio History Connection.

59　Murray, "A Bibliography of Negro Literature," draft manuscript, n.d., Daniel Murray Papers, reel 24, frame 24, 2, Wisconsin Historical Society.

60　Murray, "Bibliography of Negro Literature," 5, 6.

61　Advertisement for "Bibliographia Africana; or History of Afro-American Literature," in Hilyer, *Twentieth Century Union League Directory*, 15. Murray wrote to Harper & Brothers publishers about a "forthcoming Bibliography of Books by Afro-American and Afro-European Authors," and received a response from them on September 4, 1902: "From your description we infer that your idea would be to make it as Subscription book, for which form of publication, we think, better suited than for distribution through the usual channels of the book trade." The publisher asked to see "some material portion of the MS." and asked him to tell them "what measure you would propose to take to secure a subscription for five thousand copies of the work in advance?" Letter from Harper & Brothers to Murray, September 4, 1902, Daniel Murray Papers, reel 1, frame 150, Wisconsin Historical Society. Murray solicited a number of publishers, and received positive replies from many of them in addition to Harpers, including, for instance, the Funk and Wagnalls Company and the Singer Company (see March 24, 1903, and June 8, 1908, respectively; both letters are from reel 1 of the Daniel Murray Papers) Over the years he prepared for the book's publication, sending, for instance, a flurry of letters at the end of October 1910 to prominent African American journalists, educators, and clergy in hopes of soliciting their help in developing a network of people who would promote the work in their communities; he received many responses. For a sample of what was most likely a form letter seeking friends and acquaintances to help sell his book, see Murray to Barber, October 29, 1910, Daniel Murray Papers, reel 1, frame 318, Wisconsin Historical Society. Two examples of the responses he received are Bowen to Murray, November 2, 1910, Daniel Murray Papers, reel 1, frame 331; and Johnson to Murray, November 2, 1910, Daniel Murray Papers, reel 1, frame 333.

62　Murray, "Bibliography of Negro Literature," 1.

63　See, for instance, the letter from Mr. Richard Moss of the Trow Press to Daniel Murray, October 1, 1915, which includes details about a proposed print run of a six-volume collection, titled "Murray's Historical and Biographical Encyclopedia" (Daniel Murray Papers, reel 1, frames 521–22); and the inquiry from the A. B. Caldwell Publishing Company to Daniel Murray, dated December 14, 1917, which asked, "Have you ever yet made any arrangement for the publication of your Encyclopedia of the Colored race?" (Daniel Murray Papers, reel 1, frame 544).

64 Du Bois to Daniel Murray, November 10, 1922, Daniel Murray Papers, reel 1, frame 635.

65 Du Bois to Daniel Murray, November 16, 1922, Daniel Murray Papers, reel 1, frame 637.

66 Du Bois, "American Negro at Paris," 576.

67 Du Bois, *Autobiography*, 221.

68 Du Bois, "American Negro at Paris," 577.

69 This was a standard phrase used to explain the rationale for the Atlanta University Studies. See, for instance, the introduction to Du Bois, *Some Efforts of American Negroes*, 3.

70 Quoted in Lewis, *W. E. B. Du Bois*, 224.

71 Du Bois, *College-Bred Negro*, 5.

72 Du Bois, *College-Bred Negro*, 5.

73 Du Bois, *Negro Common School*, 1.

74 See, for instance, the introduction to Du Bois, *Negro Common School*, 1.

75 The 1900 bibliography begins on page 6 of *The College-Bred Negro* and runs through page 9. Page numbers will hereafter be cited parenthetically.

76 Manguel, *Library at Night*, 76. For the importance of categorization and a history of the way that effective systems of organization were imposed on collections of African American materials in the early twentieth century, see Laura Helton's work on Howard University librarian Dorothy Porter, whose adjustments to the Dewey Decimal system she analyzes in "On Decimals, Catalogues, and Racial Imaginaries." I thank Helton for sparking my thinking on lists and bibliographies.

77 Mary Roberts Smith to Du Bois, February 24, 1903, W. E. B. Du Bois Collection, http://credo.library.umass.edu/view/full/mums312-b005-i104 (accessed November 13, 2020); John H. Gray to Du Bois, May 24, 1903, W. E. B. Du Bois Collection, http://credo.library.umass.edu/view/full/mums312-b002 -i304 (accessed November 13, 2020).

78 Du Bois, *Negro Common School*, 4. The bibliography is found on 5–13.

79 Du Bois's bibliographic entries often abbreviate titles and sometimes record titles inaccurately. I have listed the titles correctly here.

80 Cobb, *Law of Negro Slavery*, 46.

81 Du Bois, *Negro Public School*, 1.

82 For more on the *Peter Halket* story, see Liz Stanley and Helen Dampier, "She Wrote Peter Halket." The authors discuss the Hanging Tree on page 63.

83 Du Bois, *Select Bibliography of the American Negro*, 6. Subsequent references to this text will be cited parenthetically.

84 Du Bois, "My Evolving Program," 47.

85 This letter is included in both the W. E. B. Du Bois Papers at the University of Massachusetts Amherst, and the Booker T. Washington papers at the

Library of Congress. It is also included in Washington, *Booker T. Washington Papers*, 5:480.

86 Du Bois's extensive bibliographic work includes a hand-written bibliography of his own family name. See Du Bois, "Du Bois Family Bibliography, 1905?," W. E. B. Du Bois Collection.

87 W. E. B. Du Bois, "Bibliography of Negro Folk Song in America, ca. 1903," W. E. B. Du Bois Collection.

88 Letter from Dodd, Mead & Company to Du Bois, February 24, 1906, W. E. B. Du Bois Collection.

CHAPTER THREE. WASHINGTON'S GOOD FORTUNE

Abbreviations used in notes for this chapter:

BTW: Booker T. Washington

BTW: LOC: Booker T. Washington Papers, Library of Congress, Washington, DC

BTWP: *The Booker T. Washington Papers*, vols. 1–14. Edited by Louis R. Harlan, John W. Blassingame, Pete Daniel, Stuart B. Kaufman, Raymond W. Smock, and William M. Welty. (Urbana: University of Illinois Press, 1972–1989).

1 On ghostwriting and the discourse surrounding it, see Riley and Brown, "Crafting a Public Image"; and Brandt, "Who's the President?"

2 Thornbrough's *T. Thomas Fortune* is to date the only biography of Fortune's life. There is also a helpful chronology of his life in Alexander, *Afro-American Agitator*, xxxix–xli.

3 *New York Freeman*, February 28, 1885, quoted in Thornbrough, *T. Thomas Fortune*, 33.

4 Thornbrough, *T. Thomas Fortune*, 33.

5 Thornbrough, *T. Thomas Fortune*, 45.

6 *New York Freeman*, November 23, 1884, quoted in Thornbrough, 79.

7 T. Thomas Fortune, "The Virtue of Agitation," *New York Globe*, August 18, 1883, n.p. Reprinted in Alexander, *T. Thomas Fortune, the Afro-American*, 116.

8 Fortune, *Black and White*, 12.

9 See, for instance, *New York Globe*, March 3, 10, and 17, 1883; and May 12 and 19, 1883, n.p.

10 T. Thomas Fortune, *New York Age*, June 1889.

11 *Springfield Republican*, quoted in the *New York Freeman*, December 20, 1884, n.p.

12 John E. Bruce, "Book Notice," *Washington Grit*, September 27, 1884, 2.

13 Tameka Bradley Hobbs, afterword to Fortune, *After War Times*, 68.

14 T. Thomas Fortune, *New York Age*, December 21, 1889, n.p.

15 Harlan, *Booker T. Washington*, 192.

16 Harlan, *Booker T. Washington*, 192–93.

17 Fortune to BTW, September 21, 1891, BTW: LOC, reel 9.

18 BTW, *My Larger Education*; quotes are from 127, 116, and 113, respectively.

19 These autobiographical observations are from Fortune's *After War Times*, 55.

20 This wording comes from S. Laing Williams, who served as BTW's attorney at the beginning of the twentieth century. See Williams to BTW, December 4, 1903, BTW: LOC, reel 89.

21 Fortune to BTW, March 2, 1899, BTWP 5:49. Fortune recognized the value of industrial education or, more to the point, the lack of opportunities for African Americans with higher education, writing that "to educate him [a black child] for a lawyer when there are no clients[,] for medicine when the patients[,] although numerous[,] are too poor to give him a living income[,] to fill his head with Latin and Greek as a teacher when the people he is to teach are to be instructed in the abcs[,] such education is a waste of time and a senseless expenditure of money" (Fortune, *Black and White*, 81).

22 Fortune to BTW, September 26, 1895, BTWP, 4:31.

23 Fortune to BTW, 7 March 1896, BTWP 4:131.

24 See Fortune to BTW, March 31, 1896, BTWP 4:152. *"Our friends in the north* [emphasis in original] want me to establish a newspaper here which shall cover the whole South and which they will back until I can get it on a paying basis. You know my opinion of longer residing in the north," he wrote to Washington, expressing his reluctance to live there. "I write now because you are my good friend and I want your candid opinion of the undertaking."

25 Fortune to BTW, March 7, 1896, BTWP 4:131.

26 Armistead Pride's PhD dissertation, "A Register and History of Negro Newspapers in the United States," remains a good source for estimating the number of African American newspapers that existed in the second half of the nineteenth century. He calculated that between 1865 and 1899, 1,187 Black papers were started. The peak year for launching African American newspapers was 1896, when 82 newspapers were started (406).

27 Fortune to BTW, March 7, 1896, BTWP 4:131.

28 Fortune to BTW, March 13, 1896, BTWP 4:136.

29 Walter Hines Page to BTW, July 15, 1896, BTWP 4:200.

30 Page to BTW, July 15, 1896.

31 Page to BTW, July 15, 1896.

32 Page to BTW, July 15, 1896; Walter Hines Page to BTW, August 22, 1896, BTW: LOC, reel 13.

33 Washington, *Up from Slavery*, 295.

34 Page to BTW, August 22, 1896.

35 Page to BTW, October 14, 1896, BTW: LOC, reel 13. Interestingly, Page later made a similar proposal to Charles Chesnutt, offering him serial publication of his stories first in the *Atlantic* and then in book form with Houghton, Mifflin. See Walter Hines Page to Charles Chesnutt, March 30, 1898, in Chesnutt, *Charles W. Chesnutt*, 87, 91–92.

36 Keyser, "Victoria Earle Matthews," 6.

37 Keyser, "Victoria Earle Matthews," 6.

38 For a review of BTW's staunch advocacy of Matthews's work, see Kramer, "Uplifting Our 'Downtrodden Sisterhood,'" especially 254–55.

39 Matthews, "Value of Race Literature," 177.

40 Fortune to BTW, March 13, 1896, BTWP 4:136.

41 Fortune to BTW, April 6, 1898, BTW: LOC, reel 45.

42 Fortune to BTW, April 6, 1898.

43 Fortune to BTW, May 17, 1898, BTW: LOC, reel 45.

44 Fortune to BTW, May 23, 1898, BTW: LOC, reel 45.

45 Fortune to BTW, May 23, 1898.

46 Fortune to BTW, May 17, 1898.

47 Fortune to BTW, June 3, 1898, BTW: LOC, reel 45.

48 Fortune to BTW, June 3, 1898. Grady's words come from the 1887 address "The South and Her Problems," which is included in Grady, *Speeches of Henry W. Grady*, 28.

49 Fortune to BTW, June 3, 1898.

50 Fortune, introduction to *Black-Belt Diamonds*, xi–xii.

51 Fortune to BTW, June 3, 1898. The publishers of *Black-Belt Diamonds* are listed as "Fortune and Scott, Publishers," with offices cited as 4 Cedar Street (the address of the *New York Age*), but I have not been able to determine who "Scott" was in this case. Fortune's partner in publishing at this time was Jerome B. Peterson, with whom he co-owned the newspaper, and there is no evidence to suggest that the "Scott" to which this refers was Washington's personal assistant, Emmett Scott. The first edition of *Black-Belt Diamonds* bears the name of a printer in Cambridge, Massachusetts, John Wilson and Son. Presumably, this was John Wilson, described in his obituary as "one of the foremost printers of the country." "JOHN WILSON DEAD," *Cambridge Tribune* 26, no. 11 (May 16, 1903): 6.

52 BTW to Emmett Scott, August 7, 1898, BTW: LOC, reel 71.

53 Fortune to BTW, August 9, 1898, BTW: LOC, reel 45.

54 Fortune to BTW, August 14, 1898, BTW: LOC, reel 45.

55 Fortune to BTW, August 30, 1898, BTW: LOC, reel 45. *Black-Belt Diamonds* was listed for $1.00 in the August 6, 1898, issue of the *Publisher's Weekly*, 172.

56 Fortune to BTW, December 27, 1898, BTW: LOC, reel 45.

57 Fortune to BTW, July 27, 1898, BTW: LOC, reel 45.

58 Fortune to BTW, July 27, 1898.

59 John Hertel to BTW, November 15, 1897, BTWP 4:341.

60 Walter Hines Page to BTW, January 5, 1898, BTW: LOC, reel 13.

61 Page to BTW, January 5, 1898, emphasis added.

62 Fortune to BTW, March 4, 1899, BTW: LOC, reel 45.

63 Fortune to Emmett Scott, May 22, 1899, BTW: LOC, reel 45.

64 Fortune to Emmett Scott, May 25, 1899, BTW: LOC, reel 45.

65 This is from a second letter Fortune wrote to Scott on May 25, 1899, BTW: LOC, reel 45.

66 Both quotes are from the same letter: Fortune to BTW, June 1, 1899, BTW: LOC, reel 45.

67 Fortune to BTW, June 29, 1899, BTW: LOC, reel 45.

68 Fortune to BTW, August 15, 1899, BTW: LOC, reel 45.

69 Fortune to BTW, June 1, 1899, BTW: LOC, reel 45.

70 Fortune to Emmett Scott, June 24, 1899, BTW: LOC, reel 45.

71 Fortune to BTW, June 1, 1899.

72 Fortune to Scott, June 24, 1899.

73 Fortune to BTW, June 1, 1899.

74 BTW to Fortune, September 24, 1899, BTW: LOC, reel 45.

75 BTW to Fortune, September 24, 1899.

76 Both quotes are from the same source: Fortune to BTW, September 27, 1899, BTW: LOC, reel 45.

77 BTW, preface to *Future of the American Negro*, n.p.

78 All quotes from this paragraph are from the same source: BTW to Fortune, September 24, 1899. Writing to BTW on September 28, 1899, Fortune said, "The title is of much importance. I do not like the term Negro because it is inaccurate—means too much in one way and not enough in another.'The Afro-American's Future' would be far better, provided you dealt *only* with the future phase of the subject. But we can determine that later on" (BTW: LOC, reel 45; emphasis in original). Fortune's desire that the book's title more accurately reflect its subject may be one reason the title was eventually shifted to "The Future of the American Negro."

79 Fortune to Emmett Scott, October 14, 1899, BTW: LOC, reel 45.

80 Fortune to BTW, October 13, 1899, BTW: LOC, reel 45.

81 Fortune to BTW, October 13, 1899.

82 Fortune to BTW, October 26, 1899, BTW: LOC, reel 45.

83 Fortune to BTW, October 13, 1898, BTW: LOC, reel 45.

84 Fortune to BTW, October 25, 1899, BTW: LOC, reel 45.

85 Fortune to Emmett Scott, October 31, 1899, BTW: LOC, reel 45.

86 Fortune to BTW, November 8, 1899, BTW: LOC, reel 45.

87 Fortune to Scott, October 14, 1899.

88 Fortune to Scott, October 14, 1899.

89 Fortune to BTW, October 30, 1899, BTW: LOC, reel 45.

90 All quotes in this paragraph are from the same source: Fortune to BTW, October 26, 1899, BTW: LOC, reel 45.

91 Fortune to BTW, October 13, 1889.

92 Jarrett, *Deans and Truants*, 36.

93 Fortune to BTW, September 25, 1899, BTW: LOC, reel 45.

94 Fortune to BTW, September 27, 1899 BTW: LOC, reel 45.

95 Fortune to BTW, September 26, 1899, BTW: LOC, reel 45.

96 Fortune to BTW, October 7, 1899, BTW: LOC, reel 45. Fortune was able to borrow the money, writing to BTW on October 12, 1899 that he hoped the book of poems would "prove an opening wedge into higher things" (BTW: LOC, reel 45). Neely's bankruptcy was reported in the *New York Times* on October 22, 1899, 12.

97 Fortune to BTW; the date of this letter is unclear but likely to have been either October 23 or 25, 1899. It is quoted in Thornbrough, *T. Thomas Fortune*, 210.

98 Emmett Scott to BTW, November 18, 1899, BTW: LOC, reel 71.

99 Scott to BTW, November 18, 1899.

100 Scott to BTW, November 18, 1899.

101 BTW to Emmett Scott, December 1, 1899, BTW: LOC, reel 71.

102 Fortune to BTW, December 13, 1899, BTW: LOC, reel 45.

103 Fortune to BTW, January 8, 1900, BTW: LOC, reel 45.

104 Fortune to BTW, January 11, 1900, BTW: LOC, reel 45.

105 Edgar Webber to Fortune, January 22, 1900, BTW: LOC, reel 45.

106 Webber to Fortune, January 22, 1900.

107 Fortune to BTW, March 30, 1900, BTW: LOC, reel 45; John A. Hertel to Fortune, May 7, 1900, BTW: LOC, reel 161. I have corrected the word "rush," which appears in Hertel's letter as "rish."

108 Page to BTW, January 19, 1900, BTW: LOC, reel 13.

109 Page to BTW, January 5, 1900, BTW: LOC, reel 13.

110 Page to BTW, January 19, 1900.

111 Page to BTW, January 19, 1900.

112 Fortune to BTW, June 1, 1900, BTW: LOC, reel 45.

113 Typed memorandum, undated and unsigned, BTWP, 1:xxiv.

114 As Fortune summarized the situation in a letter to BTW, "The Nichols people contracted to publish a book for $1 and to give you 6 cents a copy. They violate the contract by publishing the book for $1.50, $2.00 and $2.50 and you should have recovery of 6 cents on the dollar and not on the book." As he saw it, BTW "should get a royalty of 20% instead of 6 cents a book," since "for all business transactions of [this] character, the dollar is the unit of royalty and not the book." (Fortune to BTW, September 24 and September 26, 1900, BTW: LOC, reel 46). He was therefore of the opinion that BTW should "write the [other autobiography] whether the Nichols people consent or not" (September 24, 1900).

115 BTW to Fortune, September 11, 1900, BTW: LOC, reel 46.

116 Fortune to BTW, September 26, 1900.

117 BTW to John A. Hertel, September 22, 1900, BTWP 4: 642–63.

118 BTW to Hertel, September 22, 1900.

119 John A. Hertel to BTW, December 6, 1900, BTWP 4: 689–90.

120 Bly, "Navigating the Print Line," 215.

121 E. E. Miller (General Manager of J. L. Nichols & Co.) to BTW, October 7, 1905, BTW: LOC, reel 13. Hertel was clear that the employment of African Americans was directly related to the success of sales of *The Story of My Life and Work*. When BTW received his royalty payment for the period from July 1

to October 1, 1908—a paltry $2.12—Hertel wrote by way of explanation, "Negro books are not selling very fast this year, as members of the race in many instances seem to be out of employment and not able to buy." See J. L. Nichols & Co. to BTW, October 21, 1908, BTW: LOC, reel 15.

122 J. L. Nichols & Co. to BTW, December 6, 1905, BTW: LOC, reel 15.

123 BTW to J. L. Nichols & Co., November 24, 1905, BTW: LOC, reel 15.

124 E. E. Miller to BTW, December 6, 1905, BTW: LOC, reel 15.

125 Miller to BTW, November 28, 1905, BTW: LOC, reel 15.

126 BTW to J. L. Nichols & Co., November 24, 1905.

127 E. E. Miller to BTW, November 28, 1905.

128 Fortune did receive some compensation for his work on *The Story of My Life and Work*. He received $50 for reading the manuscript, although he expected at least another $50 for reading the proofs, which he appears not to have received.

129 BTW to J. E. MacBrady, July 3, 1900, BTWP 5:576. In correspondence between Emmett Scott and BTW on this matter, the spelling "McBrady" and "Mac-Brady" are both used.

130 I have found no sources of information on MacBrady or on the American Publishing House, one of the many subscription publishers located in and around Chicago that our critical disregard for the industry has rendered historically insignificant. MacBrady's calculated effort to misrepresent the volume as BTW's work set up a lasting fiction: just as it was intended to mislead buyers of *A New Negro for a New Century* in 1900, it has continued to mislead scholars across the twentieth and into the twenty-first century. See, for instance, Gates, "Trope of a New Negro," especially 136–40.

131 BTW to J. E. MacBrady, July 3, 1900, BTWP, 5:570.

132 BTW to Emmett Scott, July 25, 1900, BTWP, 5:591.

133 BTW to J. E. MacBrady, July 3, 1900.

134 S. Laing Williams to BTW, August 27, 1900, BTW: LOC, reel 89. Several letters outlining Washington's agreement with the American Publishing House were lost, compounding the difficulty of Williams's job. The missing correspondence had the greatest repercussions for Fortune, who believed the letters would definitively prove he was entitled to more money than he had received. See Fortune to BTW, September 7, 1900, and Fortune to Emmett Scott, November 22, 1900, both BTW: LOC, reel 46.

135 See Fortune to BTW, September 7, 1900, and Fortune to Scott, November 22, 1900.

136 S. Laing Williams to BTW, September 21, 1900, BTW: LOC, reel 81.

137 Williams to BTW, August 27, 1900.

138 Williams to BTW, August 27, 1900. All of the quotes in this paragraph are from this source.

139 Williams to BTW, December 10, 1900, BTW: LOC, reel 89.

140 Williams to BTW, October 30, 1900; S. Laing Williams to Emmett Scott, December 11, 1901, both BTW: LOC, reel 89.

141 Williams to Scott, December 11, 1901.

142 Williams to Scott, December 11, 1901.

143 "Our Book Table," *Record of Christian Work* 19, no. 12 (December 1900): 911.

144 BTW to Emmett Scott, March 20, 1900, BTW: LOC, reel 71.

145 Fortune to BTW, April 27, 1900, BTW: LOC, reel 45.

146 Emmett Scott to BTW, August 3, 1900, BTW: LOC, reel 71.

147 Smith, "Photographic Messages," 139.

148 BTW, *Working with the Hands*, 59.

149 Fortune to Emmett Scott, October 31, 1899, BTW: LOC, reel 45. Here, Fortune implies that what needs "reform" is his propensity to overwork himself for Washington: he had been with "the Wizard most of the day," which he characterized to Scott as twelve "lost" hours. But Fortune also struggled to control his addiction to alcohol during these years, and so his recognition here that he needed to "reform" can be read in multiple ways.

150 Fortune to Scott, October 31, 1899.

151 Fortune to BTW, May 9, 1900, BTW: LOC, reel 45.

152 Fortune to BTW, May 19, 1901, BTW: LOC, reel 46.

153 See, for instance, Fortune's letter to BTW dated June 26, 1901, BTW: LOC, reel 46: "The Abbey Press wants to run out my verse but wish me to bear half ($240) the expense, which is out of the question at this time."

154 Fortune to BTW, October 12, 1899, BTW: LOC, reel 45.

155 Fortune cites Page's correspondence in a letter to BTW, May 28, 1901, BTW: LOC, reel 46.

156 Fortune to BTW, May 28, 1901.

157 Fortune to BTW, June 5, 1901, BTW: LOC, reel 46.

158 Jarrett, *Deans and Truants*, 41.

159 Fortune to BTW, February 10, 1900, BTWP, 5:439.

160 J. W. Johnson, *Along This Way*, 160–61.

161 Fortune is included in Joan Sherman's *Invisible Poets* as one of many poets whose work has been neglected by scholars. Her analysis of his poetry stands as the only critical assessment of it to date. See Sherman, *Invisible Poets*, 141–53.

162 Fortune to BTW, June 6, 1901, BTW: LOC, reel 46.

163 Fortune to BTW, September 29, 1901, BTW: LOC, reel 46.

164 Fortune to BTW, September 26, 1901, BTW: LOC, reel 46. As was typically the case after a disagreement, Fortune reached out to Washington to initiate a reconciliation, writing on September 28, 1901, "No reply to telegrams hope we may straighten matters satisfactorily" (BTWP 6:219).

165 Fortune to BTW, November 3, 1902, BTW: LOC, reel 46.

166 Fortune to Emmett Scott, July 27, 1903, BTW: LOC, reel 46. Fortune's list of possible titles for the proposed book included "Is this your Sen, Sir?," "The Black Man's Burden," and "The Sword of Damocles."

167 Fortune wrote and published in the *Age* a tribute to Scott and his family commending him for his part in the success of Tuskegee and of BTW—something he perhaps recognized was not done with enough frequency for those like himself that supported BTW's rise to power and his leadership. See "Notes of the South," *New York Age*, November 2, 1905, 4.

168 *Chicago Conservator*, August 23, 1903, quoted in Thornbrough, *T. Thomas Fortune*, 246–47.

169 Fortune to Emmett Scott, March 28, 1904, quoted in Thornbrough, *T. Thomas Fortune*, 258.

170 Fortune to BTW, October 28, 1903, BTW: LOC, reel 46.

171 See Fortune to BTW, May 19, 1901, BTW: LOC, reel 46.

172 In 2014, historian Daniel Weinfeld reprinted these serialized articles in a collection titled *After War Times*; see especially his editor's note for an assessment of "After War Times" as a response to Joel Chandler Harris's 1899 *The Chronicles of Aunt Minervy Ann* (xxv–xxix).

173 J. W. Johnson, *Autobiography of an Ex-Colored Man*, 187, 207. Johnson, a fellow Floridian, included his earliest memory of Fortune in *Along This Way*, remembering him as he "sat at a desk writing, covering sheet after sheet that he dropped on the floor, all the while running his fingers through his long hair" (48).

174 Fortune to Emmett Scott, January 2, 1905, quoted in Thornbrough, *T. Thomas Fortune*, 292.

175 See, for instance, Chironi and Tomasello, "Living Labour and Social Movements," 520.

176 Here I echo Susanna Ashton's conclusions—that BTW "wrote, but wasn't a writer"—but with a different meaning. Ashton's study focuses on BTW's fraught relationship with print, and the ways he sought to be "free from the fixedness of textual representation." My own interest lies in the ways that BTW took advantage of the authority of authorship, essentially without writing. See Ashton, "Signs of Play," 19.

177 Gardner, "African American Literary Reconstructions," 440.

CHAPTER FOUR. THE CASE OF MARY CHURCH TERRELL

Abbreviations used in parenthetical citations in this chapter:

BBB: Mary Church Terrell, "Betsy's Borrowed Baby," unpublished manuscript, Mary Church Terrell Papers (MCTP), box 32, reel 23, 3, Library of Congress, Washington, DC.

CW: Mary Church Terrell. *A Colored Woman in a White World* (New York: G. K. Hall, [1940] 1996).

JJ: Mary Church Terrell, "Did Jeff Jackson Hear Caruso?," unpublished manuscript, Mary Church Terrell Papers (MCTP), box 32, reel 23, 1, Library of Congress, Washington, DC.

wss: J. Berg Esenwein. *Writing the Short-Story: A Practical Handbook on the Rise, Structure, Writing, and Sale of the Modern Short-Story* (New York: Hinds, Noble and Eldredge, 1908).

1 Repplier's "The Happiness of Writing an Autobiography" appeared in the *Atlantic Monthly*, February 1924, 200–207.

2 Mary Church Terrell, letter to Agnes Repplier, February 19, 1924, Mary Church Terrell Papers (MCTP), box 7, reel 5, Library of Congress, Washington, DC.

3 Muñoz, *Cruising Utopia*, 174. For a full articulation of the nuances of queer failure and the related concept of queer virtuosity, see 169–84.

4 Terrell to the editor of *Harper's Magazine*, March 29, 1922, MCTP, box 6, reel 5.

5 This will certainly reorient, but also significantly expand and deepen, the study of African American literary history. Adrienne Brown and Britt Rusert's work on the unpublished short fiction of W. E. B. Du Bois is one example of the kind of scholarship that will be made possible by attention to manuscript materials: see, for instance, their introduction to the Du Bois's "The Princess Steel" in "Little-Known Documents," 819–20. Prioritizing manuscript materials will also ensure that scholars take greater advantage of less well-known and underused manuscript collections, such as those housed in historically Black colleges and universities.

6 Terrell, *Colored Woman*, 1. Subsequent citations from this text will be made parenthetically as CW.

7 Jennifer M. Wilks's translation of Terrell's diary is invaluable. See "French and Swiss Diaries." I have subsequently cited from this source by the diary's dated entries.

8 September 2, 1888.

9 September 12, 1888.

10 October 29, 1888.

11 September 17, 1888.

12 October 29, 1888.

13 September 20–21, 1899.

14 See, for instance, diary entry for November 30, 1888.

15 October 29, 1888. In this entry, Terrell writes that Robert Terrell had been surprised that she "did not aspire to write for the press" (25). Terrell clearly understood that journalism was the kind of writing that was expected of women who wished to write, although it was not her ambition. In another entry (October 3, 1888), she rhetorically asks of herself, "Where is my ambition to write for the newspapers?" (22).

16 November 4, 1888.

17 September 12, 1888.

18 February 3, 1889.

19 November 30, 1888.

20 November 30, 1888.

21 February 3, 1889.

22 November 30, 1888.

23 Terrell, "Mission of Meddlers." Terrell's understanding of herself as a "meddler" is usefully contrasted with T. Thomas Fortune's no less gendered term for his own activism and that of Black men, who he considered "agitators."

24 Correspondence between Robert H. Terrell and his father-in-law, Robert Church, provides evidence that, in April 1902, Terrell arranged for a loan to repay approximately $2,000 that he had borrowed from the Capital Savings Bank. The bank failed in November 1902. Details of the bank's failure, which was in part due to what M. Sammye Miller describes as "misappropriations and looting" by several directors, can be found in Miller, "Early Venture in Black Capitalism"; the quote is from 364.

25 Booker T. Washington to Robert H. Terrell, February 20, 1906, Robert Heberton Terrell Papers, box 1, reel 1, Manuscript Division, Library of Congress, Washington, DC.

26 Booker T. Washington to Robert H. Terrell, April 27, 1910, reprinted in *Booker T. Washington Papers*, 10:323.

27 Terrell, "Samuel Coleridge-Taylor," 669.

28 Logan, *Negro in American Life*, 240.

29 Page, "Lynching of Negroes," 37.

30 Page, "Lynching of Negroes," 45.

31 Hall, "Introduction," *Revolt against Chivalry*, xx.

32 Wells, *Southern Horrors*, n.p.

33 Ida B. Wells, "Editorial," *Free Speech and Headlight* (Memphis), April 21, 1892, n.p. Original text reprinted in Wells, *Crusade for Justice*, 52.

34 Wells, *Red Record*; quotes are from last page of the chapter "The Case Stated," 15.

35 Campbell, "Power of Hegemony," 48.

36 Terrell, "Lynching from a Negro's Point of View," 855. For a reading that explores how gender and class also play a role in Terrell's essay, see Martha Solomon Watson, "Mary Church Terrell vs. Thomas Nelson Page."

37 Cited in Goldsby, *Spectacular Secret*, 100. Wells married Ferdinand Barnett in 1895 and was thereafter known as Ida B. Wells-Barnett. To avoid confusion, I have used "Wells," the name by which she was known early in her career, throughout.

38 Goldsby, *Spectacular Secret*, 64.

39 NAACP, *Thirty Years of Lynching*, 5.

40 It was not until December 18, 2018, that legislation was passed making lynching a federal crime. The Justice for Lynching Act classifies lynching, which it describes as "the ultimate expression of racism in the United States," as a hate crime. U.S. Congress, Senate Committee on the Judiciary, Justice for Victims of Lynching Act, www.congress.gov/bill/115th-congress/senate-bill/3178/text (accessed November 30, 2020).

41 Terrell, "Misrepresentations of the Colored People," ca. 1913, Mary Church Terrell Collection, boxes 102–3, folder 85, 6.

42 Terrell, "Misrepresentations of the Colored People."

43 Ryan, "Reform," in Burgett and Hendler, *Keywords in American Cultural Studies*, 197.

44 Edgar Allan Poe, "To Charles Anthon," November 2, 1844, letter 186 of *Letters of Edgar Allan Poe*, 268.

45 In *The Culture and Commerce of the American Short Story*, Andrew Levy describes the extent to which, by the end of the nineteenth century, "the short story had become a seminal tool for both authors and editors who consciously sought to bring the fringes of American life to mainstream audiences" (41).

46 Levy notes that the Home Correspondence School, in which Terrell was enrolled, published "at least nine different books on short story writing between 1912 and 1918" (85).

47 Esenwein, *Writing the Short-Story*, xi. (Subsequent references to this work will be cited parenthetically as wss.) Esenwein drew his authority from the fact that he was the editor of *Lippincott's Magazine*. According to Levy, *Writing the Short-Story* was so popular that it "went through sixteen editions in fifteen years, between 1908 and 1923" (wss 86). Subsequent citations from this text will be made parenthetically.

48 Mary Church Terrell, "Venus and the Night Doctors," *Washington Post*, April 7, 1901, E14.

49 Terrell to F. Arthur Metcalf, president, Home Correspondence School, May 25, 1916, MCTP, box 5, reel 4.

50 Terrell, French diary, September 12, 1888.

51 Terrell, "What It Means to Be Colored in the Capital of the United States," *Independent*, January 24, 1907, 184.

52 Terrell, "What It Means," 181.

53 Mary Church Terrell, "Did Jeff Jackson Hear Caruso?," unpublished manuscript, MCTP, box 32, reel 23, 1. Subsequent references to this manuscript will be cited parenthetically as JJ.

54 An example of this is the dime-novel character "Black Tom the Negro Detective," who is a white detective disguised as a Black man. The story appears in the novel *Black Tom, the Negro Detective; or, Solving a Thompson Street Mystery* (1893), which is issue number 486 of the Norman Munro series *Old Cap. Collier Library* (1883–99).

55 Washington's 1895 Atlanta Exposition speech is reprinted in his autobiography *Up from Slavery*, 224.

56 See, for instance, Terrell's entry in the French diary for September 28, 1888.

57 Mary Church Terrell, "Betsy's Borrowed Baby," unpublished manuscript, MCTP, box 32, reel 23, 3. Subsequent references to this manuscript will be cited parenthetically as BBB.

58 Parker, "Picture of Health," 179.

59 Mary Church Terrell, diary entry, February 22, 1905, MCTP, box 1, reel 1.

60 Terrell, "Lynching," 865.

61 Terrell's decision to send her fiction to the nation's elite literary journals is reminiscent of Charlotte Forten Grimké's similar choice, in the second half of the nineteenth century, to seek publication for her writing in the "quality monthlies" that supported a national literary culture in the postbellum era. Carla Peterson's essay "Reconstructing the Nation" chronicles this aspect of Forten's literary practice in contrast with Frances E. W. Harper's commitment to writing from within and for the Black community.

62 In *Uncle Tom's Cabin and the Reading Revolution*, Barbara Hochman cogently unpacks the importance of Harriet Beecher Stowe's novel for Terrell. See especially Hochman's Epilogue, "Devouring *Uncle Tom's Cabin*," 231–51.

63 Page, "Literature in the South," 752.

64 Howard B. Wells, editor for Harper and Brothers Publishers, to Mary Church Terrell, July 31, 1907, MCTP, box 4, reel 3.

65 Hamilton Holt to Mary Church Terrell, August 3, 1909, MCTP, box 4, reel 3.

66 William English Walling to Mary Church Terrell, April 7, 1910, MCTP, box 4, reel 4.

67 Both books were a part of a series of books focused on the art of writing and the process of seeing written work into publication. Esenwein, *Writing the Short-Story*.

68 Mary Church Terrell, diary entry, August 4, 1909, MCTP, box 1, reel 1.

69 Terrell to F. Arthur Metcalf, May 25, 1916.

70 F. Arthur Metcalf, president, Home Correspondence School, to Mary Church Terrell, June 1, 1916, MCTP, box 5, reel 4.

71 Muñoz, *Cruising Utopia*, 173.

72 Mary Church Terrell to the editor of *Harper's Magazine*, March 29, 1922, MCTP, box 6, reel 5.

73 Terrell to *Harper's*, March 29, 1922.

74 Terrell to F. Arthur Metcalf, May 25, 1916.

75 Terrell to *Harper's*, March 29, 1922.

76 Terrell to *Harper's*, March 29, 1922.

77 Here I rely on Jack Halberstam's formulation of queer time in *In a Queer Time and Place*, as that which "challenges conventional logics of development" (13).

78 As did many Black intellectuals in the first decades of the twentieth century, Terrell employed a clipping service, Henry Romeike Inc., to ensure that she kept up with her own published writing and that which appeared about her. What she received from the service she annotated, leaving a record of her reaction to her press coverage. As Joan Quigley notes in *Just Another Southern Town*, Terrell herself at times considered this a tedious chore (56). But the meticulousness with which she kept records serves to underscore the extent to

which she believed in building an archive of her words, her activities, and her accomplishments.

CODA. UNDERGROUND RAILROADS OF MEANING

1 William Stanley Braithwaite to Mary Church Terrell, October 6, 1922; reprinted in Butcher, *William Stanley Braithwaite Reader*, 266–67.

2 William Stanley Braithwaite to Charles W. Chesnutt, November 29, 1902; reprinted in Butcher, *William Stanley Braithwaite Reader*, 240.

3 Butcher, *William Stanley Braithwaite Reader*, 266.

4 Kinohi Nishikawa puts this another way in describing the process of "writing a history of obsolescence wherein past failures yield meaningful insights on their own terms." See "Archive on Its Own," 178.

5 Young, *Grey Album*, 11–19; see especially 11–15.

6 Young, *Grey Album*, 19.

BIBLIOGRAPHY

MANUSCRIPT COLLECTIONS

W. E. B. Du Bois Collection, MS 312. Special Collections and University Archives, University of Massachusetts Amherst Libraries.

T. Thomas Fortune Scrapbook, Sc MG287. Schomburg Center for Research in Black Culture, Manuscripts, Archives, and Rare Books Division, New York Public Library, New York, NY.

Daniel Murray Papers, Micro 577. Wisconsin Historical Society, Division of Libraries, Archives, and Museum Collections, Madison, WI.

George A. Myers Papers, MSS 70. Ohio History Connection, Columbus, OH.

Naperville Heritage Collection. Naperville Public Library, Naperville, IL.

Publishers' Canvassing Books. Special Collections and Archives, Kent State University Libraries, Kent, OH.

Mary Church Terrell Collection, MS 62–3874. Howard University, Moorland-Spingarn Research Center, Washington, DC.

Mary Church Terrell Papers. Library of Congress, Washington, DC.

Mary Church Terrell Papers, 1884–2004, 2009. Oberlin College Archives, Oberlin College, Oberlin, OH.

Robert Heberton Terrell Papers. Library of Congress, Washington, DC.

Booker T. Washington Papers. Library of Congress, Washington, DC.

Zinman Collection of Canvassing Books. Kislak Center for Special Collections, Rare Books and Manuscripts, University of Pennsylvania, Philadelphia, PA.

BOOKS AND ARTICLES

Adger, Robert M. "A Portion of a Catalogue of Rare Books and Pamphlets, Collected by R. M. Adger, Phila., upon Subjects Relating to the Past Condition of the Colored Race and the Slavery Agitation in This Country" (1894). In

Early Black Bibliographies, 1863–1918, edited by Betty Kaplan Gubert, 71–74. New York: Garland, 1982.

Aikin, Jane. "Referred to the Librarian, with the Power to Act: Herbert Putnam and the Boston Public Library." In *Windsor, Dewey, and Putnam: The Boston Experience*, edited by Donald G. Davis Jr., Kenneth E. Carpenter, Wayne A. Wiegand, and Jane Aikin, 27–37. Champaign: Board of Trustees at the University of Illinois, 2002.

Alexander, Elizabeth. *The Black Interior*. St. Paul, MN: Graywolf, 2004.

Alexander, Shawn Leigh, ed. *T. Thomas Fortune, the Afro-American Agitator: A Collection of Writings, 1880–1928*. Gainesville: University Press of Florida, 2008.

Alexander, William T. *History of the Colored Race in American*. Kansas City: Palmetto, 1887.

American College and Public School Directory, vol. 16. N.p.: C. H. Evans, 1893.

Anderson, James D. *The Education of Blacks in the South, 1860–1935*. Chapel Hill: University of North Carolina Press, 1988.

Andrews, William L. *The Literary Career of Charles W. Chesnutt*. Baton Rouge: Louisiana State University Press, 1980.

Arbour, Keith. *Canvassing Books, Sample Books, and Subscription Publishers' Ephemera, 1833–1951, in the Collection of Michael Zinman*. Ardsley, NY: Haydn Foundation for the Cultural Arts, 1996.

Ashton, Susanna. "Booker T. Washington's Signs of Play." *Southern Literary Journal* 39, no. 2 (Spring 2007): 1–23.

Atlanta Exposition Souvenir Cook Book: A Safe Guide to Ordering and Cooking. Washington, DC: R. L. Pendleton, 1895.

Bacon, Alice M. *The Negro at the Atlanta Exposition*. Trustees of the John F. Slater Fund, Occasional Papers No. 7. Baltimore, MD: Trustees of the John F. Slater Fund, 1896.

Bailey, Julius H. *Around the Family Altar: Domesticity in the African Methodist Episcopal Church, 1865–1900*. Gainesville: University Press of Florida, 2005.

Bailey, Julius H. *Race Patriotism: Protest and Print Culture in the A. M. E. Church*. Knoxville: University of Tennessee Press, 2012.

Ball, Wendy, and Tony Martin, eds. *Rare Afro-Americana: A Reconstruction of the Adger Library*. Boston: G. K. Hall, 1981.

Barton, Edmund M. "Report of the Librarian." *Proceedings of the American Antiquarian Society* 13, no. 3 (December 1900): 364–65.

Battle-Baptiste, Whitney, and Britt Rusert, eds. *W. E. B. Du Bois's Data Portraits: Visualizing Black America*. New York: Princeton Architectural Press, 2018.

Bay, Mia. *The White Image in the Black Mind: African American Ideas about White People, 1830–1925*. New York: Oxford University Press, 2000.

Belknap, Robert E. *The List: The Uses and Pleasures of Cataloguing*. New Haven, CT: Yale University Press, 2004.

Benjamin, Michael. "A 'Colored Authors Collection' to Exhibit to the World and Educate a Race." In *Education and the Culture of Print in Modern America*, edited by Adam R. Nelson and John H. Rudolph, 36–56. Madison: University of Wisconsin Press, 2010.

Benjamin, Michael. "In Search of the Grail: The Conceptual Origins of the 'Encyclopedia Africana.'" *Information and Culture* 49, no. 2 (2014): 204–33.

Bieze, Michael. *Booker T. Washington and the Art of Self-Representation*. New York: Peter Lang, 2008.

Bly, Anthony. "Navigating the Print Line: Shaping Readers' Expectations in Booker T. Washington's Autobiographies." *Alabama Review* 61, no. 3 (July 2008): 190–215.

Bowen, J. W. E. *An Appeal to the King: The Address Delivered on Negro Day in the Atlanta Exposition*. Atlanta: n.p., 1895.

Braddock, Jeremy. *Collecting as Modernist Practice*. Baltimore, MD: Johns Hopkins University Press, 2013.

Brandt, Deborah. "'Who's the President?': Ghostwriting and Shifting Values of Literacy." *College English* 69, no. 6 (July 2007): 549–71.

Brantlinger, Patrick. "Kipling's 'The White Man's Burden' and Its Afterlives." *English Literature in Translation, 1880–1920* 50, no. 2 (2007): 172–91.

Brodhead, Richard. *Cultures of Letters: Scenes of Reading and Writing in Nineteenth-Century America*. Chicago: University of Chicago Press, 1993.

Brown, Adrienne, and Britt Rusert. Introduction to "The Princess Steel" by W. E. B. Du Bois. "Little-Known Documents." PMLA 130, no. 3 (May 2015): 819–20.

Brown, Emily Clark. *Book and Job Printing in Chicago*. Chicago: University of Chicago Press, 1931.

Brown, Lois. *Pauline Elizabeth Hopkins: Black Daughter of the Revolution*. Chapel Hill: University of North Carolina Press, 2008.

Bruce, Dickson D., Jr. *Black American Writing from the Nadir: The Evolution of a Tradition, 1877–1915*. Baton Rouge: Louisiana State University Press, 1989.

Butcher, Philip, ed. *The William Stanley Braithwaite Reader*. Ann Arbor: University of Michigan Press, 1972.

Butler, H. R. "What Is the Negro Doing." *Atlanta Constitution*, October 13, 1895, 3.

Calloway, Thomas. "The American Negro Exhibit at the Paris Exposition." *Colored American*, November 3, 1900, 2.

Calloway, Thomas. "The American Negro Exhibit at the Paris Exposition." *Hampton Negro Conference* 5 (1901): 74–80.

Campbell, Karlyn Kohrs. "The Power of Hegemony: Capitalism and Racism in the 'Nadir of Negro History.'" In *Rhetoric and Community: Studies in Unity and Fragmentation*, edited by J. A. Michael Hogan, 36–61. Columbia: University of South Carolina Press, 1998.

Cardon, Nathan. *A Dream of the Future: Race, Empire, and Modernity at the Atlanta and Nashville World's Fairs*. New York: Oxford University Press, 2018.

Carroll, H. K. "The American Negro in the Twentieth Century." In *Addresses and Proceedings of the Congress on Africa*, edited by J. W. E. Bowen, 161–62. Atlanta, GA: Press of the Franklin Printing and Publishing Co., 1896.

Catalogue of Atlanta University, Atlanta, Georgia, with a Statement of Courses of Study, Expenses, Etc., 1901–1902. Atlanta, GA: Atlanta University Press, 1902.

Chakkalakal, Tess. "Reading in Sutton E. Griggs." In *Jim Crow, Literature, and the Legacy of Sutton E. Griggs*, edited by Tess Chakkalakal and Kenneth W. Warren, 143–56. Athens: University of Georgia Press, 2013.

Chakkalakal, Tess, and Kenneth W. Warren, eds. Introduction to *Jim Crow, Literature, and the Legacy of Sutton E. Griggs*, edited by Tess Chakkalakal and Kenneth W. Warren, 1–20. Athens: University of Georgia Press, 2013.

Chesnutt, Charles W. "A Multitude of Counselors." *Independent*, April 2, 1891, 4–5.

Chesnutt, Helen. *Charles W. Chesnutt: Pioneer of the Color Line.* Chapel Hill: University of North Carolina Press, 1952.

Chironi, Daniela, and Federico Tomasello. "Living Labour and Social Movements: A Dialogue with Antonio Negri." *Anthropological Theory* 17, no. 4 (2017): 518–25.

Cobb, Thomas R. R. *Law of Negro Slavery in the United States of America.* Vol. 1. Philadelphia: T. & J. W. Johnson, 1858.

Collins, William J., and Robert A. Margo. "Historical Perspectives on Racial Differences in Schooling in the United States." In *Handbook of the Economics of Education*, vol. 1, edited by Eric A. Hanushek and Finis Welch, 107–54. Amsterdam: North Holland, 2006.

Conway, James. *America's Library: The Story of the Library of Congress, 1800–2000.* New Haven, CT: Yale University Press in association with the Library of Congress, 2000.

Cooper, Anna Julia. *A Voice from the South, by a Black Woman of the South.* Xenia, OH: Aldine, 1892.

Crawford, Natalie Margo. *Black Post-Blackness: The Black Arts Movement and Twenty-First-Century Aesthetics.* Urbana: University of Illinois Press, 2017.

Crogman, William. *Talks for the Times.* Atlanta, GA: Press of Franklin Printing and Publishing, 1896.

Crogman, William, and Henry F. Kletzing. *Progress of a Race; or, The Remarkable Advancement of the Afro-American Negro, from the Bondage of Slavery, Ignorance and Poverty to the Freedom of Citizenship, Intelligence, Affluence, Honor and Trust.* Naperville, IL: J. L. Nichols, 1898.

Crummell, Alexander. "The Attitude of the American Mind toward the Negro Intellect." Annual Address to the American Negro Academy, December 28, 1897. Accessed October 2, 2018. www.blackpast.org/african-american-history/1898 -alexander-crummell-attitude-american-mind-toward-negro-intellect.

Cunningham, Virginia. *Paul Dunbar and His Song.* New York: Biblo & Tannen, 1969.

Dickson, Bruce D., Jr. *Black American Writing from the Nadir: The Evolution of a Tradition, 1877–1915.* Baton Rouge: Louisiana State University Press, 1989.

Dietrich, Lucas. "Charles W. Chesnutt, Houghton Mifflin, and the Racial Paratext." *MELUS* 41, no. 4 (December 2016): 166–95.

Dorsey, Allison. *To Build Our Lives Together: Community Formation in Black Atlanta, 1875–1906.* Athens: University of Georgia Press, 2004.

Du Bois, W. E. B. "The American Negro at Paris." *American Monthly Review of Reviews* 22, no. 5 (November 1900): 575–77.

Du Bois, W. E. B. *The Autobiography of W. E. B. Du Bois: A Soliloquy on Viewing My Life from the Last Decade of Its First Century.* New York: International Publishers, 1968.

Du Bois, W. E. B., ed. *The College-Bred Negro: A Social Study Made under the Direction of Atlanta University by the Fifth Atlanta Conference.* Atlanta, GA: Atlanta University Press, 1900.

Du Bois, W. E. B. "My Evolving Program for Negro Freedom" (1944). *Clinical Sociology Review* 8, no. 1 (1990): 47.

Du Bois, W. E. B., ed. *The Negro Common School: Report of a Social Study Made under the Direction of Atlanta University.* Atlanta, GA: Atlanta University Press, 1901.

Du Bois, W. E. B. "The Negro in Literature and Art." *Annals of the American Academy of Political and Social Science* 49, no. 1 (1913): 233–37.

Du Bois, W. E. B., ed. *A Select Bibliography of the American Negro.* Atlanta, GA: Atlanta University Press, 1905.

Du Bois, W. E. B., ed. *Some Efforts of American Negroes for Their Own Social Betterment.* Atlanta, GA: Atlanta University Press, 1898.

Du Bois, W. E. B. *The Souls of Black Folk.* New York: Penguin, [1903] 1989.

Dunbar, Erica Armstrong. *A Fragile Freedom: African American Women and Emancipation in the Antebellum City.* New Haven, CT: Yale University Press, 2008.

Dunbar, Paul Laurence. "March 15, 1897." In "Unpublished Letters of Paul Laurence Dunbar to a Friend," *Crisis* 20 (1920): 73–76.

"Editorial." *Crisis: Record of the Darker Races* 1, no. 1 (November 1910): 10.

Edwards, Brent Hayes. *The Practice of Diaspora: Literature, Translation, and the Rise of Black Internationalism.* Cambridge, MA: Harvard University Press, 2003.

Esenwein, J. Berg. *Writing the Short-Story: A Practical Handbook on the Rise, Structure, Writing, and Sale of the Modern Short-Story.* New York: Hinds, Noble & Eldredge, 1908.

Esenwein, J. Berg, and Arthur Leeds. *Writing the Photoplay.* Springfield, MA: Home Correspondence School, 1913.

Farrington, Lynne. "A Very Good Book Indeed: Selling Bibles by Subscription in Nineteenth-Century America." *Printing History* 25 (January 2019): 19–44.

Fisher, Laura R. "Head and Hands Together: Booker T. Washington's Vocational Realism." *American Literature* 87, no. 4 (2015): 709–37.

Fortune, T. Thomas. *After War Times: An African American Childhood in Reconstruction-Era Florida.* Edited by Daniel Weinfeld. Tuscaloosa: University of Alabama Press, 2014.

Fortune, T. Thomas. *Black and White: Land, Labor, and Politics in the South*. New York: Fords, Howard & Hulbert, 1884.

Fortune, T. Thomas. Introduction to *Black-Belt Diamonds: Gems from the Speeches, Addresses, and Talks to Students of Booker T. Washington*, by Booker T. Washington, v–xii. New York: Fortune and Scott, 1898.

Fortune, T. Thomas. "The Virtue of Agitation." In *T. Thomas Fortune, the Afro-American Agitator: A Collection of Writings, 1880–1928*, edited by Shawn Leigh Alexander, 115–17. Gainesville: University Press of Florida, 2008.

Foster, Frances Smith. "'It Behooves Us to Struggle.'" Review of *Schomburg Library of Nineteenth-Century Black Writers: Supplement*, in *Tulsa Studies in Women's Literature* 11, no. 2 (1992): 349–54.

Foster, Frances Smith. "A Narrative of the Interesting Origins and (Somewhat) Surprising Developments of African American Print Culture." *American Literary History* 17, no. 4 (2005): 714–40.

Franklin, John Hope. *George Washington Williams: A Biography*. Chicago: University of Chicago Press, 1885.

Frissell, H. B. "Progress of Negro Education." *South Atlantic Quarterly* 6 (January–October 1906): 39.

Gaines, Kevin. *Uplifting the Race: Black Leadership, Politics, and Culture in the Twentieth Century*. Chapel Hill: University of North Carolina Press, 1996.

Gardner, Eric. "African American Literary Reconstructions and the 'Propaganda of History.'" *American Literary History* 30, no. 3 (Fall 2018): 426–49.

Gardner, Eric. *Black Print Unbound: The Christian Recorder, African American Literature, and Periodical Culture*. New York: Oxford University Press, 2015.

Garvey, Ellen Gruber. *Writing with Scissors: American Scrapbooks from the Civil War to the Harlem Renaissance*. New York: Oxford University Press, 2013.

Gaskell, G. A. *Gaskell's Compendium of Forms, Educational, Social, Legal and Commercial*. St. Louis, MO: Richard S. Peale, 1881.

Gates, Henry Louis, Jr. "Foreword: In Her Own Write." In *The Schomburg Library of Nineteenth-Century Black Women Writers*, vii–xxii. New York: Oxford University Press, 1988.

Gates, Henry Louis, Jr. "Trope of a New Negro and the Reconstruction of the Image of the Black." *Representations* 24 (Autumn 1988): 129–55.

Gates, Henry Louis, Jr., and Gene Andrew Jarrett. Introduction to *The New Negro: Readings on Race, Representation, and African American Culture, 1892–1938*, edited by Henry Louis Gates Jr. and Gene Andrew Jarrett, 1–20. Princeton, NJ: Princeton University Press, 2007.

Gibson, J. W. *A Junior History of the United States*. Chicago: A. Flanagan, 1907.

Gikandi, Simon. "Editor's Column: The Fantasy of the Library." *PMLA* 128, no. 1 (2013): 9–20.

Gilgenbach, Cara. Introduction to "Publishers' Canvasing Books: In Special Collections and Archives, Kent State University Libraries," 2012, ii. Accessed December 1, 2020. www.library.kent.edu/files/CanvassingBookletPRINT.pdf.

Gitelman, Lisa. *Paper Knowledge: Toward a Media History of Documents*. Durham, NC: Duke University Press, 2014.

Goldsby, Jacqueline. *A Spectacular Secret: Lynching in American Life and Literature*. Chicago: University of Chicago Press, 2006.

Goldsby, Jacqueline. "Keeping the 'Secret of Authorship': A Critical Look at the 1912 Publication of James Weldon Johnson's *The Autobiography of an Ex-Colored Man*." In *Print Culture in a Diverse America*, edited by James P. Danky and James A. Wiegand, 244–72. Champaign: University of Illinois Press, 1998.

Goody, Jack. *The Domestication of the Savage Mind*. Cambridge: Cambridge University Press, 1977.

Grady, Henry Woodfin, ed. *The Speeches of Henry W. Grady*. Atlanta, GA: Chas P. Byrd, 1895.

Graff, Gerald. *Professing Literature: An Institutional History*. Chicago: University of Chicago Press, 1987.

Graff, Gerald, and Michael Warner, eds. *The Origins of Literary Studies in America: A Documentary Anthology*. New York: Routledge, 1989.

Gubert, Betty Kaplan, ed. *Early Black Bibliographies, 1863–1918*. New York: Garland, 1982.

Hager, Christopher, *Word by Word: Emancipation and the Act of Writing*. Cambridge, MA: Harvard University Press, 2013.

Halberstam, Jack. *In a Queer Time and Place: Transgender Bodies, Subcultural Lives*. New York: New York University Press, 2005.

Halberstam, Jack. *The Queer Art of Failure*. Durham, NC: Duke University Press, 2011.

Haley, James T., ed. *The Afro-American Encyclopædia; or the Thoughts, Doings, and Sayings of the Race*. Nashville, TN: Haley and Florida, 1895.

Hall, Jacqueline Dowd. "Introduction." In *Revolt against Chivalry: Jesse Daniel Ames and the Women's Campaign against Lynching*, xv–xxxviii. New York: Columbia University Press, 1993.

Hall, Stephen G. *A Faithful Account of the Race: African American Historical Writing in Nineteenth-Century America*. Chapel Hill: University of North Carolina Press, 2009.

Handy, Moses P., ed. *The Official Directory of the World's Columbian Exposition*. Chicago: W. B. Conkey, 1893.

Harlan, Louis R. *Booker T. Washington: The Making of a Black Leader, 1856–1901*. New York: Oxford University Press, 1972.

Harney, Stefano, and Fred Moten. *The Undercommons: Fugitive Planning and Black Study*. Brooklyn, NY: Autonomedia, 2013.

Harper, Frances E. W. *Iola Leroy, or, Shadows Uplifted*. New York: Oxford University Press, [1892] 1988.

Harris, Eugene. "Vital Statistics of the Negro Race." *American Missionary* 51, no. 3 (March 1897): 84–86.

Harris, Joel Chandler. *The Chronicles of Aunt Minervy Ann*. New York: Charles Scribner's Sons, 1899.

Hartman, Saidiya. "Venus in Two Acts." *Small Axe* 12, no. 2 (2008): 1–14.

Hastings, Charles H. "Some Recent Events and Tendencies in Bibliography." In *Year-Book of the Bibliographical Society of Chicago, 1899–1900*, 10–18. Chicago: Bibliograpical Society of Chicago, 1900.

Helton, Laura E. "Making Lists, Keeping Time: Infrastructures of Black Inquiry, 1900–1950." In *Against a Sharp White Background: Infrastructures of African American Print*, edited by Bridgette Fielder and Jonathan Senchyne, 82–108. Madison: University of Wisconsin Press, 2019.

Helton, Laura E. "On Decimals, Catalogues, and Racial Imaginaries of Reading." PMLA 134, no. 1 (January 2019): 99–120.

Herringshaw's Encyclopedia of American Biography of the Nineteenth Century. Chicago: American Publishers' Association, 1901.

Hilyer, Andrew F., and The Union League, eds. *Twentieth-Century Union League Directory*. Washington, DC, January 1901.

Hingham, John. *History: Professional Scholarship in America*. Baltimore, MD: Johns Hopkins University Press, 1965.

Hochman, Barbara. *Uncle Tom's Cabin and the Reading Revolution*. Amherst: University of Massachusetts Press, 2011.

Hopkins, Pauline E. *Contending Forces: A Romance Illustrative of Negro Life North and South*. New York: Oxford University Press, [1900] 1988.

Howells, William Dean. "Life and Letters." *Harper's Weekly*, June 27, 1896, 630.

Howells, William Dean. "Mr. Charles W. Chesnutt's Stories. A Review." *Atlantic Monthly* 85 (May 1900): 699–701.

Howells, William Dean. "A Psychological Counter-Current in Recent Fiction." *North American Review* 173 (December 1901): 872–88.

Jarrett, Gene Andrew. *Deans and Truants: Race and Realism in African American Literature*. Philadelphia: University of Pennsylvania Press, 2007.

Jarrett, Gene Andrew. "What Is Jim Crow?" PMLA 128, no. 2 (March 2013): 388–90.

Johnson, Edward A. *A School History of the Colored Race in America, from 1619 to 1890*. Raleigh, NC: Edwards & Broughton, 1890.

Johnson, James Weldon. *Along This Way: The Autobiography of James Weldon Johnson*. New York: Viking, 1933.

Johnson, James Weldon. *The Autobiography of an Ex-Colored Man*. New York: Sherman, French, 1912.

Johnson, Rossiter, ed. *A History of the World's Columbian Exposition, Held in Chicago in 1893*. Vol. 2. New York: D. Appleton, 1897.

Jones, Beverly Washington. *Quest for Equality: The Life and Writing of Mary Eliza Church Terrell, 1863–1954*. Brooklyn, NY: Carlson, 1990.

Josephson, Aksel G. S. "Introductory Remarks at the Organization Meeting, October 23, 1899." In *Year-Book of the Bibliographical Society of Chicago, 1899–1900*, 7–9. Chicago: Bibliographical Society of Chicago, 1900.

Keyser, Frances Reynolds. "Victoria Earle Matthews." *New York Age*, March 14, 1907, 6.

Knight, Alisha. "Putting Them on the Map: Mapping the Agents of the Colored Co-operative Publishing Company." Department of English, Washington College. Accessed December 1, 2020. www.arcgis.com/apps/MapSeries /index.html?appid=665eb933117f4ed68f0535b4560b5744.

Koehler, Robby Daniel. "How the School Became Common: Literature, Pedagogy, Politics, 1776–1840." PhD diss., New York University, 2018.

Kostlevy, William, ed. *A to Z of the Holiness Movement*. Lanham, MD: Scarecrow, 2010.

Kramer, Steve. "Uplifting Our 'Downtrodden Sisterhood': Victoria Earle Matthews and New York City's White Rose Mission, 1897–1907." *Journal of African American History* 91, no. 3 (Summer 2006): 243–66.

Lee, Edwin A. "Daniel Murray: Bibliographer of Afro-American Literature in the Library of Congress." *Colored American Magazine* 5, no. 6 (October 1902): 432–40.

Lee, George. *Beale Street: Where the Blues Began*. College Park, MD: McGrath, [1934] 1969.

Levy, Andrew. *The Culture and Commerce of the American Short Story*. New York: Cambridge University Press, 1993.

Lewis, David Levering. *W. E. B. Du Bois: Biography of a Race, 1868–1919*. New York: Henry Holt, 1993.

Logan, Rayford W. *The Negro in American Life and Thought: The Nadir, 1877–1901*. New York: Dial, 1954.

Loos, William H. "The Forgotten 'Negro Exhibit': African American Involvement in Buffalo's Pan-American Exposition, 1901." Buffalo, NY: Buffalo and Erie County Public Library and the Library Foundation of Buffalo and Erie County, 2001.

Loudin, Frederick. "Editorial." In *The Reason Why the Colored American Is Not in the World's Columbian Exposition*, edited by Robert W. Rydell, n.p. Urbana: University of Illinois Press, [1893] 1999.

Maffley-Kipp, Laurie F. *Setting Down the Sacred Past: African American Race Histories*. Cambridge, MA: Harvard University Press, 2010.

Manguel, Alberto. *The Library at Night*. New Haven, CT: Yale University Press, [2006] 2008.

Margaret Brown's French Cookery Book. Washington, DC: Rufus H. Darby, 1886.

Matthews, Victoria Earle. "The Value of Race Literature: An Address Delivered at the First Congress of Colored Women of the United States, at Boston, Mass., July 30th, 1895." *Massachusetts Review* 27 (Summer 1986): 169–91.

McCaskill, Barbara, and Caroline Gebhard, eds. *Post-Bellum, Pre-Harlem: African American Literature and Culture, 1877–1919*. New York: New York University Press, 2006.

McElrath, Joseph R. "W. D. Howells and Race: Charles Chesnutt's Disappointment of the Dean." *Nineteenth-Century Literature* 51, no. 4 (March 1997): 474–99.

McHenry, Elizabeth. "The Case of Mary Church Terrell." *American Literary History* 19, no. 2 (Summer 2007): 381–401.

McHenry, Elizabeth. *Forgotten Readers: Recovering the Lost History of African American Literary Societies.* Durham, NC: Duke University Press, 2002.

Miller, M. Sammye. "An Early Venture in Black Capitalism: The Capital Savings Bank in the District of Columbia, 1888–1902." *Records of the Columbia Historical Society, Washington, DC* 50 (1980): 359–66.

Mitchell, Edward C. "Higher Education and the Negro." In *Report of the Commissioner of Education for the Year 1894–1895.* Vol. 2, 1360–66. Washington, DC: Government Printing Office, 1896.

Mitchell, Michelle. *Righteous Propagation: African Americans and the Politics of Racial Destiny after Reconstruction.* Chapel Hill: University of North Carolina Press, 2004.

Moody, Joycelyn, and Howard Rambsy II. "Guest Editors' Introduction: African American Print Cultures." *MELUS* 40, no. 3 (Fall 2015): 1–11.

Moody-Turner, Shirley. "'Dear Doctor Du Bois': Anna Julia Cooper, W. E. B. Du Bois, and the Gender Politics of Black Publishing." *MELUS* 40, no. 3 (Fall 2015): 47–68.

Moody-Turner, Shirley. "Recovery: Nineteenth Century and Now." *Legacy* 36, no. 2 (2019): 249–52.

Morris, Robert C. *Reading, 'Riting, and Reconstruction: The Education of Freedmen in the South, 1861–1970.* Chicago: University of Chicago Press, 1976.

Mossell, N. F. [Gertrude Bustill]. *The Work of the Afro-American Woman.* New York: Oxford University Press, [1894] 1988.

Muñoz, José Esteban. *Cruising Utopia: The Then and There of Queer Futurity.* New York: New York University Press, 2009.

Murphy, Gretchen. *Shadowing the White Man's Burden: US Imperialism and the Problem of the Color Line.* New York: New York University Press, 2010.

Murray, Daniel. "A Bibliography of Negro Literature." *AME Church Review* 16 (July 1900): 19–27.

National Association for the Advancement of Colored People. *Thirty Years of Lynching in the United States, 1889–1919.* New York: National Association for the Advancement of Colored People, 1919.

Nishikawa, Kinohi. "The Archive on Its Own: Black Politics, Independent Publishing, and *The Negotiations.*" *MELUS* 40, no. 3 (2015): 176–201.

Nyong'o, Tavia. *Afro-Fabulations: The Queer Drama of Black Life.* New York: New York University Press, 2019.

Page, Thomas Nelson. "Literature in the South since the War." *Lippincott's Monthly Magazine: A Popular Journal of General Literature* 48 (July–December 1891): 740–56.

Page, Thomas Nelson. "The Lynching of Negroes: Its Cause and Its Prevention." *North American Review* 178 (January 1904): 33–48.

Parfait, Claire. "'The Grandest Book Ever Written': Advertising Joseph T. Wilson's *Black Phalanx* (1888)." In *Writing History from the Margins: African Americans and the Quest for Freedom*, edited by Claire Parfait, Hélène Le Dantec-Lowry, and Claire Bourhis-Mariotti, 13–24. New York: Routledge, 2017.

Parker, Alison M. "'The Picture of Health': The Public Life and Private Ailments of Mary Church Terrell." *Journal of Historical Biography* 13 (Spring 2013): 164–207.

Parks, Edward I. "Biographical Sketch of Professor W. H. Crogman, A. M." In *Talks for the Times*, by W. H. Crogman, ix–xxiii. Atlanta, GA: Press of Franklin Printing and Publishing, 1896.

Parrington, Paul. *The Moon Illustrated Weekly: Black America's First Weekly Magazine*. Thornton, CO: C & M, 1986.

Parrington, Paul. "The *Moon Illustrated Weekly*: The Precursor of the *Crisis*." *Journal of Negro History* 48, no. 3 (July 1963): 206–16.

Penn, I. Garland. *The Afro-American Press and Its Editors*. Springfield, MA: Wiley, 1891.

Penn, I. Garland. "Awakening of a Race: The Moral and Industrial Development of the Negro as Shown at the Exposition." *Atlanta Constitution*, September 22, 1895, 24–25.

Pennington, James W. C. *A Text Book of the Origin and History, &c. &c. of the Colored People*. Hartford, CT: L. Skinner, 1841.

Perdue, Theda. *Race and the Atlanta Cotton States Exposition of 1895*. Athens: University of Georgia Press, 2010.

Peterson, Carla. "Reconstructing the Nation: Frances Harper, Charlotte Fortune, and the Racial Politics of Periodical Publication." *Proceedings of the American Antiquarian Society* 107, no. 2 (1998): 301–34.

Peterson, Carla. "Subject to Speculation: Assessing the Lives of African American Women in the Nineteenth Century." In *Women's Studies in Transition: The Pursuit of Interdisciplinarity*, edited by Kate Conway-Turner, Suzanne Cherrin, Kathleen Doherty Turkel, and Jessica Schiffman, 109–17. Newark: University of Delaware Press, 1998.

Poe, Edgar Allan. "To Charles Anthon, November 2, 1844." In *Letters of Edgar Allan Poe*, vol. 1, edited by John Ward Ostrom, 268. New York: Gordian, 1966.

Porter, Dorothy. "Bibliography and Research in Afro-American Scholarship." *Journal of Academic Librarianship* 2, no. 2 (May 1976): 77–81.

Price, Leah. *How to Do Things with Books in Victorian Britain*. Princeton, NJ: Princeton University Press, 2012.

Pride, Armistead. "A Register and History of Negro Newspapers in the United States." PhD diss., Northwestern University, 1951.

Provenzo, Eugene F., Jr. *W. E. B. Du Bois's Exhibit of American Negroes: African Americans at the Beginning of the Twentieth Century*. Lanham, MD: Rowman and Littlefield, 2013.

Quashie, Kevin. *The Sovereignty of Quiet: Beyond Resistance in Black Culture*. New Brunswick, NJ: Rutgers University Press, 2012.

Quigley, Joan. *Just Another Southern Town: Mary Church Terrell and the Struggle for Racial Justice in the Nation's Capital*. New York: Oxford University Press, 2016.

Rawick, George P., ed. *The American Slave: A Composite Autobiography*. Vol. 5. Westport, CT: Greenwood, 1972.

Reed, Christopher Robert. *"All the World Is Here!": The Black Presence at White City*. Bloomington: Indiana University Press, 2000.

Report of the Commissioner of Education for the Year 1894–1895. Vol. 2. Washington, DC: Government Printing Office, 1896.

Repplier, Agnes. "The Happiness of Writing an Autobiography." *Atlantic Monthly*, February 1924, 200–207.

Riley, Linda A., and Stuart C. Brown. "Crafting a Public Image: An Empirical Study of the Ethics of Ghostwriting." *Journal of Business Ethics* 15, no. 7 (July 1996): 711–20.

Rosenberg, Jane Aikin. *The Nation's Great Library: Herbert Putnam and the Library of Congress, 1899–1939*. Urbana: University of Illinois Press, 1993.

Roy, Michaël. "The Slave Narrative Unbound." In *Against a Sharp White Background: Infrastructures of African American Print*, edited by Bridgette Fielder and Jonathan Senchyne, 259–76. Madison: University of Wisconsin Press, 2019.

Rusert, Britt. "Disappointment in the Archives of Black Freedom." *Social Text* 33, no. 4 (December 2015): 19–33.

Rusert, Britt. "From Black Lit to Black Print: The Return to the Archive in African American Literary Studies." *American Quarterly* 68, no. 4 (December 2016): 993–1005.

Rusert, Britt. *Fugitive Science: Empiricism and Freedom in Early African American Culture*. New York: New York University Press, 2017.

Rusert, Britt. "W. E. B. Du Bois, Aesthetics, and the Weird." Black Perspectives, February 20, 2018. www.aaihs.org/w-e-b-du-bois-aesthetics-and-the-weird.

Ryan, Susan M. "Reform." In *Keywords in American Cultural Studies*, edited by Bruce Burgett and Glenn Hendler, 196–99. New York: New York University Press, 2007.

Rydell, Robert W., ed. *The Reason Why the Colored American Is Not in the World's Columbian Exposition* (1893). Urbana: University of Illinois Press, 1999.

"Sales Talk for Progress of a Race." In *Progress of a Race; or, The Remarkable Advancement of the Afro-American Negro*. Naperville, IL: J. L. Nichols, 1920.

Santamarina, Xiomara. "'Are We There Yet?': Archives, History and Specificity in African American Literary Studies." *American Literary History* 20, nos. 1–2 (Spring/Summer 2008): 304–16.

Shermann, Joan. *Invisible Poets: Afro-Americans of the Nineteenth Century*. Urbana: University of Illinois Press, 1974.

Sinche, Brian. "The Walking Book." In *Against a Sharp White Background: Infra-structures of African American Print*, edited by Bridgette Fielder and Jonathan Senchyne, 277–97. Madison: University of Wisconsin Press, 2019.

Sinnette, Elinor Des Verney, W. Paul Coates, and Thomas C. Battle, eds. *Black Bibliophiles and Collectors: Preservers of Black History*. Washington, DC: Howard University Press, 1990.

Smethurst, James. *The African American Roots of Modernism: From Reconstruction to the Harlem Renaissance*. Chapel Hill: University of North Carolina Press, 2010.

Smith, Shawn Michelle. "Booker T. Washington's Photographic Messages." *English Language Notes* 51, no. 1 (Spring/Summer 2013): 137–46.

Spofford, Ainsworth Rand, ed. *The American Almanac and Treasury of Facts, Statistical, Financial, and Political for the Year 1880*. New York: American News, 1880.

Stafford, Marjorie. "Subscription Book Publishing in the United States, 1865–1930." Master's thesis, University of Illinois at Urbana-Champaign, 1943.

Stanley, Liz, and Helen Dampier. "'She Wrote Peter Halket': Fictive and Factive Devices in Olive Shreiner's Letters and *Trooper Peter Halket of Mashonaland*." In *Narratives and Fiction: An Interdisciplinary Approach*, edited by David Robinson, Noel Gilzean, Pamela Fisher, Tracey Yeadon-Lee, Sarah Daly, and Pete Woodcock, 61–69. Huddersfield, UK: University of Huddersfield Press, 2008.

Stewart, Jeffery C. *The New Negro: The Life of Alain Locke*. New York: Oxford University Press, 2018.

Sullivan, Patricia. "Research on Literacy in Practice: Domains, Maps, and Emerging Challenges." In *Literacy in Practice: Writing in Public, Private, and Working Lives*, edited by Patrick Thomas and Pamela Takayoshi, 230–42. New York: Routledge, 2016.

Summers, Martin. *Manliness and Its Discontents: The Black Middle Class and the Transformation of Masculinity, 1900–1930*. Chapel Hill: University of North Carolina Press, 2004.

Tankard, Paul. "Reading Lists." *Prose Studies* 28, no. 3 (December 2006): 337–60.

Tanselle, Thomas G. *Essays in Bibliographical History*. Charlottesville: Bibliographical Society of the University of Virginia, 2013.

Taylor, Elizabeth Dowling. *The Original Black Elite: Daniel Murray and the Story of a Forgotten Era*. New York: HarperCollins, 2017.

Tebbel, John. *A History of Book Publishing in the United States: The Expansion of an Industry, 1865–1919*. Vol. 2. New York: R. R. Bowker, 1975.

Terrell, Mary Church. *A Colored Woman in a White World*. New York: G. K. Hall, [1940] 1996.

Terrell, Mary Church. "Lynching from A Negro's Point of View." *North American Review* 178 (1904): 853–54.

Terrell, Mary Church. "Mission of Meddlers." *Voice of the Negro* (August 1905): 566–68.

Terrell, Mary Church. "Samuel Coleridge-Taylor, the Anglo African Composer." *Voice of the Negro* 2 (1905): 665–69.

Terrell, Mary Church. "Venus and the Night Doctors." *Washington Post*, April 7, 1901, E14.

Terrell, Mary Church. "What It Means to Be Colored in the Capital of the United States." *Independent*, January 24, 1907, 181–86.

Thomas, Amy M. "There Is Nothing So Effective as a Personal Canvas: Revaluing Nineteenth Century American Subscription Books." *Book History* 1 (1998): 140–55.

Thornbrough, Emma Lou, *T. Thomas Fortune: Militant Journalist*. Chicago: University of Chicago Press, 1972.

Tuerk, Richard. "The Short Stories of Jacob A. Riis." *American Literary Realism* 13, no. 2 (Autumn 1980): 259–65.

U.S. Bureau of the Census. *Historical Statistics of the United States, Colonial Times to 1970*. Washington, DC: US Government Printing Office, 1975.

Warren, Kenneth W. *What Was African American Literature?* Cambridge, MA: Harvard University Press, 2012.

Washington, Booker T. *Black-Belt Diamonds: Gems from the Speeches, Addresses, and Talks to Students of Booker T. Washington*. New York: Fortune & Scott, 1898.

Washington, Booker T. *The Booker T. Washington Papers*. 14 vols. Edited by Louis R. Harlan, John W. Blassingame, Pete Daniel, Stuart B. Kaufman, Raymond W. Smock, and William M. Welty. Urbana: University of Illinois Press, 1972–2014.

Washington, Booker T. *The Future of the American Negro*. Boston: Small, Maynard, 1899.

Washington, Booker T. "Industrial Education of the Blacks." In the US Bureau of Education's *Report of the Commissioner of Education*. Vol. 2, 1894–95, 1356–60. Washington, DC: Government Printing Office, 1895.

Washington, Booker T. *My Larger Education: Being Chapters from My Experience*. Toronto: McLelland & Goodchild, 1911.

Washington, Booker T. *The Story of My Life and Work*. Naperville, IL: J. L. Nichols, 1900.

Washington, Booker T. *Up from Slavery*. New York: Doubleday, Page, 1902.

Washington, Booker T. "Why Push Industrial Education in the South?" *Public Opinion*, June 11, 1896, 750–51.

Washington, Booker T. *Working with the Hands: Being a Sequel to Up from Slavery Covering the Author's Experiences in Industrial Training at Tuskegee*. New York: Doubleday, Page, 1904.

Watson, Martha Solomon. "Mary Church Terrell vs. Thomas Nelson Page: Gender, Race, and Class in Anti-Lynching Rhetoric." *Rhetoric and Public Affairs* 12, no. 1 (Spring 2009): 65–89.

Wells, Ida B. *Crusade for Justice: The Autobiography of Ida B. Wells*. Edited by Alfreda M. Duster. Chicago: University of Chicago Press, 1970.

Wells, Ida B. *The Red Record: Tabulated Statistics and Alleged Causes of Lynching in the United States* (1895). In *On Lynchings: Southern Horrors; A Red Record; Mob Rule in New Orleans*, 1–100. New York: Arno Press, 1969.

Wells, Ida B. *Southern Horrors: Lynch Law in All Its Phases*. New York: New York Age, 1892.

White, Trumbull, and William Igleheart. *The World's Columbian Exposition, Chicago, 1893: A Complete History of the Enterprise, a Full Description of the Buildings and Exhibits in All Departments and a Short Account of Previous Exhibitions*. Boston: John K. Hastings, 1893.

Wilks, Jennifer M. "The French and Swiss Diaries of Mary Church Terrell, 1888–89: Introduction and Annotated Translation." *Palimpsest: A Journal on Women, Gender, and the Black International* 3, no. 1 (2014): 8–32.

Williams, Heather Andrea. *Self-Taught: African American Education in Slavery and Freedom*. Chapel Hill: University of North Carolina Press, 2005.

Williams, Raymond. *Marxism and Literature*. Oxford: Oxford University Press, 2009.

Wilson, Mabel O. *Negro Building: Black Americans in the World of Fairs and Museums*. Berkeley: University of California Press, 2012.

Woodson, Carter G., ed. *The Works of Francis J. Grimké*. Vol. 4. Washington, DC: Associated Publishers, 1942.

"Works by Negro Authors." *Report of the Commissioner of Education for the Years 1893–94*, vol. 1, 60–65. Washington, DC: Government Printing Office, 1896. Reprinted in *Early Black Bibliographies, 1863–1918*, edited by Betty Kaplan Gubert. New York: Garland, 1982.

Year-Book of the Bibliographical Society of Chicago, 1899–1900. Chicago: Bibliographical Society of Chicago, 1900.

Young, Kevin. *The Grey Album: On the Blackness of Blackness*. Minneapolis: Graywolf, 2012.

Young, Patricia A. "Roads to Travel: A Historical Look at the *Freedman's Torchlight*—An African American Contribution to 19th-Century Instructional Technologies." *Journal of Black Studies* 31, no. 5 (May 2001): 671–98.

INDEX

Du Bois, W. E. B.: 1900 bibliography, 111–16; 1901 bibliography, 116–21; 1905 bibliography, 121–25; bibliographic work of, 82; bibliographies of, 17; on A. Crummell, 74; failure in relation to, 5–6; literacy and, 24; relations with D. Murray, 109; on Murray project, 101; on Negro literature, 21; printing business of, 1–2, 20, 126; use of bibliography, 110; B. T. Washington compared to, 38

Dunbar, Erica Armstrong, 35

Dunbar, Paul Laurence, 8–9, 119, 124, 127, 181–82, 190, 240n18

Eames, Wilberforce, 99

Edwards, Brett Hayes, 58

Elementary Spelling Book (Webster), 242n15

Emancipation: Its Course and Progress (J. Wilson), 68

English, literary, 181

"English" as a discipline, 10

"Enlightening the Race" (illustration), 53, 54

Esenwein, J. Berg, 211, 224

Exhibit of American Negroes: Du Bois and, 110; origin, 94–95; at the Pan-American Exposition, 252n54; photo, 102; responses to, 101, 103; *The Story of My Life and Work* in, 167. *See also* Murray's bibliographic project

Ezel, Lorenzo, 32, 242n15

failure: causes, 221, 225; infrastructures and, 236; politics of, 228–31; queer failure, 5–6, 190, 231–32; significance, 18; terms and conditions of, 190–91. *See also* authorship

Faithful Account of the Race, A (Hall), 27

Farrington, Lynne, 246n54

fiction: appeal of, 209–10; in bibliographies, 119; Fortune on, 160; historical, 106; of T. N. Page, 204–5; slavery in, 222–23. *See also* Terrell's short stories

First Lessons in Greek (Scarborough), 85

Foote, Julia A., 85

Foreman, P. Gabrielle, 241n34

Forgotten Readers (McHenry), 242n14

Fortune, Emanuel, 132

Fortune, T. Thomas: biography, 255n2; career, 134–35; creative writing, 160–62, 259n96; early life, 132–33; education, 137–38; in *Invisible Poets*, 261n161; literary aspirations, 180–85; relations with D. Murray, 92; portrait, 134; relations with Scott, 159, 183, 262n167; Scott correspondence, 155, 171, 180, 184, 185; significance, 17, 21, 130–31; M. C. Terrell compared to, 264n23

Fortune-Washington partnership: *Black-Belt Diamonds*, 147–52; impact on T. T. Fortune, 179–84, 261n149; *The Future of the American Negro*, 157–61; V. E. Matthews and, 144–46; *A New Negro for a New Century*, 155–56, 171–77; origin and purpose, 136, 138, 140–42; W. H. Page on, 153–54; significance, 17, 131, 185–87, 237; *Sowing and Reaping*, 177–87; *The Story of My Life and Work*, 52, 65, 164–70, 174–76; "Western" publishers and, 162–63; *Working with the Hands*, 178–79. *See also* Washington, Booker T.

Forum, 204

Foster, Frances Smith, 3–4, 13, 241n35

Freedman's Torchlight, 32–37, 243n19

freedmen's schools, 34

Freedom's Journal, 29, 242n14

Freeman, 134

Free Public Library of Philadelphia, 89

French Cook Book (Brown), 105

Frissell, Hollis, 36, 140

Fugitive Science (Rusert), 242n14

Funk and Wagnalls Company, 253n61

Future of the American Negro, The (Washington), 157–62

Gammon Theological Seminary, 42

Gardner, Eric, 12, 186–87

Garvey, Ellen Gruber, 70–71

infrastructure of African American literary culture, 11, 20, 236–37
Invisible Poets (Sherman), 261n161
Iola Leroy (Harper), 24, 124

Jacksonville Daily Union, 133
Jacobs, Harriet, 12, 105
Jarrett, Gene, 4, 161, 181
Jenkins, A. N., 47–48, 52
Jim Crow, Literature, and the Legacy of Sutton E. Griggs (Warren), 4
Jim Crow era, 11
J. L. Nichols Company. *See* Nichols Company
Johnson, Edward A, 68
Johnson, Georgia Douglas, 235
Johnson, James Weldon, 182, 184–85, 262n173
Johnson, Mrs. Harvey, 85
Johnston, Frances Benjamin, 57, 178, 179
John Wilson and Son, 257n51
journalism, 118–19, 263n15
Journal of Proceedings and Addresses, 69
Just Another Southern Town (Quigley), 266n76
Justice for Lynching Act, 264n40
Just Teach One: Early African American Print, 12–13, 241n33

Kent State University Library collection of Publishers' Canvassing Books, 30
Keyser, Frances, 145
Kletzing, E. L., 66
Kletzing, Henry Frick, 27, 28, 59, 65–67, 72, 248n89. *See also Progress of a Race* (Crogman and Kletzing)
Koehler, Robby Daniel, 249n96

Lanier, Henry Wysham, 163
Lenox Library, 99
Levy, Andrew, 210, 265n45
lexical lists, 80
librarians and archivists, 82, 250n17, 254n76
library associations, 88

Library of Congress: acquisitions, 100–101; mission and administration, 91–92; H. Putnam at, 94–95, 97; Terrell Collection at, 189–90. *See also* Murray, Daniel; Murray's bibliographic project
lists and bibliographies: authority of, 118; authorship, 130; emergence, 88–89; gendered aspects, 82–83; imperative, 127–28; as intellectual practice, 115; nature and significance, 78–80; proliferation, 86–87; purpose, 81; racial identity and, 88, 110; "A Select Bibliography of the American Negro for General Readers," 111–26; significance of, 16–17, 21; *The Work of the Afro-American Woman*, 83. *See also* Murray's bibliographic project
"Lists of Afro-American Publications" (Mossell), 84–86
literacy and illiteracy: critical thinking and, 43–44; data on, 242n5; definitions of, 242n10; *Freedman's Torchlight* role in, 32–37; in Georgia, 47; C. Hager on, 19; literary study in relation to, 24–26, 76; literature in relation to, 243n19; origin of, 25–26; in relation to *Progress of a Race*, 15–16
literary English, 181
literary marketplace: African American representation in, 204–6; commercial viability in, 181–82; racial politics of, 131; terms and conditions of, 190–91; M. C. Terrell in, 223–30; B. T. Washington and T. T. Fortune in, 162–71
literature, definition of, 25–26
Logan, Rayford, 6, 204
longue durée, 6–7
Loudin, Frederick, 244n32
lynching, 207–9, 264n40
"Lynching from a Negro's Point of View" (Terrell), 188–89, 192, 204, 220
"Lynching of Negroes, The" (T. N. Page), 204–5
Lyons, Maritcha, 145